Reasons as Defaults

" Ah! What awaits the classic bent
And what the cultured word,
Against the undoctored incident
That actually occurred."
            — Rudyard Kipling —

" An honest politician is one who,
when he is bought
    will stay bought." — Simon Cameron

" He travels the fastest who travels alone"
            — Rudyard Kipling —

" Injustice is relatively easy to bear;
what stings is justice."
            — HL. Mencken —

Reasons as Defaults

John F. Horty

OXFORD
UNIVERSITY PRESS

OXFORD
UNIVERSITY PRESS

Oxford University Press is a department of the University of Oxford.
It furthers the University's objective of excellence in research,
scholarship, and education by publishing worldwide.

Oxford   New York

Auckland   Cape Town   Dar es Salaam   Hong Kong   Karachi
Kuala Lumpur   Madrid   Melbourne   Mexico City   Nairobi
New Delhi   Shanghai   Taipei   Toronto

With offices in

Argentina   Austria   Brazil   Chile   Czech Republic   France   Greece
Guatemala   Hungary   Italy   Japan   Poland   Portugal   Singapore
South Korea   Switzerland   Thailand   Turkey   Ukraine   Vietnam

Oxford is a registered trade mark of Oxford University Press in the UK
and certain other countries.

Published in the United States of America by
Oxford University Press
198 Madison Avenue, New York, NY 10016

© Oxford University Press 2012

First issued as an Oxford University Press paperback, 2014.

Library of Congress Cataloging-in-Publication Data
Horty, John Francis.
Reasons as defaults / John F. Horty.
p.   cm.
Includes bibliographical references.
ISBN 978-0-19-974407-7 (hardcover : alk. paper);
978-0-19-939644-3 (paperback : alk. paper)
1. Reason. 2. Rationalism. 3. Explanation. 4. Justification (Theory of knowledge)
5. Reasoning. I. Title.
B833.H75   2012
128'.33—dc23   2011024385

For Lynn Karen Baumeister

"I am coming to believe that laws are the prime cause of unhappiness. It is not merely a case of born under one law, required another to obey—you know the lines: I have no memory for verse. No, sir: it is born under half a dozen, required another fifty to obey. There are parallel sets of laws in different keys that have nothing to do with one another and that are even downright contradictory. You, now—you wish to do something that the Articles of War and (as you explained to me) the rules of generosity forbid, but that your present notion of the moral law and your present notion of the point of honour require. This is but one instance of what is as common as breathing. Buridan's ass died of misery between equidistant mangers, drawn first by one then by the other . . .

"So much pain; and the more honest the man the worse the pain. But there at least the conflict is direct: it seems to me that the greater mass of confusion and distress must arise from these less evident divergencies: the moral law, the civil, military, common laws, the code of honour, custom, the rules of practical life, of civility, of amorous conversation, gallantry, to say nothing of Christianity for those that practise it. All sometimes, indeed generally, at variance; none ever in an entirely harmonious relation to the rest; and a man is perpetually required to choose one rather than another, perhaps (in his particular case) its contrary. It is as though our strings were each tuned according to a completely separate system—it is as though the poor ass were surrounded by four and twenty mangers."

Patrick O'Brian
Master and Commander

Acknowledgments

This book explores some of the ways in which ideas from nonmonotonic logic, a discipline originating within computer science, can be applied to central areas of philosophy, including moral philosophy. I have been thinking about this topic for several years, off and on, and have accumulated a number of debts, which it is now a pleasure to acknowledge.

My work on nonmonotonic reasoning began twenty five years ago, as part of a collaborative project with Chuck Cross, Rich Thomason, and Dave Touretzky, supported by the National Science Foundation, and aimed at understanding the logic of nonmonotonic inheritance networks, a formalism for knowledge representation in artificial intelligence. Most of what I know about nonmonotonic reasoning I learned in those project meetings, and much of what I know about research as well. I am very grateful to Rich and Dave for inviting me to participate in the project, and to Rich in particular for helping me to continue thinking about these problems ever since; I have been deeply influenced by his vision of logic, and of what computer science can contribute to philosophy.

In the 1980's, the study of nonmonotonic logic had not yet achieved the status it now enjoys as a normal science. At that time, there were a number of wildly different paradigms under consideration whose merits, demerits, and interrelations were explored in an intense series of workshops involving an extraordinary collection of computer scientists, logicians, and philosophers. I owe much to early discussions with Gerd Brewka, Jim Delgrande, Jon Doyle, David Etherington, Hector Geffner, Matt Ginsberg, David Israel, Hank Kyburg, Vladimir Lifschitz, Ron Loui, David Makinson, John McCarthy, Leora Morgenstern, Donald Nute, Judea Pearl, John Pollock, David Poole, Ray Reiter, Eric Sandewall, Bart Selman, and Lynn Stein; and then to later discussions with Aldo Antonelli, Horacio Arló-Costa, Nicholas Asher, Chita Baral, Johan van Benthem, Dan Bonevac, Craig Boutilier, Dov Gabbay, Rob Koons, Jorge Lobo, Jack Minker, Michael Morreau, Don Perlis, and Rohit Parikh.

My own work on nonmonotonic logic, like the subject itself, began in computer science. At some point around 1990, however, I read Bas van Fraassen's "Values and the heart's command" (1973), a seminal paper on moral conflicts, and realized both that the formal system described there could be interpreted very naturally in one of the most familiar nonmonotonic logics, and also that some of the central difficulties facing nonmonotonic logic could then be seen, in light of this interpretation, as advantages. This paper changed my thinking entirely: rather than viewing nonmonotonic logic simply as a tool for codifying a relation of defeasible consequence, I began to suspect that it might provide a more general framework within which we could explore the connections between reasons, including normative reasons, and the actions or conclusions they support.

In working out the details of this interpretation, I was fortunate to have the aid of four accomplished ethicists.

Michael Slote, a colleague during the initial stages of the project, could not have been more helpful. In addition to guiding me through the relevant ethical literature, Michael was always available to answer countless questions, and to read countless drafts. I am grateful for his encouragement of my formal work, in a field in which it is not always welcome, but also for his ability to see through the formalism to what really mattered.

Henry Richardson read a flawed, early draft of some of these chapters and discussed them with me extensively; his insight and enthusiasm, coming at a time when my thinking was confused and my confidence low, kept me working on a project that I would not have finished without him.

Jonathan Dancy read the same flawed draft (in the form of a long paper by an unknown author, arriving on his desk out of the blue), sent me a remarkably perceptive set of comments, and then invited me to present some of the material at a particularism workshop in Austin, where I was able to discuss it with an audience of experts.

And Mark Schroeder has been helpful beyond all measure in a series of conversations spanning several years. Perhaps his most concrete contribution was to insist, again and again, that I needed to pay serious attention to undercutting defeat, which I had set aside as a distraction. Eventually, I concluded that I needed to pay serious attention to undercutting defeat—and this has turned out to be, I believe, one of the most valuable aspects of the work. But Mark's aid and influence go well beyond that single piece of advice. Many of the key ideas in this book were formed during our conversations, either in sympathy with or in reaction to Mark's own views, and his support has been invaluable.

There were many others, of course. To name a few: Paul Pietroski discussed drafts of the central chapter on moral conflicts with me, supplying comments that were both wise and sane. Chuck Cross was able to locate a technical error that I suspected might be there but was unable to find myself. Nuel Belnap saved me from advancing an unfortunate analysis by saying, at just the right moment, "That seems like a trick." Ray Reiter sent several sets of comments on early drafts, and was particularly useful in helping me sort out, to the extent that I have, the difficulties presented by floating conclusions. I have not arrived at a settled view of prioritized default reasoning, but would understand the issues much less well than I do were it not for a voluminous correspondence with Jörg Hansen, who has his own, very sophisticated view of the topic. And my understanding of default reasoning more generally has been substantially enriched over the years by a running discussion with Henry Prakken, much of it centered around the issues discussed in this book—indeed, it is Henry's work on default reasoning in argumentation theory, as well as Jörg's work on priorities in input/output logic, that I am most sorry to neglect.

Bas van Fraassen, Lou Goble, Paul Pietroski, Mark Schroeder, and Marek Sergot all read the final manuscript, or significant parts of it, and pointed out further difficulties—not all of which I have been able to address, but all of which I hope to think about. Ryan Millsap and Heidi Tiedke Savage, who signed up only for proof-reading, introduced several stylistic and substantive improvements. The neuroscientist and artist Daphne Soares took a moment away from her own research on sensory organs in cavefish to draw the diagrams, and the incomparable Boris Veytsman helped to refine the final LaTeX presentation.

Although this book has been written to stand alone, from beginning to end, parts of it draw on previous work. In particular: Chapters 3 and 4 draw on my (1994a) and (2003), from the *Journal of Philosophical Logic* and *Nous*, respectively; Chapters 5 and 6 draw on my (2007b), from the *Philosopher's Imprint*; Chapter 7 draws on my (2002), from *Artificial Intelligence*; and Chapter 8 draws on my (2001b) and (2007a), from *Artificial Intelligence and Law* and again from the *Journal of Philosophical Logic*.

My work on this project was supported early on by grants from the National Science Foundation, and later by a fellowship from the National Endowment for Humanities (which asks me to note that any views, findings, conclusions, or recommendations expressed in this publication do not necessarily reflect those of the National Endowment for the Humanities). Finally, I was fortunate to have the opportunity to complete this manuscript in the ideal working conditions provided by two remarkable institutions. The first is the Netherlands Institute for Advanced Study in the Humanities and Social Sciences, in Wassenaar, the Netherlands. The second is the Center for Advanced Study in the Behavioral Sciences at Stanford University.

Contents

Introduction

Philosophy has given us two grand formal theories to help account for the processes of deliberating about or justifying actions or conclusions. The first is deductive logic. The second is decision theory, along with the closely allied fields of probability theory and inductive logic. In most ordinary cases, however, our deliberation or justification does not conform to either of these two theories. What we ordinarily do—in deliberation, for example—is simply focus on the *reasons* that favor or oppose some action or conclusion, and attempt to arrive at a decision on that basis. Why should we have dinner at Obelisk tonight? Because, even though it is expensive, the new chef is getting excellent reviews. Why do we think raccoons have found their way into the back yard? Because the garbage was knocked over and those tracks look like raccoon prints.

If the action under consideration is adopted, or the conclusion accepted, the set of supporting reasons identified during deliberation can likewise function as a justification. Supposing, for example, that a skeptical friend wonders why we would pay so much to dine at Obelisk, we might try to justify our decision by citing the excellent reviews.

Of course, it is possible that the reasoning involved in cases like this really is best thought of, at bottom, as logical or decision theoretic. Maybe our choice of restaurant is best analyzed in terms of a decision matrix, with all the utilities and probabilities filled in, and our conclusion about the raccoons as something like a deduction from a complicated knowledge base about animals and their behavior. Perhaps, then, our appeal to reasons in deliberation and justification is nothing but an abbreviated manner of speaking about these more intricate structures—maybe an allusion to the most salient features of the decision matrix, or the most salient patterns in the deduction. This could all be right; and even so, the study of the salient features or patterns associated with our talk of reasons might still be telling. But it could also be wrong. We cannot just discount the way we talk. Perhaps it is our ordinary way of speaking about deliberation and justification, directly in terms of reasons, that best captures what is going on.

The idea that our talk of reasons should be taken seriously has been especially influential in ethical theory, where several important writers have either argued or assumed that the concept of a reason is basic to the

1

normative realm, a fundamental concept in terms of which other normative notions can then be analyzed. Something like this picture can be found already in W. D. Ross, at least if we accept the standard, and attractive, interpretation of Ross's principles of prima facie duty as providing reasons for action; the idea was developed in various ways toward the middle of the last century by writers including Kurt Baier, Roderick Chisholm, Thomas Nagel, and Joseph Raz; and it figures prominently in the contemporary work of Jonathan Dancy, Derek Parfit, T. M. Scanlon, Mark Schroeder, and many others.[1] As a result, there is now a large literature on what is sometimes called practical reasoning, or more generally, the theory of reasons. Much of this literature, however, is devoted to a cluster of complex philosophical issues, such as, for example, the relation between reasons and motivation, desires, and values, the issue of internalism versus externalism in the theory of reasons, the objectivity or subjectivity of reasons, and even the question of how aspects of the world could ever come to function as reasons for cognitive agents at all.

In this book, I do my best not to take a stand on any of these issues—I hope to remain neutral—but concentrate instead on the orthogonal topic, which has received surprisingly little attention, of developing a precise, concrete theory of the way in which reasons interact to support their outcomes. The goal of the book, more exactly, is to present a framework that allows us to answer questions like these: What are reasons, and how do they support actions or conclusions? Given a collection of individual reasons, possibly suggesting conflicting actions or conclusions, how can we determine which course of action, or which conclusion, is supported by the collection as a whole? What is the mechanism of support?

One way to appreciate these questions is to consider some possible lines of response. I begin with one that I call the *weighing conception*, since

---

[1]See, for example, Baier (1958), Chisholm (1964), Dancy (2004), Nagel (1970), Parfit (2011), Raz (1975), Ross (1930), Scanlon (1998), and Schroeder (2007). A vocabulary note: the term "reason" is used in this literature to refer to a consideration that supports an action or conclusion, though not necessarily in a definitive or conclusive way, and that can exist in conjunction with reasons supporting contrary actions or conclusions. Reasons of this kind are sometimes referred to as "prima facie" reasons, echoing Ross's talk of prima facie duties (though this phrase carries the unfortunate suggestion that they may be reasons only "at first glance," and so not really reasons at all); such reasons are also frequently referred to as "pro tanto" reasons, or reasons "as far as that goes," and Dancy has recently described them as "contributory" reasons. Throughout this book I will drop all qualifiers and refer to these supporting considerations simply as reasons. None of this is to deny that there is a further use of the term "reason" according to which it does, in fact, refer to the most salient aspect of a complex explanation. We might naturally say, for example, that the reason the axiomatic system known as Peano arithmetic, in contrast to Robinson's arithmetic, allows us to prove the commutativity of addition is that it contains an induction schema. Here, there seems to be nothing prima facie or pro tanto going on at all; instead, the term "reason" is used only to highlight the particular difference between the two axiomatic systems that would figure most prominently in a full explanation of the fact that one, but not the other, supports commutativity.

Wgh'g cncptn

it is based on the view that reasons support actions or conclusions by
contributing a kind of normative or epistemic weight, and that the goal is
then to select those options whose overall weight is greatest. This general
picture is almost certainly ancient, but we know that it goes back at least
to 1772, where we can find a version of the weighing conception described
with some elegance in a letter from Benjamin Franklin to his friend Joseph
Priestley, the chemist. Priestley had written to Franklin for advice on a
practical matter. In his reply, Franklin regrets that he has no help to offer
on the specific matter at hand, since he is not sufficiently familiar with
the facts, but recommends a general technique for reaching decisions in
situations of the kind facing his friend:

> My Way is to divide half a Sheet of Paper by a Line into two
> Columns; writing over the one Pro, and over the other Con.
> Then during the three or four Days Consideration, I put down
> under the different Heads short Hints of the different Motives,
> that at different Times occur to me, for or against the Measure.
> When I have thus got them all together in one View, I endeavor
> to estimate their respective Weights; and where I find two, one
> on each side, that seem equal, I strike them both out: If I
> find a Reason pro equal to some two Reasons con, I strike out
> the three. If I judge some two Reasons con, equal to three
> Reasons pro, I strike out the five; and thus proceeding I find
> at length where the Balance lies; and if after a Day or two of
> farther Consideration nothing new that is of Importance occurs
> on either side, I come to a Determination accordingly.[2]

I suspect that most of us would now regard Franklin's picture as
quixotic, or at least extraordinarily optimistic, both in its assumption that
the force of reasons can be captured through an assignment of numerical
weights, and in the accompanying assumption that practical reasoning can
then be reduced to an application of arithmetic operations (Franklin goes
on to characterize his technique as a "moral or prudential algebra"). But
neither of these assumptions is actually essential. A number of contemporary writers are still willing to endorse a generalized form of the weighing
conception—like Franklin's, but without the commitment to a precise numerical representation, or to arithmetic operations. According to this view,
reasons can still be thought of as supporting conclusions by contributing
weights, of a sort; the weights contributed by different reasons can still be
thought of as combined in some way, even if the combination function is not
arithmetic; and these combined weights can still be balanced against each
other, with the correct outcome defined as that whose weight is greatest.
One example of the generalized weighing conception, distinguished by its

---

[2] This passage, along with a description of the circumstances in which it was written,
can be found in a recent biography of Priestly by Steven Johnson (2008, p. 95); see also
Franklin (1772, pp. 348–349).

exceptional clarity, can be found in a recent paper by John Broome, who summarizes his position as follows:

> Each reason is associated with a metaphorical weight. This weight need not be anything so precise as a number; it may be an entity of some vaguer sort. The reasons for you to ϕ and those for you not to ϕ are aggregated or weighed together in some way. The aggregate is some function of the weights of the individual reasons. The function may not be simply additive ... It may be a complicated function, and the specific nature of the reasons may influence it. Finally, the aggregate comes out in favor of your ϕing, and that is why you ought to ϕ.[3]

My objection to this picture is not so much that it is a version of the weighing conception—although, in fact, the theory I present in this book is set out as an alternative to this view. Instead, my objection is that the generalized weighing conception as described here is simply incomplete as an account of the way in which reasons support conclusions. Broome distances himself from the more objectionable features of the quantitative weighing conception—numbers, additive functions—but fails to tell us what should take their place. If the weights associated with reasons are not numbers, what are they; what are these entities of a vaguer sort? If these weights are not aggregated through simple addition, how are they aggregated; what is this more complicated function?

In raising this objection, I do not mean to criticize Broome, who surely does not intend to present anything like a complete account of his generalized weighing conception in the paper I have cited, but only to outline the view before getting on with other work. Nevertheless, I do feel that the objection highlights a real problem for contemporary advocates of the generalized weighing conception, and one that I have not seen addressed. Once we move past the level of a rough outline, it will not do to say only that reasons lend some kind of weight to conclusions, and that these weights are assembled somehow. A theory of the relation between reasons and their outcomes should be subject to the same standards of rigor that Frege brought to the study of the relation between premises and their consequences.

Another line of response—one that I call the *force conception*—is based on the metaphor of reasons as normative or epistemic forces, analogous in some ways to physical forces, and of the actions or conclusions they support as outcomes resulting from the interactions among the various

---

[3]Broome (2004, p. 37). Other examples of the generalized weighing conception, of some historical importance, are presented by Baier (1958), particularly in Chapters 3 and 12, and also by Nagel (1970), particularly in Chapters 7 and 8, who describes the function through which reasons are combined to yield an outcome as a "combinatorial function." Shelly Kagan (1988) refers to this function as a "governing function" and argues that it is not additive.

KE CNCPTN — METAPHOR $ RSNS AS NORMTV or epistemic gds
SALAGADS (somehow) to physical fce's
· SEE (XNS or CONCLNS) the support as outcomes
(rESULTING frm inter XNS AMONG
the VArious)

INTRODUCTION   5

forces at work in some situation. In fact, a picture like this was already
hinted at by some of Ross's remarks on the way in which his principles of
prima facie duty support overall judgments of right and wrong. On Ross's
view, a particular situation might trigger a number of these prima facie
principles, presenting the agent with a number of different, and conflicting,
reasons for action; he describes a case, for example, in which an agent can
relieve distress only by breaking a promise, and says of such an action that
"in virtue of being the breaking of a promise ... it tends to be wrong;
in virtue of being an instance of relieving distress it tends to be right."[4]
Faced with these various reasons for action, the agent must find some way
of reaching an overall judgment, and Ross writes at one point as if the
normative forces carried by these different reasons might combine to yield
a determinate outcome in much the same way as divergent physical forces:

> Another instance of the same distinction may be found in the
> operation of natural laws. *Qua* subject to the force of grav-
> itation towards some other body, each body tends to move in
> a particular direction with a particular velocity; but its actual
> movement depends on *all* the forces to which it is subject.[5]

In classical mechanics, the forces operating on a body can be represented
as vectors, with their overall effect calculated through simple vector arithmetic. And what this passage seems to suggest is that there might be
similar "force composition" principles at work to explain how the various
reasons, or normative forces, present in some particular situation could
result in an overall judgment.[6]

My only objection to this metaphor of reasons as normative forces is
that it is, in fact, nothing more than a metaphor; the way in which reasons
interact to support actions or conclusions is generally described only at
the highest possible level of abstraction. But that will not do. If we are
to think of reasons as normative or epistemic forces, operating in accord
with something like force composition principles, then we should be able to
ask what, exactly, those force composition principles are, how they work,
and what outputs they yield for a given set of inputs. Classical physics
would not have been a successful theory if it had said simply that the
various forces acting on a body interact somehow to yield a resultant force.
Those advocating a force conception of reasons should not be content to
say anything like that either.

---

[4] Ross (1930, p. 28).

[5] Ross (1930, pp. 28–29).

[6] It is worth noting that this picture of the way in which reasons combine to support
conclusions—common as it is, and in spite of the support it seems to receive from the
cited passage—does not necessarily represent the most accurate interpretation of Ross
himself, who felt that the resolution of the different reasons, or prima facie duties, at
work in a particular situation is achieved through a process more like perception, rather
than through the application of uniform force composition principles, such as those from
vector arithmetic; see Dancy (1991) for discussion.

Let us return to our initial questions: What are reasons, and how do they support conclusions? What is the mechanism of support? The answer I propose is that reasons are provided by default rules, and that they support the conclusions they do in accord with the logic of default reasoning, a species of nonmonotonic logic. The goal of this book is to articulate and develop this answer in some detail, but it is worth beginning with a few words to establish even its initial plausibility. Why should nonmonotonic logic—a form of logic that originated, after all, in the field of computer science—have anything whatsoever to do with the theory of reasons, and particularly with the appeal to reasons in ethics?

Well, it is true that nonmonotonic logic was first developed within computer science, but it was within artificial intelligence, rather than computer science more generally, and indeed within a particular subfield of artificial intelligence that is of special relevance to philosophy: the logical study of common sense reasoning. The initial idea driving this subfield—going back to the early days of artificial intelligence, and associated in particular with the work of John McCarthy—was that our everyday, or "commonsense," knowledge could be represented in a logical formalism, and that intelligence could then be achieved through the application of theorem proving technologies.[7] Much has changed since then, particularly the idea that our commonsense knowledge can be represented in a uniform fashion, or that general purpose theorem provers have any substantial role to play. These days, the basic information is represented in a more modular way, with special-purpose reasoners or limited, efficient logics adapted to the separate modules. But the overall research program remains in place: important aspects of our everyday knowledge are represented explicitly in a formalism that makes crucial use of logic, and much of the further information necessary for intelligent action is then supposed to be derived through a variety of reasoning mechanisms. The logical formalization of commonsense knowledge remains a vibrant subfield of artificial intelligence, overlapping what is generally thought of as philosophical logic, but with substantial differences as well.

One of the first problems encountered in the study of commonsense reasoning concerned the logical treatment of generalizations. Ordinary classical logic was developed by a series of mathematicians—beginning, of course, with Frege—for the explicit purpose of analyzing the patterns of reasoning found in mathematics; and it is a notable feature of this particular field that any generalization, in order to be classified as acceptable, must hold universally. The statement "Equilateral triangles are equiangular," for ex-

---

[7] The study of commonsense reasoning as a subfield of artificial intelligence was first identified with the publication of McCarthy (1959); later, more reflective descriptions of the goals and initial results of this program were presented by McCarthy and Patrick Hayes (1969), and then again by McCarthy (1977). Richmond Thomason (1991) relates McCarthy's program to the tradition of "logicism" within philosophy; further discussion, along with an overview of the current state of the logicist program in artificial intelligence, can be found in Thomason (2009).

ample, can be said to express a mathematical truth only because it holds of every single instance, without exception. It quickly became apparent to researchers in artificial intelligence, however, that neither classical logic nor any of its standard variants could be used to model our commonsense reasoning, precisely because, once we leave the domain of mathematics, so much of this reasoning seems to be guided by generalizations that are indeed subject to exceptions. Statements such as "Birds fly," for instance, or "The car starts when you turn the key" seem to express generalizations that are useful for our ordinary reasoning, though neither holds without fail. Not every bird flies, as we all know, and sometimes the car fails to start even when you turn the key.

Of course, philosophers have often appealed to generalizations like these—usually called *defeasible* generalizations—particularly in ethics and epistemology. It is, arguably, generalizations of exactly this kind that are expressed by Ross's principles of prima facie duty, such as the principle that promises ought to be kept. Going back further, it was part of Aristotle's philosophy—his metaphysics and philosophy of science, as well as his ethics—that important regularities might hold, not always or of necessity, but only "for the most part." And in contemporary epistemology, it is often argued that the relation between premises grounded in perception and conclusions about the world is mediated by generalizations of this kind as well, such as the generalization that things that appear to be red actually are red, which can then be defeated in the face of aberrant facts—the fact that the ambient lighting is red, for example. Still, in spite of the frequent appeal to defeasible generalizations within philosophy, it was not until the practical need arose within artificial intelligence for actually reasoning with this kind of information that serious logical attention was focused on the problem; and it then became clear that the resulting theories would have to differ considerably from standard classical logic or its usual variants.

The most important of these differences concerns the logical property known as *consequence monotonicity*—or more simply, *monotonicity.* In standard logics, the conclusions derivable from a particular set of premises are preserved when that premise set is supplemented with new information; the addition of new premises may lead to new conclusions, but never to the withdrawal of conclusions already established. Because of this, the set of conclusions, or consequences, supported by these logics is said to increase monotonically with the set of premises from which these conclusions are derived. It seems clear, however, that any sensible notion of defeasible consequence would have to violate this monotonicity property—here, the addition of new premises often does lead to the withdrawal of previously established conclusions. MONOTONICITY

This point can be illustrated with a couple of examples, which we return to on various occasions throughout the book. Suppose, first, that our premise set contains the defeasible generalization that birds fly, and imagine that we are told only that Tweety is a bird. Then it seems reasonable to conclude from this information that Tweety flies. But this conclusion would have to be withdrawn if we were provided with the additional information that Tweety is a penguin—or a baby bird, or a dead bird, or a bird with its feet stuck in cement. Or suppose, second, that our premise set contains the defeasible principle that promises ought to be kept, and imagine that Jack has promised to meet Jo for lunch. Then it seems reasonable to conclude that Jack ought to meet Jo for lunch. But once again, we would be apt to withdraw this conclusion if we were to learn that Jack is faced with an emergency, such as the need to rescue a drowning child—or if we were to learn that the promise was extracted under duress, or perhaps that Jo habitually extracts such promises from her friends and has no intention of meeting Jack at all. In each case, a conclusion that seems to follow from a defeasible generalization, or a defeasible moral principle, is naturally withdrawn in the face of further information, in violation of monotonicity.

The property of consequence monotonicity flows from assumptions that are deeply rooted in both the proof theory and the semantics, not only of classical logic, but of most of the standard philosophical logics as well. Systems that abandon this property must also abandon these basic assumptions, introducing fundamentally new logical ideas. Because of their intrinsic interest and practical importance, the study of these *nonmonotonic logics* has now grown into a significant area of research, with a variety of applications.

I do not intend to provide anything like a survey of this complex field here, of course.[8] Instead, I will follow only a single thread, beginning with ideas first mapped out in Raymond Reiter's *default logic*, one of the original approaches to nonmonotonic reasoning, but developed along lines

---

[8]Traditional nonmonotonic logics can be classified into two broad categories: first, there are *model-preference* theories, beginning with the theory of circumscription from McCarthy (1980), but now generalized in such a way that they have a close connection with standard logics of conditionals; second, there are *fixed-point* theories, including the default logic developed by Raymond Reiter (1980) as well as the original "nonmonotonic" logic due to Drew McDermott and Jon Doyle (1980). A brief overview of these traditional approaches, emphasizing motivation and conceptual issues, can be found in Horty (2001c); for a more complete account, with extensive references to the literature, I recommend David Makinson's (2005). Standing alongside these standard nonmonotonic logics, there is a separate, though related, tradition, which has some importance in this book, of logics for what might be called *argument-based* defeasible reasoning. This tradition encompasses the original defeasible logics due to Donald Nute, beginning with Nute (1988) and summarized in Nute (1994); the various systems for defeasible reasoning proposed by John Pollock, beginning with Pollock (1987) and developed in his extensive subsequent work on the topic, most notably Pollock (1995); and the research on logics for nonmonotonic inheritance reasoning initiated by David Touretzky (1986) and then developed in a series of papers by Thomason, Touretzky, and myself, especially including Touretzky, Horty, and Thomason (1987) and Horty, Thomason, and Touretzky (1990). Surveys of our own and related work on nonmonotonic inheritance reasoning can be found in Thomason (1992) and in Horty (1994b); a survey of argument-based defeasible reasoning more generally, with special emphasis on Pollock's work and on the ideas emanating from a seminal paper by Phan Minh Dung (1995), is provided by Henry Prakken and Gerard Vreeswijk (2002).

default logic

not anticipated in that theory—allowing for priorities among defaults, for the ability to reason about these priorities within default logic itself, as well as about the exclusion of certain defaults from consideration, and all the while emphasizing the normative interpretation of the theory as much as its original epistemic interpretation.[9]

The basic idea underlying default logic is straightforward: an ordinary logic is to be supplemented with a special set of *default rules*, which can then be used to represent defeasible generalizations. If an ordinary rule of inference, with X as its premise and Y as its conclusion, tells us to conclude Y whenever we have established X, then what a default rule tells us is simply that, whenever we have established X, we should conclude Y by default. The default rule corresponding to the defeasible generalization that birds fly, for example, would tell us that, once it has been established that some object is a bird, we should conclude by default that it flies; the default rule corresponding to the principle that promises ought to be kept would tell us that, once a promise has been made, we should conclude by default that it ought to be kept.

As it turns out, a default logic of this kind provides a very natural platform for the construction of a theory of reasons and their interaction, since—although this was not the original interpretation—a default rule with X as its premise and Y as its conclusion can sensibly be taken to mean that X functions as a reason for Y. The epistemic default corresponding to the generalization that birds fly, for example, can be taken to mean that being a bird functions as a reason for the conclusion that an object flies; the default corresponding to the principle that promises ought to be kept can be taken to mean that, if an agent has promised to perform some action, then that promise functions as a reason for performing the action.

But if reasons are to be explicated in terms of default rules—if default logic is to be used in accounting for reasons and their interaction—we must first understand these default rules themselves: what does it actually mean to say that a conclusion Y follows from a premise X by default? At this stage, the question can be answered only to a first approximation. To say that Y follows from X by default is to say something like this: if it has been established that X, so that we are presented with a reason for Y, we should then endorse Y as well, unless the default that provides X as a reason for Y has been excluded from consideration, or unless we have also endorsed another reason, no weaker than X, that supports a conflicting conclusion—in which case, according to the theory to be developed here,

---

[9]The canonical presentation of default logic can be found, once again, in Reiter (1980); the normative interpretation of this theory is first developed in Horty (1994a). The treatment of priorities among defaults, as well as the process of reasoning about these priorities, has various connections to the literature, which are described throughout the text; the treatment of exclusion set out here is new with this book.

we can sometimes say that X is defeated as a reason for Y, and sometimes only that it is conflicted.

That is already complicated, and quickly becomes worse once we move past the level of a first approximation. The other reasons defeating or conflicting with X may themselves be defeated or conflicted, or they might be excluded as well. The excluding reasons may likewise be defeated or conflicted, or themselves excluded, and any reason may be strengthened or weakened in the presence of others. The reasons present in any given situation support the actions or conclusions they do through a complex system of interactions; the goal of this book is to describe these interactions precisely and in detail, and then to show how the resulting theory both relates to some traditional topics in the theory of reasons and also suggests new topics for exploration.

The book is divided into four parts, of two chapters each.

The first part sets the stage by introducing default rules and laying out the formal material necessary for developing a very simple default logic. In contrast to Reiter's original approach, the default rules belonging to the logic presented here are *prioritized*; and I introduce the preliminary idea that the impact of this prioritization can be accommodated simply by allowing lower priority default rules to be defeated by conflicting rules of higher priority—so that the default representing the statement "Birds fly," for example, might be defeated by the default representing the statement "Penguins don't fly." One of the most striking features of default logics is that they can be associated with, in a sense, multiple conclusion sets, and I consider some of the conceptual issues presented by this possibility. Finally, once our simple default logic has been set out, I show how it can serve as the foundation for a concrete theory of reasons, and then compare the resulting theory to some other formal or semi-formal treatments of reasons from the literature.

In the second part of the book, drawing on the familiar idea that the truth or falsity of ought statements is grounded, ultimately, in reasons, I explore two different ways of defining a logic of normative concepts—a deontic logic—in terms of the prioritized default logic developed in the first part. These two deontic logics reflect different strategies for handling the multiple conclusion sets from default logic. One of them, it turns out, allows for normative conflicts, or dilemmas, while the other does not; and once the two logics have been formulated, I examine some of the most important arguments against moral dilemmas within the framework they provide. My conclusion is that, setting aside whatever constraints might be imposed by some particular ethical theory, there is no logical or conceptual reason for ruling out such dilemmas.

The third part is, in many ways, the heart of the book. The version of default logic presented in the first part is a *fixed priority* theory, in which the priority relations among default rules are fixed in advance, and all defaults are, in addition, universally applicable. But in fact, some of the most important things we reason about, and reason about defeasibly, are the priorities among the very default rules that guide our defeasible reasoning, and indeed, in many situations, about whether certain default rules should be applicable at all. My goal here is to explain how this more complicated reasoning can be modeled. More exactly, I define two variants of the earlier account: first, a *variable priority* default logic, in which our reasoning is guided by a set of default rules subject to a priority ordering, but in which the priority ordering among these default rules is itself established through the process of defeasible reasoning they serve to guide; and second, an *exclusionary* default logic, in which this same process of reasoning is likewise used to determine whether, in particular situations, certain default rules are to be excluded from consideration entirely. Once these new logics have been defined, I investigate connections among some of the concepts involved, such as priorities and exclusion, and then show both how these concepts can be used to elaborate our earlier theory of reasons, and also how they can help to illuminate some important philosophical issues: the notion of undercutting defeat in epistemology, Raz's theory of exclusionary reasons, and, especially, Dancy's particularist arguments that principles have no place in moral reasoning.

In the fourth part of the book, I return to two problems left open in the first part. The initial problem concerns, once again, the topic of reasoning with the multiple conclusion sets allowed by default logics. The most common proposal is that a statement should be accepted as a "real" conclusion just in case it is contained in each of these sets. But what if the statement is supported in these different conclusion sets by different, and incompatible, arguments? Here our intuitions fragment, and I explore the nature of the fragmentation. The second problem concerns the way in which the prioritization among default rules should affect our reasoning. A very simple proposal, though adequate to guide our discussion throughout the body of the book, is presented in the first part. But this simple proposal quickly runs into difficulties when more complex examples are considered; and in this final part of the book, I examine some more refined proposals.

There are two appendices. The first relates the default theories defined here to Reiter's original account, and establishes some straightforward properties of these theories; the second relates the present deontic logics to more familiar approaches from the literature.

I am aware that a book like this presents a balanced pair of risks. There is the risk that those who do not care for formal work may be put off by the whole approach: how could technical definitions and results of this kind possibly have any bearing on fundamental issues in the theory of reasons? And there is the risk that those who enjoy formal work will wonder why there is not more of it: where is the detailed, technical exploration of the default logics presented here, and of their connections to other nonmonotonic logics?

I have tried to manage these risks as well as possible. The philosophical goal, once again, is to show how ideas from default logic can form the foundation of a precise, concrete theory of reasons and their interaction, and I know of no way to achieve this goal without actually presenting a default logic, and then using this logic to construct such a theory. Still, the logic at work here is developed in the simplest possible way; only those formal properties directly relevant to the current philosophical project are mentioned at all, and proofs are set off in the appendices. The entire book should be accessible to any reader with a good understanding of ordinary classical logic.

There is, of course, a third risk, and this is that, by developing a precise, concrete theory of reasons and their interaction, I allow for the possibility that the theory can then be shown, in a precise and concrete way, to be mistaken. But this is a risk I welcome. I have more faith in the overall idea—that default logic, and nonmonotonic logics more generally, can serve as the foundation for a useful theory of reasons—than in the details of the particular proposal set out here. Indeed, I have done my best to highlight the weaknesses of the current theory, as well as open issues. If others are willing to work with this theory carefully enough to identify errors and suggest alternative approaches, I can only be grateful.

Part I

Default logic

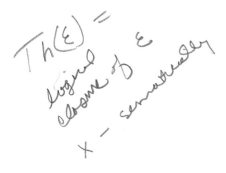

Chapter 1

A primer on default logic

We start with fundamentals, concentrating first on default logic itself, and then on some basic aspects of the account of reasons to be built from this theory. The goal of this first chapter, then, is to motivate and develop a very simple prioritized default logic. The chapter begins by introducing default rules as well as prioritized default theories, structures containing a prioritized set of these default rules along with more ordinary information: it then moves through a series of definitions leading to the crucial notion of an extension for such a theory, and finally explores the relation between this concept of an extension and the more usual logical concept of a conclusion set.

1.1 Basic concepts

1.1.1 Default rules

We take as background an ordinary logical system in which ∧, ∨, ⊃, and ¬ are the operations of conjunction, disjunction, material implication, and negation, and in which ⊤ is the trivially true proposition—or "the true," as Frege might say. The turnstile ⊢ indicates ordinary logical consequence: where $\mathcal{E}$ is a set of propositions and X is an individual proposition, $\mathcal{E} \vdash X$ means that X is derivable from $\mathcal{E}$ according to the rules of classical logic, or equivalently, that X is semantically implied by $\mathcal{E}$. We can then define $Th(\mathcal{E})$ as the logical closure of $\mathcal{E}$, the set of propositions that follow from $\mathcal{E}$ through ordinary logical consequence, by stipulating that

$$Th(\mathcal{E}) = \{X : \mathcal{E} \vdash X\}.$$

A set of propositions like this, closed under logical consequence, is sometimes described as a *belief set*, since it can be used to represents the beliefs of an ideal reasoner, a reasoning agent that can perform logical inference instantaneously. Ideal reasoners do not exist, of course, but the myth is nevertheless useful as a competence model for actual reasoners, and it is a model that we will rely on throughout—we are studying default reasoning, after all, not resource-bounded reasoning.

A further simplification: although I have spoken of propositions, our default logic is to be thought of as developed within the setting of an underlying formal language, containing sentences of the usual logical style, constructed in the usual way from their grammatical constituents. The overall goal, however, is to formulate a precise theory of reasons, not necessarily a pedantic theory of reasons, and there are certain things that it is possible to be relaxed about. One of these is use and mention. We will arrive, eventually, at a view, according to which reasons are cast as certain propositions—rather than sentences, of course—and so it will be easiest by far simply to speak at the level of propositions throughout. Accordingly, although uppercase italicized letters should, technically, be understood as referring to sentences from the underlying formal language, I will speak almost uniformly as if they refer, instead, to the propositions expressed by these sentences. Thus, for example, I will say "the proposition X" when what I really mean to speak of is the proposition expressed by the sentence X, and occasionally even quantify over "all propositions X" when what I really mean to quantify over is all sentences X.

Now, against this background, and with these conventions in mind, let us begin with a standard example, already alluded to in the Introduction, and known as the Tweety Triangle.[1] If an agent is told only that Tweety is a bird, it would be natural for the agent to conclude that Tweety is able to fly. Why is that? It is because the fact that Tweety is a bird is a reason for the conclusion that Tweety is able to fly; and on the view recommended here, this reason relation is captured by a rule according to which, given the information that Tweety is a bird, the agent should normally conclude that Tweety can fly by default. Indeed, our everyday reasoning seems to be governed by a general default according to which birds, normally, are able to fly. But suppose the agent is later told, in addition, that Tweety is a penguin, a fact that functions as a reason for the conclusion that Tweety cannot fly. This reason relation now corresponds to a different default rule, according to which the information that Tweety is a penguin normally leads to the conclusion that Tweety cannot fly—a default that ultimately derives, once again, from the everyday generalization that penguins, normally, cannot fly. Since it is natural to suppose that the default about penguins is stronger than the default about birds, reflecting the relative strength of the two reasons, the agent should withdraw its initial judgment that Tweety flies, and conclude instead that Tweety cannot fly.[2]

---

[1] It is called this because of its triangular shape, soon to become apparent, when depicted as an inference graph.

[2] In an effort to find language that is both gender neutral and unobtrusive, I often speak as if the agent under discussion is an impersonal reasoning device, such as a

Note that I speak here, loosely, of default rules as capturing, or corresponding to, reason relations, and will continue to do so throughout this chapter. In the next chapter, once the appropriate technical concepts have been set out, the nature of this correspondence is described with more care.

Where X and Y are arbitrary propositions, let us now take $X \to Y$ as the *default rule* that allows us to conclude Y, by default, once X has been established. It is important to note that, although written horizontally, a default rule of the form $X \to Y$ is a rule, like modus ponens, with a premise and a conclusion, not a formula, like the material conditional, with an antecedent and a consequent.[3] To illustrate the function of these default rules by returning to our example: if we suppose that B is the proposition that Tweety is a bird and F the proposition that Tweety can fly, then $B \to F$ is the rule that allows us to conclude that Tweety can fly, by default, once it has been established that Tweety is a bird. If we suppose, more particularly, that B can be expressed as $Bird(t)$ and F as $Fly(t)$, where t is Tweety, then the default $B \to F$ can likewise be expressed as $Bird(t) \to Fly(t)$. This particular default rule can therefore be thought of as an instance for Tweety of some general default rule of the form $Bird(x) \to Fly(x)$, allowing us to conclude, for an arbitrary object x, that x can fly, by default, once it has been established that x is a bird.

It is, in many ways, easier to understand general defaults like this— *defeasible*, or *default*, generalizations—than it is to understand their particular instances: the general default $Bird(x) \to Fly(x)$, for example, can be taken to approximate the meaning of the generic truth "Birds fly," while it is harder to find any simple English statement to carry the meaning of a particular instance of this rule, such as $Bird(t) \to Fly(t)$. And in fact, it would be possible to work with general default rules of this sort directly; indeed, this was the standard practice in many of the initial papers on default logic. In order to avoid the complexities involved in the treatment of variables and instantiation in default logic, however, we will follow the more common practice of focusing only on instances of these general rules. Rather than including a general default itself in some formalization, that is, we will instead include each of its particular instances, though these instances should always be thought of as reflecting the general defaults that they instantiate.

We assume two functions—*Premise* and *Conclusion*—that pick out the premises and conclusions of default rules: if δ is the default $X \to Y$, then *Premise*(δ) is the proposition X and *Conclusion*(δ) is the proposition Y. The second of these functions can be lifted from individual defaults to sets

---

computer, which can appropriately be referred to with the pronoun 'it'. When this is just too awkward, I randomize between masculine and feminine pronouns.

[3] For those familiar with standard default logic: the rule that I write as $X \to Y$ represents a *normal* default rule, typically written as $(X : Y / Y)$, in which the proposition X functions as "prerequisite," the first instance of Y functions as "justification," and the second as "conclusion." The relation between the default logics presented here and Reiter's original theory of normal defaults is discussed in Appendix A.3.

Practical Name — name for
Epistemic RSNS — name for XNS
                            conclusions
18   CHAPTER 1.   A PRIMER ON DEFAULT LOGIC

of defaults in the obvious way, so that the conclusion of a set of defaults is
the set of conclusions of the defaults belonging to the original set; or more
formally, where $\mathcal{S}$ is some set of defaults, we stipulate that

$$Conclusion(\mathcal{S}) = \{\, Conclusion(\delta) : \delta \in \mathcal{S} \,\}$$

is the set of conclusions of those defaults belonging to $\mathcal{S}$.

Throughout this book, we will be slipping back and forth, rather casu-
ally, between what might be called *practical* and *epistemic* reasons—reasons
for actions, versus reasons for conclusions. The information that Tweety is
a bird might be said to provide an epistemic reason supporting the conclusion that Tweety flies. By contrast, if Jack promises to meet Jo for lunch,
his promise is most naturally interpreted as providing a practical reason. It
does not necessarily support the conclusion that he will meet her for lunch,
but provides him with a reason for doing so.

Various theses could be advanced concerning the relation between these
two kinds of reasons. One thesis is that epistemic reasons should be subsumed as a species under the genus of practical reasons. On this view,
our reason for the conclusion that Tweety flies does not, in fact, support a
proposition, but actually recommends an action: perhaps the action of *concluding* that Tweety flies. Another thesis is that practical reasons should
be subsumed as a species under the genus of epistemic reasons. On this
view, Jack's reason to meet Jo for lunch does not recommend an action but
actually supports a proposition: perhaps the proposition that Jack *ought* to
meet Jo for lunch. Yet a third thesis is that neither practical nor epistemic
reasons can be subsumed under the genus of the other, but that they are
simply distinct kinds of reasons, though strikingly similar in many of their
important logical properties.

The account set out here is intended to be independent of any of these
theses, or others, concerning the relation between practical and epistemic
reasons; it can be adapted, I believe, to accommodate a variety of different
positions on the topic. Although I will not, therefore, try to address the
relations between practical and epistemic reasons, or the complicated topic
of their interactions, I will, at various points, be discussing each of these
two kinds of reasons individually, and will then use the same notation in
both cases, relying on context to indicate whether the conclusion Y in a
default of the form $X \rightarrow Y$ is supposed to represent a recommended action
or a supported proposition. For expository convenience—simply because
the theory is more naturally motivated in this way—I will begin by focusing
primarily on epistemic reasons, and then turn to practical reasons later on.

1.1.2   Priority relations

As we have seen, some defaults, as well as the reasons to which they correspond, are naturally taken to have greater strength, or higher priority, than
others. This information will be represented, in the first instance, through

an ordering relation $<$ on default rules, where the statement $\delta < \delta'$ means that the default δ' has a higher priority than the default δ. Later, once the correspondence between reasons and defaults has been defined precisely, the priority relation can then be transferred from default rules to reasons themselves. Two questions now arise concerning these priority relations: first, where do they come from, and second, what properties can they be expected to satisfy?

The priority relations among defaults, and their corresponding reasons, can have different sources. In the Tweety Triangle, for example, the priority of the default about penguins over the default about birds has to do with specificity: a penguin is a specific kind of bird, and so information about penguins in particular takes precedence over information about birds in general. But even in the epistemic domain, there are priority relations that have nothing to do with specificity. Reliability is another source. Both the weather channel and the arthritis in my left knee provide reasonably reliable predictions of oncoming precipitation, but the weather channel is more reliable: in case these two sources of information support conflicting conclusions, I will favor the conclusion supported by the weather channel. And once we move from epistemic to practical reasons, then authority provides yet another source for priority relations. National laws typically override state or provincial laws, and more recent court decisions have more authority than older decisions; direct orders override standing orders; and orders from the Colonel override orders from the Major.

Finally, one of the most important sources of priority is our very own reasoning, indeed our default reasoning, about which defaults, or reasons, have higher priority than others. Just as we reason about ordinary things in the world—birds, penguins, the weather—so we reason about our own reasons, offering further reasons for taking some of our reasons more seriously than others, and still further reasons for evaluating those. This process, through which the priorities among defaults are themselves established through default reasoning, or through which the strength of reasons is established by appeal to further reasons, is studied in detail in Chapter 5.

We turn now to the properties we should expect to be satisfied by the overall priority ordering, whatever its source. It is natural, first of all, to suppose that this ordering relation should satisfy the *transitivity* property,

$$\delta < \delta' \quad \text{and} \quad \delta' < \delta'' \quad \text{imply} \quad \delta < \delta'',$$

according to which the default δ'' has a higher priority than δ whenever δ'' has a higher priority than δ', and δ' itself has a higher priority than δ; and it seems equally natural to assume that the ordering satisfies the property of *irreflexivity*, according to which

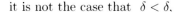

it is not the case that $\delta < \delta$,

so that no default can ever have a higher priority than itself. An ordering relation that is both transitive and irreflexive is referred to as a *strict partial ordering*.

Should we assume any other properties in the priority orderings? In particular, should we assume that this ordering satisfies the property of *connectivity*, according to which we would have

$$\text{either} \quad \delta < \delta' \quad \text{or} \quad \delta' < \delta$$

whenever δ and δ' are distinct defaults? Here we reach an important branch point in our discussion. On one hand, this connectivity assumption would allow for a straightforward resolution to any potential conflicts among default rules. What the assumption tells us is that, of any two such rules, and their corresponding reasons, one is always stronger than the other; and so it would be natural, in case of a conflict, to settle the matter simply by favoring the stronger of the two. On the other hand, connectivity is not particularly plausible, in either the practical or the epistemic domain, and for two reasons.

First of all, some reasons seem simply to be incommensurable. The canonical example in the practical domain is Jean-Paul Sartre's description of a student during the Second World War who felt for reasons of patriotism and vengeance (his brother had been killed by the Germans) that he ought to leave home to fight with the Free French, but who also felt, for reasons of sympathy and personal devotion, that he ought to stay at home to care for his mother.[4] Sartre presents the situation in a vivid way that really does make it seem as if the reasons confronting the student derive from entirely separate sources of value—duty to country, versus duty to family—and cannot meaningfully be compared in importance.

It is more difficult to construct a plausible example of incommensurability in the epistemic domain, but consider a hypothetical election between two candidates in an isolated southern congressional district. Suppose that the Associated Press poll strongly favors Candidate 1 while an experienced local politician, who is neutral in the contest, confidently predicts a victory for Candidate 2. Modern statistical polling is exacting and scientific, but it can yield incorrect results in unfamiliar situations, where parameters might not have been set properly to reflect local circumstances. The politician, by contrast, has an intuitive and historically-grounded sense of his community, which we can suppose he has relied on throughout his successful career, but opinions might have shifted in ways of which he is not aware, and which a survey would detect. A situation like this, then, would seem to present us with conflicting epistemic reasons, deriving from entirely different sources, which are at least arguably incomparable.

The second reason for questioning connectivity is that, even if two conflicting defaults, along with their corresponding reasons, are in fact comparable in strength, they might nevertheless violate the connectivity property,

---

[4]The example is from Sartre (1946).

according to which one or the other must be stronger, simply by having equal strength. As an example from the practical domain, suppose I have inadvertently promised to have a private dinner tonight with each of two identical and identically situated twins, both of whom would now be equally disappointed by my cancellation; the situation can be made arbitrarily symmetrical.[5] I now face two reasons, my promises, that favor two conflicting actions: having a private dinner with Twin 1, or having a private dinner with Twin 2. Since these reasons are of exactly the same kind, they can meaningfully be compared in priority. But given the symmetry of the situation, how could I possibly assume that the priority assigned to either reason should be higher than the priority assigned to the other?

It is, again, a bit harder to find convincing examples of equally weighted, conflicting reasons in the epistemic domain, but consider this. Suppose I have two friends, both equally reliable, and that the three of us plan to meet for lunch at a place selected by the two of them. As lunch time approaches, I receive two text messages, one from each friend. The first reads, "We'll be at Mark's Kitchen, meet us there," and the second, "We'll be at Everyday Gourmet, meet us there." Although the two messages are displayed on my cell phone in some sequence, of course, a check of their time stamps shows that they were sent simultaneously—and at this point my phone battery dies, so that I can neither inquire nor receive any further corrections. I am now faced with a practical decision: Where should I go? But the answer hinges on an epistemic question: Where will my friends be? And in considering this question I seem to be faced once again with two reasons, the text messages sent by my equally reliable friends, identical in strength but supporting conflicting conclusions.

I do not know of anyone who has argued that conflicts like this among epistemic reasons must always be resolvable, but in the case of practical conflicts there are some important precedents. Although they did not use the technical language of ordering or connectivity, some historical figures—F. H. Bradley, several of the British intuitionists, such as Ross—did seem to feel that moral reasons, at least, could always be ranked in such a way that any conflicts would be resolved, if not abstractly, then at least in their application to a particular situation.[6] However, both the process through which such a ranking could be arrived at and the grounds on which it might be defended have always remained somewhat mysterious. Notoriously, Bradley and Ross themselves, both influenced by Aristotle, imagined that the relative priority of the reasons at work in a particular situation could be discovered, and perhaps justified, simply through an intuitive appraisal—a kind of perceptual judgment made by the practically wise person, or in the case of Bradley, by the person who has properly identified his will with the spirit of the community. Of course, other writers in the pluralist tradition

---

[5]The importance of symmetrical cases like this in practical reasoning was emphasized by Ruth Barcan Marcus (1980).

[6]See Bradley (1927) and Ross (1930).

have attempted to describe more theoretically transparent, and rationally defensible, procedures through which conflicts might be adjudicated. Still, although I do not know of any general argument against this possibility, I do think it is fair to say that all of the procedures that have been elaborated to date either fail to guarantee that these conflicts will actually be resolved, or else rely, at some point, on a kind of moral insight no less obscure than that suggested by Bradley and Ross.

In light of the apparent counterexamples to connectivity, then, and lacking any real justification for the idea, we will assume throughout the remainder of this book that the priority relation on default rules and their corresponding reasons satisfies only the two strict partial ordering constraints, transitivity and irreflexivity, allowing for the possibility of conflicting defaults that are either incomparable or identical in priority.

1.1.3 Theories and scenarios

We concentrate in this chapter on *fixed priority* default theories—default theories, that is, in which all priorities among default rules are fixed in advance, so that there is no need to consider either the source of these priority relations or the way in which they are established, but only their effect on the conclusions reached through default reasoning. A theory of this kind contains three components: the first is a set W of ordinary propositions, taken to represent the agent's fixed background information; the second is a set $\mathcal{D}$ of default rules; the third is a priority ordering $<$ on these default rules.

Definition 1 (Fixed priority default theories) A fixed priority default theory Δ is a structure of the form $\langle W, \mathcal{D}, < \rangle$, in which W is a set of ordinary propositions, $\mathcal{D}$ is a set of default rules, and $<$ is a strict partial ordering on $\mathcal{D}$.

Such a structure—a collection of ordinary propositions together with an ordered collection of default rules—is supposed to represent the initial data provided to the agent as a basis for its reasoning.

The development of nonmonotonic logic was originally driven by the epistemic interpretation of defaults, and so began, as we will here, with the problem of characterizing the belief sets supported by default theories—the conclusions that an ideal reasoner might settle upon when the hard information from W is supplemented with the defaults from $\mathcal{D}$. On this interpretation, defaults are best thought of as special rules of inference that can be used to extend the conclusions derivable from the propositions belonging to W beyond their standard logical consequences, and for this reason, the belief sets supported by default theories are generally referred to as *extensions* of those theories. Much of the research in default logic is aimed at developing appropriate definitions for this technical concept of an extension, mapping out alternatives and exploring their properties.

We will approach the matter in a somewhat roundabout way, focusing here, not directly on the concept of an extension, but instead on the more fundamental notion of a *scenario*, where a scenario based on a default theory $\Delta = \langle W, D, < \rangle$ is defined simply as some subset S of the set D of defaults contained in that theory. From an intuitive standpoint, a scenario is supposed to represent the particular subset of available defaults that have actually been selected by the reasoning agent as providing sufficient support for their conclusions—the particular subset of defaults, that is, to be used by the agent in extending the initial information from W to a full belief set, which we can then speak of as the belief set that is generated by the scenario. More exactly, where S is a scenario based on the default theory $\Delta = \langle W, D, < \rangle$, we can say that the belief set $\mathcal{E}$ is *generated* by that scenario just in case

$$\mathcal{E} = Th(W \cup Conclusion(S));$$

the agent arrives at the belief set $\mathcal{E}$ generated by the scenario S by first extracting the conclusions from the defaults belonging to that scenario, then combining this set of conclusions with the hard information from W, and finally taking the logical closure of the entire thing.

Not every scenario based on a default theory is intuitively acceptable, of course; some scenarios might contain what seems to be the wrong selection of defaults. The central task of this chapter is to characterize, as we will say, the *proper scenarios*—those sets of defaults that might be accepted by an ideal reasoning agent, on the basis of the information contained in some particular default theory. Once this notion of a proper scenario is in place, the traditional concept of an extension of a default theory can then be defined quite simply as a belief set that is generated by a proper scenario.

All of this will be explained more carefully in the remainder of the chapter, but the ideas at work can be illustrated by returning to our initial example of the Tweety Triangle, with P, B, and F as the propositions that Tweety is a penguin, that Tweety is a bird, and that Tweety flies. Let us take δ_1 and δ_2 as the defaults $B \to F$ and $P \to \neg F$, instances for Tweety of the general default rules that birds fly and that penguins do not. The information from this example can then be captured by the default theory $\Delta_1 = \langle W, D, < \rangle$, where $W = \{P, P \supset B\}$ and $D = \{\delta_1, \delta_2\}$, and where $\delta_1 < \delta_2$. The set W contains the basic information that Tweety is a penguin, and that this entails the fact that he is a bird; the set D contains the two defaults; and the ordering tells us that the default about penguins has higher priority than the default about birds.

It is often possible, and where possible it is often helpful, to depict default theories as *inference graphs*, with nodes representing propositions and links between nodes representing both ordinary and default entailment

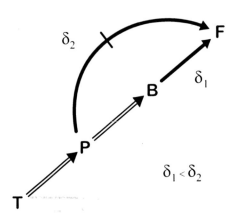

Figure 1.1: The Tweety Triangle

relations between these propositions.[7] The conventions for interpreting
these graphs are as follows: A strict link of the form $X \Rightarrow Y$ indicates that,
according to the theory under consideration, the proposition X materially
implies the proposition Y; as a special case, the link $\top \Rightarrow Y$ indicates that
Y is materially implied by the true proposition, or more simply, that Y
is true. In order to make the inference relations among propositions more
perspicuous, a strict positive link $X \Rightarrow \neg Y$, with a negated proposition
on its tail, is often written as the strict negative link $X \not\Rightarrow Y$, and two
strict negative links of the form $X \not\Rightarrow Y$ and $Y \not\Rightarrow X$ are often merged
into a single link $X \not\Leftrightarrow Y$, indicating that the propositions X and Y are
inconsistent, that each implies the negation of the other. A defeasible link of
the form $X \rightarrow Y$ indicates that the proposition Y follows from X by default,
where, again, the defeasible positive link $X \rightarrow \neg Y$, pointing at a negated
proposition, is often abbreviated as the defeasible negative link $X \not\rightarrow Y$.
Given these conventions, the theory currently under consideration—Δ_1, or
the Tweety Triangle—can now be depicted as in Figure 1.1.

It is clear that this theory allows four possible scenarios—$\mathcal{S}_1 = \emptyset$, $\mathcal{S}_2 =$
$\{\delta_1\}$, $\mathcal{S}_3 = \{\delta_2\}$, or $\mathcal{S}_4 = \{\delta_1, \delta_2\}$—corresponding to the situations in which
the reasoning agent endorses neither of the two available defaults, only the
first default, only the second, or both. From an intuitive standpoint, of
course, it seems that the agent should endorse the default δ_2, and only

---

[7]The graphical notation employed here is drawn from the literature on nonmonotonic inheritance networks, a formalism for representing information pioneered by Scott
Fahlman (1979), first analyzed in detail by Touretzky (1986), and then developed in the
series of papers by Thomason, Touretzky, and myself mentioned earlier. A very similar graphical formalism for the representation of defeasible information was developed
independently by Pollock, beginning with Pollock (1987).

that default, leading to the conclusion that Tweety does not fly. Therefore, only the third of these four scenarios, $\mathcal{S}_3 = \{\delta_2\}$, should be classified as proper. Following our recipe, we can then define the extension of this default theory, the belief set generated by its proper scenario, as the set

$$
\begin{aligned}
\mathcal{E}_3 &= Th(\mathcal{W} \cup Conclusion(\mathcal{S}_3)) \\
&= Th(\{P, P \supset B\} \cup \{\neg F\}) \\
&= Th(\{P, P \supset B, \neg F\}),
\end{aligned}
$$

arrived at by combining the conclusion of the single default rule from $\mathcal{S}_3$, the proposition $\neg F$, with the hard information from $\mathcal{W}$, the propositions P and $P \supset B$, and then taking the logical closure of the result.

As this example shows, the process of constructing an extension from a proper scenario, once one has been identified, is routine. The real work lies in the task, to which we now turn, of providing a general definition of the proper scenarios themselves.

1.2 Central definitions

1.2.1 Binding defaults

We begin with the concept of a binding default. If default rules correspond to reasons in general, then the binding defaults are supposed to correspond to those that can be classified as *good* reasons, in the context of a particular scenario. This reference to a scenario is not accidental: according to the theory developed here, the set of defaults that might correspond to good reasons will depend on the set of defaults already endorsed, the agent's current scenario.

The concept of a binding default is defined in terms of three preliminary ideas, which we consider first—triggering, conflict, and defeat.

Not every default is even applicable in every scenario, of course. The default that birds fly, for example, provides no reason at all for an agent to conclude that Tweety flies unless that agent is already committed to the proposition that Tweety is a bird. The *triggered* defaults are supposed to represent those that are applicable in the context of a particular scenario; they are defined as the defaults whose premises are entailed by that scenario—those defaults, that is, whose premises follow from the initial information belonging to the underlying default theory together with the conclusions of the defaults already endorsed.

Definition 2 (Triggered defaults) Let $\Delta = \langle \mathcal{W}, \mathcal{D}, < \rangle$ be a fixed priority default theory and $\mathcal{S}$ a scenario based on this theory. Then the defaults from $\mathcal{D}$ that are triggered in the context of the scenario $\mathcal{S}$ are those belonging to the set

$$
Triggered_{\mathcal{W}, \mathcal{D}}(\mathcal{S}) = \{\delta \in \mathcal{D} : \mathcal{W} \cup Conclusion(\mathcal{S}) \vdash Premise(\delta)\}.
$$

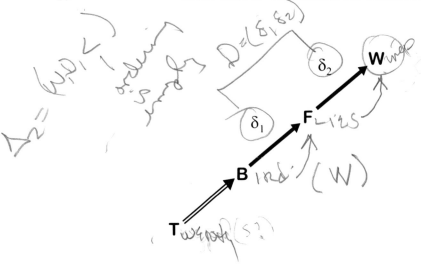

Figure 1.2: Chaining defaults

To illustrate: take B, F, and W respectively as the propositions that Tweety is a bird, that Tweety flies, and that Tweety has wings; and let δ_1 and δ_2 be the defaults $B \to F$ and $F \to W$, instances for Tweety of the general defaults that birds fly and that flying things tend to have wings. Now consider the default theory $\Delta_2 = \langle \mathcal{W}, \mathcal{D}, < \rangle$, depicted in Figure 1.2, where $\mathcal{W} = \{B\}$, where $\mathcal{D} = \{\delta_1, \delta_2\}$, and where the ordering $<$ is empty. Suppose the reasoning agent has not yet endorsed any of the defaults from $\mathcal{D}$, so that its initial scenario is simply $\mathcal{S}_1 = \emptyset$, the empty set. Since $\mathcal{W} \cup Conclusion(\mathcal{S}_1) \vdash Premise(\delta_1)$ and it is not the case that $\mathcal{W} \cup Conclusion(\mathcal{S}_1) \vdash Premise(\delta_2)$, we then have $Triggered_{\mathcal{W},\mathcal{D}}(\mathcal{S}_1) = \{\delta_1\}$. In the context of this initial scenario, then, only the default δ_1 is triggered, providing the agent with a reason for its conclusion, the proposition F. Now suppose the agent accepts this default, and so moves to the new scenario $\mathcal{S}_2 = \{\delta_1\}$. Since $\mathcal{W} \cup Conclusion(\mathcal{S}_2) \vdash Premise(\delta_2)$, we have $Triggered_{\mathcal{W},\mathcal{D}}(\mathcal{S}_2) = \{\delta_1, \delta_2\}$, so that the default δ_2 is now triggered as well, providing a reason for the new conclusion W.

This discussion of triggered defaults leads to a terminological question. Suppose, as in this example, that an agent's background theory contains the default $B \to F$, an instance for Tweety of the general default that birds fly, together with B, the proposition that Tweety is a bird, so that the default is triggered. It seems plain that there is then a reason for the agent to conclude that Tweety flies. But how, exactly, should this reason be reified? Should it be identified with the default $B \to F$, or with the proposition B? More generally, should reasons be identified with default rules themselves, or with the propositions that trigger them?

This question, like many questions concerning reification, is somewhat artificial. Evidently, both the default and the proposition are involved in providing the agent with a reason for concluding that Tweety flies. The default would have no bearing if it were not triggered by some proposition to which the agent is committed; the proposition would be nothing but an incidental feature of the situation if it did not trigger some default. When it comes to reification, then, the reason relation could, strictly speaking, be projected in either direction, toward default rules or the propositions that trigger them, and the choice is largely arbitrary.

Still, it corresponds most closely with ordinary usage to reify reasons as propositions, rather than rules. Our discussion throughout this book will therefore be based on an analysis according to which *reasons are identified with the premises of triggered defaults*; and we will speak of these triggered defaults, not as reasons themselves, but as *providing* certain propositions—their premises—as reasons for their conclusions. To illustrate this terminology: in the case of our example, we will say that B, the proposition that Tweety is a bird, is a *reason* for the conclusion that Tweety flies, and that this reason is *provided by* the default $B \rightarrow F$.

Triggering is a necessary condition that a default must satisfy in order to be classified as binding in a scenario, but it is not sufficient. Even if some default is triggered, it might not be binding, all things considered—the reason it provides might not be a good reason. Two further aspects of the situation could interfere.

The first is easy to describe. A default will not be classified as binding in a scenario, even if it happens to be triggered, if that default is *conflicted*—that is, if the agent is already committed to the negation of its conclusion.

Definition 3 (Conflicted defaults) Let $\Delta = \langle W, D, < \rangle$ be a fixed priority default theory, and S a scenario based on this theory. Then the defaults from D that are conflicted in the context of the scenario S are those belonging to the set

$$Conflicted_{W,D}(S) = \{\delta \in D : W \cup Conclusion(S) \vdash \neg Conclusion(\delta)\}.$$

The intuitive force of this restriction can be illustrated through another standard example, which can be thought of as an epistemic analog to a moral dilemma. The example, first introduced in the early days of nonmonotonic logic, when the memory of the 37th President of the United States was still fresh, is known as the Nixon Diamond. Suppose that Q, R, and P are the propositions that Nixon is a Quaker, that Nixon is a Republican, and that Nixon is a pacifist; and let δ_1 and δ_2 be the defaults $Q \rightarrow P$ and $R \rightarrow \neg P$, instances for Nixon of the generalizations that Quakers tend to be pacifists and that Republicans tend not to be pacifists. The Nixon Diamond can then be represented through the theory $\Delta_3 = \langle W, D, < \rangle$, depicted in Figure 1.3, where $W = \{Q, R\}$, where $D = \{\delta_1, \delta_2\}$, and where the ordering $<$ is empty; neither default has a higher priority than the other.

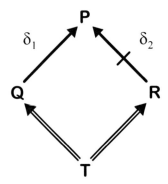

Figure 1.3: The Nixon Diamond

Suppose that the reasoning agent has not yet accepted either of these two defaults, so that its initial scenario is $\mathcal{S}_1 = \emptyset$. In this situation, we have $\textit{Triggered}_{\mathcal{W},\mathcal{D}}(\mathcal{S}_1) = \{\delta_1, \delta_2\}$. Both defaults are triggered, providing the agent with reasons for their conclusions. The default δ_1 provides Q, the proposition that Nixon is a Quaker, as a reason for the conclusion P, that Nixon is a pacifist; the default δ_2 provides R, the proposition that Nixon is a Republican, as a reason for the conclusion $\neg P$, that Nixon is not a pacifist. Still, although these two defaults support conflicting conclusions, neither is, according to our definition, conflicted in the initial scenario. Since it is not the case that $\mathcal{W} \cup \textit{Conclusion}(\mathcal{S}_1) \vdash \neg \textit{Conclusion}(\delta_1)$, the agent is not yet committed to denying the conclusion of the first default, and likewise for the second. The set of conflicted defaults is therefore empty: $\textit{Conflicted}_{\mathcal{W},\mathcal{D}}(\mathcal{S}_1) = \emptyset$. Both defaults seem to provide good reasons for their conclusions, and so the agent must find some way of dealing with the conflict presented by its current scenario.

Now imagine that, on whatever grounds, the agent decides to endorse one of these two defaults—say δ_1, supporting the conclusion P, that Nixon is a pacifist—and so moves to the new scenario $\mathcal{S}_2 = \{\delta_1\}$. In the context of this new scenario, the other default—δ_2, supporting the conclusion $\neg P$, that Nixon is not a pacifist—will now be conflicted: since $\mathcal{W} \cup \textit{Conclusion}(\mathcal{S}_2) \vdash \neg \textit{Conclusion}(\delta_2)$, we now have $\textit{Conflicted}_{\mathcal{W},\mathcal{D}}(\mathcal{S}_2) = \{\delta_2\}$. From the standpoint of the new scenario, then, the reason provided by δ_2 will no longer be classified as a good reason, since the agent has already settled on a default that provides a reason for a conflicting conclusion.

The second restriction governing the notion of a binding default is that, even if it is triggered, and even if it is not conflicted, a default still cannot be classified as binding if it happens to be *defeated*. Although, as we will see later on, in Chapter 8, the concept of a defeated default is considerably more difficult to define than that of a conflicted default, the basic idea is simple enough: very roughly, a default will be defeated whenever there is a stronger triggered default that supports a conflicting conclusion.[8]

This idea can be illustrated by returning to the Tweety Triangle—that is, the theory $\Delta_1 = \langle \mathcal{W}, \mathcal{D}, < \rangle$, depicted in Figure 1.1, where $\mathcal{W} = \{P, P \supset B\}$, where $\mathcal{D} = \{\delta_1, \delta_2\}$ with δ_1 and δ_2 as the defaults $B \to F$ and $P \to \neg F$, and where $\delta_1 < \delta_2$. As a reminder: P, B, and F are the propositions that Tweety is a penguin, that Tweety is a bird, and that Tweety flies. Let us suppose once again that the agent has not yet endorsed either of the two defaults, so that its initial scenario is $\mathcal{S}_1 = \emptyset$. In this situation, we again have $Triggered_{\mathcal{W},\mathcal{D}}(\mathcal{S}_1) = \{\delta_1, \delta_2\}$. Both defaults are triggered, with δ_1 providing B as a reason for the conclusion F while δ_2 provides P as a reason for the conclusion $\neg F$. And we again have $Conflicted_{\mathcal{W},\mathcal{D}}(\mathcal{S}_1) = \emptyset$, so that neither of these defaults is itself conflicted. In some ways, then, this situation is like the Nixon Diamond, where the agent is confronted with a pair of triggered defaults supporting conflicting conclusions, neither of which is itself conflicted. Here, however, it does not seem that the agent should be free, as with the Nixon Diamond, to settle this conflict in favor of either one of the two defaults. Instead, it seems appropriate to say, on intuitive grounds, that the default δ_1, supporting the conclusion F, is defeated by the default δ_2, since this default is also triggered, it is stronger than δ_1, and it supports the conflicting conclusion $\neg F$.

Motivated by this example, we can now generalize our basic idea into a preliminary definition, according to which a default is defeated in a scenario if that scenario triggers some stronger default with a conflicting conclusion.

Definition 4 (Defeated defaults: preliminary definition) Let $\Delta = \langle \mathcal{W}, \mathcal{D}, < \rangle$ be a fixed priority default theory, and $\mathcal{S}$ a scenario based on this theory. Then the defaults from $\mathcal{D}$ that are defeated in the context of the scenario $\mathcal{S}$ are those belonging to the set

$$Defeated_{\mathcal{W},\mathcal{D},<}(\mathcal{S}) =$$
$$\{\delta \in \mathcal{D} : \quad \text{there is a default } \delta' \in Triggered_{\mathcal{W},\mathcal{D}}(\mathcal{S}) \text{ such that}$$
$$(1) \ \delta < \delta',$$
$$(2) \ \mathcal{W} \cup \{Conclusion(\delta')\} \vdash \neg \ Conclusion(\delta)\}.$$

In a case like this, where one default δ is defeated by another default δ', we can speak of δ' as a *defeating default* for δ, or more simply, as a *defeater*.

---

[8]Many writers distinguish between *rebutting* defeat and *undercutting* defeat—a contrast originally due to Pollock—where rebutting defeat corresponds, roughly, to the concept described in the text, and where undercutting defeat is a separate notion, according to which a consideration defeats a reason for a conclusion, not by supporting a contradictory conclusion, but by challenging the reason relation itself. As I use it in this book, the term "defeat" refers only to rebutting defeat, but we will return in Chapter 5 to consider how the important notion of undercutting, or *exclusionary*, defeat can be accommodated within the framework of this book.

This preliminary definition yields the correct results in the Tweety Triangle, where we can see that, as desired, the default δ_1 is defeated in the context of the scenario $\mathcal{S}_1$, with δ_2 as its defeater: it follows from the definition that $Defeated_{\mathcal{W},\mathcal{D},<}(\mathcal{S}_1) = \{\delta_1\}$, since $\delta_2 \in Triggered_{\mathcal{W},\mathcal{D}}(\mathcal{S}_1)$ and we have both (1) $\delta_1 < \delta_2$ and (2) $\mathcal{W} \cup \{Conclusion(\delta_2)\} \vdash \neg Conclusion(\delta_1)$. Indeed, this preliminary definition is adequate for a wide variety of ordinary examples, and in order to avoid unnecessary complication, we will rely on it as our official definition throughout the bulk of this book. There are also, however, some more complex cases in which this simple definition of defeat fails to yield correct results. The problem of accounting for the impact of prioritization in default logic, whether by refining the simple concept of defeat or in some other way, is difficult, and in spite of a good deal of effort, still not entirely resolved; we will return to consider the issue in more detail in Chapter 8.

Once the underlying notions of triggering, conflict, and defeat are in place, we can define the set of defaults that are classified as *binding* in the context of a particular scenario quite simply, as those that are triggered in that scenario, but neither conflicted nor defeated.

Definition 5 (Binding defaults) Let $\Delta = \langle \mathcal{W}, \mathcal{D}, < \rangle$ be a fixed priority default theory, and $\mathcal{S}$ a scenario based on this theory. Then the defaults from $\mathcal{D}$ that are binding in the context of the scenario $\mathcal{S}$ are those belonging to the set

$$Binding_{\mathcal{W},\mathcal{D},<}(\mathcal{S}) \;=\; \{\delta \in \mathcal{D}: \quad \delta \in Triggered_{\mathcal{W},\mathcal{D}}(\mathcal{S}),$$
$$\delta \notin Conflicted_{\mathcal{W},\mathcal{D}}(\mathcal{S}),$$
$$\delta \notin Defeated_{\mathcal{W},\mathcal{D},<}(\mathcal{S})\}.$$

The concept can again be illustrated with the Tweety Triangle, under the assumption that the agent's initial scenario is $\mathcal{S}_1 = \emptyset$. Here, the default δ_1, providing a reason for the conclusion F, that Tweety flies, is triggered in the context of this scenario, and it is not conflicted, but as we have just seen, it is defeated by the default δ_2; and so it cannot be classified as binding. By contrast, the default δ_2, supporting the conclusion $\neg F$, that Tweety does not fly, is likewise triggered in the scenario, not conflicted, and in this case not defeated either—there is no stronger triggered default that supports a conflicting conclusion. This default, therefore, is binding.

1.2.2   Proper scenarios and extensions

Let us return to our central task of defining the proper scenarios based on particular default theories—those sets of defaults that might be endorsed by ideal reasoning agents—as well as the extensions they generate.

The binding defaults, we recall, are supposed to represent the good reasons, in the context of a particular scenario. It is therefore natural to isolate the concept of a *stable scenario* as one containing all and only the defaults that are binding in the context of that very scenario.

Definition 6 (Stable scenarios) Let $\Delta = \langle \mathcal{W}, \mathcal{D}, < \rangle$ be a fixed priority default theory, and $\mathcal{S}$ a scenario based on this theory. Then $\mathcal{S}$ is a stable scenario based on the theory Δ just in case

$$\mathcal{S} = \mathit{Binding}_{\mathcal{W}, \mathcal{D}, <}(\mathcal{S}).$$

An agent who has accepted a set of defaults that forms a stable scenario is in an enviable position. Such an agent has already endorsed exactly those defaults that it recognizes as providing good reasons in the context of that scenario; the agent, therefore, has no incentive either to abandon any of the defaults it has already endorsed, or to endorse any others.

As this characterization makes clear, a scenario can fail to achieve stability in two ways: by including defaults that are not classified as binding in the context of that scenario, or by excluding defaults that are. Both defects can be illustrated by returning to the previous theory $\Delta_2 = \langle \mathcal{W}, \mathcal{D}, < \rangle$, depicted in Figure 1.2, where $\mathcal{W} = \{B\}$, where $\mathcal{D} = \{\delta_1, \delta_2\}$ with δ_1 as the default $B \rightarrow F$ and δ_2 as the default $F \rightarrow W$, and where the ordering $<$ is empty. Consider the four possible scenarios based on this theory: $\mathcal{S}_1 = \emptyset$, $\mathcal{S}_2 = \{\delta_1\}$, $\mathcal{S}_3 = \{\delta_2\}$, and $\mathcal{S}_4 = \{\delta_1, \delta_2\}$. Here it is easy to see that none of $\mathcal{S}_1$, $\mathcal{S}_2$, or $\mathcal{S}_3$ is a stable scenario, the first because it excludes the default δ_1, which is binding in the context of $\mathcal{S}_1$, the second because it excludes the default δ_2, which is binding in the context of $\mathcal{S}_2$, and the third because it includes the default δ_2, which is not binding in the context of $\mathcal{S}_3$, and also because it excludes δ_1, which is binding. What about $\mathcal{S}_4 = \{\delta_1, \delta_2\}$—is this a stable scenario? Yes, at last: every default that is binding in the context of $\mathcal{S}_4$ is included in this scenario, and every included default is binding.

Evidently, the set of defaults belonging to a stable scenario is highly interdependent. Including one default may lead to the classification of another as binding, which must then be included as well; alternatively, including one default might just as easily rule out the possible inclusion of another. The first possibility can be illustrated by continuing with the same example and returning to the scenario $\mathcal{S}_2 = \{\delta_1\}$. As we have seen, this set is not stable, since, once δ_1 has been included, the default δ_2 is now triggered and neither conflicted nor defeated, and so binding, but not included. The second possibility—that the inclusion of one default forces the exclusion of another—was already illustrated in our discussion of the Nixon Diamond, the theory $\Delta_3 = \langle \mathcal{W}, \mathcal{D}, < \rangle$, depicted in Figure 1.3, where $\mathcal{W} = \{Q, R\}$, where $\mathcal{D} = \{\delta_1, \delta_2\}$ with δ_1 as $Q \rightarrow P$ and δ_2 as $R \rightarrow \neg P$, and where the ordering $<$ is empty. Here, both δ_1 and δ_2 are binding in the context of the scenario $\mathcal{S}_1 = \emptyset$, triggered but neither conflicted nor defeated. Either, therefore, could reasonably be accepted, but the acceptance of either rules out acceptance of the other. If the reasoning agent accepts the default δ_1, for example, and so moves to the scenario $\mathcal{S}_2 = \{\delta_1\}$, then the default δ_2 is conflicted in this new context, and so no longer binding.

Now the proper scenarios, we recall, are supposed to be those sets of defaults that might be endorsed by an ideal reasoner on the basis of the information contained in a default theory. As we have seen, an agent that has accepted a stable scenario is in a state of epistemic equilibrium, at least, with no motivation either to expand or to contract its set of accepted defaults. Can we, then, simply identify the proper scenarios with the stable scenarios? I offer two answers to this question, a preliminary answer and a more complete answer.

The preliminary answer is that, in the vast range of ordinary cases, including all of those to be considered in the body of this book, we can indeed identify the proper scenarios with the stable scenarios. This preliminary answer can be solidified in the following rather boring preliminary definition.

Definition 7 (Proper scenarios: preliminary definition)   Let $\Delta = \langle \mathcal{W}, \mathcal{D}, < \rangle$ be a fixed priority default theory, and $\mathcal{S}$ a scenario based on this theory. Then $\mathcal{S}$ is a proper scenario based on the theory Δ just in case $\mathcal{S}$ is a stable scenario based on this theory.

Unfortunately, the more complete answer is that there are also certain aberrant default theories which allow stable scenarios that cannot really be classified as proper—that is, as scenarios that an ideal reasoner would accept. These aberrant theories contain defaults, or chains of defaults, that are, in a sense, self-triggering, with the result that the stable scenarios they support are not properly grounded in the hard information from the underlying theories. Since the problems presented by theories like these are essentially technical, and have little bearing on the more philosophical issues that concern us in this book, we can safely rely on our preliminary definition, which simply identifies proper and stable scenarios, throughout the body of this book. For the sake of completeness, however, we return to consider these aberrant default theories in Appendix A.1, which provides a more generally applicable definition of proper scenarios for fixed priority default theories.

At this point, then, having introduced at least a working idea of the proper scenarios, we can now officially define the extensions of default theories—those belief sets that an ideal reasoner might arrive at—as the belief sets that are generated by the proper scenarios based on these theories.

Definition 8 (Extensions) Let $\Delta = \langle \mathcal{W}, \mathcal{D}, < \rangle$ be a fixed priority default theory. Then $\mathcal{E}$ is an extension of the theory Δ just in case, for some proper scenario $\mathcal{S}$ based on this theory,

$$\mathcal{E} = Th(\mathcal{W} \cup Conclusion(\mathcal{S})).$$

With these formal definitions in place, let us return to our informal discussion of the Tweety Triangle—again, the theory $\Delta_1 = \langle \mathcal{W}, \mathcal{D}, < \rangle$, depicted in Figure 1.1, where $\mathcal{W} = \{P, P \supset B\}$, where $\mathcal{D} = \{\delta_1, \delta_2\}$ with

δ_1 the default $B \rightarrow F$ and δ_2 the default $P \rightarrow \neg F$, and where $\delta_1 < \delta_2$. In our earlier discussion, we noted that, of the four possible scenarios based on this theory—that is, $\mathcal{S}_1 = \emptyset$, $\mathcal{S}_2 = \{\delta_1\}$, $\mathcal{S}_3 = \{\delta_2\}$, and $\mathcal{S}_4 = \{\delta_1, \delta_2\}$—only the third seemed attractive from an intuitive point of view; and we are now in a position to verify that this scenario, and only this scenario, is proper.

The argument proceeds by enumeration. The first scenario, $\mathcal{S}_1 = \emptyset$, cannot be proper since it fails to contain the default δ_2, which is binding in the context of this scenario—triggered, but neither conflicted nor defeated. The second, $\mathcal{S}_2 = \{\delta_1\}$, cannot be proper since it contains the default δ_1, which is defeated in the context of that scenario, and so not binding. And the fourth, $\mathcal{S}_4 = \{\delta_1, \delta_2\}$, cannot be proper either, since each of the two defaults it contains conflicts with the other, so that both are conflicted and neither is binding. Only the third scenario, $\mathcal{S}_3 = \{\delta_2\}$, is proper, containing all and only the defaults that are binding in the context of that scenario. As in our previous discussion, we can then verify that $\mathcal{E}_3 = Th(\{P, P \supset B, \neg F\})$ is the unique extension of this default theory, generated by its unique proper scenario.

Our various definitions allow us to establish a number of important formal properties of extensions, of which I will mention only two here, because of their relevance to our later treatment of deontic logic. The first is the property of *closure*, according to which extensions are closed under logical consequence. More exactly: if $\mathcal{E}$ is an extension of some default theory that contains the statement X, and if $X \vdash Y$—that is, if Y is an ordinary logical consequence of X—then $\mathcal{E}$ likewise contains the statement Y. The second is the property of *consistency*, according to which an extension of a default theory is consistent just in case the set of ordinary propositions from that theory is itself consistent; the application of default rules cannot introduce inconsistency. More exactly: if $\mathcal{E}$ is an extension of the default theory $\Delta = \langle \mathcal{W}, \mathcal{D}, < \rangle$, then $\mathcal{E}$ is consistent just in case the set $\mathcal{W}$ of ordinary propositions from this default theory is itself consistent.

The first of these properties, closure, follows immediately from the definition of an extension of a default theory itself in terms of logical closure. The verification of the second property, consistency, is slightly more complicated, having two parts. To see, first of all, that $\mathcal{E}$ must be inconsistent if $\mathcal{W}$ is, we note that, if $\mathcal{E}$ is an extension, it must be the case that $\mathcal{E} = Th(\mathcal{W} \cup Conclusion(\mathcal{S}))$ for some proper scenario $\mathcal{S}$, so that $\mathcal{E}$ is a superset of $\mathcal{W}$. Since any superset of an inconsistent set is itself inconsistent, $\mathcal{E}$ must be inconsistent if $\mathcal{W}$ is. To establish the other direction, that $\mathcal{W}$ must be inconsistent if $\mathcal{E}$ is, we can reason as follows. If $\mathcal{E} = Th(\mathcal{W} \cup Conclusion(\mathcal{S}))$ is inconsistent, then the set $\mathcal{W} \cup Conclusion(\mathcal{S})$ entails every formula, and so the negation of every formula as well. Therefore, every default from $\mathcal{D}$ is conflicted in the context of $\mathcal{S}$, the generating scenario: $Conflicted_{\mathcal{W}, \mathcal{D}}(\mathcal{S}) = \mathcal{D}$. Since a default can be binding only if it is not conflicted, it follows that the set of defaults that are binding in this scenario is empty: $Binding_{\mathcal{W},\mathcal{D},<}(\mathcal{S}) = \emptyset$. And since a scenario can be proper only if every default it contains is binding, it likewise follows that the scenario $\mathcal{S}$ itself must be empty: $\mathcal{S} = \emptyset$. From this we have $Conclusion(\mathcal{S}) = \emptyset$, of course, and so $\mathcal{E} = Th(\mathcal{W})$. But if $\mathcal{E}$ contains nothing more than the logical consequences of $\mathcal{W}$, and $\mathcal{E}$ is inconsistent, then $\mathcal{W}$ must be inconsistent as well.

1.3   Extensions and conclusions

Let us now look more carefully at the relation between the extensions of default theories and their conclusions, or consequences. Given the information contained in a default theory, what should an agent actually conclude? How should we define the consequences of such a theory? These may seem like odd questions. Why not simply stipulate that the conclusions, or consequences, of default theories are the propositions contained in their extensions?

This suggestion is reasonable in many cases. Consider again the Tweety Triangle—that is, the theory $\Delta_1 = \langle \mathcal{W}, \mathcal{D}, < \rangle$ from Figure 1.1, where $\mathcal{W} = \{P, P \supset B\}$, where $\mathcal{D} = \{\delta_1, \delta_2\}$ with δ_1 and δ_2 as the defaults $B \to F$ and $P \to \neg F$, and where $\delta_1 < \delta_2$. As we have seen, this theory yields the unique proper scenario $\mathcal{S}_3 = \{\delta_2\}$, which then generates the unique extension $\mathcal{E}_3 = Th(\{P, P \supset B, \neg F\})$. It therefore seems very natural to identify the consequences of this default theory with the propositions contained in this extension, which supplements the initial facts P and $P \supset B$, that Tweety is a penguin and therefore a bird, with the default conclusion $\neg F$, that Tweety cannot fly.

Unfortunately, this simple suggestion—that the consequences of default theories can be identified with the propositions contained in their extensions—runs into difficulties in other cases. The reason for this is that the present account, like many others in nonmonotonic reasoning, defines a relation between default theories and their extensions that is anomalous from a more conventional perspective: certain default theories are associated with multiple extensions, while others have no extensions at all.

1.3.1   Theories with multiple extensions

The canonical example of a default theory with multiple extensions is the Nixon Diamond—the theory $\Delta_3 = \langle \mathcal{W}, \mathcal{D}, < \rangle$, depicted in Figure 1.3, where $\mathcal{W} = \{Q, R\}$, where $\mathcal{D} = \{\delta_1, \delta_2\}$ with δ_1 and δ_2 as the defaults $Q \to P$ and $R \to \neg P$, and where $<$ is empty. This theory yields two proper scenarios, both the scenario $\mathcal{S}_1 = \{\delta_1\}$, considered earlier, and the scenario $\mathcal{S}_2 = \{\delta_2\}$. These two proper scenarios generate the two extensions $\mathcal{E}_1 = Th(\{Q, R, P\})$ and $\mathcal{E}_2 = Th(\{Q, R, \neg P\})$. Both of these extensions contain Q and R, the initial information that Nixon is a Quaker and a Republican, but the first contains P, the proposition that he is a pacifist, while the second contains $\neg P$, the proposition that he is not. In light of these two extensions, what should the reasoning agent actually conclude from the original default theory: is Nixon a pacifist or not? More generally, when a default theory leads to more than one extension, how should we define its consequences?

The question is vexed, and has not been adequately addressed even in the literature on nonmonotonic reasoning. I cannot hope to resolve the issue here, but will simply describe three broad strategic options, in order to illustrate the range of possibilities.

The first option is to interpret the different extensions associated with a default theory simply as different equilibrium states that an ideal reasoner might arrive at on the basis of the initial information from that theory. The agent could then be expected to select, arbitrarily, a particular one of these extensions and endorse the conclusions supported by it. In the case of the Nixon Diamond, for example, the agent could appropriately select either the extension $\mathcal{E}_1$ or the extension $\mathcal{E}_2$, endorsing either the conclusion that Nixon is a pacifist, or else the conclusion that he is not.

This option—which I will call the *choice* option—is highly nonstandard from the perspective of more familiar logics, but not, I think, incoherent.[9] It involves viewing the task of a default logic, not as guiding the reasoning agent to a unique set of appropriate conclusions, but as characterizing different, possibly conflicting conclusion sets as rational outcomes based on the initial information provided to the agent. Viewed from this standpoint, default logic could then be seen as analogous to other fields, such as game theory, for example, that allow multiple equilibrium states in their characterization of rationality. And regardless of its theoretical pedigree, it seems that something like this choice option is, in fact, frequently employed in our everyday reasoning. Given conflicting defeasible rules, we often simply do adopt some internally coherent point of view in which these conflicts are resolved in some particular way, in spite of the fact that there are other coherent points of view in which the conflicts are resolved in different ways.

Still, although this reasoning policy may be sensible, it is hard to see how the choice option could be codified in a formal consequence relation. Suppose some default theory allows multiple extensions. If the choice of extension really is arbitrary, different reasoning agents might then select different ones of these extensions, or the same reasoning agent might select different extensions at different times. Which extension, then, could be said to represent the actual conclusion set of the original theory?

The second option—which I refer to as the *credulous* option—can be developed in a number of different ways, but each involves endorsing either a proposition, or else one of its variants, as a conclusion of a default theory

---

[9]The labeling of this reasoning strategy as the "choice" option is due to Makinson (1994).

whenever that proposition is contained in some extension of the theory.[10]
Unlike the choice option, this credulous option can indeed be codified in a
consequence relation, but if the option is developed in the most straightforward way—with the propositions found in extensions themselves taken
as conclusions—then the consequence relation would be a peculiar one: it
might well lead to a situation in which the set of conclusions associated with
a default theory is inconsistent even though that default theory itself is consistent. Consider the Nixon Diamond once again. Here, the information
contained in the original default theory seems to be consistent—indeed, it
seems to be true. But according to this straightforward understanding of
the credulous option, the set of conclusions associated with this consistent
default theory would contain the flatly inconsistent propositions that Nixon
is a pacifist and that he is not, since P is found in one extension of the
theory while $\neg P$ is found in the other.

One way of avoiding this peculiar feature of the credulous option is to
suppose that the real conclusions of a default theory are, not the propositions themselves that belong to its various extensions, but rather, certain
more complex propositions that result when these initial propositions are
nested within some kind of modal operator, which then shields them from
direct contradiction. To illustrate: suppose we take $\mathcal{B}(X)$ as the proposition that X is believable, where the propositions that are *believable* on the
basis of a default theory are defined as those included in some extension
of that theory, representing some internally coherent point of view. We
might then define the conclusions of a default theory as the set that supplements the original information from the theory with $\mathcal{B}(X)$ whenever the
proposition X belongs to any one of these extensions.

This way of developing the credulous option has some interest. It results
in a conclusion set that is consistent as long as the set of hard information from the underlying default theory is itself consistent, and indeed,
Reiter's original paper on default logic provides a verification procedure,
sound and complete under certain conditions, that could be used in determining whether a statement belongs to the conclusion set as defined here.[11]
Unfortunately, however, by doing things in this way, with an epistemic operator, we also manage to sidestep our original question. We had originally
wanted to know what conclusions a reasoning agent should actually draw
from the information provided by a default theory—whether, for example,
the information from the Nixon Diamond should lead the agent to conclude
that Nixon is, or is not, a pacifist. But according to the current version of
the credulous option, we are told only what is believable—that both $\mathcal{B}(P)$

---

[10]This reasoning strategy was first described as "credulous" by Touretzky, Horty, and
Thomason (1987); the same strategy had earlier been labeled as "brave" by McDermott
(1982), and is sometimes called "liberal" as well. There is some inconsistency in the
literature and the term "credulous" has also been used to characterize the reasoning
strategy described here as the choice option.

[11]See Section 4 of Reiter (1980).

and $\mathcal{B}(\neg P)$ belong to the conclusion set, so that it is believable on the basis of the information from the initial theory that Nixon is a pacifist, and also believable that he is not. This may be useful information; not everything is believable. But it is still some distance from telling us whether the agent should conclude that Nixon is, or is not, a pacifist.

Yet another way of developing the credulous option is to think of the modal operator that is wrapped around the propositions drawn directly from extensions, and so preventing outright contradiction, not as an epistemic operator $\mathcal{B}$, indicating something like believability, but as a deontic operator $\bigcirc$, indicating what ought to be the case. This approach, as it turns out, leads to an attractive deontic logic, which is explored in more detail in Chapters 3 and 4.

The third option for handling multiple extensions—now typically described as the *skeptical* option—is based on the general idea that a reasoning agent should simply withhold judgment concerning any statement that is treated differently in different extensions.[12] Again, this general idea can be developed in different ways. By far the most common, however, is what I call the *proposition intersection* approach, according to which a proposition is classified as a conclusion of a default theory just in case it belongs to every extension of that theory—just in case, that is, the proposition belongs to the intersection of these various extensions.

This approach has several virtues. It is simple. It is logically coherent, leading to a unique conclusion set, and to a conclusion set that will be consistent as long as the hard information from the underlying default theory is itself consistent. It does not require the appeal to any modal operator, and it yields results that tend to have a good deal of intuitive attraction. In the case of the Nixon Diamond, for example, a reasoning agent following this approach would conclude neither that Nixon is a pacifist nor that he is not, since neither P nor $\neg P$ is contained in both extensions of this theory. Instead, the agent would remain skeptical concerning Nixon's pacifism, and draw no new conclusions at all beyond the hard information from the original theory.

Although the skeptical option does not require the appeal to a modal operator, it allows for such an appeal, and, as with the previous believability interpretation, an analog to this skeptical approach can likewise be developed into an attractive deontic logic, which is again explored in detail in Chapters 3 and 4. In Chapter 7, we consider some cases in which the proposition intersection approach to skepticism leads to more questionable results.[13]

---

[12]The use of the label "skeptical" to describe this general reasoning strategy, as well as some related strategies, in nonmonotonic logic is again due to Touretzky, Horty, and Thomason (1987); a similar strategy had earlier been labeled as "cautious" by McDermott (1982).

[13]Having set out these three options—choice, credulous, and skeptical—for defining the consequences of a default theory with multiple extensions, it is worth asking which option Reiter himself endorsed in (1980). Interestingly, he neither answers nor seems

1.3.2   Theories without extensions

As an example of a default theory with no extensions at all, let δ_1 be the default $\top \to A$ and δ_2 the default $A \to \neg A$, and consider the theory $\Delta_4 = \langle \mathcal{W}, \mathcal{D}, < \rangle$, depicted in Figure 1.4, where $\mathcal{W} = \emptyset$, where $\mathcal{D} = \{\delta_1, \delta_2\}$, and where $<$ orders these two defaults so that $\delta_1 < \delta_2$. By our definition of an extension, any extension of this theory would have to be generated by some proper scenario based on the theory. But we can verify by enumeration that no subset of $\mathcal{D}$ is a proper scenario: $\mathcal{S}_1 = \emptyset$ is not proper, since δ_1 is binding in the context of this scenario, but not included; $\mathcal{S}_2 = \{\delta_1\}$ is not proper, since it includes δ_1, which is defeated in this context by δ_2, a stronger triggered default, and so not binding; $\mathcal{S}_3 = \{\delta_2\}$ is not proper, since it contains δ_2, which is not triggered and not binding; and $\mathcal{S}_4 = \{\delta_1, \delta_2\}$ is not proper, since both of the defaults it includes are conflicted, and so not binding. Since there are no proper scenarios based on this theory, and extensions are generated by proper scenarios, the theory cannot have any extensions either.

There are several ways of responding to the possibility of default theories without extensions, which, again, I will simply mention.

We can observe, first of all, that the problem springs, quite generally, from the presence of "vicious cycles" among default rules, in which we are required to endorse one default, but where this endorsement initiates a chain of reasoning that leads, ultimately, to the endorsement of another that defeats the first. In our simple example, this vicious cycle is compressed into the single default δ_2, but it is easy to see that such a cycle could be arbitrarily long. One option, then, is to argue that the presence of vicious cycles renders a default theory incoherent. This is plausible in the case of our example. The default δ_1 is trivially triggered, providing

---

even to recognize this question; and even more interestingly, his informal discussion suggests that he is drawn, at separate points, to each of the three options defined here. Early on, in Section 1.3 of the paper, he sets out an example, like the Nixon Diamond, involving two incomparable but potentially conflicting defaults—that people tend to live where their spouses live, but also tend to live where their employers are located—and he considers the case of Mary, whose spouse lives in Toronto but whose employer is located in Vancouver. Properly formalized, this example would lead, just as with the Nixon Diamond, to two extensions, one containing the statement that Mary lives in Toronto and the other containing the statement that Mary lives in Vancouver; and what Reiter writes of the example is that "one can choose to believe that Mary's hometown is Toronto or that it is Vancouver, but not both." This remark clearly suggests the first of our three options, the choice option. The second, or credulous, option, and in particular the believability interpretation, is supported by the verification procedure that Reiter presents in Section 4 of his paper, which is meant to show that a statement belongs to some extension of a default theory, and which he explicitly describes as establishing that such a statement "can be believed." Finally, Reiter alludes to the third, or skeptical, option again in Section 1.3, in a footnote to his discussion of Mary, where he notes that the agent might "refuse to choose between the Toronto extension and the Vancouver extension," and conclude only that Mary lives in Toronto or that she lives in Vancouver—the strongest statement on the subject that is contained in both extensions.

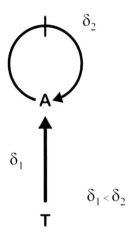

Figure 1.4: An incoherent theory

a reason for A, and is, at least to begin with, neither conflicted nor defeated, so that we must accept this default; but once we do, the default δ_2 is triggered as well, providing a stronger reason for $\neg A$ and so defeating the default that triggered it. How could we possibly make sense of a situation like that? If we think of an extension of a default theory as representing some coherent point of view based on the information contained in that theory, then the idea behind this option is to accept the lack of extensions as an indication that the underlying theory simply does not allow for a coherent interpretation at all.

For those who favor this strategy, it is then natural to attempt to formulate precise syntactic conditions ruling out the kind of vicious cycles that render default theories incoherent. This line of exploration has a long history in nonmonotonic reasoning, and generally involves defining some sort of stratification of default rules, implicit or explicit.[14] In the present setting, the goal would be to find the weakest and most plausible syntactic restrictions necessary to guarantee the existence of proper scenarios, and so of extensions, for the default theories defined here.

From a more general perspective, the strategy behind this first option is reminiscent of Tarski's idea of circumventing the semantic paradoxes by

---

[14]Some initial milestones along these lines are Reiter's (1980) proof that extensions are guaranteed for "normal" default theories, Touretzky's (1986) proof that "acyclic" inheritance networks must have extensions, and the work by Krzysztof Apt, Howard Blair, and Adrian Walker (1988) on the semantics of "stratified" logic programs. These three concepts—normality, acyclicity, and stratification—can all be understood as formal, syntactic conditions guaranteeing the coherence of theories expressed in different nonmonotonic logics.

postulating a linguistic hierarchy to rule out vicious self-reference. It is
also possible, however, to explore the idea of allowing vicious cycles among
defaults, not imposing any syntactic restrictions at all, and then attempting
to modify the underlying theories so as to generate extensions even when
these cycles are present. An approach along these lines—to continue the
analogy—would be similar to more recent work on the semantic paradoxes,
and might well use tools developed in that work.[15]

Finally, again returning to the idea that theories without extensions are
simply incoherent, it may be possible to allow these theories all the same
if one happens to favor the proposition intersection approach to skeptical
reasoning. According to this approach, as we have seen, the conclusions
of a default theory are identified with the propositions that belong to the
intersection of its various extensions. But since an incoherent theory has
no extensions—and since the intersection of an empty set of sets is defined
as containing every element in the domain—any formula at all would then
lie in the intersection of these extensions. An incoherent default theory,
then, just like an inconsistent theory in ordinary logic, could naturally be
viewed as having every formula as a conclusion.

---

[15] As an example, Aldo Antonelli (1999) adapts ideas from Kripke's treatment of the
paradoxes to modify Reiter's original default logic, without priorities but containing non-
normal defaults, so that existence of extensions is guaranteed. There are also, of course,
a variety of default logics formulated without any reference to the semantic paradoxes,
but for which extensions are guaranteed; a good entry point into this literature   is
provided by James Delgrande, Torsten Schaub, and W. Ken Jackson (1994).

Chapter 2

From defaults to reasons

The goal of this chapter is to show how default logic can be adapted to serve as a foundation for a concrete theory of reasons. In the previous chapter, I spoke loosely of a correspondence between default rules and reasons. Having introduced a number of technical concepts in the course of developing our simple default logic, I now consider this correspondence in more detail, as well as the overall account of reasons that emerges from the underlying default logic.

2.1   An austere theory of reasons

My proposal is that the reason relation can be defined in terms of defaults and their properties. More exactly, and to repeat the idea sketched in Section 1.2, my proposal is that: given a background default theory $\Delta = \langle W, \mathcal{D}, < \rangle$ and a scenario $\mathcal{S}$ based on this theory, the proposition X should be defined as a *reason for Y in the context of $\mathcal{S}$* just in case there is some default δ of the form $X \to Y$ from the underlying set $\mathcal{D}$ that is triggered in the context of $\mathcal{S}$—just in case, that is, δ belongs to $\mathit{Triggered}_{W,\mathcal{D}}(\mathcal{S})$. In a situation like this, once again, we will say that the default δ *provides* a reason for Y, and that the reason it provides is X.

This proposal calls for three preliminary remarks.

First, the reason relation is often spoken of, not simply as a dyadic relation between two propositions, or between a proposition and an action, but as a triadic relation specifying, in addition, the agent for whom the reason holds, and sometimes as a quadratic relation also specifying the time at which it holds. The fact that Jack promised to meet Jo for lunch is a reason for him to meet her, but not a reason for me to do so; the fact that there is food in the kitchen may be a reason for me to go there at lunch time, when I am hungry, but not later on, when I am no longer hungry. In treating the reason relation as dyadic, I do not mean to deny that reasons hold *for* an agent, and perhaps *at* a time, but only to abstract away from these complexities. I am not concerned here with the question

of what makes a proposition a reason for one agent but not another, or
with the dynamics of reasons. Rather, focusing only on the reasons that
happen to hold for a fixed agent, and at a fixed time, I am concerned to
explore both the relations among these reasons and the way in which they
support actions or conclusions.

Second, in defining reasons in terms of default rules, am I saying that
the reason relation holds only because of these defaults, that it is somehow
due to the defaults? No—no more than ordinary inference relations among
propositions are due to Frege's logic, or the physical relations among objects
in the world are due to our formulation of physical theories. Instead, my
picture is the standard one. Some propositions stand in a reason relation
to other propositions, or to actions—the source of these relations is not
my concern. My proposal is simply that default logic provides a suitable
formalism for the theorist to use in representing and reasoning about these
relations.

And third, reasons are identified with the premises of triggered defaults,
but how, exactly, are we to understand default rules themselves? My answer is that a default of the form $X \rightarrow Y$, which I regard as primitive, can
best be understood as meaning that X is a consideration that *counts in
favor of Y*, or simply that X *favors Y*—a phrase that, at least as I intend
it, carries no implication that X is either true or something to which we
are committed.[1] The concept of a reason at work here thus has two components: a favoring relation, which is supplied by an underlying default,
together with the presumption of premise truth, which then triggers, or
activates, that favoring relation.

It is worth noting that at least one previous writer relies on a fundamental normative relation, much like that carried by our default rules,
that explicitly withholds any commitment to premise truth; in an important early paper, Chisholm proposes as his primitive ethical concept the
notion of "requirement," a relation between propositions of which he takes
an expansive view:

> Requirement may be illustrated by the following: promise-
> making requires—or calls for—promise-keeping; being virtuous,
> according to Kant, requires being rewarded; the dominant sev-
> enth requires the chord of the tonic; one color in the lower left
> calls for a complementary color in the upper right.[2]

---

[1] I borrow the language of favoring from Scanlon (1998, p. 17) and Dancy (2004,
p. 75).

[2] Chisholm (1964, p. 147). And even more expansively, he compares his notion of
requirement to the idea of "completion" from Gestalt's psychology, citing Maurice Mandelbaum's (1955, pp. 95–96) discussion of the way in which "A curve may demand a
certain completion and seem to reject all others; this completion appears as appropriate
to the nature of the curve ... In perceptual experience we find things belonging together, demanding and rejecting certain completions, appropriately and inappropriately
organized."

Indeed, Chisholm's concept of requirement bears several points of analogy with the notion of favoring explored here, and carried by default rules. He notes, first of all, that requirement is likewise defeasible, in the sense that one requirement can be defeated or overridden by a stronger requirement. Second, he notes that the statement "X requires Y" does not imply a commitment to the truth of X; to block any such a suggestion, he writes that the language "X would require Y" might be less misleading.[3] As with favoring, the notion of requirement is supposed to be activated by premise truth: from the idea that X requires Y—or "would" require Y—we then reach the conclusion that Y is actually required, that there is a requirement for Y, by supplementing the initial idea with the further information that X is the case.[4] Finally, and again as in the present framework, Chisholm highlights the parallel between the normative notion of requirement and a corresponding epistemic relation, "confirmation," which could likewise be represented as a default; here too he stresses both defeasibility—the statement "X confirms Y" is consistent with the statement "X *and* Z confirms not-Y," which is itself consistent with "X *and* Z *and* W confirms Y"—and lack of commitment to premise truth, noting again that the statement "X would confirm Y" might be preferable.[5]

With these preliminary remarks in place, let us now return to the proposal itself—that reasons are to be identified with the premises of triggered defaults. I want to emphasize two features of the resulting account of reasons. The account is, first of all, *austere*, in the sense that what counts as a reason for what is tied very closely to the particular set of default rules belonging to the underlying theory. And second, the account is *relative*, in the sense that the reason relation depends, not only on an underlying default theory, but also on a particular scenario based on that theory.

---

[3]To keep notation as uniform as possible, I have substituted the uppercase variables used here for the lowercase variables that actually appear in Chisholm's paper.

[4]Chisholm in (1964) represents the notion of requirement through an R-relation, so that "XRY" is taken to mean that X requires Y in the sense discussed here, where there is no commitment to the truth of X; he then represents the idea that there is a requirement for Y—that the antecedent of such an R-relation holds—through a propositionally quantified formula of the form $\exists X(X \ \& \ XRY)$, which affirms the existence of the antecedent fact. Ten years later, Chisholm (1974, p. 119) confuses things slightly by continuing to treat his formal R-relation in this noncommittal way, but now explicating our ordinary notion of requirement in such a way that it does carry a commitment to antecedent truth; in this later paper, the phrase "X requires Y" is now defined to mean "X obtains and XRY."

[5]With regard to the idea that we might have both "X confirms Y" and "X *and* Z confirms not-Y," Chisholm (1964, p. 148) writes: "We do not say, in such cases, that one confirmation has been 'overridden' or 'defeated' by another, but we could." Although this remark—that we "could" say this—sounds odd to our ears, since talk of overriding and defeat is so prevalent in contemporary epistemology, it was not such an odd thing to say when Chisholm wrote it. A useful historical discussion of defeasibility and defeat in contemporary philosophy is presented by Ronald Loui (1995), who argues that these ideas originated in the philosophy of law, especially with H. L. A. Hart's (1948), moving from that field first into ethics, and only later to epistemology.

To illustrate the austerity of the proposed account, imagine a situation in which I have promised to lend $5 to a friend tomorrow and also to donate $5 to charity, so that I have reasons to do both of these things. In accord with the current account, we can suppose that these reasons are provided by triggered defaults from an underlying default theory. But imagine also that I now have only $15, with no immediate prospects of getting more, and that a movie costs $7; this is part of the background information from that same default theory. Then it seems to follow that I ought not to see a movie tonight. But do I have any reason not to see a movie? No, not according to the current account—not unless there happens to be some other default from the underlying theory that provides such a reason. So this is one way in which the analysis of reasons provided by the current account is austere: the things we have reason to do cannot be combined together, or combined with our background information, to yield reasons for doing other things. My reasons for lending $5 to a friend and donating $5 to charity cannot be combined together with the information about the price of a movie, and the fact that I have only $15, to yield a reason not to see a movie.

Or consider Jack once again, who has promised to meet Jo for lunch, and so has a reason to do so, where this reason is provided by a default from the underlying theory. And suppose that, in order to meet Jo on time, he must now get into his car; this is part of the background information from that theory. Surely Jack ought to get into his car, but does he have a reason to do so? Again, no—not unless there is a separate default to provide the reason. So this is another way, even more striking, in which the proposed analysis is austere: it is not closed under ordinary consequence. Even though Jack has a reason for meeting Jo, and meeting Jo entails getting into his car, it does not follow that Jack has any reason to get into his car.

Austerity is a virtue, of course, but as these examples indicate, the very austere conception of reasons proposed here presents some intuitive difficulties—certainly it seems odd to say, in the circumstances, that I have no reason at all not to see a movie tonight, or that Jack has no reason to get into his car. To this complaint I have two responses. The first is a generic response, often applicable to efforts that involve the philosophical explication of an ordinary concept, but always worth remembering: even though our theoretical work originates with ordinary linguistic usage, and is meant to systematize that usage, the resulting theory cannot be required to conform to our ordinary usage in every detail. In this case, we are trying to get at the truth underlying our ordinary talk of reasons, not to provide an account of that talk itself—the enterprise is philosophy, not linguistics. There will be various points of slippage between the theoretical account provided here and our ordinary talk of reasons; and one of these is that our ordinary talk sometimes, though not always, seems to allow the things we have reason for to be combined and then closed under consequence, while the theoretical account presented here does not.

Still, where there is slippage between the theoretical reconstruction of some concept and our ordinary way of speaking, it is best if that slippage can be explained. My second response, then, is to suggest a hypothesis as to why our ordinary talk seems so natural—why it seems so natural to say that I have a reason not to see a movie, or that Jack has a reason to get into his car—even though these statements are not supported by the current theory. The hypothesis is this: the ought statements corresponding to these reason statements are indeed correct, and so we tend to think that the reason statements should be correct as well, simply because we assume too close a connection between reasons and oughts—we tend to assume that, for each ought, there must be a reason. In particular, then, I agree that I ought not to see a movie, and that Jack ought to get into his car; and if we assume that each of us must have some reason for doing anything that he or she ought to do, or ought to refrain from, then it follows that Jack and I must have reasons for doing, or not doing, these things. The assumption that there must be a reason for every ought, however, is one that I am able to reject, as we will see in the following chapter, once we begin to map out the connections between reasons and oughts in detail.

Let us turn, now, to the relativity of the proposed account. Since I define reasons as the premises of triggered defaults, and different defaults might be triggered in different scenarios, the proposed analysis of a reason must be relativized, not only to an underlying default theory, but also to a particular scenario based on that theory: what counts as a reason for what might vary from one scenario to another. This is, I think, correct as a fundamental analysis, and for the most part it is this relative reason relation that we will be working with. Furthermore, the relativization leads to no difficulties at all in the case of default theories that allow for only a single proper scenario. There we can naturally define an *absolute* reason relation, according to which X is classified as a reason for Y in an absolute sense just in case, in the relative sense already established, X is a reason for Y in the unique proper scenario based on the underlying default theory—just in case, that is, there is a default of the form $X \rightarrow Y$ from the underlying theory that is triggered in the context of this unique proper scenario.

But what of default theories that allow for multiple proper scenarios—how could we define an absolute reason relation for these theories? Here, there seem to be only two options with any plausibility, roughly corresponding to the skeptical and credulous approaches, discussed earlier, for characterizing the conclusions of theories with multiple extensions. Given a default theory allowing for multiple proper scenarios, we could say that X is to be classified as a reason for Y in the absolute sense just in case, in the relative sense already established, X is a reason for Y in all—or, alternatively, in some—of the proper scenarios based on the underlying default theory.

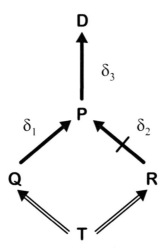

Figure 2.1: Nixon and disarmament

In order to get a sense of the difference between these options, we need to consider a case in which different defaults are triggered in different proper scenarios. The original Nixon Diamond, from Figure 1.3, will not do, since, although this theory does allow for two proper scenarios, both of the defaults it contains are triggered in both of these scenarios. But suppose that the Nixon Diamond is extended with δ_3 as the additional default $P \to D$, an instance for Nixon of the generalization that pacifists tend to favor disarmament, where P is the familiar proposition that Nixon is a pacifist and D is the new proposition that Nixon favors disarmament. The resulting theory is then $\Delta_5 = \langle \mathcal{W}, \mathcal{D}, < \rangle$, depicted in Figure 2.1, where $\mathcal{W} = \{Q, R\}$, where $\mathcal{D} = \{\delta_1, \delta_2, \delta_3\}$ with δ_3 as above and with δ_1 as $Q \to P$ and δ_2 as $R \to \neg P$, and where the ordering $<$ is empty; once again, Q and R are the propositions that Nixon is a Quaker and a Republican.

This new default theory allows exactly two proper scenarios: $\mathcal{S}_1 = \{\delta_1, \delta_3\}$ and $\mathcal{S}_2 = \{\delta_2\}$. And just as in the original Nixon Diamond, even though the default δ_1 belongs only to the first scenario and δ_2 belongs only to the second, both of these defaults are triggered in both scenarios, since their premises are already present in the background theory. As a result, our relative theory tells us that Q is a reason for P and that R is a reason for $\neg P$ in the context of $\mathcal{S}_1$, and also in the context of $\mathcal{S}_2$. The new default δ_3, however, is triggered only in the context of $\mathcal{S}_1$, not in the context of $\mathcal{S}_2$, since its premise, the proposition P, is available only once the default δ_1 has been accepted. Our relative theory of reasons therefore tells us that P is a reason for D—the fact that Nixon is a pacifist is a reason for concluding that he favors disarmament—only in the context of S_1, not in the context of S_2 as well.

This example, then, allows us to distinguish between the two options for defining an absolute reason relation, dependent only on the background default theory, and not also on a particular scenario. According to the first option, which requires that the relative reason relation hold in each proper scenario, we would have to say that P is not a reason for D in the absolute sense, since the corresponding relative relation fails to hold in the context of the scenario S_2. But according to the second option, which requires only that the relative relation hold in some proper scenario, we could then say that P is a reason for D, since the corresponding relative relation holds in the context of S_1.

Which option is preferable? Given only the information provided in the original default theory, and displayed in Figure 2.1, would we or would we not say that there is a reason for D, the proposition that Nixon favors disarmament? The example strains our intuitions, perhaps past the breaking point, and I have no desire to try to legislate in a borderline case like this. My own feeling, however, is that we would be inclined to say that there is some reason, at least, for the conclusion that Nixon favors disarmament. After all, it follows from the underlying default theory that he may well be a pacifist—there is an extension containing this conclusion; it is a "believable" proposition, according to one version of the credulous approach. And my feeling is that our intuitions about an absolute reason relation in the face of multiple proper scenarios may track this same credulous path, so that we are inclined to regard even the mere believability of the proposition that Nixon is a pacifist, the fact that it could well be true, as a reason for the conclusion.

2.2 Developing the theory

2.2.1 Conflict, strength, and defeat

Having defined the bare concept of a reason in terms of ideas from an underlying default theory, we can now begin to develop the account by lifting some of the other formal ideas originally defined only for default theories to our ordinary talk of reasons. As we will see, the process is entirely straightforward.

We begin with the notion of conflict. Suppose that X is classified as a reason for Y, in the context of some scenario—that is, the underlying default theory contains a default δ of the form $X \rightarrow Y$ that is triggered in the context of that scenario. Then we can say that X is *conflicted* as a reason for Y, in the context of that scenario, just in case the default δ that provides X as a reason for Y is itself conflicted. This idea receives its classic illustration in the Nixon Diamond—once again, the theory $\Delta_3 = \langle \mathcal{W}, \mathcal{D}, < \rangle$, depicted in Figure 1.3, where $\mathcal{W} = \{Q, R\}$, where $\mathcal{D} = \{\delta_1, \delta_2\}$ with δ_1 and

δ_2 as the defaults $Q \rightarrow P$ and $R \rightarrow \neg P$, and where $<$ is empty. Now consider the scenario $\mathcal{S}_1 = \{\delta_1\}$ based on this theory. In the context of this scenario, the proposition R, that Nixon is a Republican, is classified as a reason for $\neg P$, the proposition that he is not a pacifist; this reason is provided by the default δ_2, which is triggered in any scenario based on the original theory. However, R is conflicted as a reason for $\neg P$ in the context of $\mathcal{S}_1$, since this scenario already contains δ_1, which provides Q, the proposition that Nixon is a Quaker, as a reason for the conflicting conclusion P.

Next, strength of reasons. Suppose that, in the context of some scenario, X is a reason for Y, provided by the default δ, and W is a reason for Z, provided by the default δ'. Then we can say that W is a *stronger* reason for Z than X is for Y, or that W has *higher priority* as a reason for Z than X has as a reason for Y, just in case $\delta < \delta'$—just in case, that is, the default δ', which provides W as a reason, itself has a higher priority than δ, which provides X as a reason. This time, of course, the classic illustration is provided by the Tweety Triangle— again, the theory $\Delta_1 = \langle \mathcal{W}, \mathcal{D}, < \rangle$, depicted in Figure 1.1, where $\mathcal{W} = \{P, P \supset B\}$, where $\mathcal{D} = \{\delta_1, \delta_2\}$ with δ_1 and δ_2 as the defaults $B \rightarrow F$ and $P \rightarrow \neg F$, and where $\delta_1 < \delta_2$. Here, the proposition B, that Tweety is a bird, is classified as a reason for F, the conclusion that he flies, while the proposition P, that Tweety is a penguin, is classified as a reason for $\neg F$, the conclusion that he cannot fly. The first of these reasons is provided by the default δ_1 and the second by the default δ_2, both of which are triggered in any scenario based on the original theory. But according to our definition, P is a stronger reason for $\neg F$ than B is for F, since $\delta_1 < \delta_2$—the default δ_2, which provides P as a reason, is itself stronger than the default δ_1, which provides B.

The notion of strength leads immediately to that of defeat, which can be defined in two equivalent ways. Suppose as before that X is a reason for Y, provided by the default δ, triggered in the current scenario. Then we can say, first of all, that X is *defeated* as a reason for Y in the context of this scenario if the default δ, which provides X as a reason, is itself defeated by some other default δ'. Or second, working entirely at the level of reasons, without delving into the substructure of defaults, we can say that X is defeated as a reason for Y whenever there is some other reason W for a conclusion that contradicts Y when taken together with the background information, where W is, in addition, a stronger reason for this contradicting conclusion than X is for Y; in this case, we can describe W as a *defeating reason* for X, or simply as a *defeater*.

The reader can verify that these two definitions of defeat are indeed equivalent, and both can be illustrated with the Tweety Triangle. Here, as we have seen, the default δ_1 provides the proposition B, that Tweety is a bird, as a reason for the conclusion F, that Tweety flies. But this reason is defeated according to our first definition because, as verified earlier, the default δ_1 is itself defeated by the default δ_2, in any scenario based on the underlying theory. And B is likewise defeated as a reason for F by our second definition, since, as we have also noted, there is another reason P, the proposition that Tweety is a penguin, that offers stronger support for the conflicting conclusion $\neg F$, that Tweety cannot fly, than B does for F. The proposition that Tweety is a bird is thus classified as a reason for the conclusion that he flies, but the proposition that Tweety is a penguin functions as a defeater for this reason.

Finally, we turn to the concept of a good reason, which again can be provided with two equivalent definitions, one that appeals directly to the underlying default theory and another that involves only the concepts we have introduced to characterize reasons themselves. Suppose once more that X is a reason for Y in the context of some scenario, provided by the default δ. Then we can say, first, that X is a *good reason* for Y in the context of that scenario if δ is binding in the context of that scenario; or second, simply echoing our definition of a binding default at the level of reasons, we can say that X is a good reason for Y if it is indeed a reason for Y, and a reason that is neither conflicted nor defeated. To illustrate, return to the Tweety Triangle, and consider, for example, the empty scenario, containing no defaults at all. In the context of that scenario, we can now verify that P, the proposition that Tweety is a penguin, is not only a reason for the conclusion $\neg F$, that he cannot fly, but a good reason for this conclusion. For, by the first definition, the default δ_2 that provides P as a reason is not just triggered but binding in the context; and by the second definition, the proposition P is not just a reason for its conclusion, but a reason that is neither conflicted nor defeated.

The definitions of these various concepts—conflicted reasons, defeated reasons, good reasons—are all relative, dependent on some particular scenario. I leave to the reader the straightforward task of developing the corresponding absolute concepts in the way suggested by our earlier discussion, by relativizing the definitions already presented to the unique proper scenario supported by an underlying default theory, if there is one, and otherwise by handling the case of multiple proper scenarios in whatever way he or she thinks best. Even in its relative version, however, one of these initial concepts, the crucial notion of defeat, calls for some immediate comments.

The language of defeasibility and defeat is, by now, part of the folk vocabulary of professional philosophy, though it is used in strikingly different ways by different writers. The definitions presented here are meant to explicate what I think of as the core ideas underlying this language, though I do not intend for these definitions to correspond to any particular one of these established usages, nor will I try to survey them all. Still, in order to highlight the distinctive features of my approach, it will be useful to compare the present treatment of defeat with two others from the literature—both, as it happens, due to John Pollock, who has done so much to develop this idea and to emphasize its importance.

In some of his informal work in epistemology, Pollock introduces the concept of a defeater with the following definition: if X is a reason to believe Y, then Z is a defeater for this reason just in case $X \wedge Z$ is not a reason to believe Y.[6] Definitions of this general form are not uncommon. But it is easy to see that nothing along these lines will work, at least in conjunction with the austere treatment of reasons presented here. Suppose that B, the proposition that Tweety is a bird, is a reason for F, the proposition that he flies—that is, there is a triggered default of the form $B \rightarrow F$ in the underlying default theory. Now let R be the proposition that Tweety is a red thing so that $B \wedge R$ is the proposition that Tweety is a red bird. Then, because the austere theory ties the reason relation so closely to the structure of default rules, this theory will not, in fact, classify the proposition $B \wedge R$ as a reason for F, not unless the underlying default theory also happens to contain a default rule of the form $(B \wedge R) \rightarrow F$. And from this it would follow by Pollock's proposed definition of defeat that R is a defeater for B as a reason to conclude F. But that cannot be right. The proposition that Tweety is red should not defeat the proposition that Tweety is a bird as a reason for the conclusion that Tweety flies.

It may be tempting to blame the austere theory of reasons itself for this odd result: perhaps, if B is classified as a reason for F, then $B \wedge R$ should be classified as a reason for F as well. But surely not just any arbitrary proposition can be conjoined with an existing reason without disturbing the reason relation; for example, the proposition $B \wedge P$, that Tweety is both a bird and a penguin, cannot continue to count as a reason for concluding that he flies. Why, then, can R be conjoined with B but not P—how can we separate the propositions that can be safely conjoined with an existing reason from those that cannot? I see no way of answering this question without appealing to some antecedent distinction between those propositions that function as defeaters of the original reason and those that do not. But in that case the project is circular, since this concept of a defeater is the very idea that Pollock hopes to explicate, by appeal to a prior understanding of the propositions that can or cannot be conjoined into existing reasons without disturbing their force as reasons.

Rather than blaming the odd result on the austere theory, therefore, I prefer to locate the problem with Pollock's informal definition of defeat itself. From an intuitive standpoint, what it means to say that Z is a defeater of X as a reason for Y—the core of the idea—is that Z interferes, in some way, with the support that X offers for Y. To say that Z is *not* a defeater of X as a reason for Y, then, is simply to say that Z does not interfere with the support that X offers for Y. But this does not require, as Pollock would have it, that Z itself must be part of the reason for Y, that

---

[6]See, for example, Pollock and Joseph Cruz (1999, p. 37); I have modified the definition in the text only by omitting mention of the subject for whom X is or is not a reason to believe Y. This definition goes back at least to Pollock (1974, pp. 41–42), and is anticipated by Chisholm (1966, p. 53).

Z itself must provide any positive support for this conclusion or be part of a complex that does. In the case of our example, being a red thing does not interfere with the support that being a bird provides for the conclusion that Tweety flies. But that does not imply that being red should form any part of the reason for this conclusion, or provide any positive support for it—being a red thing simply has nothing to do with being able to fly, one way or the other.

In addition to his informal definition of the defeat relation, however, Pollock also offers an entirely different, formal definition of a notion he describes as "rebutting" defeat, which plays an important role in his technical theories of defeasible reasoning.[7] In these various theories, reasons are organized into inference graphs, very much like those presented here to display default theories, with nodes in the graphs representing reasons and directed links between these nodes representing reason relations. Reasons are assigned strengths, much as in the current framework, and Pollock's notion of defeat, transposed into our current notation, can then be approximated as follows: Z is a rebutting defeater for X just in case (1) X is a reason of strength m supporting some proposition Y, (2) Z is reason of strength n supporting some proposition that is inconsistent with Y, and (3) it is not the case that $n < m$.[8]

This definition of Pollock's is similar to my own, easily comparable, and may even appear to be more sensible. The chief difference lies with the strength requirements that each of us places on the notion of defeat. Suppose that X is a reason for Y and that Z is a reason for some contradictory conclusion. Then what I require in order for Z to defeat X is that Z should actually be a stronger reason for the conflicting conclusion than X is for Y, while Pollock requires only that Z should not be a weaker reason than X. Pollock, therefore, allows X to be defeated by Z as a reason for Y when the strength of Z for the conflicting conclusion is either equal to or incomparable with that of X, while I do not. The difference between these two accounts can be illustrated by the Nixon Diamond from Figure 1.3,

---

[7] As noted earlier, in Section 1.2.1, Pollock has also introduced a separate notion of "undercutting" defeat, which we consider at length in the third part of this book.

[8] Definitions of rebutting defeat along these lines appear throughout Pollock's work, but this particular approximation is based on the definition from his (1995, p. 103). Some of the ways in which the version of this definition presented in the text is only an approximation, and in which Pollock's overall architecture differes from the current framework, are these: First, Pollock relativizes reasons to a background set of suppositions, allowing for something like conditional proof. Second, Pollock assigns strength to nodes, or reasons, rather than to the links representing reason relations; as a result, it seems to follow that the same reason, or consideration, cannot lend different degrees of support to different conclusions. And third, since the strengths Pollock assigns to reasons are supposed to interact with the probability calculus, these strengths are represented as real numbers, and are therefore totally ordered (1995, p. 94). What Pollock actually requires in his analog to my clause (3), then, is that $m \leq n$—not simply that n is not weaker than m, but that n is actually at least as strong as m. I have relaxed this clause in my approximation of Pollock's definition to allow it to apply more sensibly to the case in which the strengths, or priorities, among reasons are only partially ordered.

where Q and R, the propositions that Nixon is a Quaker and a Republican, stand as reasons for the conflicting conclusions P and $\neg P$, that he is a pacifist, and that he is not a pacifist. These two reasons are provided, as we recall, by the respective defaults $Q \to P$ and $R \to \neg P$, which are incomparable in strength, so that the reasons they provide are incomparable as well. According to my account, then, neither of these two reasons, P or Q, is defeated, since, although they support contradictory conclusions, neither reason is actually stronger than the other. According to Pollock's account, by contrast, both reasons are defeated, since they support contradictory conclusions and, for each of the two reasons, the other is not weaker.

It is situations like this that make it appear as if Pollock's definition of defeat may be more sensible than my own. Why? Well, if the core idea underlying defeat is, once again, that Z defeats X as a reason for Y whenever Z interferes with the support that X provides for Y—or that Z somehow blocks our tendency to draw Y as a conclusion even though we have accepted X—then the Nixon Diamond would seem to qualify. After all, if we knew only Nixon's religion, that he is a Quaker, we would be likely to draw the conclusion that he is a pacifist, since Quakers tend to be pacifists. But since Republicans tend not to be pacifists, if we were to learn of Nixon's political affiliation as well, we would then be likely to withdraw this initial conclusion and, I suspect, simply remain agnostic, or puzzled, about his pacifism, in light of the conflicting evidence. The proposition that Nixon is a Quaker, therefore, acts as a reason for the conclusion that he is a pacifist, and the proposition that he is a Republican seems to act like a defeater for this reason in at least this sense: it blocks our tendency to reach the conclusion that Nixon is a pacifist, even though we have accepted the proposition that he is a Quaker. Since this proposition acts like a defeater, why should it not be classified as a defeater, just as Pollock's definition suggests?

To this argument I can offer two responses. My first response is that there seems to be an intuitive difference between situations in which Pollock and I both recognize a relation of defeat and situations in which Pollock recognizes defeat and I do not—that is, between situations in which, on one hand, a consideration Z offers stronger support for some contradictory conclusion than X does for Y, and situations in which, on the other hand, Z offers support for a contradictory conclusion that is either equal to or incomparable in strength with the support offered by X for Y. Situations of the first sort are illustrated by the Tweety Triangle, where both Pollock and I agree that the proposition that Tweety is a penguin defeats the information that Tweety is a bird as a reason for the conclusion that he flies. In situations like this, the outcome is usually clear and uncontroversial; in this case, there is no question that the correct conclusion is that Tweety cannot fly. Situations of the second sort are illustrated by the Nixon Diamond, where Pollock would claim that the proposition that Nixon is a Republican defeats the information that Nixon is a Quaker as a reason for the conclusion that he is a pacifist, but I would not. Situations like this typically lead to puzzlement and agnosticism; here, we find it hard to say whether Nixon is a pacifist or not. Since the relations among reasons in these two kinds of situations are so different, then, and since our reactions are different as well—clarity, versus puzzlement and agnosticism—I believe that it is a conceptual mistake to group them both together under the single rubric of defeat.

My second response is this. The virtue claimed for Pollock's treatment of defeat is that it allows us to explain our agnosticism in cases such as the Nixon Diamond by classifying each of the two reasons involved—that Nixon is a Quaker, and also a Republican—as a defeater of the other, so that neither then yields a firm conclusion. But that is not the only way to explain our agnosticism, and perhaps not the best way. On my own view, neither of these reasons defeats the other. The two reasons are provided by defaults belonging to two different proper scenarios, leading to two different extensions, one of which contains the statement that Nixon is a pacifist and one of which contains the statement that he is not. Even adhering to the current notion of defeat, therefore, our agnosticism can still be explained simply by adoption of the skeptical approach, discussed earlier, toward theories with multiple extensions, which supports as conclusions only those propositions contained in the intersection of the various extensions, and so refrains in this case from any commitment, one way or the other, on the matter of Nixon's pacifism.

2.2.2 Reasons and enablers

I now want to consider a distinction, due to Dancy, between reasons themselves and *enablers*, where an enabler is an external consideration that allows a reason to do its job.[9] Dancy's point in drawing this distinction is to counter the tendency to assimilate enablers to reasons, and more generally, to show that there are various roles for considerations to play in practical and epistemic reasoning, not just the role of reasons. I cannot hope here to explore the ramifications of this distinction within ethics and epistemology, as Dancy himself does, but only to show that it is supported by the current account of reasons.

Let us begin with the chain of reasoning that Dancy uses to introduce the distinction:

1. I promised to do it.
2. My promise was not given under duress.
3. I am able to do it.
4. There is no greater reason not to do it.
5. So I ought to do it.[10]

---

[9]The distinction is discussed throughout Chapter 3 of Dancy (2004).

[10]Dancy (2004, p. 38); note that I have substituted Dancy's 5* for his 5, in order to avoid the issue of what it might mean for an argument to terminate in an action.

Here, Dancy argues, only the first proposition, that I promised to do it, counts as a reason for the conclusion that I ought to do it; the other three considerations—that my promise was not given under duress, that I am able to do it, that there is no greater reason not to—are not themselves reasons for the conclusion, or even parts of reasons, but instead three different kinds of enablers, which play three different roles in allowing the initial reason to support its conclusion. The reason why I ought to do it, then, is supposed to be the simple consideration that I promised to, not the more complex consideration that I promised to, there was no duress, I am able to, and there is no greater reason not to.

In fact, even this pedestrian case of ordinary practical reasoning raises issues that we are not yet prepared to handle. The way in which reasons support ought statements is not described until Chapter 3, and likewise the relation between oughts and ability; and the precise role of the second consideration, that my promise was not given under duress, will not become clear until Chapter 5. A full discussion of this example is therefore deferred until Section 5.3.3, once all of the necessary concepts have been introduced.

For the moment, I want to concentrate only on the role of the fourth consideration in Dancy's example—that there is no greater reason not to do it—and show both that the current account does not, in fact, classify this consideration as part of the reason why I ought to do it, and also that this classification is sensible. The point can be illustrated most simply with a purely epistemic example, from which the additional complicating considerations have been removed, so consider:

1. Tweety is a bird.
2. There is no better reason for thinking Tweety does not fly.
3. Therefore Tweety flies.

And suppose, as a further simplification, that the only consideration so far recognized as a reason for concluding that a bird would not fly is the fact that it might also be a penguin, a specific kind of flightless bird.

In that case, then, again taking P, B, and F as the propositions that Tweety is a penguin, a bird, and a thing that flies, the information underlying this chain of reasoning could naturally be represented as the default theory $\Delta_6 = \langle W, \mathcal{D}, < \rangle$, where $W = \{B, P \supset B\}$, where $\mathcal{D} = \{\delta_1, \delta_2\}$ with $\delta_1 = B \rightarrow F$ and $\delta_2 = P \rightarrow \neg F$, and where $\delta_1 < \delta_2$. The theory is like the Tweety Triangle, except that W contains only the information that Tweety is a bird, not the additional information that he is a penguin as well, together with an instance of the truth that all penguins are birds; once more, $\mathcal{D}$ contains instances for Tweety of the defaults that birds fly and penguins do not, and $<$ tells us that the default about penguins carries a higher priority than the default about birds.

This default theory now yields the single proper scenario $\mathcal{S}_1 = \{\delta_1\}$, supporting F, the conclusion that Tweety flies. And according to the account presented here, the reason for this conclusion is simply the proposition B, that Tweety is a bird; this is the premise of δ_1, the only default triggered in the scenario. But then, what of the second consideration in our example—that there are no better reasons for thinking that Tweety does not fly, or, given our simplification, that we do not possess the information that Tweety is a penguin? According to our account, this is not a reason for concluding that Tweety flies, nor is it part of such a reason. Instead, it is simply an observation that a particular fact, which would have defeated the current reason if it were present, is not present. It is, as Dancy says, an enabler—a consideration that enables the current reason to support its conclusion, though not a reason itself.

Now of course, this analysis of the situation, according to which the proposition that Tweety is not a penguin is not part of the reason for concluding that he flies, but simply an enabling consideration, is itself dependent on our formalization of the example. In the proposed theory, the conclusion that Tweety flies is due to the default δ_1—that is, $B \rightarrow F$—which provides the proposition that Tweety is a bird as a reason for this conclusion. But this default could just as easily have been replaced with a default of the form $(B \wedge \neg P) \rightarrow F$. There is nothing wrong with complex reasons. One might say, for example, that the reason Muhammad Ali was a great fighter is that he was quick, strong, smart, and able to take a punch—where all four of these features were necessary to assure his greatness. Why not suppose, then, that what favors the conclusion that Tweety flies is, not the simple proposition that he is a bird, but instead the complex proposition that he is a bird and not a penguin?

There is, I think, nothing wrong with this suggestion in principle.[11] Encoding a body of information properly into a default theory is something of a craft, and it can often be hard to tell whether some particular consideration should be represented as part of a more complex reason, or instead, as an enabling condition that allows a simpler reason to have the right effect. As far as I know, there is no general test to determine the matter, and individual proposals must be evaluated case by case. Still, I believe that, at least in this case, it is plain that the idea of replacing the simple default $B \rightarrow F$ with the more complex $(B \wedge \neg P) \rightarrow F$ is mistaken. There are at least two problems with this idea.

The first becomes apparent the moment we step away from our simplifying assumption that the only flightless birds are penguins. There are also, of course, ostriches, emus, cassowaries, kiwis, flightless steamer ducks, and many other species of birds that do not fly by nature. Furthermore, there are birds that may fly by nature, but are unable to fly due to particular circumstances: baby birds, sick birds, birds with their wings clipped, birds with their feet stuck in cement, birds attached by wires to heavy lead weights—and this list is truly open-ended. Once it is agreed that our default rule should contain the clause that Tweety is not a penguin, it is hard

---

[11] And Dancy (2004, p. 39) agrees, referring to his own example.

to see why the rule should not also require that Tweety does not fall into
any of these other categories either. The result would be a rule of staggering complexity, or at least staggering length, stipulating not only that
Tweety cannot belong to any of the known species of flightless birds, but
also that he should fail to meet every one of the other imaginable conditions
that might prevent a bird from flying.

No one, speaking naturally, would ever refer to the premise of such a
complex rule as the reason for concluding that Tweety flies.[12] It is just
possible, I suppose, that some theorist might require a default rule to have
this complex form all the same, yet reserve the ordinary term "reason"
for the particular conjunct from the premise of the rule that is somehow
most salient—that Tweety is a bird.[13] In that case, though, it is natural
to wonder what all the other conjuncts are doing—that Tweety is not a
penguin, not an ostrich, not an emu, that his wings are not clipped, his feet
are not stuck in cement, and so on. I can only imagine that a theorist who
insists that all of these further qualifications should be included within
the premise of a default must be confusing a default rule with a correct
universal generalization, and imposing on the former conditions that are
needed only for the latter.

The second problem with the idea of replacing the simple default $B \to F$
with the more complex $(B \wedge \neg P) \to F$ is more subtle, and would arise even
if we were to maintain our simplifying assumption that the only condition
that could interfere with the conclusion that Tweety flies, given that he is
a bird, is that he might also be penguin—although it becomes much more
striking once that simplifying assumption is dropped. The problem is this:
any proposition that forms the premise of a default rule must be verified in
order for that rule to be applied. And it does seem reasonable, if we want
to be able to infer that Tweety flies because birds fly, that we should first
have to verify that Tweety is a bird. But it seems much less reasonable
that we should also have to verify that Tweety is not a penguin before
concluding, by default, that Tweety flies, and entirely unreasonable—once
we drop our simplifying assumption—that we should then have to verify
that Tweety does not belong to any of the countless other classes of birds
that do not fly. The inference from the premise that Tweety is a bird to

---

[12]Without pretending to speak naturally, Raz (1975, pp. 22–25; 2000, p. 59n) introduces the technical term "complete reason" to refer to this kind of fully-qualified
premise.

[13]It is also possible that Raz himself is such a theorist. In the course of introducing
complete reasons as fully-qualified premises of conditionals, he suggests that we allude
to these extensive conjunctions by citing only certain conjuncts, writing, for example,
that: "In ordinary conversation, we almost never make a full and complete statement
of our reasons. We state only a part of them, our choice of which part to state being
determined by pragmatic considerations" (1975, p. 22). But here we must be careful.
We can accept both the ideas that reasons can be conjunctive, and that we often allude
to conjunctive reasons by citing only certain of their conjuncts—an idea that I defend
later, in Section 6.3.1—without committing ourselves to the further idea that the reasons
alluded to must therefore be fully-qualified, complete reasons.

the conclusion that he flies is supposed to be based on the assumption, not the explicit verification, that Tweety is not an odd sort of bird, such as a penguin or a bird with its feet stuck in cement.

This second problem can be illustrated in the simplest case by noting that, if we did replace the default $B \to F$ with the more complex $(B \wedge \neg P) \to F$ in the earlier Δ_6, then the resulting default theory would no longer support F, the conclusion that Tweety flies. Why not? Because the other information from the theory does not actually tell us that Tweety is not a penguin—it merely fails to tell us that he is a penguin—and so the new default would no longer be triggered, or applicable. In order for the new default to be triggered, the fact that Tweety is not a penguin would now have to be explicitly encoded into the underlying default theory, perhaps by supplementing the hard information from the theory with the further proposition $\neg P$. And of course, this is the simplest case. If we then drop our simplifying assumption, and move from $(B \wedge \neg P) \to F$ to a fully-qualified default, with a premise stipulating that Tweety does not belong to any known class of exceptional bird, then each of the various ways in which Tweety is not exceptional—that he is not an ostrich, not an emu, that his feet are not stuck in cement, and so on—would likewise have to be explicitly encoded in the underlying default theory, in order for us to reach the conclusion that Tweety flies.

The contrast between what needs to be verified, or explicitly asserted, and what can simply be assumed is a central theme in nonmonotonic reasoning. It is apparent, for example, in this passage from an early paper by McCarthy, arguing that the contrast reflects communication conventions deeply embedded in our language:

> Suppose A tells B about a situation involving a bird. If the bird cannot fly and this is relevant, then A must say so. Whereas if the bird can fly, there is no requirement to mention the fact. For example, if I hire you to build me a bird cage and you don't put a top on it, I can get out of paying for it even if you tell the judge that I never said my bird could fly. However, if I complain that you wasted money by putting a top on a cage I intended for a penguin, the judge will agree with you that if the bird couldn't fly I should have said so.[14]

Indeed, Dancy's distinction between reasons and enablers in ethics and epistemology is itself anticipated by a similar distinction in nonmonotonic reasoning, and artificial intelligence more generally, though the motivation for the distinction is different in the two fields.

Within artificial intelligence, the initial point of concern is with useful rules, which might actually play some role in the deliberation of cognitive agents; and here the distinction between reasons and enablers—though

---

[14]McCarthy (1986, p. 91).

this is not the terminology employed—is found especially in discussions of the *qualification problem*, the problem of formulating useful rules for commonsense reasoning amidst a sea of qualifications and exceptional circumstances.[15] Imagine, for example, a robot relying on its knowledge of the world to construct a plan for getting to work in the morning, where a plan is, say, a sequence of actions leading to the desired outcome: the robot is at work. The robot's knowledge might include a rule that we would put most naturally by saying something like, "If you turn the key, the car will start." It is not hard to imagine that this rule could figure prominently in the robot's planning, and that, if it decides to drive to work, the robot might even include the action "Turn the key" in its eventual plan, in order to start the car.

But of course, the rule as stated is incorrect, at least if it is interpreted as an ordinary conditional. Even if you turn the key, the car will not start if there is no gas in the tank, if the battery is dead, if the distributor has been removed, if the valves have been jammed, the crank shaft is broken, or if there is a potato in the tailpipe—again, the list is open-ended.[16] So consider these various conditions: the key is turned, the battery is not dead, the distributor is intact, and so on. Each is necessary for the car to start. Yet they are not all on a par. It makes sense for the first condition, that the key is turned, to figure in the antecedent of a useful rule about starting cars, and for the robot to place the action "Turn the key" in its plan for getting to work. But a rule that contained all of the other various conditions in its antecedent—that the battery is not dead, the distributor is intact, there is no potato in the tailpipe, and so on—would not be useful at all, but entirely unmanageable; and the robot would never get to work if it actually tried to guarantee all of these conditions as part of its plan.

The study of nonmonotonic logic arose, in part, from an effort to understand the rules we actually use in our reasoning, not the fully-qualified rules that might be correct from a more conventional perspective, but that we never do actually use; and what I am suggesting with my overall analysis is that those propositions that stand as premises of these useful rules coincide with the propositions that are to be classified as reasons, rather than mere enablers. Continuing with our example: the rule that the car starts when you turn the key could naturally be captured as a default, and in explaining the event, we would naturally say that the reason the car started is that the robot turned the key; the condition that there should be no potato in the tailpipe would have no place in a useful default rule, and it would be odd to find any allusion to this fact—a mere enabler, not a reason—in any explanation of the event.

---

[15] See McCarthy (1977) for the canonical description of this problem.

[16] Because of this example, the qualification problem in artificial intelligence is sometimes referred to as the "potato in the tailpipe" problem; some historical reflections on the problem are provided by Matthew Ginsberg (1993, p. 281, fn. 27).

In his own treatment of reasons, Dancy does not, of course, begin with
a logical account of the rules that might be useful for cognitive agents, or
with any study of the literature from artificial intelligence or default logic.
Instead, he tends to speak as if the reason relation—that some propositions
are or are not reasons for others, or for actions—is simply an aspect of the
world that is there for us to discern, or to fail to discern. Suppose, however,
that I am right in thinking that the class of reasons, as identified by Dancy
and others, coincides with the class of propositions that serve as premises
for rules of the sort that we find to be useful, studied in artificial intelligence
and represented here as defaults. In that case, the coincidence would be
too striking not to require explanation, but the explanation could move in
either direction. It may be that these rules are useful precisely because they
do represent the reason relation that is already, somehow, present in the
world; or conversely, it may be that there is no such antecedently-existing
reason relation, and that what we think we see when we look for it results
only from projecting onto the world a relation suggested by the default
rules that happen to be most useful for cognitive agents like ourselves.

2.2.3   Reason amalgamation

I close this chapter by simply mentioning, and acknowledging the importance of, a topic that I do not have much to say about—the way in which,
as it sometimes seems, weaker reasons may combine together to defeat a
stronger reason.

Consider an example: I have been invited to the wedding of a distant
relative at a difficult time of year. I am not particularly close to this
relative, and, since the wedding falls at such an inconvenient time, I would
rather not go. But suppose I learn that the guests will include my two old
aunts, Olive and Petunia, whom I enjoy and who I know would like to see
me. Here it is perfectly sensible to imagine that, even though I would still
choose not to attend the wedding if only one of the two aunts were going,
the chance to see both Aunt Olive and Aunt Petunia in the same trip offers
enough value to compensate for the inconvenience of the trip itself.

Now, one way of representing this situation would be by taking the
individual reasons arising from the presence of Olive and Petunia as ex-
haustive. More exactly, let O be the proposition that Aunt Olive will be
at the wedding, and P the proposition that Aunt Petunia will be there;
let I be the proposition that the trip is inconvenient, and W the proposi-
tion that I actually attend the wedding. And take $\Delta_7 = \langle \mathcal{W}, \mathcal{D}, < \rangle$, where
$W = \{I, O, P\}$, where $\mathcal{D} = \{\delta_1, \delta_2, \delta_3\}$, with δ_1 as $O \rightarrow W$, with δ_2 as
$P \rightarrow W$, and with δ_3 as $I \rightarrow \neg W$, and where the priority ordering tells us
both that $\delta_1 < \delta_3$ and that $\delta_2 < \delta_3$. According to this theory, then, the
hard information is that the trip is inconvenient, Aunt Olive will be there,
and Aunt Petunia will be there; the fact that Olive will be there is a reason
to attend the wedding, as is the fact that Petunia will be there, but the

inconvenience of the trip is a reason, stronger than either of these, not to attend the wedding.

It is easy to see that this theory yields $S_1 = \{\delta_3\}$ as its unique proper scenario, supporting the conclusion that I ought not to attend the wedding because of the inconvenience of the trip—a reason that is strong enough to defeat the presence of Aunt Olive as a reason for attending, and also the presence of Aunt Petunia. But of course, this is the wrong result. It is part of the story that, although the inconvenience would outweigh the benefits of seeing either Olive or Petunia individually, it does not outweigh the benefit of seeing them together.

From a more general perspective, the difficulty is that, although the current theory is formulated as an alternative to the weighing conception, there are situations, like this one, in which something like the weighing conception seems exactly right. One can almost picture a scale on which the inconvenience of the trip is balanced against, and outweighs, the benefits of seeing Aunt Olive alone, and then watching as the value of seeing Aunt Petunia as well is added to the scale and the balance slowly tips to the other side, favoring the trip after all. The problem with the current theory is that it does not allow the priorities associated with a number of different defaults, or reasons, to be combined—much as weights can be combined—to defeat another default that is capable of defeating each of them individually.

In fact, the wedding example itself can be coded into the framework of default logic. Let δ_4 be the new default $O \wedge P \rightarrow W$, and take $\Delta_8 = \langle W, D, < \rangle$, where W is just as before, where D now contains δ_4 as well as the previous δ_1, δ_2, and δ_3, and where the priority ordering tells us everything it did before but also that $\delta_3 < \delta_4$. This new theory, then, contains all of the earlier information together with the new information that the presence of both Aunt Olive and Aunt Petunia is a reason to attend the wedding, and a reason strong enough to defeat the inconvenience of the trip as a reason not to attend. The theory therefore yields $S_2 = \{\delta_4\}$ as its unique proper scenario, supporting the desired conclusion that I ought to attend the wedding because both Olive and Petunia will be there.

In a way, though, this representation of the example simply relocates the issue. The question, now, concerns the relation between the new default δ_4 and the previous δ_1 and δ_2, or between the new reason arising from the presence of Olive and Petunia together, and the previous reasons arising from the presence of Olive, and also of Petunia. One option is to suppose that these defaults are entirely independent, that they have nothing to do with each other—and likewise, that the reason arising from the presence of Olive and Petunia together has nothing to do with the separate reasons arising from the presence of Olive, and of Petunia. This option has the advantage of simplicity, and, as its sole disadvantage, a significant degree of implausibility: can we really say that the reason arising from the presence of Olive and Petunia together has nothing at all to do with the separate reasons arising from the presence of Olive, and of Petunia?

The other option, of course, is to suppose that the new default δ_4, along with its place in the priority ordering, is somehow derived from the previous defaults δ_1 and δ_2, and their priorities—or that the complex reason arising from the presence of Olive and Petunia together is formed by amalgamating, somehow, the simpler reasons arising from the presence of Olive, and of Petunia. This option carries more initial plausibility, perhaps, but raises a number of difficult issues. Surely, not just any two reasons favoring some outcome can be amalgamated together to form a stronger reason favoring that outcome, and sometimes reasons that favor a particular outcome when taken individually favor another outcome entirely when taken together. Suppose, for example, that Symptom 1 is a reason for the administration of Drug A, since it suggests Disease 1, for which Drug A is appropriate, and that Symptom 2 is also a reason for the administration of Drug A, since it suggests Disease 2, for which Drug A is also appropriate; still, it might be that Symptoms 1 and 2 appearing together suggest Disease 3, for which Drug A is not appropriate. Or as a more concrete example, suppose I am deliberating about an afternoon run, and that both heat and rain, taken individually, function as negative reasons, arguing against a run; still, the combination of heat and rain together might function as a positive reason, favoring the run as refreshing.

If reasons do indeed amalgamate, it is clear that they often behave differently under amalgamation, at least: some complex reasons, such as Olive and Petunia, form stronger reasons supporting the same conclusions as their components, while others, such as Symptoms 1 and 2, or heat and rain, actually interfere with the support provided by their component reasons. Anyone favoring the option of reason amalgamation would therefore, at some point, have to provide a careful description of the process, and of the constraints governing this process. Which reasons can properly be amalgamated and which cannot? And how is the priority of a complex, or amalgamated, reason influenced by the priority of its components? These are difficult questions. I am not aware of any successful attempt to answer them in the literature, nor do I have anything to offer myself.[17]

---

[17] Among writers who have discussed this issue, most take the first of our two options: Pollock (1995, pp. 101–102) treats complex, or amalgamated, reasons, along with their priorities, as independent of the simpler reasons that might naturally be taken as their components; Delgrande and Schaub (2004) introduce a variant of default logic in which priorities are defined among sets of defaults, rather than among individual defaults, but present no systematic procedure for relating the priority assigned to a set of defaults to the priorities assigned to the singleton-sets containing the individual defaults from the original set; and Schroeder (2007, Chapter 7) works with a formal model in which weights are assigned directly to sets of reasons, rather than to individual reasons, but again does not relate the weight of a set of reasons to the weight of the singleton sets constructed from the reasons belonging to that set. Recently, Prakken (2005) has sketched a new framework in which a sort of default logic is applied to the process of reason amalgamation itself; the system is promising, but also complex, and has to date been presented only in outline.

Part II

Deontic logic

Chapter 3

Reasons and oughts

This second part of the book has two goals. The first, and primary, goal is to explain how the various reasons at work in a situation can support conclusions about what an agent ought to do—in the language of Ross, how prima facie duties, or prima facie oughts, can lead to all things considered oughts, or more simply, to oughts *sans phrase*. Ross's own view, of course, is that this step is accomplished through an application of moral intuition, insight, or perception. And as we will see later, in our discussion of particularism, I agree that, on certain occasions, we must appeal to something like moral intuition—or at least to a process that I do not know how to describe. However, I would like to delay any such appeal as long as possible, and to constrain its application to special circumstances, rather than supposing that it is at work on a day-to-day basis, and in the vast run of cases.

In the current chapter, therefore, I describe a systematic procedure, applicable in the broad range of ordinary cases, through which ought statements can be derived from default theories and the reasons they provide. Indeed, I present two such procedures—two deontic logics—one that allows for the possibility of conflicting all things considered oughts and one that does not.

The second goal is to explore the possibility of moral conflicts within the general framework provided by these two deontic logics. Although I do not pursue this second goal in any serious way until the following chapter, it is useful to begin with some preliminary discussion now, since it will help shape our understanding of the logics themselves.

Let us say that a *normative conflict* is a situation in which an agent ought to perform an action X, and also ought to perform an action Y, but in which it is impossible for the agent to perform both X and Y. Not all normative conflicts are moral conflicts, of course. It may be that the agent ought to perform the action X for reasons of personal generosity, but ought to perform the action Y for reasons of prudence: perhaps X involves buying a lavish gift for a friend, while Y involves depositing a certain amount of money in the bank. Our practical deliberation is shaped by a concern with a variety of morally neutral goods—not just generosity and prudence, but any number of others, such as etiquette, aesthetics, fun. I mention these ancillary values, however, only to put them aside. We will be concerned here, not with normative conflicts more generally, but precisely with *moral conflicts*—situations in which, even when our attention is restricted entirely to moral reasons for action, it is nevertheless true that an agent ought to do X and ought to do Y, but cannot do both.

It is often argued that moral conflicts, defined in this way, simply cannot occur, that they are impossible. The justifications offered for this conclusion fall into two broad categories. Some writers contend that, although there might be normative conflicts more generally, the possibility of specifically moral conflicts is ruled out by the special nature of moral reasons, or by special constraints on these reasons. Arguments along these lines generally proceed by identifying as genuinely moral reasons for action only those supported by some particular moral theory—usually a Kantian or utilitarian theory—that itself rules out the possibility of conflicts. Alan Donagan, for example, argues against moral conflicts by advancing a kind of rationalist theory, developed through a process of dialectical reasoning, according to which it is very nearly analytic that such conflicts cannot arise: whenever an apparent conflict is discovered, this is supposed to show only that the theory as developed thus far is defective, requiring further revision until the conflict is avoided.[1] And of course, it is most natural also for an advocate of the utilitarian approach to be drawn toward Mill's own conclusion that the principle of utility, the ultimate moral reason, provides a common standard through which any apparent moral conflicts can be resolved.[2]

I will have very little to say about this first style of argument, which denies the possibility of moral conflicts by appealing to considerations concerning the kinds of reasons for action that might be supplied by the correct moral theory; the general line of thought is sensible, of course, but the project of developing any such argument in detail would be a substantial task, since it requires the defense of some particular moral theory as correct. I will concentrate, instead, on a different style of argument, which denies the possibility of moral conflict, not so much by appealing to a particular moral theory, but rather on the basis of broader conceptual considerations, sometimes, but not always, involving issues in deontic logic.

Generally, those who argue in this way—including Philippa Foot, John Searle, Judith Jarvis Thomson, and more recently, David Brink and Paul Pietroski—begin by partitioning certain terms from our ethical language into two distinct classes, with the members of these classes playing different

---

[1] See Donagan (1984; 1993).

[2] Although some writers, such as Michael Slote (1985), suggest that utilitarianism can allow for the possibility of moral conflicts, I do not know of any conclusive arguments along these lines; I show in Horty (2001a) that situations of the sort described by Slote, while certainly anomalous, do not lead to moral conflicts in the sense defined here.

roles.[3] Although the exact character of this distinction varies from one writer to the next, and there is some disagreement about which terms fall in which class, the basic idea is plain. Certain ethical terms are supposed to signal, or at least allow for, what we might call a *weak* use, according to which they do little more than indicate moral reasons, which may well conflict. To illustrate, recall the earlier example, from Section 1.1.2, in which I have inadvertently promised to have a private dinner tonight with each of two twins, Twin 1 and Twin 2. In that case, it is natural to say that I have an "obligation" to dine with Twin 1, due to my promise, and also with Twin 2. It can likewise be said that I have a "prima facie duty" to dine with Twin 1, and also with Twin 2, or that dining with Twin 1 is something I ought to do "other things being equal," as is dining with Twin 2.

In addition to terms like these, which invite a weak reading— representing only moral reasons for action, and allowing conflicts—there are also supposed to be other ethical terms, particularly "ought" and "must," that signal a *strong* use, indicating the judgment that results once all of these various reasons are taken into consideration. This strong use is sometimes indicated by talk of what an agent ought to do "on balance" or "all things considered," or of what an agent "really" ought to do, though the use of the word "ought" alone is often enough to force the strong interpretation. Ought statements of this strong kind are supposed to be, in a sense, derived from the weaker variety, since they are based on the moral reasons at work in a given situation. But since they are also supposed to reflect the result of integrating and balancing these various reasons, it is thought that there can be no conflicts among these strong oughts—that we cannot accept, for example, the statement "All things considered, I ought to dine with Twin 1" along with the statement "All things considered, I ought to dine with Twin 2."

My concern, then, is with the position that, although there may be conflicts between the various forms of weak, or prima facie, ethical statements, there can be no conflicts involving strong, or all things considered, oughts; and I focus special attention on a proposal—hinted at by Donagan and Foot, explicitly defended by Brink—which will be described here as the "disjunctive account." The most powerful case for moral conflicts seems to arise in situations in which the reasons for performing each of two incompatible actions, X and Y, are either evenly balanced or else incommensurable. According to the disjunctive account, the correct all things considered conclusion to draw in these situations is, not that the agent ought to perform the action X and ought also to perform the action Y, but simply that the agent ought to perform either X or Y. In the twins case, for example, the disjunctive account would lead me to conclude, not that I ought to dine with Twin 1 and also that I ought to dine with Twin 2,

---

[3]See Brink (1994), Foot (1983), Pietroski (1993), Searle (1980), and Thomson (1990).

but simply that I ought to dine either with Twin 1 or with Twin 2, that I am not permitted to break both my promises and dine alone, say, or with someone else entirely.

Of the two deontic logics presented in this chapter, one allows conflicts among all things considered oughts while the other rules out such conflicts precisely by developing a disjunctive account—providing, as far as I know, the first accurate formulation of this view.

3.1   The two logics

I begin by introducing a conditional deontic operator $\bigcirc$ intended to represent the strong, or all things considered, ought: if X and Y are propositions expressible in the background language, then $\bigcirc(Y/X)$ is the statement that, all things considered, Y ought to be the case under the circumstances X.

This notation calls for two immediate comments. First, although the ought operator introduced here is conditional, it is easy enough, as well as standard practice, to define its unconditional analog as a conditional ought that happens to be conditional only on $\top$, the trivially true proposition. Thus, the simple ought statement $\bigcirc(Y)$, according to which Y simply ought to be the case, can be identified with the conditional ought statement $\bigcirc(Y/\top)$, according to which Y ought to be the case in any circumstance in which the trivially true proposition holds. Indeed, although simple oughts are officially defined from conditional oughts in this way, we will, in fact, for the sake of clarity and ease of exposition, approach the matter in exactly the opposite direction, focusing first on the simple ought operator as if it were primitive, and then later treating the conditional version of this operator as a generalization.

As a second comment, the reader may have noticed that I have now shifted from an informal discussion largely focused on questions concerning what various agents ought to do to a formal notation containing statements only about what ought to be the case—an impersonal ought, rather than a personal ought. What should we make of this gap between our informal talk and our formal theory? My suggestion is that we should ignore it. Although it may well be important, for various purposes, to distinguish personal from impersonal oughts—statements about what agents ought to do, from statements about what ought to be the case—I believe that the issues raised by that distinction are orthogonal to the problems considered here: conflicts can arise concerning either personal or impersonal oughts, and a strategy for handling conflicts of either kind should be applicable also to the other. I therefore follow a policy of intentional but, I hope, harmless equivocation, sliding back and forth between the personal and the impersonal.[4] I will generally rely on personal oughts in informal discussion,

---

[4] There is, of course, a perspective from which this strategy involves no equivocation at all. It is often suggested that personal oughts can be analyzed directly in terms of imper-

for the simple reason that they allow for the formulation of more natural examples; but in order to avoid the extraneous complications involved in a proper treatment of personal agency, which would be necessary for a full logical representation of these examples, the formal development itself will be restricted to the simpler case of impersonal oughts.[5]

With these preliminaries behind us, we can now turn to the general problem at issue in this chapter: given a background default theory, how do we determine which all things considered oughts are supported by this theory and the reasons it provides? If we think of oughts as following, or derived, from reasons, this problem can be cast as a logical question: how can we define a *consequence relation* telling us whether a simple ought statement of the form $\bigcirc(Y)$—or more generally, a conditional ought statement of the form $\bigcirc(Y/X)$—follows from the information contained in some background default theory?

3.1.1 Simple oughts

There is a standard answer to the question of how all things considered oughts are generated by reasons. The simplest form of the standard answer—found in Chisholm, for example—is that an agent ought to perform an action if there is an undefeated reason for the agent to perform that action.[6] A more general form of the standard answer—found in Baier, Gilbert Harman, Schroeder, and many others—is that an agent ought to

---

sonal oughts. According to a view I have described elsewhere as the "Meinong/Chisholm thesis," after two prominent proponents, the statement that an agent ought to perform some action is to be understood as meaning only that it ought to be the case that the agent performs that action—the statement that I ought to dine with Twin 1, for example, is supposed to mean only that it ought to be the case that I dine with Twin 1. For advocates of this thesis, or of any similar way of reducing personal to impersonal oughts, the gap between our informal talk of personal oughts and the impersonal ought operator of our formal theory is illusory. The formal theory can then be taken at face value as an account of impersonal ought statements, which can itself be understood, in accord with the Meinong/Chisholm thesis or some related reduction, as providing the proper analysis of the personal ought statements found in our ordinary talk. Of course, the Meinong/Chisholm thesis is not simply an analytic truth, but a substantive philosophical thesis, perhaps even a linguistic thesis, about the relation between personal and impersonal oughts, with both advocates and opponents. It is a thesis that I argue against in Horty (2001a), though my arguments depend on a particular account of both agency and the ought operator; Schroeder (2011b) offers some more general objections. Recent advocates of the Meinong/Chisholm thesis, or something very close, include Broome (1999) and Ralph Wedgwood (2006).

[5] For an illustration of the complications that a treatment of personal agency might introduce, the interested reader can consult the recent, sustained study of the concept by Nuel Belnap, Michael Perloff, and Ming Xu (2001).

[6] See Chisholm (1964, p. 149) and (1974, p. 125); note that Chisholm uses the term "overridden" for our "defeated," and that—as an advocate of the Meinong/Chisholm thesis—he is explicitly talking about what ought to be the case, rather than, in the first instance, what agents ought to do. An interesting variant of this view is presented by Raz (1975, p. 30), who argues that saying that an agent ought to perform some action actually means nothing more than that the agent has some reason to perform the action,

perform an action when the reasons that favor performing that action outweigh the reasons that oppose doing so.[7]

It is important to realize, however, that, as long as we adhere to the
austere theory of reasons developed in the previous chapter, this standard
account of the way in which oughts are generated by reasons is not going
to work, in either of its versions. To see this, we need only recall the movie
example from Section 2.1, according to which: I have promised to lend a
friend $5 tomorrow, and to donate another $5 to charity; I currently have
only $15, with no prospects of getting any more, and seeing a movie tonight
would cost $7. It seems to follow from this information that I ought not to
see a movie tonight. But given the austere theory of reasons, the standard
account does not yield this result. According to the austere theory, I do
not have an undefeated reason to refrain from seeing a movie, nor do my
reasons to refrain from seeing a movie outweigh my reasons for seeing one.
Indeed, according to this theory, I do not have any reason to refrain from
seeing a movie at all. What I have, due to my two promises, is a reason
for lending $5 to my friend and another reason for donating $5 to charity,
period.

Or recall our other example along the same lines: Jack has promised to
meet Jo for lunch, and in order to do that, he must now get into his car.
It seems to follow that Jack ought to get into his car. But this ought will
not be generated by the standard account, since, according to the austere
theory, Jack has no reason to get into his car, let alone an undefeated
reason, or a set of reasons that outweighs his set of reasons not to get into
the car. All Jack has is a reason, due to his promise, for having lunch with
Jo.

Evidently, the difficulty is this: the standard account of the way in
which oughts are generated from reasons requires very direct support—
there must be some particular reason for each of the things we ought to
do—but the austere theory, precisely because of its austerity, simply does
not supply enough reasons to generate the appropriate oughts. And just as
evidently, there are two routes toward a resolution of this difficulty. First,
we could abandon the austere theory, and instead search for some way
to inflate our set of reasons until we have enough to generate the desired
oughts. Perhaps, in the movie example, I might be able to derive a reason
not to see a movie from my antecedent reasons to lend money to my friend
and donate to charity; perhaps Jack could derive a reason for getting into
his car from his existing reason to have lunch with Jo. Following this first
path would involve defining a sort of logic of reasons—some systematic
method for deriving reasons from other reasons. I have nothing against
the idea in principle. My only objection is that I have never seen it done,

but that the use of the word "ought" carries the pragmatic implication that the reason
is undefeated.

[7]See, for example, Baier (1958, p. 102), Harman (1975, p. 112), and Schroeder (2007,
p. 130).

and I do not know how to do it myself. I therefore follow a second path in this book, maintaining the austere theory of reasons but searching for a more relaxed view of the relation between reasons and oughts, one that abandons the requirement of direct support and allows for the possibility that an agent ought to perform an action even though there may be no explicit reason to do so.

The most straightforward way of developing this idea would be to imagine that the actions an agent ought to perform include, not just those that the agent has explicit reason to perform, but all of those whose performance is, under the circumstances, required for—or entailed by—the actions that the agent has explicit reason to perform. This straightforward approach works well in many examples. In the movie case, for instance, I have explicit reasons to give $5 to a friend and to give $5 to charity, in a situation in which I have only $15 and a movie costs $7. Under these circumstances, then, performing the actions I have explicit reason to perform requires, or entails, that I not see a movie; and so seeing a movie would be something I ought not to do. Or again, if Jack has an explicit reason to meet Jo, and this entails getting into his car, then getting into his car would be something Jack ought to do.

Unfortunately, this straightforward strategy leads to problems in any situation in which an agent is confronted with reasons for conflicting actions. The point can be illustrated by returning once again to the twins example, which we now represent as a default theory. Take A_1 and A_2 as the propositions that I have arranged to dine with Twins 1 and 2, respectively, and D_1 and D_2 as the propositions that I do in fact dine with Twins 1 and 2, respectively. The example can then be encoded in the default theory $\Delta_9 = \langle W, D, < \rangle$, depicted in Figure 3.1, where $W = \{A_1, A_2, \neg(D_1 \wedge D_2)\}$, where $D = \{\delta_1, \delta_2\}$, with δ_1 and δ_2 as the defaults $A_1 \rightarrow D_1$ and $A_2 \rightarrow D_2$, and where the ordering $<$ is empty; neither default has a higher priority than the other. Here the defaults from D tell us that arranging to dine with either of the two twins favors doing so, while the background information from W tells us that I have, in fact, arranged to dine with each of the two twins, but that, sadly, I cannot dine with both.

In this situation, of course, I have a reason to dine with each twin; that is, there are reasons supporting D_1 and D_2. But under the circumstances of the example, which includes the statement $\neg(D_1 \wedge D_2)$ as background information, these two propositions are inconsistent, and therefore entail any other proposition at all, according to ordinary classical logic. If we suppose, therefore, that the actions I ought to perform are those whose performance is, under the circumstances, entailed by the actions I have reason to perform, it seems to follow—since the propositions D_1 and D_2 together entail any other—that I ought to perform every action whatsoever. But that cannot be right. Even if I have run into a sort of local difficulty by overbooking my evening, it would be odd to conclude from this that I ought to do absolutely everything.

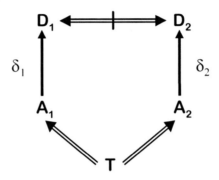

Figure 3.1: The twins

What this example shows is that we cannot, in general, define the actions an agent ought to perform as those that are required for, or entailed by, those actions the agent has explicit reason to perform. At times, the agent will have explicit reason to perform conflicting actions, in which case the performance of all of those actions—an inconsistent set—would entail the performance of every action. In such a situation, then, what can we say the agent ought to do?

Well, if an agent cannot perform all of the actions supported by its entire set of reasons, perhaps the agent could isolate some coherent subset of its reasons, at least, and perform the actions supported by the reasons from that set, as well as any others required for, or entailed by, those actions. This seems like a sensible suggestion, but what, exactly, is a coherent set of reasons? The hypothesis I explore here is that, against the background of a particular default theory, a *coherent* set of reasons can be defined as the collection of reasons provided by some proper scenario based on that theory.[8] And in that case, the all things considered oughts derivable from a default theory—the actions or propositions supported by coherent sets of reasons, along with their consequences—can then be thought of as determined by the extensions of that default theory, the statement sets generated by its proper scenarios.

Even this hypothesis, however, does not yet determine a unique approach, since, as we know, default theories can allow multiple proper scenarios, and so multiple extensions. As a result, there are two natural ways in which the general hypothesis could be developed, corresponding to the credulous and skeptical approaches explored earlier for reasoning with multiple extensions. We might decide, as a first alternative, to endorse a

---

[8]The notion of coherence is discussed further, and contrasted with that of a mere consistency, in Section 4.1.1.

proposition as an all things considered ought just in case it is supported by some one of the theory's proper scenarios, or contained in some one of its extensions. This alternative, corresponding to the credulous treatment of multiple extensions, will be described here as the *conflict account*, since it allows for conflicts among all things considered oughts.

Definition 9 (Simple oughts: the conflict account) Let $\Delta = \langle \mathcal{W}, \mathcal{D}, < \rangle$ be a default theory. Then the simple ought statement $\bigcirc(Y)$ follows from Δ according to the conflict account just in case $Y \in \mathcal{E}$ for some extension $\mathcal{E}$ of this theory.

Or, as a second alternative, we might decide to endorse a proposition as an all things considered ought just in case it is supported by every scenario based on an underlying default theory, or contained in each of that theory's extensions. This alternative, corresponding to the skeptical treatment of multiple extensions, will be described as the *disjunctive account* since it avoids conflicts in accord with the disjunctive strategy sketched earlier. Although it differs from the first alternative only in a single word—"some" is replaced by "each"—the second alternative is set out separately here for the sake of thoroughness.

Definition 10 (Simple oughts: the disjunctive account) Let $\Delta = \langle \mathcal{W}, \mathcal{D}, < \rangle$ be a default theory. Then the simple ought statement $\bigcirc(Y)$ follows from Δ according to the disjunctive account just in case $Y \in \mathcal{E}$ for each extension $\mathcal{E}$ of this theory.

The differences between these two accounts, conflict and disjunctive, can be illustrated by returning to the twins example, the theory Δ_9 depicted in Figure 3.1. It is easy to verify that this theory yields two proper scenarios $\mathcal{S}_1 = \{\delta_1\}$ and $\mathcal{S}_2 = \{\delta_2\}$, generating the two extensions

$$\begin{aligned} \mathcal{E}_1 &= Th(\{A_1, A_2, \neg(D_1 \wedge D_2), D_1\}), \\ \mathcal{E}_2 &= Th(\{A_1, A_2, \neg(D_1 \wedge D_2), D_2\}). \end{aligned}$$

Since D_1 belongs to the first of these extensions and D_2 to the second, the conflict account thus supports both the statements $\bigcirc(D_1)$ and $\bigcirc(D_2)$. The result is a conflict among all things considered oughts, telling me that I ought to dine with Twin 1, and also that I ought to dine with Twin 2, though I cannot do both. According to the disjunctive account, on the other hand, neither $\bigcirc(D_1)$ nor $\bigcirc(D_2)$ is supported, since neither D_1 nor D_2 belongs to each extension of the theory. But of course, since each extension does contain either D_1 or D_2, and extensions are closed under logical consequence, each extension also contains the proposition $D_1 \vee D_2$, and so the disjunctive account yields $\bigcirc(D_1 \vee D_2)$ as an all things considered ought. In the case of this example, then, where I have arranged to dine with each twin but cannot do so, rather than telling me that I ought to dine with Twin 1 and also that I ought to dine with Twin 2, and so face a moral conflict, the disjunctive account tells me only that what I ought to do, all things considered, is dine with one twin or the other. And this particular example indicates the general pattern: where the conflict account yields moral conflicts, the disjunctive account yields only disjunctive obligations.

3.1.2   Conditional oughts

Each of these accounts—conflict, disjunctive—can now be extended from simple to conditional oughts in the same way. The basic idea is this. Start with a default theory $\Delta = \langle \mathcal{W}, \mathcal{D}, < \rangle$. In evaluating a simple ought $\bigcirc(Y)$, we looked to see if the proposition Y is contained in the extensions of this theory, either some or all, depending on whether we have embraced the conflict or disjunctive account. In the case of a conditional ought $\bigcirc(Y/X)$, we now look to see if Y is contained in the extensions, not of the original theory itself, but of the new theory $\langle \mathcal{W} \cup \{X\}, \mathcal{D}, < \rangle$, arrived at by supplementing the hard information $\mathcal{W}$ from the original theory with the antecedent X of the conditional. To simplify notation, we let

$$\Delta[X] = \langle \mathcal{W} \cup \{X\}, \mathcal{D}, < \rangle$$

represent the result of supplementing, or updating, the hard information from Δ with the additional statement X. Our account of conditional oughts, both conflict and disjunctive, can then be presented as follows, again in two separate definitions, though they differ only in a single word.

Definition 11 (Conditional oughts: the conflict account) Let $\Delta = \langle \mathcal{W}, \mathcal{D}, < \rangle$ be a default theory. Then the conditional ought statement $\bigcirc(Y/X)$ follows from Δ according to the conflict account just in case $Y \in \mathcal{E}$ for some extension $\mathcal{E}$ of $\Delta[X]$.

Definition 12 (Conditional oughts: the disjunctive account) Let $\Delta = \langle \mathcal{W}, \mathcal{D}, < \rangle$ be a default theory. Then the conditional ought statement $\bigcirc(Y/X)$ follows from Δ according to the disjunctive account just in case $Y \in \mathcal{E}$ for each extension $\mathcal{E}$ of $\Delta[X]$.

This treatment of conditional oughts can be illustrated by embellishing the story of Jack, who has promised to meet Jo for lunch, with the familiar complication—perhaps too familiar—that Jack may encounter a drowning child on his way to meet Jo, and that rescuing that child would then interfere with their lunch date. The example will be formalized, however, in such a way that neither Jack's promise to meet Jo nor the child's need is built into the underlying default theory, but only the fact that it is impossible for Jack both to meet Jo and rescue the child.

Suppose, then, that P is the proposition that Jack promises to meet Jo for lunch, that M is the proposition that he actually meets her, that N is the proposition that the child needs to be rescued, and that R is the

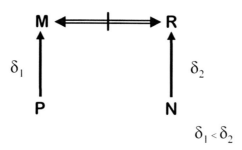

Figure 3.2: The drowning child

proposition that Jack carries out the rescue. Suppose also that δ_1 is the default $P \to M$, according to which Jack's promise to meet Jo favors doing so, and that δ_2 is the default $N \to R$, according to which the child's need favors Jack's carrying out the rescue. The example can then be encoded into the default theory $\Delta_{10} = \langle W, \mathcal{D}, < \rangle$, depicted in Figure 3.2, where $W = \{\neg(M \wedge R)\}$, where $\mathcal{D} = \{\delta_1, \delta_2\}$, and where $\delta_1 < \delta_2$: the hard background information contains only the fact that Jack cannot both meet Jo and rescue the child, and the ordering stipulates that rescuing the child is more important than meeting Jo.

This theory, as it stands, does not lead to any interesting simple oughts. Neither default is triggered, and so there is no reason for Jack either to meet Jo or to rescue the child. However, the theory does yield, as a conditional ought, the conclusion that Jack ought to meet Jo given that he has promised to do so. This can be seen by noting that the supplemented theory $\Delta_{10}[P]$—that is, $\langle W \cup \{P\}, \mathcal{D}, < \rangle$—leads to the unique proper scenario $\mathcal{S}_1 = \{\delta_1\}$, which then generates the unique extension $\mathcal{E}_1 = Th(\{\neg(M \wedge R), P, M\})$. Since the proposition M belongs to the unique extension of the supplemented theory $\Delta_{10}[P]$, it follows that the original theory Δ_{10} supports the conditional ought $\bigcirc(M/P)$ as a conclusion—and it supports this conclusion according to both accounts, conflict and disjunctive, since the extension is unique.

Now suppose that Jack has promised to meet Jo, but also, in this case, that the child needs to be rescued—that is, the antecedent under consideration is the proposition $P \wedge N$. Under these conditions, as we can see, the theory yields the conclusion that Jack ought to rescue the child rather than meet Jo. For in this case, the appropriately supplemented theory is $\Delta_{10}[P \wedge N]$, which supports $\mathcal{S}_2 = \{\delta_2\}$ as its unique proper scenario; the default δ_1 is triggered, providing a reason for Jack to meet Jo, but this reason is defeated by the stronger reason provided by δ_2 for rescuing the child. The scenario $\mathcal{S}_2$ then generates $\mathcal{E}_2 = Th(\{\neg(M \wedge R), P \wedge N, R\})$ as the unique extension of the supplemented theory $\Delta_{10}[P \wedge N]$. This extension contains the proposition R, of course, and since it is closed under consequence, the proposition $\neg M$ as well, from which we can conclude that both the conditional oughts $\bigcirc(R/P \wedge N)$ and $\bigcirc(\neg M/P \wedge N)$ follow from the original theory Δ_{10}. What this theory tells us, then, is that, under the condition that Jack has promised to meet Jo for lunch but the child needs to be rescued, what Jack actually ought to do is rescue the child and not meet Jo.

3.1.3   Some history

We have considered two different ways of defining all things considered oughts in terms of the reasons provided by an underlying default theory, a conflict account and a disjunctive account, both of which generalize to include conditional as well as simple oughts. In fact, the ideas behind the conflict account can be traced back to an early proposal by Bas van Fraassen, though the relation to default logic is more recent; the connections among these ideas is described in detail in Appendix B.1.[9] The present formulation of the disjunctive account is new, however, and calls for some immediate comments.

As we can see from our discussion of the twins example, there are actually two separate elements to the disjunctive account. The first is the idea that, even when each of two actions is supported by an undefeated reason, it is not necessary to accept either of the corresponding all things considered oughts, if they conflict—as in this case, where neither the statement that I ought to dine with Twin 1 nor the statement that I ought to dine with Twin 2 is supported. The second element is the additional idea that a disjunction of the conflicting claims actually should be accepted as an all things considered ought—in this case, that I ought to dine either with Twin 1 or with Twin 2. These two elements have not always occurred together.

A view that seems to contain the first of these two elements without the second was proposed by Earl Conee, who agrees that there are cases in which "competing moral considerations have exactly the same force," but writes that: "there is no need to count each of these alternatives as morally required. We have the familiar option of holding that when moral factors are equal, each act is permitted and none is absolutely obligatory."[10] What Conee suggests here is that, in a sense, the two counterbalanced moral claims cancel each other out, so that neither of the conflicting acts is obligatory, in accord with the first element of the disjunctive account; but although each of these acts is permitted, there appears to be no hint, in Conee's discussion, of the second element of the disjunctive account,

---

[9]See van Fraassen (1973) for his initial proposal, and Horty (1994a) for the link between this proposal and default logic.

[10]Conee (1982, pp. 243–244).

according to which one or the other of the two conflicting acts must actually be performed.

A similar approach, containing the first but not the second element of the disjunctive account, was advanced by Foot, who considers a situation in which there are undefeated reasons for feeling that one ought to perform each of two incompatible actions, A and B; but rather than supposing that "both judgments have to be affirmed," as the conflict account would have it, she is instead reluctant to draw either conclusion: "What we must ask, therefore, is whether in cases of irresolvable moral conflict we have to back both the judgment in favor of A and the judgment in favor of B, although doing B involves not doing A. Is it not possible that we should rather declare that the two are incommensurable, so that we have nothing to say about the overall merits of A and B, whether because there is nothing that *we* can say or because there is no truth of the matter and therefore nothing to *be* said."[11] Again, Foot's idea seems to be that we should refrain—on either epistemic or metaphysical grounds—both from the judgment that one ought to perform the action A and from the judgment that one ought to perform the action B, but there is no suggestion at all that we should endorse the disjunctive judgment that one ought to perform either A or B.

As far as I know, this second element of the disjunctive account was first explicitly advanced by Donagan, in the course of commenting on an example involving conflicting but symmetrical moral reasons, much like the conflict created by my dinner arrangements with the two twins, but more dramatic: "Where the lives of identical twins are in jeopardy and I can save one but only one, every serious rationalist moral system lays down that, whatever I do, I must save one of them ... Certainly there is no moral conflict: from the fact that I have a duty to save either a or b, it does not follow that I have a duty to save a and a duty to save b."[12] This passage, at last, contains both elements of the disjunctive account: not only that the agent faces no real moral conflict in cases like this, but that one of the two actions, rescuing either a or b, must actually be performed. Still, although the passage does set out the full disjunctive idea, it is advanced only in terms of a particular example, from a very different, rationalist perspective; and no precise account is provided of the way in which the output duties are supposed to be derived from the input rules supplied by Donagan's rationalist moral system.

It was not until a more recent paper by Brink that the disjunctive account received a full-scale defense from a more general perspective, where Brink's "all things considered obligations" are thought of as derived from

---

[11]Foot (1983, p. 267); here and elsewhere in my discussion of Foot, I have, once again for notational uniformity, substituted uppercase variables for the lowercase variables that appear in Foot's text.

[12]Donagan (1984, pp. 286–287). And he continues: "Can it be seriously held that a fireman, who has rescued as many as he possibly could of a group trapped in a burning building, should blame himself for the deaths of those left behind, whose lives could have been saved only if he had not rescued some of those he did?"

an underlying set of reasons, which he refers to as "prima facie obligations," but without any particular rationalist constraints on the nature of these reasons.[13] As in the current treatment, Brink supposes that these all things considered oughts are to be generated from undefeated reasons, but he rejects the idea that each undefeated reason, or prima facie obligation, should generate a corresponding all things considered ought—an idea that can be seen as a rudimentary version of our conflict account. Instead, he endorses a view that is supposed to coincide in its outcome, at least, with the disjunctive account as defined here:

> Ordinarily, an undefeated prima facie obligation does constitute an all-things-considered obligation. But not always. Where there is an undefeated competitor, we can conclude that neither obligation is an all-things-considered obligation. This may seem to leave the agent confronting an insoluble conflict with no all-things-considered obligations, and this may seem puzzling to some. But the agent does face an all-things-considered obligation: it is to perform one or the other of the prima facie obligations.[14]

Furthermore, unlike Donagan, Brink actually goes on to propose a procedure for specifying this desired outcome, deriving the all things considered oughts from the underlying reasons, or prima facie obligations. However, the procedure proposed by Brink is different from that set out here, and yields a result that fails to agree, I believe, both with that of the disjunctive account as defined here and with Brink's own desired outcome.

In the present framework, as we have seen, the disjunctive account is defined by appeal to undefeated reasons—more exactly, to coherent sets of undefeated reasons, those provided by the proper scenarios, which then generate extensions. These are, of course, exactly the same sets of reasons that figure in the definition of the conflict account; the sole difference between the two accounts is that, rather than supporting a statement as an ought whenever it is contained in some extension, the disjunctive account requires that an ought must be contained in every extension. On Brink's approach, by contrast, the set of undefeated reasons is bypassed in favor of a different set entirely—the "overriding" reasons, or prima facie obligations, which, in addition to being undefeated themselves, also defeat all others with which they conflict:

> An all-things-considered obligation represents what one ought to do in light of *all* morally relevant factors, including alternatives. If so, then only prima facie obligations that are undefeated *and* defeat all competitors are all-things-considered obligations. In other words, to be an all-things considered obliga-

---

[13]See Brink (1994).
[14]Brink (1994, p. 238).

tion, a prima facie obligation must be *overriding* and not simply
not overridden.[15]

The idea behind this suggestion, adapted to the present setting, seems
to be that an all things considered ought statement of the form $\bigcirc(Y)$ is
supported by a background set of reasons just in case the statement Y is
entailed by the actions for which the agent has overriding reasons—reasons
that defeat all competitors.[16] It is, however, easy to see the problem with
this suggestion by returning to the twins example, the theory Δ_9 depicted in
Figure 3.1, where I have reasons for dining with each of two twins, actions
captured through the propositions D_1 and D_2. Since it is impossible to
dine with both twins, the actions supported by my reasons conflict, but
since these reasons are either equally weighted or incomparable, neither
is defeated by the other. Each of the two reasons is thus undefeated, but
each likewise fails to defeat its competitor. Since an overriding reason must
itself be undefeated, but must also defeat each of its competitors, neither
reason, therefore, can be classified as overriding.

The upshot is this. Because, according to Brink's proposal, an all things
considered ought statement $\bigcirc(Y)$ is supported whenever Y is entailed by
the propositions for which there are overriding reasons, and there are no
overriding reasons at all in this case, it follows that neither $\bigcirc(D_1)$ nor
$\bigcirc(D_2)$ is supported. The proposal thus successfully avoids generating a
moral conflict. It does not tell me that I ought to dine with one twin,
and also that I ought to dine with the other. But by exactly the same
argument—because oughts must be supported by overriding reasons, and
there are no overriding reasons—the proposal likewise fails to support the
disjunctive obligation $\bigcirc(D_1 \vee D_2)$. It does not tell me that, since I cannot
dine with both, at least I ought to dine with one twin or the other.

Brink's own definitional procedure, then, appears to capture only the
first, not the second, element of the disjunctive account—successfully avoiding a conflict among all things considered oughts, but also failing to generate the appropriate disjunctive oughts. I conclude that the idea of defining
the disjunctive account by appeal to a new set of reasons, the overriding
reasons, is an error. The disjunctive account should instead be defined
directly from the undefeated reasons, exactly as it is in this book. The
undefeated reasons are first organized into coherent sets—those provided
by proper scenarios, which generate extensions. The oughts supported by

---

[15] Brink (1994, p. 240).

[16] A view similar to Brink's was suggested earlier by Harman, who presents his "good-
reasons" analysis of ought statements as follows: "to say that P ought to do D is to
say that P has sufficient reasons to do D that are stronger than the reasons he has to
do something else. If what you mean is that P morally ought to do D, you mean that
P has sufficient *moral* reasons to do D that are stronger than the reasons he has to do
anything else" (1978, p. 118). What Harman seems to be telling us here is that oughts
are to be defined in terms of reasons that are actually stronger than any conflicting
reasons—that is, in terms of overriding reasons—rather than simply in terms of reasons
for which there are no stronger conflicting reasons, the undefeated reasons.

the disjunctive account can then be identified with those propositions contained in each of the various extensions, not just those belonging to some extension or another.

3.2   Properties of the logics

Although not a central concern of this book, it will be useful for the sake of perspective to note some formal properties of the two accounts defined here, considered as logics for deriving all things considered oughts from a background default theory. As a preliminary step, where $\Delta = \langle \mathcal{W}, \mathcal{D}, < \rangle$ is an underlying default theory, we let $\hspace{0.1em}\vdash_C$ and $\hspace{0.1em}\vdash_D$ represent the consequence relations defined by these two logics, so that the statements $\Delta \hspace{0.1em}\vdash_C \bigcirc (Y/X)$ and $\Delta \hspace{0.1em}\vdash_D \bigcirc (Y/X)$ are taken to mean that the all things considered ought $\bigcirc(Y/X)$ follows from the information contained in Δ according to the conflict or disjunctive accounts, respectively. We use the unadorned symbol $\hspace{0.1em}\vdash$—as in the statement $\Delta \hspace{0.1em}\vdash \bigcirc (Y/X)$—when we wish to speak of both the conflict and disjunctive accounts indiscriminately.

The first thing to note about the two logics set out here is that neither allows for *strengthening of the antecedent*. Although it may be reasonable to conclude from the default theory Δ that a proposition Y ought to hold under circumstances characterized only through the proposition X, it need not follow that Y ought to hold when the circumstances are characterized more fully through the proposition $X \wedge Z$—or, put formally, from the fact that $\Delta \hspace{0.1em}\vdash \bigcirc (Y/X)$, it need not follow that $\Delta \hspace{0.1em}\vdash \bigcirc (Y/X \wedge Z)$. This point was, in fact, already illustrated by our example of Jack, Jo, and the drowning child, encoded earlier as the default theory $\Delta_{10} = \langle \mathcal{W}, \mathcal{D}, < \rangle$, depicted in Figure 3.2, where $\mathcal{W} = \{\neg(M \wedge R)\}$, where $\mathcal{D} = \{\delta_1, \delta_2\}$ with δ_1 as $P \rightarrow M$ and δ_2 as $N \rightarrow R$, and where $\delta_1 < \delta_2$. Here, as we saw, both of the two logics tell us that $\Delta_{10} \hspace{0.1em}\vdash \bigcirc (M/P)$; if the situation is described only as one in which Jack has promised to meet Jo for lunch, it is reasonable to conclude that he ought to do so. But it does not follow from this that $\Delta_{10} \hspace{0.1em}\vdash \bigcirc (M/P \wedge N)$. When the situation is described as one in which Jack has promised to meet Jo but is also needed to rescue the child, we no longer conclude that he ought to meet Jo; instead, both of the two logics now tell us $\Delta_{10} \hspace{0.1em}\vdash \bigcirc (\neg M/P \wedge N)$, that Jack ought not to meet Jo.

In failing to allow for strengthening of the antecedent, the accounts set out here agree with those logics of conditional obligation that are developed as a species of conditional logic, within the framework of possible worlds semantics.[17] But there is another, deeper way in which the accounts developed here differ even from these conditional logics—namely, in failing to satisfy the property of consequence monotonicity, discussed in the In-

---

[17]The study of conditional deontic logics of this variety began with the work of Brian Chellas (1974), Dagfinn Føllesdal and Risto Hilpinen (1971), Bengt Hansson (1971), David Lewis (1973), and van Fraassen (1972); a useful comparison of these various logics can be found in Lewis (1974).

troduction to this book. In classical logic, as well as most philosophical logics, including standard conditional logics and conditional deontic logics, the set of derivable conclusions grows monotonically with the information from which these conclusions are derived, the set of premises: increasing the information contained in a premise set will never lead to the abandonment of a previously supported conclusion—or, put more formally, if the premise set Γ' contains all the information found in the premise set Γ, and perhaps more, it follows that X will be a consequence of Γ' whenever X is a consequence of Γ.

If we now take the background default theories as analogous to premise sets, however, this property of consequence monotonicity fails for the present logics. Here, a default theory $\Delta' = \langle \mathcal{W}', \mathcal{D}', <' \rangle$ can naturally be thought of as containing all the information found in the default theory $\Delta = \langle \mathcal{W}, \mathcal{D}, < \rangle$ whenever $\mathcal{W}'$ contains each proposition belonging to $\mathcal{W}$, whenever $\mathcal{D}'$ contains each default belonging to $\mathcal{D}$, and whenever the ordering relation $<'$ is at least as strong as $<$. Yet it is possible, even if Δ' contains all the information found in Δ, that Δ might support an all things considered ought that is not supported by Δ'.

Again, this point can be illustrated by returning to Jack, Jo, and the drowning child, but this time beginning with a variant of the original example. Let the new theory $\Delta_{11} = \langle \mathcal{W}, \mathcal{D}, < \rangle$ be like the original Δ_{10}, depicted in Figure 3.2, except that, while the new $\mathcal{W} = \{\neg(M \wedge R)\}$ coincides with the hard information from the original theory, the new $\mathcal{D} = \{\delta_1\}$ contains only a single default, and the new $<$ is empty. The theory Δ_{11} thus agrees with Δ_{10} except that it fails to contain the default δ_2, according to which the child's need favors rescuing the child, or any priority information concerning this default. And here, it is easy to see that $\Delta_{11} \mathrel{\vdash\mkern-7mu\sim} \bigcirc (M/P \wedge N)$. According to both accounts, conflict and disjunctive, the new theory yields the conclusion that Jack ought to meet Jo for lunch given his promise, even in light of the drowning child's need, since the theory contains no default that is triggered by this need; the child's need is thus nothing but a bland fact, providing no reason for any particular action. Now, returning to the original $\Delta_{10} = \langle \mathcal{W}, \mathcal{D}, < \rangle$, in which, once again, $\mathcal{D} = \{\delta_1, \delta_2\}$ and $\delta_1 < \delta_2$, it is clear that this theory contains all the information—all the facts, defaults, and ordering constraints—found in Δ_{11}. Nevertheless, as we have seen, we do not have $\Delta_{10} \mathrel{\vdash\mkern-7mu\sim} \bigcirc (M/P \wedge N)$, since Δ_{10} now contains the default δ_2, which is triggered by the child's need, and which, in fact, defeats the default δ_1 that provides Jack with a reason for meeting Jo.

This example at last shows, formally, that both the conflict and the disjunctive accounts defined here can be classified as nonmonotonic logics. They cannot, therefore, be articulated in any simple way within the modal, or intensional, framework that is so often appealed to as a foundation for deontic logic, since theories developed within this framework support consequence monotonicity. Still, even though a full development of the conflict and disjunctive accounts requires an appeal to default logic, or some other technique for nonmonotonic reasoning, it is worth noting that both of these two accounts offer *conservative extensions* of standard deontic logic in the sense that, roughly speaking, when applied to a situation in which there are no conflicting reasons, the two accounts agree both with standard deontic logic and with each other; these results are formulated precisely and established in Appendix B.2.

Although the definitions of consequence for the conflict and disjunctive accounts presented thus far specify the notion only for atomic ought statements of the form $\bigcirc(Y/X)$, the idea can be extended to boolean combinations of these statements in the obvious way, by stipulating that

$$\Delta \hspace{0.3em}\vdash\hspace{-0.9em}\sim\hspace{0.3em} \phi \wedge \psi \text{ just in case } \Delta \hspace{0.3em}\vdash\hspace{-0.9em}\sim\hspace{0.3em} \phi \text{ and } \Delta \hspace{0.3em}\vdash\hspace{-0.9em}\sim\hspace{0.3em} \psi,$$

$$\Delta \hspace{0.3em}\vdash\hspace{-0.9em}\sim\hspace{0.3em} \neg\phi \text{ just in case it is not the case that } \Delta \hspace{0.3em}\vdash\hspace{-0.9em}\sim\hspace{0.3em} \phi,$$

where the ϕ and ψ range over boolean combinations of atomic oughts. It is then easy to verify that both of the resulting logics defined here are *noncontradictory*, in the sense that neither will allow a consequence statement of the form $\Delta \hspace{0.3em}\vdash\hspace{-0.9em}\sim\hspace{0.3em} \phi \wedge \neg\phi$. No underlying default theory, no matter what its nature, will ever support a logical contradiction between simple ought statements or their boolean combinations.

It is particularly important, in the case of the conflict account, to bear in mind the distinction between moral conflicts, of the sort that are allowed by this account, and logical contradictions, which are ruled out. According to the conflict account, it is possible for a default theory to support two oughts of the form $\bigcirc(Y/X)$ and $\bigcirc(\neg Y/X)$, telling us both that it ought to be that Y under the condition X, and also that it ought to be that $\neg Y$ under the same condition; this is simply an all things considered moral conflict, of the sort that the conflict account is designed to allow. But since the conflict account is noncontradictory, as we have just seen, it can never support two statements of the form $\bigcirc(Y/X)$ and $\neg \bigcirc(Y/X)$, telling us both that it ought to be that Y under the condition X, and also that it is not the case that it ought to be that Y under the very same condition; that would be a logical contradiction.

Continuing our survey of logical properties, we can see also that both the conflict and disjunctive accounts defined here are characterized by a notion of consequence for all things considered oughts that is itself *closed under logical consequence*, in the sense that, whenever we know both that $\Delta \hspace{0.3em}\vdash\hspace{-0.9em}\sim\hspace{0.3em} \bigcirc(Y/X)$ and that $Y \vdash Z$—that is, if Z is an ordinary logical consequence of Y—we must also have $\Delta \hspace{0.3em}\vdash\hspace{-0.9em}\sim\hspace{0.3em} \bigcirc(Z/X)$. Why is this? Well, consider the conflict account. According to this account, $\Delta \hspace{0.3em}\vdash\hspace{-0.9em}\sim\hspace{-0.2em}_C \bigcirc(Y/X)$ holds just in case Y belongs to some extension $\mathcal{E}$ of the theory $\Delta[X]$ that results from supplementing the hard information from Δ with the proposition X as an additional fact. But extensions themselves, as noted in Section 1.2.2, are closed under ordinary logical consequence. Therefore, if Y belongs to the extension $\mathcal{E}$, and Z is a logical consequence of Y, then Z will belong to $\mathcal{E}$ as well, so that we must have $\Delta \hspace{0.3em}\vdash\hspace{-0.9em}\sim\hspace{-0.2em}_C \bigcirc(Z/X)$ if we have $\Delta \not\hspace{-0.3em}\sim_C \bigcirc (Y/X)$. The argument for the disjunctive account is identical, except that, instead of reasoning about one particular extension of the supplemented default theory, we must reason about all such extensions.

It is sometimes easier to grasp the intuitive force of the property that oughts are closed under logical consequence by considering a sort of converse case, supposing that $\Delta \hspace{-0.1em}\sim \bigcirc (Y/X)$ and $U \vdash \neg Y$, so that closure under consequence would then lead to the conclusion that $\Delta \hspace{-0.1em}\sim \bigcirc (\neg U/X)$. Here, the idea is that anything that entails the negation of what ought to be the case had better not be the case itself—for example, and in terms of actions: if I ought to pay you the money I owe you tomorrow, and going to a movie tonight entails that I will not be able to do that, then I ought not to go to a movie tonight.[18]

Finally, it is easy to see that both the conflict and disjunctive accounts support the principle that *ought implies can*, sometimes known as the *volunteerist* principle, according to which only consistent propositions can be enjoined as oughts, no matter what inconsistencies might be found among the reasons used to generate these oughts. Put formally, what the principle tells us is that, if $\Delta = \langle \mathcal{W}, \mathcal{D}, < \rangle$ is the background default theory, then whenever $\Delta \hspace{-0.1em}\sim \bigcirc (Y/X)$, it follows that the enjoined statement Y must be consistent—as long as the underlying set $\mathcal{W}$ of hard information from Δ is itself consistent, and also consistent with the conditioning proposition X.

Again, we can see why this principle should hold most easily by focusing on the conflict account. So suppose $\Delta \hspace{-0.1em}\sim_C \bigcirc (Y/X)$, where $\mathcal{W}$ is consistent with X. What this means, once again, is that Y belongs to some extension $\mathcal{E}$ of the theory $\Delta[X]$ that results when the hard information $\mathcal{W}$ from Δ is supplemented with X. Any extension based on a default theory containing a consistent set of hard facts will itself be consistent, as we saw in Section 1.2.2. And by hypothesis, the set of hard facts from the supplemented theory $\Delta[X]$ is consistent, since $\mathcal{W}$ is consistent with X. The extension $\mathcal{E}$

---

[18]The idea that oughts are closed under consequence is also, of course, a feature of standard deontic logic, but one of its more contentious features, which has generated considerable opposition. A recent statement of the opposing view, with references to this literature, is presented by Sven Ove Hansson (2001, p.141 ff.), who describes closure under consequence as the property of "necessitation," argues that necessitation is responsible for "most of the major deontic paradoxes" (Ross's paradox, the paradox of commitment, the Good Samaritan paradox, the knower paradox), and then takes pains to develop a deontic logic in which necessitation fails; another such logic is developed by Frank Jackson (1985). On the other hand, closure under consequence has recently been defended by Brink (1994, p. 234, fn. 29) and by Thomson (1990, pp. 156–157). My own view is that cases such as this movie example, drawn from Section 2.1, show that some form of closure under consequence is unavoidable: how else could I conclude that I ought not to see a movie tonight, except by using logic, arithmetic, and whatever other reasoning tools I might possess to see that doing so is inconsistent with paying you the money I owe tomorrow? As for the deontic paradoxes, which are so often used to justify the rejection of closure under consequence, many of these seem more like pragmatic oddities than true paradoxes, and in any case, it is suggested by Horty and Belnap (1995, pp. 620–622) that at least some can be handled more appropriately by adjusting the underlying logic of agency, rather than adjusting the deontic logic itself.

will therefore be consistent, from which it follows that the enjoined statement Y must be consistent as well, since a consistent set cannot contain an inconsistent statement. Again, the argument in the case of the disjunctive account follows suit, except that we must reason about all extensions of the supplemented default theory, not just one.

Both the conflict and disjunctive accounts, then, block the support of inconsistent all things considered oughts, given a consistent set of hard facts. But these two accounts block inconsistency in interestingly different ways, reflected in their different treatments of a principle characterized by Bernard Williams as the rule of *agglomeration*, according to which any conjunction formed from enjoined propositions must be enjoined as well.[19] Formally, and in full generality, the rule of agglomeration allows us to conclude that $\Delta \mathrel{\v;\sim} \bigcirc (Y \wedge Z/X)$ whenever we have both $\Delta \mathrel{\v;\sim} \bigcirc (Y/X)$ and $\Delta \mathrel{\v;\sim} \bigcirc (Z/X)$, but it is perhaps more easily recognizable in its unconditional form, according to which it allows us to conclude $\Delta \mathrel{\v;\sim} \bigcirc (Y \wedge Z)$ from $\Delta \mathrel{\v;\sim} \bigcirc (Y)$ and $\Delta \mathrel{\v;\sim} \bigcirc (Z)$.

In order to illustrate the different ways in which the conflict and disjunctive accounts block the support of inconsistent oughts, and their different treatments of agglomeration, let us now return to the twins example— coded earlier as the theory Δ_9, depicted in Figure 3.1—in which I am faced with undefeated reasons for dining with each of the two twins, represented by the conflicting propositions D_1 and D_2. According to the conflict account, as we saw in our earlier discussion of this example, each of these two propositions is then enjoined as an all things considered ought—that is, we have both $\Delta_9 \mathrel{\v;\sim}_C \bigcirc (D_1)$ and $\Delta_9 \mathrel{\v;\sim}_C \bigcirc (D_2)$. It is therefore plain that the consequence relation associated with the conflict account cannot allow the rule of agglomeration, for agglomeration would lead us to conclude at once, in this case, that $\Delta_9 \mathrel{\v;\sim}_C \bigcirc (D_1 \wedge D_2)$, which violates the principle that ought implies can, of course, since $D_1 \wedge D_2$ is inconsistent in the context of the example. As in the approach originally advocated by Williams, the conflict account thus allows for the support of a collection of all things considered oughts that, taken jointly, are inconsistent; but it blocks the support of individual inconsistent oughts by refusing to allow these jointly inconsistent oughts to be agglomerated into one.

The disjunctive account, by contrast, does allow the rule of agglomeration: in general, we can conclude that $\Delta \mathrel{\v;\sim}_D \bigcirc (Y \wedge Z/X)$ whenever we have $\Delta \mathrel{\v;\sim}_D \bigcirc (Y/X)$ and $\Delta \mathrel{\v;\sim}_D \bigcirc (Z/X)$. Why? Because according to the disjunctive account, if we have $\Delta \mathrel{\v;\sim}_D \bigcirc (Y/X)$, this entails that Y belongs to each extension of the theory $\Delta[X]$ that results once the hard information from Δ is supplemented with X, and likewise, if $\Delta \mathrel{\v;\sim}_D \bigcirc (Z/X)$, then Z also belongs to each extension of the supplemented theory. But again, extensions are closed under ordinary logical consequence. Therefore, if both Y and Z belong to each extension of the supplemented default

---

[19]See Williams (1965); Marcus (1980) refers to the same principle as the rule of *factoring*.

theory, then the statement $Y \wedge Z$ belongs to each extension as well, and so we must also have $\Delta \vdash_D \bigcirc (Y \wedge Z/X)$.

In the particular case of the twins example, we would be able to conclude, by agglomeration, that $\Delta_9 \vdash_D \bigcirc (D_1 \wedge D_2)$ if we could establish both $\Delta_9 \vdash_D \bigcirc (D_1)$ and $\Delta_9 \vdash_D \bigcirc (D_2)$. And so it follows at once, since the disjunctive account also satisfies the principle that ought implies can, that we should not be able to establish both $\Delta_9 \vdash_D \bigcirc (D_1)$ and $\Delta_9 \vdash_D \bigcirc (D_2)$—and indeed we can establish neither, since neither D_1 nor D_2 is contained in each extension of the underlying theory. Unlike the conflict account, then, the disjunctive account does allow various supported all things considered oughts to be agglomerated into one, but in this case there is no risk that such agglomeration would lead to an individually inconsistent ought since the entire collection of supported oughts is itself jointly consistent.

Chapter 4

Moral conflicts

We now have before us two logics, reflecting two different approaches to the problem of deriving all things considered oughts from an underlying default theory and the reasons it provides: the conflict account, according to which a proposition is enjoined as an ought just in case it is contained in some extension of the underlying default theory, and the disjunctive account, according to which a proposition is enjoined as an ought just in case it is contained in each extension of the underlying default theory.

Although these two logics lead to different verdicts on the issue of all things considered moral conflict—one denying and the other affirming the possibility—they are developed within a common framework, using common ideas; and as we have seen, the resulting logics share a number of desirable properties. Both are conservative extensions of standard deontic logic, agreeing with this theory, and with each other, in the absence of conflicts among undefeated reasons. Both are noncontradictory, never yielding an all things considered ought as well as its negation. Both lead to a set of all things considered oughts that is closed under logical consequence, enjoining all the logical consequences of the enjoined propositions. Both maintain the principle that ought implies can, according to which only consistent propositions can be enjoined, as long as the hard information from the background theory is itself consistent. And both are sensitive enough to register the failure of strengthening in the antecedent, and also the failure of consequence monotonicity, that characterizes our normative reasoning.

Against the background of these two logics, and using them as tools, I now turn to an extended appraisal of the possibility—or at least the logical coherence—of all things considered moral conflicts. More precisely, the question I ask is this: setting aside arguments based on the adoption of some particular moral theory or another, are there any reasons for favoring one of these two approaches over the other, and in particular, for rejecting the conflict approach? I consider three kinds of objections to the possibility of all things considered moral conflicts, based, respectively, on considerations from deontic logic, conceptual considerations concerning the nature of all things considered oughts, and an analogy between moral and physical forces. The conclusion I reach is that, given the terms of the current discussion—that is, without appealing to any constraint on the structure of moral reasons that might be provided by some particular moral theory—there is no logical or conceptual reason to reject the possibility of moral conflict.

4.1 Logical objections

There are three standard logical objections to any theory, such as the conflict account, that allows for the possibility of conflicting all things considered oughts. Although these three objections are admirably presented, along with references to the literature, by Christopher Gowans, we will concentrate here on a more recent and extensive discussion by Brink.[1] In Brink's paper, each of these objections is presented as a "paradox"—a contradiction generated from the assumption of conflicting all things considered oughts, taken together with certain principles from standard deontic logic that are viewed as crucial to our normative reasoning. Since, as we have seen, the conflict account defined here is itself noncontradictory, any derived contradictions must depend in an essential way on these auxiliary principles, and so our assessment of these principles will likewise determine the force of the objections.

4.1.1 Agglomeration

Brink's first paradox relies on two deontic principles, both discussed in the previous section. The first is the principle that ought implies can, which is already supported by the conflict account; the second is the rule of agglomeration, which is not. It is of course easy, as we saw at the end of the previous chapter, to arrive at a contradiction when the conflict account is supplemented with agglomeration. The conflict account allows certain consistent default theories to support statements of the form $\bigcirc(Y)$ and $\bigcirc(\neg Y)$—that is, we might have both $\Delta \hspace{1pt}\vdash_C \bigcirc(Y)$ and $\Delta \hspace{1pt}\vdash_C \bigcirc(\neg Y)$, for some theory Δ whose hard information is consistent. Agglomeration would then lead us to the conclusion $\Delta \hspace{1pt}\vdash_C \bigcirc(Y \wedge \neg Y)$, enjoining the proposition $Y \wedge \neg Y$. The principle that ought implies can tells us that any proposition enjoined by a consistent theory must be consistent. But the proposition $Y \wedge \neg Y$ is not consistent.

In fact, Brink himself does not take this first paradox very seriously, since he tends to dismiss the principles through which it is generated, and agglomeration in particular, writing that: "Where there is no conflict between A and B, it seems harmless to recognize an obligation to do both as well as obligations to do each. But it also seems unnecessary; an obligation

---

[1] See Brink (1994) and Gowans (1987a).

to do each seems adequate to explain the moral situation."[2] I believe, however, that the matter is more complicated, and that we do need to allow
for some degree of agglomeration in order to understand certain aspects of
our normative reasoning, even in an account that tolerates conflicts.

The point is best illustrated with an example. Imagine that an agent's
deliberation is governed by two prima facie oughts, which provide reasons
for action: "You ought either to fight in the army or perform alternative
service" and "You ought not to fight in the army"—the first issuing from
some legal authority, perhaps, the second from religion or conscience. More
exactly, where F is the proposition that the agent fights in the army and
S the proposition that the agent performs alternative service, let δ_1 and
δ_2 be the defaults $\top \to F \vee S$ and $\top \to \neg F$, and suppose the underlying
default theory is $\Delta_{12} = \langle \mathcal{W}, \mathcal{D}, < \rangle$, where $\mathcal{W}$ is empty, $\mathcal{D} = \{\delta_1, \delta_2\}$, and
the ordering $<$ is empty. This theory leads to one proper scenario, the
set $\mathcal{S}_1 = \{\delta_1, \delta_2\}$ containing both defaults, which then generates $\mathcal{E}_1 =
Th(\{F \vee S, \neg F\})$ as an extension.

Looking only at the oughts explicitly supported by the generating defaults, we can see immediately that the default theory under consideration
yields both $\bigcirc(F \vee S)$ and $\bigcirc(\neg F)$ as all things considered oughts, telling
us that the agent ought to fight in the army or perform alternative ser-
vice, and also that the agent ought not to fight in the army. Is this a
complete description of the moral situation? I believe not. I believe that,
once we reach the conclusions that the agent ought either to fight in the
army or perform alternative service, but also that the agent ought not to
fight in the army, we are then committed to the further conclusion that the
agent ought to perform alternative service—and fortunately, the conflict
account supports this result as well. Because extensions are closed under
ordinary logical consequence, the extension $\mathcal{E}_1 = Th(\{F \vee S, \neg F\})$ contains
the proposition S, so that the conflict account yields the conclusion $\bigcirc(S)$.

Of course, one might argue that it is not necessary for the agent to derive
this further conclusion in order to perform the right action, and perhaps
this is Brink's point when he suggests that agglomeration is unnecessary
to explain the moral situation. As long as the agent satisfies the explicitly
supported oughts $\bigcirc(F \vee S)$ and $\bigcirc(\neg F)$, bringing about a situation in which
she either fights in the army or performs alternative service, but also one
in which she does not fight in the army, the agent will satisfy the derivable
ought $\bigcirc(S)$ as well, bringing about a situation in which she performs
alternative service. Since this ought will be satisfied in any case, why, then,
is it necessary for it to be derived? To argue in this way, however, would be
to limit the scope of deontic logic to a narrowly action-guiding enterprise,
rather than one that is supposed to be more fully descriptive of the moral
situation. If the formalism is to serve simply as a guide to action, it may
be sufficient for it to enjoin a set of propositions which, as long as these

---

[2]Brink (1994, p. 229).

propositions are satisfied, will lead to the achievement of a proper state of affairs. If the aim is descriptive, on the other hand, it is natural to expect a deontic logic to provide a more complete characterization of the moral situation; and in the case at hand, it is clear that such a characterization should include the information that one of the things the agent ought to do, all things considered, is perform alternative service.

The advantage of the rule of agglomeration is that, together with closure under logical consequence, it allows us to understand reasoning like this—why the explicit oughts from our example lead to the further conclusion that the agent ought to perform alternative service—while working solely at the level of all things considered ought statements, without appealing directly to underlying default theories and the properties of their extensions. In the present case, for example, if we were able to combine the enjoined propositions from the two all things considered oughts $\bigcirc(F \vee S)$ and $\bigcirc(\neg F)$ into the agglomerated result $\bigcirc((F \vee S) \wedge \neg F)$, we could then immediately derive $\bigcirc(S)$ as a conclusion, given closure under consequence, since S is a consequence of $(F \vee S) \wedge \neg F$.

Of course, as we have seen, full agglomeration cannot coherently be accommodated within the conflict account, unless we are willing to abandon the principle that ought implies can—for otherwise, once again, $\bigcirc(Y)$ and $\bigcirc(\neg Y)$ could be agglomerated into $\bigcirc(Y \wedge \neg Y)$. The literature on agglomeration in deontic logic seems to contain only arguments favoring either wholesale acceptance or wholesale rejection of the principle. Apparently, however, what is needed in a logic that allows for normative conflicts is some degree of agglomeration, but not too much, and my suggestion is that the conflict account presented here allows just the right amount.

In order to understand the delicacy of formulating an appropriately hedged principle of agglomeration—and to further our appreciation of the conflict account—it is worth considering another principle with some initial plausibility. The idea behind this principle, which we can describe as the principle of *consistent agglomeration*, is that we are free to agglomerate individual oughts as long as doing so does not lead to an inconsistent enjoined proposition. This principle could be captured, in full generality, through a rule allowing us, for any theory $\Delta = \langle \mathcal{W}, \mathcal{D}, < \rangle$, to conclude that $\Delta \mathrel{\vrule height 1.6ex depth 0pt width 0.6pt\kern-0.3pt\sim} \bigcirc(Y \wedge Z/X)$ whenever we have both $\Delta \mathrel{\vrule height 1.6ex depth 0pt width 0.6pt\kern-0.3pt\sim} \bigcirc(Y/X)$ and $\Delta \mathrel{\vrule height 1.6ex depth 0pt width 0.6pt\kern-0.3pt\sim} \bigcirc(Z/X)$, subject only to the constraint that the proposition $Y \wedge Z$, taken together with the hard information from $\mathcal{W}$, must be consistent; or in its unconditional form, allowing us to conclude $\Delta \mathrel{\vrule height 1.6ex depth 0pt width 0.6pt\kern-0.3pt\sim} \bigcirc(Y \wedge Z)$ from $\Delta \mathrel{\vrule height 1.6ex depth 0pt width 0.6pt\kern-0.3pt\sim} \bigcirc(Y)$ and $\Delta \mathrel{\vrule height 1.6ex depth 0pt width 0.6pt\kern-0.3pt\sim} \bigcirc(Z)$, subject to the same constraint. Such a rule is weak enough to avoid generating agglomerates of the form $\bigcirc(Y \wedge \neg Y)$ even when both of the individual oughts $\bigcirc(Y)$ and $\bigcirc(\neg Y)$ are supported; and it is strong enough, in the case of our example, to tell us that we are committed to the agglomerate $\bigcirc((F \vee S) \wedge \neg F)$, and so to $\bigcirc(S)$, once we have accepted the individual oughts $\bigcirc(F \vee S)$ and $\bigcirc(\neg F)$.

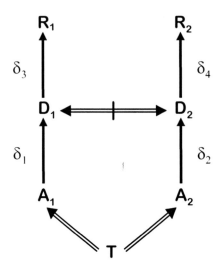

Figure 4.1: Reservations for dinner

Is the principle of consistent agglomeration correct, then? I do not think so. The problem with this principle can be illustrated by considering an elaborated version of our earlier twins example—the theory Δ_9, discussed in Section 3.1.1 and depicted in Figure 3.1. Suppose, as in the original example, that I have arranged to have a private dinner with each of the two twins, cannot have dinner with both, but that, as a further complication, the two twins prefer different restaurants: Twin 1 prefers Restaurant 1, say, while Twin 2 prefers Restaurant 2. In that case, if I am going to have dinner with Twin 1, I have a reason for making a reservation at Restaurant 1, while, if I am going to have dinner with Twin 2, I have a reason for making a reservation at Restaurant 2. Let R_1 and R_2 be the propositions that I make reservations at Restaurants 1 and 2, respectively, and recall that D_1 and D_2 are the respective propositions that I will have dinner with Twins 1 and 2. We can then take δ_3 and δ_4 as the defaults $D_1 \rightarrow R_1$ and $D_2 \rightarrow R_2$, which might provide me with reasons for making reservations. And the entire example can now be encoded into the default theory $\Delta_{13} = \langle \mathcal{W}, \mathcal{D}, < \rangle$, depicted in Figure 4.1, where $\mathcal{W} = \{A_1, A_2, \neg(D_1 \wedge D_2)\}$, with A_1 and A_2 again as the propositions that I have arranged for dinner with Twins 1 and 2, where $\mathcal{D} = \{\delta_1, \delta_2, \delta_3, \delta_4\}$, with δ_1 and δ_2 as the defaults $A_1 \rightarrow D_1$ and $A_2 \rightarrow D_2$ and with δ_3 and δ_4 as before, and where the ordering $<$ is empty.

It can now be verified (and I recommend that the reader do so) that this elaborated version of the twins example leads to the two proper scenarios

$\mathcal{S}_1 = \{\delta_1, \delta_3\}$ and $\mathcal{S}_2 = \{\delta_2, \delta_4\}$, generating the two extensions

$$\begin{aligned} \mathcal{E}_1 &= Th(\{A_1, A_2, \neg(D_1 \wedge D_2), D_1, R_1\}), \\ \mathcal{E}_2 &= Th(\{A_1, A_2, \neg(D_1 \wedge D_2), D_2, R_2\}), \end{aligned}$$

the first representing the outcome in which I have arranged to have dinner with both twins, cannot do so, choose to have dinner with Twin 1 and so make a reservation at Restaurant 1, and the second representing the outcome in which I choose Twin 2 and Restaurant 2 instead. Since D_1 and R_1 belong to one extension while D_2 and R_2 belong to the other, the conflict account yields at least the following all things considered oughts: $\bigcirc(D_1)$, $\bigcirc(R_1)$, $\bigcirc(D_2)$, and $\bigcirc(R_2)$. I ought to have dinner with Twin 1, and because of that, I ought to make a reservation at Restaurant 1. But also, I ought to have dinner with Twin 2, and because of that, I ought to make a reservation at Restaurant 2.

Now, what about agglomeration? Like the conflict account, the principle of consistent agglomeration would block the combination of $\bigcirc(D_1)$ and $\bigcirc(D_2)$ to yield $\bigcirc(D_1 \wedge D_2)$, and the reason for this, in the case of consistent agglomeration, is that the agglomerated result $D_1 \wedge D_2$ would be inconsistent, given our background assumptions: I simply cannot have dinner with both twins. On the other hand, there is nothing to prevent me from making reservations at both restaurants; that is certainly something I am able to do. Therefore, the principle of consistent agglomeration would allow us to combine $\bigcirc(R_1)$ and $\bigcirc(R_2)$ to reach the agglomerate $\bigcirc(R_1 \wedge R_2)$, according to which making reservations at both restaurants is something I ought to do. But this is a very odd conclusion. Consider that many restaurants now require a credit card deposit to hold a reservation, and suppose these restaurants are like that. I am already in trouble because I will not be able to have dinner with each twin, as promised. Why should I make things worse for myself by creating a situation in which I will inevitably incur a charge, as well as inconveniencing one restaurant or another? And this is not the only odd conclusion supported by consistent agglomeration. The rule also allows us to conclude both $\bigcirc(D_1 \wedge R_2)$ and $\bigcirc(D_2 \wedge R_1)$, since both agglomerates are consistent, telling us in each case that what I ought to do is have dinner with one twin but make a reservation at the restaurant preferred by the other.

Fortunately, the conflict account presented here allows us to avoid all of these odd agglomerates. Consider $\bigcirc(R_1 \wedge R_2)$, for example. As we recall, the conflict account allows us to endorse a proposition as an all things considered ought just in case that proposition is contained in some extension of the underlying default theory. But in this case, although R_1 is contained in one extension and R_2 is contained in another—and even though the conjunction $R_1 \wedge R_2$ is consistent—there is no single extension that contains both R_1 and R_2, or their conjunction. And the other odd agglomerates fail for just the same reason. Although D_1 belongs to one extension of the current default theory and R_2 belongs to the other, there is no single extension that contains both propositions, or their conjunction, and so we do not have $\bigcirc(D_1 \wedge R_2)$; and likewise we do not have $\bigcirc(D_2 \wedge R_1)$.

What the conflict account does allow is the agglomeration of $\bigcirc(D_1)$ and $\bigcirc(R_1)$ into the combined ought $\bigcirc(D_1 \wedge R_1)$, not just because the conjunction $D_1 \wedge R_1$ is consistent, but because both the propositions D_1 and R_1, and so their conjunction, can be found in the same extension; and likewise, it allows for the agglomeration of $\bigcirc(D_2)$ and $\bigcirc(R_2)$ into the combined ought $\bigcirc(D_2 \wedge R_2)$. Notice that these two agglomerated oughts, in addition to being consistent, can also reasonably be described as *coherent*, in a way that some of those allowed by the principle of consistent agglomeration cannot: the idea that what I ought to do is have dinner with one twin and make a reservation at the restaurant preferred by that twin is considerably more coherent than the idea that what I ought to do is have dinner with one twin but make a reservation at the restaurant preferred by the other.

The general situation can therefore be described like this. Both the principle of consistent agglomeration and the conflict account presented here block the combination of separate enjoined propositions into an agglomerate when the resulting conjunction would be inconsistent. All inconsistent conjunctions are incoherent, but some enjoined conjunctions can sensibly be classified as incoherent even though they are consistent—such as the idea that what I ought to do is have dinner with one twin but make reservations at the restaurant preferred by the other, or the idea that I ought to make reservations at both restaurants. The principle of consistent agglomeration blocks inconsistency, but allows incoherence. By requiring as a condition on agglomeration that separate enjoined propositions must belong to the same extension, the conflict account demands that enjoined conjunctions must be coherent as well.

4.1.2   Other logical objections

Let us now turn from considerations concerning appropriate constraints on agglomeration to the remaining two logical arguments against all things considered moral conflicts—Brink's remaining two paradoxes, which he does take seriously, unlike the first, since he endorses the principles involved.

The second logical objection is again based on two principles. The first is the principle of closure under logical consequence, which Brink refers to as the *obligation execution* principle, because it obliges us not to do anything that would prevent the execution of our obligations. This principle, which is supported by the conflict account, was presented earlier, in Section 3.2, as the principle allowing us to conclude, whenever we know that $\Delta \mathrel{|\!\sim} \bigcirc(Y/X)$ and $Y \vdash Z$—that is, Z is an ordinary logical consequence of Y—that $\Delta \mathrel{|\!\sim} \bigcirc(Z/X)$ should hold as well; but for the purpose of the present discussion, it will be sufficient to concentrate only on an unconditional version of the principle, allowing us to conclude, from $\Delta \mathrel{\vert\!\sim} \bigcirc (Y)$ and $Z \vdash Y$, that $\Delta \mathrel{\vert\!\sim} \bigcirc (Z)$. The second principle, which Brink describes as the *weak obligation* principle, tells us that, whenever a proposition Y is enjoined as an all things considered ought, it is not the case that $\neg Y$ can be enjoined as well—that is, that $\bigcirc (Y)$ implies $\neg \bigcirc (\neg Y)$. In the present setting, this principle can be captured as the assumption that

$$\Delta \mathrel{\vert\!\sim} \bigcirc (Y) \supset \neg \bigcirc (\neg Y)$$

should hold quite generally, for any default theory Δ and proposition Y whatsoever.

It is easy to see the troubles that result when the conflict account, which does not support the weak obligation principle, is then supplemented with this principle. Suppose that, as the conflict account allows, some default theory yields both of two inconsistent statements as all things considered oughts—that is, suppose that (1) $\Delta \mathrel{\vert\!\sim}_C \bigcirc (U)$ and (2) $\Delta \mathrel{\vert\!\sim}_C \bigcirc (V)$, where the propositions U and V are inconsistent. Since U and V are inconsistent, we can of course conclude (3) $V \vdash \neg U$—that V logically implies the negation of U. From (2) and (3), the principle of closure under logical consequence, or obligation execution, allows us to conclude that (4) $\Delta \mathrel{\vert\!\sim}_C \bigcirc (\neg U)$. From (1), however, the principle of weak obligation yields the conclusion (5) $\Delta \mathrel{\vert\!\sim}_C \neg \bigcirc (\neg U)$.[3] And then, together, (4) and (5) show that the conflict account, when it is supplemented with the weak obligation principle, leads to a contradiction—not just to the idea that conflicting propositions might both be enjoined as all things considered oughts, which is simply a moral conflict, but to the idea that the very same proposition might be both enjoined and not enjoined, which is a logical contradiction.

The third of the standard logical objections to moral conflicts—Brink's third paradox—relies on the new notion of permissibility, where the statement $\mathsf{P}(Y)$ is taken to represent the idea that the proposition Y is permissible. Typically in deontic logic, what is permissible is characterized in terms of what ought to be the case, through a definition along the lines of

$$\mathsf{P}(Y) \quad \text{just in case} \quad \neg \bigcirc (\neg Y),$$

telling us that a proposition is permissible if it is not the case that it ought not to be the case. Brink accepts this characterization of permissibility in terms of ought, not as a definition, actually, but rather as a principle relating the two ideas, which he refers to as the principle of *correlativity*. In addition, however, Brink also accepts the further and more substantive principle, which he describes as the *weak impermissibility* principle, according to which anything that ought to be the case must also be permissible—

---

[3] For the sake of tidiness, we note that this step in the argument requires that the relation $\mathrel{\vert\!\sim}_C$ should be closed under modus ponens, in the sense that, when we have both $\Delta \mathrel{\vert\!\sim}_C \phi$ and $\Delta \mathrel{\vert\!\sim}_C \phi \supset \psi$, we can then conclude that $\Delta \mathrel{\vert\!\sim}_C \psi$.

that is, according to which $\bigcirc(Y)$ implies $\mathsf{P}(Y)$.[4] This principle is best captured in the present setting through the general stipulation that

$$\Delta \mathrel{\vert\!\sim} \bigcirc(Y) \supset \mathsf{P}(Y)$$

holds for default theories and statements in general.

Again, the weak impermissibility principle is not supported by the conflict account, and as before, it is easy to see the difficulties that result when the account is supplemented with this principle by considering a case in which some theory enjoins conflicting propositions as all things considered oughts—that is, where (1) $\Delta \mathrel{\vert\!\sim}_C \bigcirc(U)$ and (2) $\Delta \mathrel{\vert\!\sim}_C \bigcirc(V)$, where U and V are inconsistent. Since U and V are inconsistent, we again have (3) $V \vdash \neg U$. From (2) and (3), the principle of closure under consequence again tells us that (4) $\Delta \mathrel{\vert\!\sim}_C \bigcirc(\neg U)$. But now, from (1), Brink's weak impermissibility principle tells us that (5) $\Delta \mathrel{\vert\!\sim}_C \mathsf{P}(U)$, which is equivalent to (6) $\Delta \mathrel{\vert\!\sim}_C \neg \bigcirc(\neg U)$ by the definition of what is permissible in terms of what ought to be. And then (4) and (6) show that the conflict account, supplemented with the weak impermissibility principle, again leads to a contradiction.

What Brink's second and third logical objections show, then, is that the conflict account is rendered inconsistent if it is supplemented with either the weak obligation principle or the weak impermissibility principle, both of which he supports. But how convincing are these objections, taken as arguments against the conflict account? The first thing to note is that it is not really surprising that these principles should lead to inconsistency in the context of the conflict account—which allows for moral conflicts, of course—since the effect of each of these principles is simply to assert that there can be no moral conflicts. The weak obligation principle, for example, supplements the set of statements supported by the conflict account with arbitrary statements of the form $\bigcirc(Y) \supset \neg \bigcirc(\neg Y)$, but any such statement is equivalent by elementary logic to a statement of the form $\neg \bigcirc(Y) \vee \neg \bigcirc(\neg Y)$, which is then equivalent to the statement $\neg(\bigcirc(Y) \wedge \bigcirc(\neg Y))$—telling us explicitly that the conflicting propositions Y and $\neg Y$ cannot both be enjoined. And the weak impermissibility principle supplements the set of supported statements with statements of the form $\bigcirc(Y) \supset \mathsf{P}(Y)$, but each of these can then be transformed, by the definition of permissibility in terms of ought, into a weak obligation statement of the form $\bigcirc(Y) \supset \neg \bigcirc(\neg Y)$, which can itself be transformed into a statement explicitly denying the existence of moral conflicts, as we have just seen.

In some ways, then, since the principles of weak obligation and weak impermissibility are both equivalent to the denial of moral conflicts, it is hard to take them seriously as components of any real argument against

---

[4]Brink refers to this principle as weak impermissibility because he formulates it as the principle that $\neg\mathsf{P}(Y)$ implies $\neg \bigcirc(Y)$, according to which anything that is not permissible cannot be obligatory either; the two formulations are equivalent, of course.

the existence of such conflicts, as opposed simply to reformulations of the view that there are none; both principles are nothing but straightforward denials of the very point at issue. Still, reformulating a view in a particular way sometimes highlights advantages to it that may not have been apparent in its original formulation, even when the original formulation and the restatement are equivalent—and perhaps the reason for denying the possibility of moral conflicts is more evident when this position is restated as the weak obligation principle, or as weak impermissibility. It is therefore important to consider the arguments that Brink actually presents in favor of the weak obligation and weak impermissibility principles; but in both cases the justification is brief, as if the truth of these principles should be almost immediately apparent. Concerning weak obligation, he says only that: "the weak obligation principle, as its name suggests, seems especially uncontroversial. If I'm obligated not to kill my neighbor, then surely it's not the case that I'm obligated to kill him."[5] And concerning weak impermissibility: "But surely that [principle] must be true. If it's impermissible for me to torture my neighbor, then surely it's not the case that I'm obliged to torture him."[6]

What Brink provides here, by way of justification, are simply concrete of instances of the abstract principles in question that are supposed to seem intuitively attractive—which is perfectly fair, of course: at some point in the justification of a set of fundamental logical principles, appeal to argument must necessarily be replaced by appeal to intuition. Still, it is difficult to establish a general principle beyond doubt by exhibiting a single instance, no matter how convincing. There is always the possibility that the truth of that particular instance could be explained through some other means, rather than by appeal to the general principle involved, or that a plausible counterexample to the principle might still be found; and in this case I feel that both avenues of criticism are available.

Here, the instances provided by Brink to illustrate the abstract principles are so alarming, and the consequents of these particular instances—that I am not obligated to kill my neighbor, or to torture my neighbor—are so palpably true that it is hard to see whether these consequents actually follow from the antecedents of the principles, or whether they are simply true on their own, lending a false credibility to the principles themselves. Furthermore, there are coherent scenarios in which the two principles could at least arguably be classified as incorrect, as we can see by returning to the twins example, where it is impossible to dine with both twins, so that dining with either entails not dining with the other. In this situation, it can be argued that, because I promised to dine with Twin 2, I ought to do so, and therefore—given closure under consequence, since dining with Twin 2 entails not dining with Twin 1—that I ought not to dine with Twin 1. But since I promised to dine with Twin 1 as well, I ought to dine with Twin 1.

---

[5]Brink (1994, p. 235).
[6]Brink (1994, p. 236).

The situation is therefore arguably one in which I ought to dine with Twin 1 but also ought not to dine with Twin 1, contrary to the principle of weak obligation. Furthermore, the definition of permissibility in terms of ought tells us that I am not permitted to dine with Twin 1 if I ought not to dine with Twin 1. And so the same situation—in which I ought to dine with Twin 1 but also ought not to dine with Twin 1—arguably illustrates a case in which I ought to dine with Twin 1 but, according to the definition, am not permitted to do so, contrary to the principle of weak impermissibility.

4.2 Conceptual objections

Our analysis has relied on a distinction between two uses of ethical terms, such as "ought" and related items, which I characterized earlier as a weak and a strong use. According to the weak, or prima facie, use, these terms merely indicate reasons; according to the strong, or all things considered, use, they register the judgments arrived at once all the various reasons at work in a particular situation are taken into consideration.

As I mentioned earlier, although some distinction along these lines is reflected in the work of a number of writers, different writers characterize the distinction in different ways. Some—such as Chisholm, or Donald Davidson—use our present vocabulary of weak, or prima facie, versus strong, or all things considered, oughts, while others present what appears to be the same distinction with other terminology.[7] For example, Searle refers to our weak oughts as "obligations," and uses the term "ought" itself only for strong oughts; the idea is that agents are subject to various obligations, possibly conflicting, which are then combined to result in a specification of what, all things considered, they ought to do.[8] In a similar fashion, Thomson describes our weak oughts in terms of the "obligations" and "commitments" we have to one another, or—echoing the language of Wesley Hohfeld—the "claims" we have against each other, and again reserves the term "ought" for the strong oughts that result when all of these weak oughts are taken into account.[9] Other writers, such as Gowans, actually use the term "ought" itself to refer to our weak oughts, and then describe our strong oughts as what we "must" do.[10] And Foot abandons any attempt to link the distinction between weak and strong oughts to familiar terms from natural language at all, speaking of them only as "type 1" and "type 2" oughts, respectively.[11]

All of these writers, then, agree with the treatment set out here in accepting the contrast between weak and strong oughts, in one guise or another. Where they differ, however, is on the following crucial point.

---

[7] See Chisholm (1964) and Davidson (1970).

[8] See Searle (1980).

[9] See Thomson (1990); the allusion is to Hohfeld (1919).

[10] See Gowans (1987a).

[11] See Foot (1983).

In the present treatment, we consider two accounts of the strong, or all things considered, ought—one of which, the conflict account, allows for moral conflicts even among strong oughts. These various writers, on the other hand, once they have drawn the distinction between weak and strong oughts, either argue or, more often, simply assume that there can be no moral conflicts involving strong oughts, almost as if the idea that conflicts must be limited to weak oughts while strong oughts remain conflict free follows at once from a mere recognition of that distinction.

An example of a writer who seems simply to assume the idea is Searle, who suggests that our moral reasoning can best be represented through the postulation of a variety of deontic operators $\bigcirc_1, \bigcirc_2, \ldots \bigcirc_n$ to represent the weak obligations deriving from different sources, together with the special deontic operator $\bigcirc^*$ representing the strong, all things considered ought.[12] Having introduced this distinction, Searle then, quite naturally, denies the validity of statements like $\bigcirc_1 A \supset \neg \bigcirc_2 \neg A$ and $\bigcirc_1 A \supset \neg \bigcirc^* \neg A$. That is, he denies, in the first case, that the fact that some action is obligatory according to one source of obligation entails that the opposite action cannot be obligatory according to another, thus allowing for conflicts among different weak obligations. And in the second case, he denies that the fact that some action is obligatory according to some particular source of obligation entails that the opposite cannot be what the agent ultimately ought to do, thus allowing for conflicts between weak obligations and the strong, all things considered moral ought. At this point, however, Searle simply notes—without comment or argument—that the statement $\bigcirc^* A \supset \neg \bigcirc^* \neg A$ should be classified as valid, ruling out the possibility of a conflict among strong oughts by asserting "that if one ought to do some particular thing, all things considered, then it is not the case that, all things considered, one ought not to do that very thing." Searle's paper, which is typical of the literature, thus contains a clear statement of the position that weak but not strong oughts should allow for conflicts, but no real argument for the position; it is taken for granted.

In fact, I can find only two writers, Thomson and Foot, who actually seem to argue for this position on the basis of conceptual considerations related to the nature of the distinction between weak and strong oughts. Thomson is, again, happy to admit that there might be conflicts among weak moral reasons for action, such as commitments or obligations, but rules out conflicts among strong oughts:

> It should be stressed that what is an odd idea is that "I ought to give C a banana" and "I ought to give D a banana" are both true [even though I have only one banana to give, and cannot give it to both C and D]. There is no oddity in the idea that "I am committed to C to giving C a banana" and "I am

---

[12]The position described in this paragraph, as well as the quotation, can be found in Searle (1980, pp. 248–249).

> committed to D to giving D a banana" are both true. Similarly
> for the ordinary English expressions "obligation" and duty."[13]

To support the conclusion that there can be no conflicts among strong
moral oughts, she sets out two arguments, the first of which appears in the
passage immediately preceding that just cited:

> Some philosophers have canvassed the idea in recent years that
> it can be the case that I ought to do alpha and ought to do beta
> despite the fact that I cannot do both alpha and beta. Should
> we agree with them? It is an odd idea. I will certainly feel you
> have been unhelpful if when I tell you about my predicament,
> and ask what I ought to do, you tell me "Well, as a matter of
> fact, you ought to give C a banana and you ought to give D a
> banana." I just told you I have only one banana.[14]

To this argument, I can offer two related replies. First, to say that your
response to Thomson's question is unhelpful—or odd, or in some other
way inappropriate—is not necessarily to say that it is false, as we know
from the theory of conversational implicature. It could easily be that your
response provides a true, or correct, statement of the moral facts, which,
unfortunately, are not particularly helpful in this case. And second, it
may be that the reason your response appears to be unhelpful, or odd,
is that the response suggests a misunderstanding of the natural sense in
which a question like Thomson's would be asked. Here it is useful to
recall Williams's distinction between what might be called the *moral* and
the *deliberative* senses of the word "ought"—between, that is, "the *ought*
that occurs in statements of moral principle, and in the sorts of moral
judgments about particular situations that we have been considering, [and]
the *ought* that occurs in the deliberative question 'what ought I to do?'
and in answers to this question, given by myself or another."[15]

As Williams points out, it is often natural to ask this kind of deliberative question even when all the moral facts are in place and agreed upon.
Imagine, for example, that I face a very weak but nonetheless clear all
things considered moral ought enjoining one action, but also have a com-
pelling but largely self-interested reason for performing a conflicting action.
Perhaps I have told my colleague Anne that I would give her comments on
her paper by tomorrow, but also, and at the last moment, have been offered tickets to take my family to a football game that we would all dearly
love to see: the Pittsburgh Steelers are playing the Baltimore Ravens for
the American Football Conference championship. To make matters worse,
suppose I happen to know that Anne is deeply mired in grading and committee work at the moment, so that, even if I should decide to stay home

---

[13]Thomson (1990, p. 83).

[14]Thomson (1990, p. 83).

[15]Williams (1965 p. 184).

and write up my comments, there is only a slight chance that she would be able to look at them before the end of the week anyway. And of course, I cannot reach Anne.

In such a situation, it might be natural for me to ask a friend what I ought to do, where the point of this deliberative question would be to solicit help in balancing what seems to be a very weak moral demand against, in this case, a much stronger demand based on my own self-interest. It would be unhelpful, and odd, for my friend to respond to this question simply by reiterating the moral demand—the moral ought—which is presumably already known and taken as a premise of the question. (A promise is a promise: what I ought to do, when the matter is considered from the moral perspective alone, is stay home and comment on Anne's paper.) The fact that such a response would be unhelpful, however, does not mean that it would be incorrect as a statement of the moral facts, only that I am not asking to be reminded of the moral facts, of which we can suppose I am painfully aware. I am asking, instead, a deliberative question about what I ought to do when a number of considerations, including the moral facts, are taken into account; to suppose that the moral facts alone determine the answer to this deliberative question is to commit oneself to what Williams calls the "necessary supremacy of the moral."[16]

A similar point can be made about Thomson's question regarding what she ought to do with the banana. Even though it might be unhelpful for you to respond to this question simply by reiterating the moral facts—that she ought to give the banana to C, but that she also ought to give the banana to D—this does not necessarily mean that your statement of the moral facts is incorrect. It may mean only that the question is naturally interpreted as deliberative, taking the moral predicament as a premise and asking what she should do now that she has found herself in such a predicament. In this case, a more helpful reply might be something like: "Well, you're stuck; what you ought to do now is flip a coin, give the banana to the winner, apologize to the loser, and offer him the very next banana you come across." Of course, it is just possible to regard this last bit of advice as itself a dictate of morality, as if morality itself specifies the appropriate behavior in the face of the conflicting oughts, so that, in a sense, there is no real moral conflict. But it is also possible to imagine that morality generates but does not resolve the conflict, and that the advice is intended simply as a deliberative, practical suggestion as to the best thing to do once one has landed in such a moral predicament.

So much, then, for Thomson's first argument in support of the view that there can be no conflicts among strong moral oughts. Her second argument occurs a few pages later, and rests on a claim about English usage:

---

[16]See also Dancy (2004, p. 43) on the possibility that a weak moral requirement might be defeated by stronger requirements, or opportunities, of other kinds.

> I think myself that it was not merely odd but patently incorrect
> to think that "I ought to give C a banana" and "I ought to give
> D a banana" can both be true compatibly with my having only
> one banana; I think we simply do not use the English word
> "ought" in such a way that that is so. In any case, I will not. I
> will throughout so use "ought" that it cannot be the case that
> I ought to do alpha and ought to do beta where I cannot do
> both alpha and beta.[17]

This argument, however, can be disposed of quickly. It is, of course, always
fair to stipulate that a term will be used in some particular way for one's
own local purposes; but as a claim about the English language, the idea
that we do not use the word "ought" in a way that allows for conflicts is
surely incorrect. There seems to be nothing especially odd to the ear about
the following sentiment, even when both oughts are evidently moral: "Oh
dear, I promised Anne comments on her paper by tomorrow, so I ought
to stay home this evening and work, but I also promised Alex to take her
to the game if the Steelers made it to the playoffs—and they have, and
it's tonight—so I really ought to do that as well." Even many of those
authors who ultimately deny the possibility of moral conflict concede that
English usage suggests otherwise, such as Foot, who writes on the basis of
considerations about ordinary English, that "it may seem surprising that
anyone should ever have denied that I can have an obligation to do A and
an obligation not to do A, or that I ought to do A and ought not to do
it."[18] And as we have seen, other writers, such as Gowans, feel that the
term "ought" itself is most naturally taken to refer to weak moral oughts,
which allow conflicts, rather than to our strong moral oughts, which are
instead supposed to be characterized as what we "must" do.

Let us now turn to Foot's own argument for the idea that weak but
not strong oughts can allow for moral conflicts; the argument is based on
the nature of the distinction she draws between weak and strong oughts,
or, as she calls them, "type 1" and "type 2" oughts, respectively.[19] In
Foot's view, type 1 oughts are analogous to "engagements"—arrangements
or commitments that we might make to perform some action. Just as we
can easily find ourselves with conflicting engagements, it is equally possible
to face a conflict among type 1 oughts. Indeed, the possibility of conflict involving type 1 oughts, commitments or obligations, is so plain, Foot claims,
that any resistance to the idea must be due largely to a confusion of type 1
oughts with type 2 oughts, which do not allow for conflicts, and which she
introduces in the following passage:

> What is a type 2 ought statement? What is it that makes 'ought
> A'(2) inconsistent with 'ought $\neg A$'(2), although 'ought A'(1) is

---

[17]Thomson (1990, p. 83).

[18]Foot (1983, p. 254).

[19]This argument is found in Foot (1983, pp. 254–257).

> consistent with 'ought $\neg A$'(1)? The explanation is that type 2 ought statements tell us *the right* thing to do, and that this means the thing that is *best* morally speaking ... It is implied that for one for whom moral considerations are reasons to act, there are better moral reasons for doing this action than for any other. As this cannot be true both of A and of $\neg A$, 'ought A'(2) is inconsistent with 'ought $\neg A$'(2). 'Ought A'(2) is not, however, inconsistent with 'ought $\neg A$'(1). I can have reason not to do something and yet have better reason to do it than I have to do anything else.[20]

Given this way of defining type 2, or strong, oughts, Foot is correct in claiming that they cannot allow conflicts. Let A and B be conflicting actions, which cannot both be performed. Unless the preference ordering among reasons for acting is circular, there cannot be better reasons for performing A than for performing B, and also better reasons for performing B than for performing A. If, in general—and here I am adapting Foot's notation—'ought Y' in the type 2 sense is supposed to mean that there are better reasons for performing the action Y than for performing any conflicting action, it follows at once that we cannot accept both 'ought A' and 'ought B'.[21]

Foot's definition, then, does indeed entail that type 2 oughts do not allow for moral conflicts, but here we must object to the definition itself, on the grounds that it yields intuitively incorrect results. In fact, Foot's definition of type 2 oughts in terms of the best moral reasons—reasons that are better than those for performing any conflicting action—is essentially equivalent to Brink's suggestion considered earlier, in Section 3.1.3, of defining all things considered oughts in terms of those prima facie oughts that are not only undefeated themselves, but also defeat all competitors—that is, the overriding oughts.

Since the two definitions are equivalent, they are subject to similar problems, as we can see by returning to our twins example. In this situation, as we recall, I have reasons, my promises, for performing each of these two conflicting actions, but since neither of these reasons is actually stronger than the other, then according to Foot's definition, neither action is something that I ought to do in the type 2 sense. The definition is thus successful in avoiding conflict, but as we saw in our earlier discussion, it also fails to provide us with any mechanism for drawing the intuitively desirable result that, given my promises, I ought at least to have dinner with one twin or the other; lacking further elaboration, there is nothing at all in

---

[20] Foot (1983, p. 256), where the difference between her type 1 and type 2 oughts is indicated by numerical adjuncts to the ought statements.

[21] This conclusion holds even if the reasons for performing A and B are either incommensurable or identical in strength, since, in that case, neither reason is actually better than the other, and so we can accept neither 'ought A' nor 'ought B'.

Foot's account to tell us that this disjunctive action is supported by some best reason.

Of course, as we now know, it is possible to avoid all things considered conflicts, while at the same time generating the appropriate disjunctive oughts, by adopting a different approach—basically, the disjunctive account as described here. Suppose, then, that we repair the technical error in Foot's definition by adopting a treatment more along the lines of our disjunctive account—stipulating, roughly, that an action is what one ought to do in the type 2 sense whenever it is supported, not by some best reason, but by each coherent set of reasons, where this idea of coherent sets of reasons is explicated in terms of proper scenarios of an underlying default theory. In that case, the definition of type 2 oughts would yield intuitively acceptable results, and it would indeed follow from this definition that type 2 oughts cannot allow for conflicts.

But what does this tell us, exactly? If we pattern the definition of type 2 oughts after something like the disjunctive account, they will be conflict free; but it is equally true that if we pattern the definition of type 2 oughts after something like the conflict account, they will allow for conflicts. Once we accept the technical emendation, Foot's paper can then be taken to show that there is, in fact, a sensible way of defining a conflict-free notion of strong oughts, in addition to a notion that allows for conflicts; but the paper does not present an argument for adopting either of these two notions in preference to the other.

4.3 Objections based on reasons as moral forces

The final argument I consider here for rejecting the idea of conflicts among all things considered oughts is based on what is, frankly, a metaphor—the metaphor of prima facie oughts, or reasons, as moral forces, analogous in some ways to physical forces, and of all things considered oughts as the outcomes resulting from interactions among the various moral forces that are active in some particular situation. This metaphor can be found already in Ross, in a well-known passage, part of which was cited in the Introduction to this book, where he compares the way in which the various moral features of an action combine to yield an overall evaluation of that action to the way in which the physical forces acting on an object combine to determine its direction and velocity:

> Any act that we do contains various elements in virtue of which
> it falls under various categories. In virtue of being the breaking
> of a promise, for instance, it tends to be wrong; in virtue of
> being an instance of relieving distress it tends to be right. Ten-
> dency to be one's duty may be called a parti-resultant attribute,
> one which belongs to an act in virtue of some one component
> in its nature. *Being* one's duty is a toti-resultant attribute, one

which belongs to an act in virtue of its whole nature and of nothing less than this.

Another instance of the same distinction may be found in the operation of natural laws. *Qua* subject to the force of gravitation towards some other body, each body tends to move in a particular direction with a particular velocity; but its actual movement depends on *all* the forces to which it is subject.[22]

As Ross himself suggests, the moral forces metaphor leads naturally to an interpretation of prima facie oughts as ceteris paribus, or "other things being equal," moral statements, telling us what all things considered oughts would hold in the absence of any other moral forces—here, for example, is his commentary on the prima facie duty of returning good for good:

What I maintain is that an act in which good is returned for good is recognized as *specially* binding on us just because it is of that character, and that *ceteris paribus* any one would think it his duty to help his benefactors rather than his enemies, if he could not do both; just as it is generally recognized that *ceteris paribus* we should pay our debts rather than give our money in charity, when we cannot do both.[23]

More exactly, the ceteris paribus interpretation of prima facie oughts, or reasons, holds that a statement of the form "Under the circumstances X, it ought prima facie to be that Y," or more simply, "X is a reason for Y," should be taken to mean that, whenever the circumstances X occur, then other things being equal—that is, in the absence of any additional moral forces—it ought all things considered to be that Y.

Of course, it will rarely occur in any real situation that additional moral forces are entirely absent, that only a single moral consideration is relevant; but this is exactly what one would expect from the analogy between moral and physical forces. Even though physical laws might imply that some object, subject to a certain force, would behave in a particular way in the absence of any additional physical forces, it is impossible to determine the exact behavior of that object in the real world until all the various forces actually influencing it are taken into account: the gravitational attraction between one object and another might imply a particular trajectory, for example, but the actual trajectory could then be influenced by friction, collisions, further gravitational attractions to other objects, and so on. In just the same way, Ross thought, one must take account of all the various moral forces to which an action is subject before arriving at an all things considered evaluation. The fact that some action—say, repaying a debt rather than donating to charity—is an instance of returning good for good tells us only that this action is what the agent ought to do in the absence

---

[22] Ross (1930, pp. 28–29).
[23] Ross (1930, p. 30).

of further moral forces. But in the usual case there will be further prima facie oughts, further moral reasons, to contend with: perhaps the agent has promised money to the charity, so that the prima facie ought concerning promising comes into play, or perhaps the charity is exceptionally benevolent and efficient in its use of contributions, so that the prima facie ought of beneficence is relevant.

The metaphor of prima facie oughts, or reasons, as moral forces, with all things considered oughts as the resulting outcomes, and also the related interpretation of prima facie ought statements as ceteris paribus moral laws are both useful, I think. They are, in any case, pervasive, lying just below the surface in several discussions of moral reasoning, and have recently been defended explicitly and in detail by Brink and Pietroski.[24] What I do not see, however, is how—as both Brink and Pietroski suggest—accepting either the moral forces metaphor or the ceteris paribus interpretation of prima facie ought statements provides any reason for rejecting the possibility of all things considered moral conflicts.[25]

To begin with, simply interpreting prima facie oughts as ceteris paribus moral laws does not tell us anything at all about the kind of conclusions we should expect to be derivable from a body of prima facie oughts as premises, and in particular, whether these conclusions can or cannot allow for conflicts; there is no generally accepted organon for reasoning with ceteris paribus laws, moral or otherwise.[26] To say that, given X, it ought to be that Y ceteris paribus is, again, to say only that, under the circumstances X, it ought to be that Y other things being equal, in the absence of any further moral considerations, or forces. But since we so rarely encounter a situation in which only a single moral force comes into play, what we really need to know, in order to give any real meaning to the moral force interpretation, is how the various moral forces that might be operative in a given situation interact with each other to determine the resulting outcomes—how the various prima facie oughts bearing on a situation interact to determine the resulting all things considered oughts.

---

[24] See Brink (1994, pp. 216–220) and Pietroski (1993).

[25] The idea that adopting the moral forces metaphor entails rejecting all things considered moral conflicts—that is, the implication between these two positions—is accepted, not only by those like Brink and Pietroski, who do adopt the metaphor and therefore reject moral conflicts, but also by some who wish to argue in the other direction. As an example, Dancy (1993, pp. 102–103), who accepts the possibility of moral conflicts, argues against the moral forces metaphor on the grounds that it does not allow for this possibility; and the same implication—that the moral forces metaphor somehow rules out conflicts—is reaffirmed in his (2004, p. 35, fn. 20), where Dancy mentions the failure to allow for an understanding of tragic dilemmas as one of the difficulties facing the view that overall oughts are to be thought of as some function of contributory, or prima facie, oughts.

[26] Indeed, I believe that the most promising logical techniques available for understanding ceteris paribus reasoning are those that have been developed within the field of nonmonotonic logic—exactly the techniques that are at work in this book.

The principles specifying the way in which input forces interact to determine the resulting outcomes in a force theory are sometimes known as "composition principles." Of course, everyone's favorite example of composition principles at work is found in classical physics, where both the input forces acting on an object and its resulting output behavior are represented as vectors, and the output is calculated from the inputs through simple vector arithmetic. The analogy with classical physics is followed rather closely by Brink, who speaks of the process through which prima facie moral forces determine all things considered oughts as "moral factor addition":

> It is not essential to the factor addition model that we always be able to assign precise numerical values to the various moral forces present in a situation. What is important is that the moral status of an act *sans phrase* results from adding the moral forces, positive and negative, contributed by the various morally relevant factors; the act with the highest moral total is all-things-considered obligatory.[27]

But it is not necessary to follow classical physics so rigidly. Force composition principles from some of the special sciences—genetics, evolutionary biology, economics, psychology—can differ substantially from those of classical physics. Often, in these special sciences, the composition principles involved are qualitative rather than quantitative, or statistical rather than deterministic; at times one force is allowed to override, or trump, another, rather than simply modifying its effect. And it is not unreasonable to expect that the principles governing the interactions among moral forces may be even more complicated.

What I would like to suggest is that both of the two accounts presented here—both the conflict account and the disjunctive account—can sensibly be regarded as supplying exactly what is needed: an approximation, at least, of an appropriate set of composition principles for moral forces. Both accounts provide a precise method, subject to reasonable logical and intuitive constraints, for calculating all things considered oughts from a background set of prima facie oughts, or reasons. If prima facie oughts are thought of as input moral forces and all things considered oughts as the resulting outputs, then both accounts can be seen as encoding principles through which outputs are determined by the input forces. And if this is so—if both the conflict and disjunctive accounts can sensibly be thought of as supplying force composition principles—then it is hard to see how the moral force metaphor could be used as a basis for favoring either of these two accounts over the other.

It is, of course, possible to argue that, for some reason, it would be unnatural to interpret the conflict account as specifying composition principles for moral forces. Although one might happily allow conflicting moral

---

[27]Brink (1994, p. 217).

forces as inputs, perhaps there is something odd about the idea of force composition principles that allow conflicts even among their outputs. Pietroski suggests as much.[28] He considers a situation in which some agent, Morty, is subject to conflicting prima facie oughts: first, to be at the train station on time to meet a friend, and second, to help a child he comes across on the way, which would then cause him to be late for the train. This situation is compared to a case in evolutionary biology in which some population is subject to conflicting ceteris paribus laws: one predicting drift in favor of some trait T, and another predicting selection in favor of a competitor trait T'. And here, Pietroski claims, the question of what Morty actually ought to do, in the all things considered sense, is analogous to the question concerning the direction in which the population will actually evolve:

> Saying that Morty ought$_{act}$ [that is, actually ought] to go to the station *and* that Morty ought$_{act}$ to help the child makes no more sense than saying that the population will actually evolve in the direction of T *and* that it will actually evolve in the direction of T'. The population will evolve in the direction of T, or it will evolve in the direction of T', or perhaps it will not evolve at all ... But the population cannot evolve in both directions. Nor can a ball simultaneously pushed north and pushed south move north and move south. Similarly, Morty ought$_{act}$ to be at the station on time, or (exclusively) he ought$_{act}$ to help the child. But it is not that case that he ought to do both.[29]

Is this a reasonable analogy? I agree, of course, that the ball will not simultaneously move north and south, and that the population will not evolve in both directions at once. These things simply cannot happen, and so any set of force composition principles predicting that they will happen would have to be rejected at once, on the grounds of predicting the impossible. But is it, in the same way, impossible to imagine that an agent might be subject to conflicting all things considered oughts, so that a theory predicting that he is would likewise have to be rejected? Again, this question—whether there can be conflicting all things considered oughts—is the very point at issue, and an answer cannot be taken for granted as a basis for argument.

Instead of physics or evolutionary biology, let us consider a different analogue for the behavior of moral forces. Suppose I have just taken a new job at, say, the Acme Corporation, to begin on Monday. Imagine that the corporate offices for Acme are located in a rural office park, so that the only practical way of getting to work is to drive there and park in the corporate parking lot. During my orientation session, the various rules governing Acme employees are explained to me. I learn that, in order to park in the corporate lot, it will be necessary to display an official Acme parking

---

[28] See Pietroski (1993, pp. 502–503).
[29] Pietroski (1993, p. 503).

decal, which is to be mailed to my home address as part of my Employee Orientation Packet: if I park in the corporate lot without displaying the decal, I will receive a ticket, resulting in a fine. I also learn that my pay will be reduced for each day of work missed: in effect, another fine. In virtue of my employment at the Acme Corporation, I am therefore subject to certain forces that, if not moral, are at least normative, in the sense that I will receive a sanction—in this case, a fine—if I fail to act appropriately. One of these normative forces compels me to report to work each day; another compels me not to park in the corporate lot without displaying a parking decal.

Now suppose that Monday arrives, but that my Orientation Packet, containing the parking decal, has not yet come in the mail. What should I do? If I fail to report to work, I will receive a fine; but going to work requires parking in the corporate lot, and I will also receive a fine if I park there without displaying a decal. At this point, it may seem reasonable for me to get in touch with Acme, so imagine that I call the Parking Coordinator to explain my situation. He understands the problem, and is sympathetic, but claims that there is little he can do; his job is simply to enforce the parking regulations, which require him to ticket any car parked in the corporate lot without a decal, and indeed, he will himself receive a fine if he fails to do so. Imagine that I then call the only other relevant Acme official, the Personnel Director, who is likewise sympathetic but unable to help; her job is simply to enforce the personnel regulations, which require her to fine an employee for each missed day of work.

In this simple example, there is a clear and concrete criterion for determining whether I have violated a norm of the Acme Corporation: I receive the relevant fine. Apparently, I am now destined to receive some fine or another, either for parking without a decal or for missing a day of work. It is therefore natural to conclude that the normative forces to which I am subject in virtue of my employment at the Acme Corporation are organized in such a way that, under the circumstances in which I find myself, I simply cannot avoid violating some norm. And perhaps the composition principles governing moral forces work in exactly the same way, so that at times—even after balancing the relevant forces to the best of our ability, and filing the appropriate appeals—we may nevertheless be faced with a situation in which we cannot avoid violating some all things considered moral ought.

One might, of course, object to this analogy by arguing that there is something deeply flawed either with the employment regulations issued by the Acme Corporation or with their administration: surely there ought to be some individual outranking both the Parking Coordinator and the Personnel Directors, with the authority to adjudicate between the relevant rules in a case like mine, so that a normative conflict is avoided. Maybe so, but not all normative systems are organized and administered as we would hope. Perhaps Acme is just badly run. Or the case could be modified by supposing that the parking concession is operated by an entirely independent organization—Consolidated Parking, say. In this new situation, I would then be violating a Consolidated regulation if I go to work and an Acme regulation if I do not; but since these two organizations are independent, there would be no reason at all to expect any degree of coordination in the formulation or administration of their policies, or any higher authority to whom I could appeal a conflict.

Alternatively, one might respond to the analogy by arguing that the rules of morality must be better organized than the employment regulations issued by the Acme Corporation—and in particular that, although it may indeed be possible for employees to face certain normative conflicts involving the Acme regulations, there can be no conflicts regarding all things considered moral oughts. What a proponent of this view would need to establish is that, because of the special nature of morality among the variety of normative systems, moral rules—unlike employment regulations, for example—must either be so carefully qualified that the antecedents of any two rules with conflicting consequents can never both apply in the same situation, or else that the preference ordering on moral rules must be strongly connected, so that in case of conflict, one of the two rules will be given precedence. Again, this is an entirely coherent position, but it requires substantive moral argument for its justification. Until such an argument is provided, it is hard to see what reason there could be for ruling out the possibility of moral conflicts, or for preferring the disjunctive account to the conflict account.

Part III

Some elaborations

Chapter 5

Variable priorities and exclusion

Let us take stock. In the first part of this book, I mapped out a very simple prioritized default logic and explored the relation between this logic and the theory of reasons. In the next part, we saw how two separate deontic logics could be defined in terms of an underlying default logic—providing a concrete illustration of the familiar idea that oughts might be defined in terms of reasons—and used the differences between these deontic logics to explore various arguments bearing on the possibility of moral dilemmas.

In this third part of the book, we will consider some ways in which the simple default logic defined earlier can be elaborated, leading to a more robust theory of reasons; we then see how this elaborated theory of reasons bears on some important philosophical concepts and issues, especially those surrounding the debate concerning moral particularism.

I begin, in this chapter, by elaborating our earlier default logic along two dimensions. First, the priorities among default rules have, so far, been taken as fixed in advance, but there are situations in which it is most natural to think of these priorities themselves as established through reasoning, and indeed through default reasoning. And second, the notion of defeat defined so far captures only one form, described here simply as "defeat," but often called "rebutting defeat," in which one default defeats another by providing a stronger reason for a conflicting conclusion. There is at least one other form, generally called "undercutting defeat," and related to the concept of an "exclusionary reason" from the literature on practical reasoning, in which one default defeats another, not by contradicting its conclusion, but by undermining its capacity to provide a reason at all.

5.1 Variable priority default theories

5.1.1 The definition

We have concentrated thus far on fixed priority default theories, in which priority relations among default rules are fixed in advance; in our earlier discussion, we considered some possible sources of this priority ordering—

specificity, reliability, authority. Given the link between reasons and defaults, the idea that the priority relations among default rules are fixed in advance corresponds to the familiar idea that the strength, or importance, of various reasons is likewise fixed, either by convention or as part of their nature.[1]

In fact, however, one of the most important things we reason about, and reason about by default, are the priorities among the very default rules that guide our default reasoning—we offer reasons for taking some of our reasons more seriously than others. This is particularly evident in well-structured normative domains, such as the law, where the resolution of a dispute often involves explicit arguments concerning the relative importance of different considerations bearing on some issue. But it occurs also in the epistemic domain. Consider reliability. In our initial discussion of priority relations, from Section 1.1.2, I mentioned by way of illustration that both the weather channel and the arthritis in my left knee are reliable indicators of oncoming precipitation, but that the weather channel is more reliable. Suppose, however, that someone disagreed and thought that my arthritis was more reliable. What would we say to such a person? I imagine that we would offer a variety of reasons favoring the reliability of the weather channel over that of my arthritis, and these reasons themselves might then have to be buttressed by appeal to further reasons.

Our first task, then, is to show how situations like this can be accommodated within the general framework presented here. What we want is an account in which, just as before, our reasoning is guided by a set of defaults subject to a priority ordering, but in which it is now possible for the priorities among defaults to be established through the same process of reasoning they serve to guide. Although this may sound complicated—perhaps forbiddingly so, perhaps circular—it turns out that the theory as presented thus far can be extended to provide such an account in four simple steps, through the adaptation of known techniques.[2]

The first step is to enrich our language of choice with the resources to enable formal reasoning about priorities among defaults: a new set of individual constants, to be interpreted as names of defaults, together with a relation symbol representing priority. For the sake of simplicity, we will assume that each of these new constants has the form d_X, for some subscript

---

[1] See, for example, Baier (1958, p. 106) for the suggestion that the strength of reasons is determined by the "social environment." John Skorupski (1997) works with a model of reasons according to which the weight of a reason is, in a sense, part of its nature.

[2] The particular approach presented here is new only in its development within the current framework of scenarios: it is based on techniques first introduced by Thomas Gordon (1993) in his analysis of legal reasoning; these techniques have been refined and developed by a number of people, notably including Gerhard Brewka (1994b; 1996) as well as Prakken and Giovanni Sartor (1995; 1996). The more general idea that a priority ordering among default rules could be determined by the default reasoning they serve to guide originated with Touretzky (1984; 1986); the idea is developed in a different way by Horty, Thomason, and Touretzky (1990), and is isolated and discussed in detail in Section 4 of Horty (1994b).

X, and that each such constant refers to the default δ_X. And we will assume also that our language now contains the relation symbol $\prec$, representing priority among defaults.

To illustrate this notation, suppose that δ_1 is the default $X \to Y$, that δ_2 is the default $Z \to \neg Y$, and that δ_3 is the default $\top \to \ d_1 \prec d_2$, where, in keeping with our convention, the new constants d_1 and d_2 refer to the defaults δ_1 and δ_2 respectively. Then what δ_3 says is that the default δ_2 has a higher priority than δ_1. As a result, we would expect that, when both of these defaults are triggered—that is, when both X and Z hold—the default δ_1 will generally be defeated by δ_2, since the two defaults have conflicting conclusions. Of course, since δ_3 is itself a default, the information it provides concerning the priority between δ_1 and δ_2 is defeasible as well, and could likewise be defeated.

The second step is to shift our attention from structures of the form $\langle \mathcal{W}, \mathcal{D}, < \rangle$—that is, from fixed priority default theories—to structures of the form $\langle \mathcal{W}, \mathcal{D} \rangle$, containing a set $\mathcal{W}$ of ordinary propositions as well as a set $\mathcal{D}$ of defaults, but no priority relation on the defaults that is fixed in advance. Instead, both $\mathcal{W}$ and $\mathcal{D}$ may contain initial information concerning priority relations among defaults, and then conclusions about these priorities, like any other conclusions, are arrived at through defeasible reasoning. Because conclusions about the priorities among defaults might themselves vary depending on which defaults the agent accepts, these new structures are known as *variable priority* default theories. It is stipulated as part of the definition that the set $\mathcal{W}$ of ordinary propositions must contain each possible instance of the irreflexivity and transitivity schemata

$$\neg(d \prec d),$$
$$(d \prec d' \wedge d' \prec d'') \supset d \prec d'',$$

in which the variables are replaced with names of the defaults belonging to $\mathcal{D}$.

Definition 13 (Variable priority default theories) A variable priority default theory Δ is a structure of the form $\langle \mathcal{W}, \mathcal{D} \rangle$, with $\mathcal{W}$ a set of ordinary propositions and $\mathcal{D}$ a set of defaults, subject to the following constraints: (1) each default δ_X is assigned a unique name d_X; (2) the set $\mathcal{W}$ contains each instance of the irreflexivity and transitivity schemata in which the variables are replaced with the names of defaults from $\mathcal{D}$.

Now suppose the agent accepts some particular scenario based on these new default theories; the third step, then, is to lift the priority ordering that is implicit in the agent's scenario to an explicit ordering that can be used in default reasoning. This is done in the simplest possible way, through the introduction of a *derived* priority ordering, with the statement $\delta <_\mathcal{S} \delta'$ taken to mean that δ' has a higher priority than δ according to the scenario $\mathcal{S}$.

Definition 14 (Derived priority orderings) Let $\Delta = \langle W, \mathcal{D} \rangle$ be a variable priority default theory and $\mathcal{S}$ a scenario based on this theory. Then the priority ordering $<_\mathcal{S}$ derived from $\mathcal{S}$ against the background of this theory is defined by taking

$$\delta <_\mathcal{S} \delta' \text{ just in case } W \cup Conclusion(\mathcal{S}) \vdash d \prec d'.$$

The force of this definition, from an intuitive standpoint, is that δ' has a higher priority than δ according to the scenario $\mathcal{S}$ just in case the conclusions of the defaults belonging to this scenario, when taken together with the hard information from W, entail the statement $d \prec d'$, according to which δ' has a higher priority than δ. Because W contains all instances of transitivity and irreflexivity, the derived priority relation $<_\mathcal{S}$ is guaranteed to be a strict partial ordering.

The fourth and final step is to define the notion of a proper scenario for variable priority default theories. This is accomplished by leveraging our previous definition of proper scenarios for fixed priority default theories, which sets out the conditions under which $\mathcal{S}$ counts as a proper scenario for the fixed priority theory $\langle W, \mathcal{D}, < \rangle$, where $<$ can be any strict partial ordering whatsoever over the defaults. Using this previous definition, we can now stipulate that $\mathcal{S}$ is a proper scenario for the variable priority theory $\langle W, \mathcal{D} \rangle$ just in case $\mathcal{S}$ is a proper scenario, in the previous sense, for the particular fixed priority theory $\langle W, \mathcal{D}, <_\mathcal{S} \rangle$, where W and $\mathcal{D}$ are carried over from the variable priority theory, and where $<_\mathcal{S}$ is now the priority relation derived from the scenario $\mathcal{S}$ itself.

Definition 15 (Proper scenarios: variable priority default theories) Let $\Delta = \langle W, \mathcal{D} \rangle$ be a variable priority default theory and $\mathcal{S}$ a scenario based on this theory. Then $\mathcal{S}$ is a proper scenario based on the theory Δ just in case $\mathcal{S}$ is a proper scenario based on the fixed priority default theory $\langle W, \mathcal{D}, <_\mathcal{S} \rangle$, where $<_\mathcal{S}$ is the priority relation derived from $\mathcal{S}$ against the background of Δ.

The intuitive picture is this. In searching for a proper scenario, the agent arrives at some scenario $\mathcal{S}$, which then entails conclusions about various aspects of the world, including priority relations among the agent's own defaults. If these derived priority relations can be used to justify the agent in accepting exactly the scenario $\mathcal{S}$ that the agent began with, then the scenario is proper.

5.1.2   Some examples

Rather than reflecting on these various definitions in the abstract, it is best to turn at once to some concrete examples.

We begin with a variant of the Nixon Diamond, in which it is useful to adopt, not the epistemic perspective of a third party trying to decide whether or not Nixon is a pacifist, but instead, the practical perspective of a young Nixon trying to decide whether or not to become a pacifist. Suppose, then, that Nixon's practical reasoning takes place against the background of the variable priority default theory $\Delta_{14} = \langle \mathcal{W}, \mathcal{D} \rangle$, where $\mathcal{W}$ contains the propositions Q and R, reminding Nixon that he is a Quaker and a Republican—along with, as always in the case of variable priority default theories, appropriate instances of irreflexivity and transitivity— and where $\mathcal{D}$ contains only δ_1 and δ_2, where δ_1 is $Q \rightarrow P$ and where δ_2 is $R \rightarrow \neg P$.[3] Given our current perspective, these two defaults should now be interpreted as providing practical, rather than epistemic, reasons: δ_1 tells Nixon that, as a Quaker, he has a reason to become a pacifist, while δ_2 tells him that, as a Republican, he has a reason not to become a pacifist. Nothing in the theory yet tells Nixon how to resolve the conflict between these two defaults, and so he is faced with a practical dilemma. The theory, as it stands, would yield two proper scenarios, the familiar $\mathcal{S}_1 = \{\delta_1\}$ and $\mathcal{S}_2 = \{\delta_2\}$, supporting the conflicting conclusions P and $\neg P$.

Imagine, however, that Nixon decides to consult with certain authorities to help him resolve his dilemma. Let us suppose that he discusses the problem first with a respected member from his Society of Friends congregation, who tells him that religious concerns are more important than political concerns, so that δ_1 should take priority over δ_2, but that he also talks with a local official of the Republican Party who tells him just the opposite, that politics trumps religion, so that δ_2 should be assigned more weight than δ_1. And suppose we let A and B represent the respective statements of these religious and political figures, the fact that they said what they did. The advice of these two authorities can then be encoded through the defaults δ_3 and δ_4, where δ_3 is $A \rightarrow d_2 \prec d_1$ and δ_4 is $B \rightarrow d_1 \prec d_2$. Here, the new default δ_3 represents the fact that the statement by the religious figure favors the assignment of more weight to δ_1 than to δ_2, while the new default δ_4 represents the fact that the statement by the political figure favors the assignment of more weight to δ_2. It is important to emphasize that, given our practical perspective, these two new defaults should be interpreted, not as evidence about the facts, but, quite literally, as advice about what to do; the default δ_3, for example, should be interpreted, not as providing Nixon with evidence that δ_1 actually *has* more weight than δ_2, but only as suggesting that he should *place* more weight on δ_1 in his deliberations.

At this point, the variable priority default theory that provides the background for Nixon's reasoning is $\Delta_{15} = \langle \mathcal{W}, \mathcal{D} \rangle$, where $\mathcal{W}$ contains the propositions A, B, Q, and R—according to which Nixon is a Quaker and a Republican, and his religious and political advisors said what they did—

---

[3]Formally, this new theory differs from the original Nixon Diamond, the theory Δ_3 depicted in Figure 1.3, in two ways: first, the Nixon Diamond contains an empty ordering on the defaults, while the current theory, as a variable priority theory, contains no ordering at all; second, the hard information from the current theory contains all instances of irreflexivity and transitivity for the two defaults belonging to this theory.

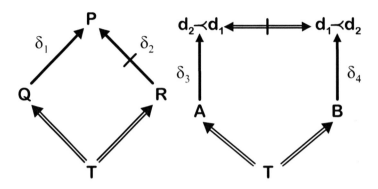

Figure 5.1: Nixon's dilemma

and where $\mathcal{D}$ now contains δ_1, δ_2, δ_3, and δ_4.[4] This theory can be depicted as in Figure 5.1. The diamond on the left represents the original conflict between Nixon's religious and political views, which provide reasons favoring and opposing pacifism. The virtual diamond on the right represents the conflict between Nixon's two advisors concerning the proper weight to be assigned to his religious and political reasons, one suggesting that his religious reason should take precedence over his conflicting political reason, the other suggesting the opposite; it follows from the irreflexivity and transitivity schemata contained in $\mathcal{W}$ that these two recommendations stand in direct contradiction.

Of course, since his chosen authorities disagree, Nixon has not yet resolved his practical dilemma, now represented by the two proper scenarios $\mathcal{S}_3 = \{\delta_1, \delta_3\}$ and $\mathcal{S}_4 = \{\delta_2, \delta_4\}$, which again favor conflicting courses of action. According to the scenario $\mathcal{S}_3$, supporting the propositions $d_2 \prec d_1$ and P, Nixon should place more weight on δ_1 than on the conflicting δ_2, and so embrace pacifism; according to the scenario $\mathcal{S}_4$, supporting the propositions $d_1 \prec d_2$ and $\neg P$, Nixon should instead place more weight on δ_2 and so renounce pacifism. What is especially interesting about this theory, however, is not that it yields two proper scenarios, favoring two courses of action, but that it yields *only* two proper scenarios, favoring *only* two courses of action. After all, the default δ_1 conflicts with δ_2, while the default δ_3 conflicts with δ_4. Since there are two conflicts, each of which can go either way, why are there not four proper scenarios, favoring four courses of action?

---

[4]The set $\mathcal{W}$ must also contain, of course, the instances of irreflexivity and transitivity for the defaults belonging to this theory; but since it is part of the definition of a variable priority default theory that its hard information contains all appropriate instances of irreflexivity and transitivity—and since these instances can be generated automatically from the defaults contained in that theory—I will no longer mention them explicitly.

The answer is that the two conflicts are not independent. Any resolution of the conflict between δ_3 and δ_4 commits Nixon to a particular priority ordering between δ_1 and δ_2, which then determines the resolution of that conflict in favor of the default that has been assigned higher priority. Thus, for example, the scenario $\mathcal{S}_3$ can be classified as proper because it contains the default δ_3, according to which δ_1 is to be assigned a higher priority than δ_2, and then contains the preferred default δ_1 itself; this scenario represents the perfectly sensible course of action in which Nixon accepts the advice of the religious authority that his religious reason takes precedence over his political reason, and then embraces pacifism on religious grounds. The scenario $\mathcal{S}_4$ is likewise proper because it contains δ_4, according to which δ_2 is to be assigned a higher priority than δ_1, and then contains the preferred δ_2 as well; this scenario represents the other sensible course of action available to Nixon, in which he accepts the advice of the political authority that his political reason takes precedence over his religious reason, and so renounces pacifism on political grounds.

From an intuitive standpoint, however, it would be incorrect—odd, irrational—for Nixon to accept a scenario that commits him to a particular priority ordering between δ_1 and δ_2, but then to resolve the conflict between these two defaults in favor of that to which he himself has assigned the lower priority. A situation of this kind can be illustrated by the scenario $\mathcal{S}_5 = \{\delta_2, \delta_3\}$, for example, which contains δ_3, according to which δ_1 is to be preferred to δ_2, but then contains δ_2 in place of δ_1; this scenario represents the course of action in which Nixon again accepts the advice of the religious authority that his religious reason should take precedence over his political reason, but then chooses all the same to renounce pacifism on the basis of his political reason, in spite of a religious reason that he himself judges to be stronger, favoring the opposite choice.

Our informal intuition that the scenario $\mathcal{S}_5$ is incorrect, or irrational, is mirrored formally by the fact that it is not, according to our definition, classified as a proper scenario based on $\Delta_{15} = \langle \mathcal{W}, \mathcal{D} \rangle$, the underlying variable priority default theory. To see this, we note first that the scenario $\mathcal{S}_5$ leads to a derived priority ordering $<_{\mathcal{S}_5}$ according to which $\delta_2 <_{\mathcal{S}_5} \delta_1$—the default providing the religious reason is classified as more important than the default providing the political reason. If we supplement our variable priority theory with this derived priority ordering to get the fixed priority theory $\langle \mathcal{W}, \mathcal{D}, <_{\mathcal{S}_5} \rangle$, we can now see that the default δ_2 is defeated in the context of $\mathcal{S}_5$ by the default δ_1, a stronger default with a conflicting conclusion. The scenario $\mathcal{S}_5$ is not, therefore, a proper scenario based on the fixed priority theory $\langle \mathcal{W}, \mathcal{D}, <_{\mathcal{S}_5} \rangle$, since it contains the default δ_2, which is defeated in the context of that very scenario; and so, according to our definition, it cannot be a proper scenario based on the original variable priority theory either.

Finally, let us imagine that the young Nixon, still faced with his conflict, continues to seek further counsel. Perhaps he turns to his wife, Pat, who

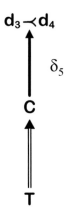

Figure 5.2: Resolving Nixon's dilemma

tells him that the party official's advice is to be preferred to that of the religious figure. If we let C stand for Pat's statement, her advice can be encoded through the new default δ_5, where δ_5 is $C \rightarrow d_3 \prec d_4$. The default theory guiding Nixon's reasoning is now $\Delta_{16} = \langle W, D \rangle$, where W contains the propositions A, B, C, Q, and R—all the previous hard information along with Pat's statement—and where D now contains δ_5, as well as the previous δ_1, δ_2, δ_3, and δ_4. This theory can be depicted by combining the previous Figure 5.1, representing all the previous information, with the new Figure 5.2, representing Pat's advice.

With this new information, Nixon's conflict is at last resolved. As the reader can verify, the variable priority default theory Δ_{16} gives rise to the single proper scenario $\mathcal{S}_6 = \{\delta_2, \delta_4, \delta_5\}$, supporting the conclusions $d_3 \prec d_4$, $d_1 \prec d_2$, and $\neg P$. The scenario corresponds to the course of action in which Nixon is moved by Pat's advice to take the advice of the party official more seriously than that of the religious figure, and so accepts the party official's advice that his political reason is to be preferred to his religious reason, and so renounces pacifism on the basis of his political reason.

Before continuing, I want to return to a point just mentioned, but not developed, in the presentation of this example: if we adopt the practical perspective, so that default rules are interpreted as providing reasons for actions rather than beliefs, this perspective can then be applied quite generally, to those defaults that indicate priority relations among default rules themselves, as well as to defaults of the more usual sort. A default with the conclusion $d \prec d'$ can then be taken as providing the agent, not with a reason for concluding that the default δ' happens to have a higher priority than δ, but rather, with a reason supporting the action of *assigning* to δ' a higher priority than that assigned to δ. And in general, the agent, in reasoning about priorities among default rules, can be interpreted, not as attempting to discover an antecedently existing ordering relation, but instead as trying to establish how priorities among the rules that guide its reasoning *ought* to be assigned.

This idea corresponds to the view previously advanced by Schroeder, according to which the weight carried by a reason in deliberation is itself a normative matter.[5] On Schroeder's view, to say that a reason carries a certain weight, or occupies a certain position in the priority ordering, is like saying that a particular person is admirable: just as the judgment about admirability is supported, not by surveying the population to find out how many individuals actually do admire that person, but instead by arguing that the person in question ought to be admired, so the judgment about weight or priority is likewise supported by a normative argument, showing that it is appropriate, or correct, for the reason to have the weight, or priority assigned to it.

And both of these ideas—Schroeder's, my own—fit together naturally with the deontic interpretation of default logic developed in the previous two chapters, which renders the normative element explicit. Consider, once again, the young Nixon, who has finally arrived at $\mathcal{S}_6 = \{\delta_2, \delta_4, \delta_5\}$ as the unique proper scenario based on the underlying default theory Δ_{16}. This scenario generates a unique extension of the theory, containing $d_3 \prec d_4$, $d_1 \prec d_2$, and $\neg P$; and since the extension is unique, both of our two deontic logics, the conflict and disjunctive accounts, yield the ought statements $\bigcirc(d_3 \prec d_4)$, $\bigcirc(d_1 \prec d_2)$, and $\bigcirc(\neg P)$ as consequences of Nixon's background information.[6] From the practical standpoint, then, in settling on $\mathcal{S}_6$ as a proper scenario, Nixon has arrived at a coherent normative perspective: what he concludes is that he ought to assign a greater priority, or more weight, to δ_4 than to δ_3, and so that he ought to assign a greater priority to δ_2 than to δ_1, and so that he ought to renounce pacifism.

Our variant of the Nixon Diamond should, I hope, serve to illustrate the workings of variable priority default theories—though perhaps not their usefulness, due to the whimsical nature of the example. For a more realistic illustration, we consider a situation from commercial law, originally

---

[5]The point is developed in Schroeder (2007), in Chapter 5, particularly pp. 100–102, and throughout Chapter 7. In addition to maintaining that the weight carried by reasons is a normative matter, Schroeder accepts the view that normative properties are themselves analyzable in terms of reasons—so that the weight of reasons is determined by other reasons, which then carry their own weight. Schroeder is thus presented with an apparent circularity similar to that confronted here, with the priority relations among defaults themselves determined by default reasoning, and offers his own solution with his treatment of "weight recursion" in pp. 136–139. It would be an interesting project to compare Schroeder's solution to the circularity problem with that presented in this book.

[6]Of course, technically, the deontic logics from the previous two chapters were formulated in terms of fixed priority default theories, not the variable priority default theories now before us; but the adaptation is immediate, simply a matter of substituting one kind of default theory for another in the definitions.

described by Thomas Gordon, but simplified and adapted for present purposes.[7]

We are to imagine that both Smith and Jones have individually lent money to Miller for the purchase of an oil tanker, which serves as collateral for both loans, so that both lenders have a "security interest" in the ship—this is defined as a right to recoup their loan value from the sale of the ship in case of default on the loan. Miller has, we imagine, defaulted on both the loans; the ship will be sold, and the practical question is which of the two lenders has an initial claim on the proceeds. Suppose Smith now asserts that his security interest in the ship has been "perfected"—roughly, that it takes priority over any security interests that might be held by others, such as Jones, so that Smith would have the initial claim to any proceeds from the sale. The specific legal issue that arises, then, is whether or not Smith's assertion that his security interest has been perfected is correct.

As it happens, there are two relevant bodies of regulation governing the situation: the Uniform Commercial Code (UCC), according to which an individual's security interest is perfected if that individual has possession of the collateral, and the Ship Mortgage Act (SMA), according to which a security interest in a ship can be perfected only by an individual who has filed certain financial documents. In this case, we are to imagine that Smith is in possession of the ship but has failed to file the necessary documents, so that the two statutes yield conflicting results: according to UCC, Smith's security interest in the ship is perfected, but according to SMA, it is not.

There are, of course, various legal principles for resolving conflicts of this kind. One is the principle of *Lex Posterior*, which gives precedence to the more recent of two regulations. Another is the principle of *Lex Superior*, which gives precedence to the regulation supported by the higher authority. Here, UCC supplies the more recent of the two regulations, having been drafted and then enacted by all the various states (except Louisiana) in the period between 1940 and 1964, while SMA dates from 1920. However, SMA derives from a higher authority, since it is federal law, rather than state law. Given only this information, then, the conflict remains: according to *Lex Posterior*, UCC should take precedence over SMA, while according to *Lex Superior*, SMA should take precedence over UCC.

But let us suppose that, for whatever reason—custom, legislation, a court decision—one of these two principles for conflict resolution has gained favor over the other: perhaps *Lex Posterior* is now favored over *Lex Superior*. In that case, the current situation is analogous in structure to the previous Nixon example, and can be represented in the same way.

---

[7]See Gordon (1993). Other realistic examples are developed by Prakken and Sartor (1996), who consider the issues surrounding a conflict between European Community and Italian law concerning the marketing of a particular product under the label of "pasta," and also a conflict between separate Italian laws concerning the renovation of historic buildings.

To aid comprehension, we use mnemonics in our formalization. Let *Perfected*, *Possession*, and *Documents* be the respective propositions that Smith's security interest in the ship is perfected, that Smith possesses the ship, and that Smith has filed the appropriate financial documents. Then the relevant portions of UCC and SMA can be represented as the defaults δ_{UCC} and δ_{SMA}, where δ_{UCC} is *Possession* → *Perfected* and δ_{SMA} is ¬*Documents* → ¬*Perfected*. The principles of *Lex Posterior* and *Lex Superior* can be captured by the general defaults

$$Later(d, d') \rightarrow d \prec d'$$
$$State(d) \wedge Federal(d') \rightarrow d \prec d',$$

telling us, quite generally, that later regulations are to be preferred over earlier regulations, and that federal regulations are to be preferred over those issued by states; the particular instances of these two principles of concern to us here can be represented as δ_{LP} and δ_{LS}, where δ_{LP} is $Later(d_{SMA}, d_{UCC}) \rightarrow d_{SMA} \prec d_{UCC}$ and δ_{LS} is $State(d_{UCC}) \wedge Federal(d_{SMA}) \rightarrow d_{UCC} \prec d_{SMA}$. Finally, we can take δ_{LSLP} as the default $\top \rightarrow d_{LS} \prec d_{LP}$, again an instance of a general principle telling us that *Lex Posterior* is to be favored over *Lex Superior*.

Now let $\Delta_{17} = \langle \mathcal{W}, \mathcal{D} \rangle$ be the variable priority default theory in which $\mathcal{D}$ contains these five defaults—δ_{UCC}, δ_{SMA}, δ_{LP}, δ_{LS}, and δ_{LSLP}—and in which $\mathcal{W}$ contains the facts of the situation—*Possession*, ¬*Documents*, $Later(d_{SMA}, d_{UCC})$, $Federal(d_{SMA})$, and $State(d_{UCC})$—telling us, again, that Smith has possession of the ship but did not file documents, that UCC is later than SMA, and that SMA is federal law while UCC is state law. This default theory then yields the set $\mathcal{S}_1 = \{\delta_{UCC}, \delta_{LP}, \delta_{LSLP}\}$ as its unique proper scenario—supporting the conclusions $d_{LS} \prec d_{LP}$, $d_{SMA} \prec d_{UCC}$, and *Perfected*—and so recommending a course of action according to which δ_{LP} is to be favored over δ_{LS}, so that δ_{UCC} is then favored over δ_{SMA}, so that Smith's security interest in the oil tanker is to be judged as perfected. As before, this example fits together very cleanly with the deontic understanding of default logic, according to which the underlying default theory supports the statements $\bigcirc(d_{LS} \prec d_{LP})$, $\bigcirc(d_{SMA} \prec d_{UCC})$, and $\bigcirc(Perfected)$, now most naturally interpreted as telling the court both how the various principles involved ought to be arranged and how the particular case at hand ought to be decided.

5.2 Exclusionary default theories

5.2.1 The definition

We have considered, thus far, only one form of defeat—generally called "rebutting" defeat—according to which a default supporting a conclusion is said to be defeated by a stronger default supporting a conflicting conclusion. There is also a second form of defeat, according to which one default supporting a conclusion is thought to be defeated by another, not because it supports a conflicting conclusion, but because it challenges the connection between the premise and the conclusion of the original default. In the literature on epistemic reasons, this second form of defeat is generally referred to as "undercutting" defeat, and was first pointed out by Pollock.[8]

The distinction between these two forms of defeat can be illustrated by a standard example. Suppose an object in front of me looks red. Then it is reasonable for me to conclude that it is red, through an application of a general default according to which things that look red tend to be red. But let us imagine two possible confounding circumstances. First of all, a reliable source—so reliable that I trust this source more than my own sense perception—might inform me that the object is not, in fact, red. (We can suppose that, as I am well aware, the reliable source may know things that I do not: the object could be illuminated by red lights, a red screen could have been inserted in front of the object, and so on.) Or second, I might have taken a drug—let us call it Drug 1—that makes everything look red.

Now, if the object looks red but the reliable source tells me otherwise, then it is natural to appeal to another default, with the conclusion that the object is not red, since what the reliable source says tends to be true and the reliable source has told me that it is not red. And because, by hypothesis, the reliable source is more reliable than perception, this new default would have to be stronger than the original, that whatever looks red tends to be red, and so would defeat this original default in the sense we have considered so far, by providing a stronger reason for a conflicting conclusion. If the object looks red but I have taken Drug 1, on the other hand, then it seems again that I am no longer entitled to the conclusion that the object is red. But in this case, the original default is not defeated in the same way. There is no stronger reason for concluding that the object is not red; instead, it is as if the favoring relation represented by the original default is itself severed, so that what was once a reason no longer provides any support for its conclusion.

This second form of defeat, or something very close to it, is discussed also in the literature on practical reasoning, where it is considered as part

---

[8]See Pollock (1970) for an initial discussion; his own treatment of this notion is developed in detail in later work, such as Pollock (1995). Within artificial intelligence, the idea of undercutting defeat has a peculiar history. It was first introduced, independently of Pollock's work, in some of the very early formalisms for knowledge representation, such as the NETL system of Fahlman (1979), but was soon eliminated by researchers attempting to make logical sense of these formalisms: although the idea is still barely present in one of the initial efforts along these lines, by David Etherington together with Reiter (1983), it seems to have disappeared entirely by the time of Touretzky (1986). This elimination of a second form of defeat was regarded, at the time, as a simplification. Having been eliminated, however, the concept of undercutting defeat was then reintroduced into artificial intelligence by writers explicitly reflecting on Pollock's work, such as Kurt Konolige and Karen Myers (1989), and now plays a major role in the study of argument systems and nonmonotonic reasoning, as detailed by Prakken and Vreeswijk (2002), for example.

of the general topic of "exclusionary" reasons, first introduced by Raz.[9] To motivate the concept, Raz provides a number of examples, but we consider here only the representative case of Colin, who must decide whether to send his son to a private school. We are to imagine that there are various reasons pro and con. On one hand, the school will provide an excellent education for Colin's son, as well as an opportunity to meet a more varied group of friends; on the other hand, the tuition is high, and Colin is concerned that a decision to send his own son to a private school might serve to undermine his support for public education more generally.

However, Raz asks us to imagine also that, in addition to these ordinary reasons pro and con, Colin has promised his wife that, in all decisions regarding the education of his son, he will consider only those reasons that bear directly on his son's interests. And this promise, Raz believes, cannot properly be viewed as just another one of the ordinary reasons for sending his son to the private school, like the fact that the school provides a good education. It must be viewed, instead, as a reason of an entirely different sort—a "second-order" reason, according to Raz, for excluding from consideration all those ordinary, or "first-order," reasons that do not bear on the interests of Colin's son. Just as, once I have taken Drug 1, I should disregard the fact that an object looks red as a reason for concluding that it is red, Colin's promise should lead him, likewise, to disregard those reasons that do not bear on the interests of his son. An exclusionary reason, on this interpretation, is nothing but an undercutting defeater in the practical domain.

Now, how can this phenomenon of undercutting, or exclusion, be understood? The standard practice is to postulate undercutting as a separate, and primitive, form of defeat, to be analyzed alongside the concept of ordinary, or rebutting, defeat; this practice is advocated, most notably, by Pollock.[10] The present account, though, takes a different approach. There remains in our logic only one form of defeat—ordinary defeat, of the sort described earlier. However, the expressive resources of our language are again expanded, ever so slightly, to allow for explicit reasoning about which defaults are, or are not, excluded from consideration; and then the definition of triggering is modified so that only defaults that are not excluded can be triggered at all.

Just as in our treatment of variable priority default theories—where we had to reason by default about the priorities that controlled our default reasoning—there is again the threat of circularity. This time, the set of

---

[9]See Section 1.2 of Raz (1975) for his initial discussion. The topic has spawned an extensive secondary literature, notably including papers by Chaim Gans (1986), Michael Moore (1989), and Stephen Perry (1987; 1989), subsequent elaborations by Raz himself, both in his (1989) and in a postscript to the second edition of his (1975), and a review of the latter by William Edmundson (1993).

[10]See Pollock (1995) and the papers cited there; a survey of the work on this topic in nonmonotonic reasoning, which largely follows the same approach, can be found in Prakken and Vreeswijk (2002).

triggered defaults now depends on our conclusions about which defaults are excluded from consideration, while the set of excluded defaults itself depends on, among other things, which defaults are or are not triggered. But as before, the apparent circularity poses no real problems and our account of undercutting, or exclusion, can be developed very naturally, this time in three steps.

All of the steps are simple, but the first is the simplest: we introduce a new predicate *Out* into our language, with the intention that, where d is the constant representing the default δ, the statement $Out(d)$ expresses the idea that δ is undercut, excluded, or otherwise taken out of consideration. To illustrate, suppose that δ_1 is the default $A \rightarrow Out(d_2)$, and that δ_2 is the default $B \rightarrow P$. Then the intuitive force of δ_1 is that the condition A favors removing the default δ_2 from consideration. As a result, given only these two defaults, and assuming both A and B, we would expect to conclude that the default δ_2 is excluded from consideration, and we would expect to conclude nothing at all about P.

An *exclusionary* default theory, then, is nothing but a default theory with the resources to apply this new *Out* predicate to constants representing its own defaults.

Definition 16 (Exclusionary default theories) An exclusionary default theory is a default theory subject to the following constraints: (1) each default δ_X is assigned a unique name d_X; (2) the background language of the theory contains the predicate *Out*.

It is worth noting that both the fixed priority default theories defined in Chapter 1 and the variable priority theories introduced in this chapter can be exclusionary, but we will concentrate in what follows on variable priority exclusionary default theories, which allow both for priorities among defaults to be adjusted and also for defaults to be excluded altogether.

The second step is to specify the defaults that are to be classified as *excluded from consideration* in the context of some particular scenario. Again, this task is straightforward: the idea is that a default δ is to be excluded from consideration in the context of a scenario just in case that scenario, taken together with the hard information from the underlying theory, entails $Out(d)$, the proposition that δ is excluded.

Definition 17 (Exclusion) Let $\Delta = \langle \mathcal{W}, \mathcal{D} \rangle$ be a variable priority default theory and $\mathcal{S}$ a scenario based on this theory. Then the set $Excluded_{\mathcal{S}}$ of defaults that are excluded from consideration in the context of the scenario $\mathcal{S}$, and against the background of the theory Δ, is defined by taking

$$\delta \in Excluded_{\mathcal{S}} \text{ just in case } \mathcal{W} \cup Conclusion(\mathcal{S}) \vdash Out(d).$$

Since this definition of exclusion involves logical entailment, whether or not a default is excluded from consideration may depend on global properties of both the scenario $\mathcal{S}$ in question and the set $\mathcal{W}$ of hard facts from the

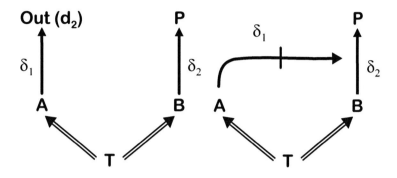

Figure 5.3: An exclusionary default theory

underlying default theory, but in the frequent case in which $\mathcal{S}$ contains a particular default δ' with the statement $Out(d)$ as its conclusion, it is natural to say that δ is *excluded*, or *undercut*, by δ', and so to speak of δ' as an *excluder*, or as an *undercutter*, for the default δ.

The third and final step is to modify the definition of a triggered default so that only those defaults that are not excluded can be triggered.

Definition 18 (Triggered defaults: revised definition) Let Δ be a default theory with $\mathcal{W}$ as its hard information and $\mathcal{D}$ as its underlying set of defaults, and let $\mathcal{S}$ be a scenario based on this theory. Then against the background of this theory, the defaults from $\mathcal{D}$ that are triggered in the context of the scenario $\mathcal{S}$ are those belonging to the set

$Triggered_{\mathcal{W},\mathcal{D}}(\mathcal{S}) =$
$\quad \{\delta \in \mathcal{D} : \delta \notin Excluded_{\mathcal{S}} \text{ and } \mathcal{W} \cup Conclusion(\mathcal{S}) \vdash Premise(\delta)\}.$

This revised notion of triggering now has two clauses. A default that is triggered in a certain scenario must, first of all, satisfy our original condition that the premise of the default is entailed in the context of that scenario, but second, the new definition also requires that the default is not excluded. It is worth noting that the revised definition of a triggered default, though formulated with exclusionary default theories in mind, is a conservative generalization of our original definition, since, in any default theory that is not exclusionary, the set of excluded defaults will be empty, so that the revised definition collapses into the original.

Once the original notion of triggering has been generalized to the revised notion, our treatment of exclusion, or undercutting, is complete. The account can be illustrated in the simplest possible case by returning to our recent example: suppose that $\Delta_{18} = \langle \mathcal{W}, \mathcal{D} \rangle$ is an exclusionary default theory in which $\mathcal{W}$ contains A and B, and in which $\mathcal{D}$ contains δ_1 and δ_2, where δ_1 is $A \to Out(d_2) \Leftrightarrow Out(d_2)$ and δ_2 is $B \to P$. Exclusionary default theories like these can be depicted as inference graphs in the standard fashion, but also in a new and somewhat more suggestive format in which each link of the form $X \to Out(d)$, where d refers to the default δ, is replaced with a link of the form $X \not\to \delta$, indicating that X favors rejecting the default itself. In the case of our example, then, the default δ_1 can be depicted through the link $A \not\to (B \to P)$; the entire theory Δ_{18} can thus be depicted in standard fashion by the diagram on the left of Figure 5.3, or in our new format by the diagram on the right.

This theory allows four possible scenarios—$\mathcal{S}_1 = \emptyset$, $\mathcal{S}_2 = \{\delta_1\}$, $\mathcal{S}_3 = \{\delta_2\}$, and $\mathcal{S}_4 = \{\delta_1, \delta_2\}$—but we can see that only the second of these, the scenario $\mathcal{S}_2 = \{\delta_1\}$, is proper. Why? Well, to begin with, the default δ_1 is binding in the context of this scenario, triggered but neither conflicted nor defeated. But the default δ_2 is excluded in this same context—δ_2 belongs to $Excluded_{\mathcal{S}_2}$—since $\mathcal{W} \cup Conclusion(\mathcal{S}_2) \vdash Out(d_2)$. It thus follows from the revised definition of triggering that δ_1, though its premise is entailed, is not triggered in the context of this scenario, and so cannot be binding either. From this, we can conclude that $\mathcal{S}_2$ is proper, since it contains all and only the defaults that are binding in that context. As for the other scenarios: it is easy to verify that both δ_1 and δ_2 are binding in the context of $\mathcal{S}_1$, but neither is contained in that scenario; the default δ_1 is binding, in the context of $\mathcal{S}_3$, but not contained in that scenario; and the default δ_2 is contained in $\mathcal{S}_3$, but excluded, and so cannot be triggered or binding.

5.2.2   Some examples

Turning now to more concrete illustrations, we begin with the epistemic example sketched earlier. Let L, R, S, and D_1 be the respective propositions that the object before me looks red, that it is red, that the reliable source has told me the object is not red, and that I have taken Drug 1; and suppose that δ_1 is $L \to R$, that δ_2 is $S \to \neg R$, and that δ_3 is $D_1 \to Out(d_1)$. According to the first of these defaults, looking red favors the conclusion that the object is red; according to the second, the statement by the reliable source favors the conclusion that the object is not red; and according to the third, having taken Drug 1 favors the conclusion that the first default should be removed from consideration.

We investigate this example by formulating two variable priority exclusionary default theories, in each of which the object looks red, but with the different confounding circumstances activated. The first theory is $\Delta_{19} = \langle \mathcal{W}, \mathcal{D} \rangle$, depicted in Figure 5.4, where $\mathcal{D}$ contains δ_1, δ_2, and δ_3, and where $\mathcal{W}$ contains, in this first case, the propositions L and S, that the object looks red but the reliable source tells me it is not, as well as the proposition $d_1 \prec d_2$, that the second default takes priority over the first—since, recall, we have stipulated that the reliable source is more

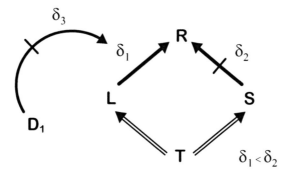

Figure 5.4: The reliable source

reliable even than my own sense perception. It is easy to verify that the unique proper scenario based on this theory is $S_1 = \{\delta_2\}$, supporting the conclusion $\neg R$, that the object is not red. Here, the default δ_1 is triggered, but this default is defeated in our ordinary sense by δ_2, a stronger default supporting a conflicting conclusion; the default δ_3 is not triggered, since its premise is not entailed in the context of the scenario.

The second theory is $\Delta_{20} = \langle \mathcal{W}, \mathcal{D} \rangle$, depicted in Figure 5.5, with $\mathcal{D}$ as before but where $\mathcal{W}$ now contains L along with D_1, rather than S, so that the object looks red but I have taken Drug 1. This theory now yields $S_2 = \{\delta_3\}$ as its unique proper scenario, supporting $Out(d_1)$ as a conclusion, but neither R nor $\neg R$, and so telling us that δ_1 is to be excluded from consideration, but nothing at all about the actual color of the object. In contrast to the previous case, where δ_1 was defeated by δ_2, the current situation is one in which δ_1 is excluded by δ_3. Neither δ_1 nor δ_2 is triggered: δ_2 because its premise is not entailed in the context of the scenario, and δ_1 because it fails to satisfy our new requirement that a triggered default cannot be excluded.

We can now record a simple observation—important in itself, but particularly important for our discussion in the following chapter—that follows from two features of our overall account: first, the account is based on the idea that reasons are to be analyzed as the premises of triggered defaults; and second, the notion of triggering has now been revised so that only defaults that are not excluded from consideration can be triggered. The observation, then, is this: the premises of excluded defaults cannot be classified as reasons for their conclusions. Consider again the previous drug example for illustration. Here, as we have seen, the default δ_1 is excluded from consideration by δ_3. This default is not, therefore, triggered, and so cannot provide L as a reason for R. Once I have taken Drug 1, the fact that the object looks red no longer counts as a reason for the conclusion

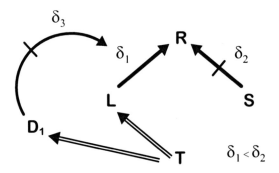

Figure 5.5: Drug 1

that it is red. It is not as if looking red is still a reason for the conclusion but is now defeated by some stronger reason—looking red is no longer any reason for the conclusion at all.

It is possible, of course, for situations to be considerably more complicated than those considered thus far: ordinary defeaters and excluders can themselves be defeated or excluded, both defeaters and excluders of defeaters and excluders can likewise be defeated or excluded, and so on. I do not intend to explore the ramifications among these possibilities in any detail here, but it is worth considering a further case that is just one degree more complex. Suppose that, as before, the object looks red and I have taken Drug 1, which makes everything look red, but that I have also taken Drug 2, an antidote to Drug 1 that neutralizes its effects. How should this situation be represented?

From an intuitive standpoint, what Drug 2 gives me is, not any positive reason for concluding that the object is red, but instead, a reason for disregarding the reason provided by Drug 1 for disregarding the reason provided by my senses for concluding that the object is red. Its associated default therefore provides a reason for disregarding a reason for disregarding a reason—an excluder excluder. Formally, then, letting D_2 be the proposition that I have taken Drug 2, the effect can be captured through δ_4, the default $D_2 \rightarrow Out(d_3)$, according to which, once I have taken the new drug, this fact provides a reason for concluding that the previous default δ_3 should be excluded from consideration. The situation can now be represented through the theory $\Delta_{21} = \langle \mathcal{W}, \mathcal{D} \rangle$, depicted in Figure 5.6, where $\mathcal{D}$ contains the new δ_4 as well as the previous δ_1 through δ_3, and where $\mathcal{W}$ contains D_2 as well as the previous L and D_1. The unique proper scenario based on this theory is $\mathcal{S}_3 = \{\delta_1, \delta_4\}$, supporting R and $Out(d_3)$ as conclusions, and so telling us that the object is red and that δ_3 should be excluded

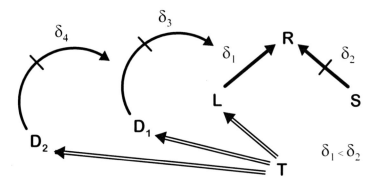

Figure 5.6: Drugs 1 and 2

from consideration. By excluding δ_3, the new δ_4 excludes the very default that had previously provided the reason for excluding δ_1, which can now, therefore, reemerge to support the conclusion that the object is red.

Turning to the practical domain, we can illustrate the use of exclusionary default theories by reconsidering the earlier case of Colin, who is deliberating about sending his son to a private school. Let S, E, and H be the propositions that Colin's son is sent to the school, that the school provides an excellent education, but that its tuition is high; and take δ_1 as the default $E \rightarrow S$ and δ_2 as $H \rightarrow \neg S$. These two defaults should be interpreted as telling Colin that the excellent education favors sending his son to the private school, while the high tuition favors not doing so. Simplifying somewhat, let us suppose that these are the only two defaults bearing directly on the issue. But there is also Colin's promise to his wife, which we can represent through the general default

$$\neg Welfare(d) \rightarrow Out(d),$$

telling Colin that, in this decision, he should disregard any considerations that do not center around his son's welfare; and suppose δ_3 and δ_4 are, respectively, $\neg Welfare(d_1) \rightarrow Out(d_1)$ and $\neg Welfare(d_2) \rightarrow Out(d_2)$, instances of the general default for δ_1 and δ_2.

Let $\Delta_{22} = \langle \mathcal{W}, \mathcal{D} \rangle$ be the exclusionary default theory in which $\mathcal{D}$ contains δ_1, δ_2, δ_3, and δ_4, and in which $\mathcal{W}$ contains E, H, and $\neg Welfare(d_2)$, telling us that: the education is excellent, the tuition is high, but δ_2, the default concerning the high tuition, does not bear directly on the welfare of Colin's son. Now if Colin were to consider only the defaults δ_1 and δ_2, concerning the excellent education versus the high tuition, it is easy to see that he would be faced with a conflict—incomparable reasons recommending different actions. Because of his promise to his wife, however, Colin's deliberation is also constrained by the default δ_4, requiring him to exclude δ_2 from consideration, and so allowing δ_1 to stand unopposed. The theory thus yields $\mathcal{S}_1 = \{\delta_1, \delta_4\}$ as its unique proper scenario, supporting S and $Out(d_2)$ as conclusions, telling Colin that he should send his son to the private school and pay no attention at all to the high tuition, since the default δ_2, which would otherwise provide this feature of the situation as an opposing reason, has been excluded from consideration.

Just as in the epistemic case, excluding defaults can themselves be excluded: perhaps Colin has promised his mistress to disregard any promises made to his wife. What I disagree with, however, is the suggestion—found in the literature on practical reasoning, and occasionally in the epistemic literature—that reasons form a kind of hierarchy, so that, just as excluding defaults provide "second-order" reasons, defaults that exclude excluding defaults provide "third-order" reasons, and so on. Perhaps there are some domains, such as the law, where this kind of stratification is the ideal, but even there I suspect that the ideal is seldom realized; and it is hard to see why we could assume any neat stratification in less regimented areas. In addition to promising his mistress to disregard all promises made to his wife, Colin might easily, and at the same time, have promised his wife to disregard all promises made to his mistress.[11] There may be other mistresses as well, and other promises. Colin's entire life, and the reasons governing it, could be a tangled mess, but the theory would apply all the same.

5.3   Discussion

5.3.1   Downward closure of exclusion

We have now generalized our previous account of default reasoning in two ways: first, by allowing the priority relations among defaults to vary, and second, by allowing certain defaults to be excluded from consideration altogether. It is natural to ask whether there is any relation between these two generalizations.

In fact, there is one very attractive view according to which the two generalizations are closely related, and indeed, according to which exclusion is simply a special case of priority adjustment. On this view, once the agent is granted the ability to reason about the priorities assigned to defaults, it is imagined that excluding a default can then be defined in terms of priority adjustment—either as assigning that default a weight of zero, or as assigning it a weight that falls below some fixed threshold value, or as assigning it a weight so low that the default is anyway hardly worth bothering with.

---

[11] Exercise: provide a formal representation of this situation. What proper scenarios does the resulting exclusionary default theory support?

This view, or something like it, has been suggested by at least four previous writers. First, Stephen Perry, the legal scholar, discussing a framework much like that developed here, with reasons for adjusting the weights or priorities assigned to other reasons, writes that "an exclusionary reason is simply the special case where one or more first-order reasons are treated as having zero weight."[12] Second, Dancy introduces the concepts of "intensifiers" and "attenuators" as considerations that strengthen or weaken the force of reasons, and then defines the further concept of a "disabler" as a consideration that attenuates the strength of a reason so thoroughly that it is "reduced to nothing."[13] Third, Schroeder argues that undercutting—he uses the epistemic term—comes in degrees, and that what is typically referred to as "undercutting" in epistemology is best analyzed as an extreme case of attenuation in the strength of reasons; he refers to this thesis as the "undercutting hypothesis."[14] And finally, in my own previous work, I have developed a detailed formal theory of exclusion, or undercutting, as the assignment to a default of a priority that falls below some particular threshold.[15]

I now feel, however, that—in spite of its economy and intuitive attractiveness—this general line of thought is incorrect, and that exclusion cannot be analyzed simply as a special case of priority adjustment. Why not? The difficulty is this: if exclusion of a default from consideration is to be analyzed as the assignment to that default of a sufficiently low priority, then it follows, of course, that any default whose priority is actually lower than that of an excluded default must be excluded as well. What this means, put a bit more formally, is that any such analysis entails the property of *downward closure for exclusion*, according to which: whenever a default δ is excluded and a default δ' is lower in priority than δ, then δ' must likewise be excluded. And as it turns out, this property of downward closure fails to hold in a number of natural cases.

Suppose that δ_1 is the default $A \to P$, that δ_2 is $B \to \neg P$, and that δ_3 is $C \to Out(d_2)$; and consider the very simple theory $\Delta_{23} = \langle W, D \rangle$, depicted in Figure 5.7, where D contains δ_1, δ_2, and δ_3, and where W contains A, B, and C, as well as the propositions $d_1 \prec d_2$ and $d_2 \prec d_3$, according to which δ_1 has a lower priority than δ_2, which itself has a lower priority than δ_3. In this situation, C is provided as hard information and nothing interferes with the default δ_3; so it seems clear that we must accept $Out(d_2)$ as a conclusion. The default δ_2 therefore has to be excluded from consideration, leaving us with no reason to reach $\neg P$ as a conclusion. Since δ_1 has an even lower priority than δ_2, however, it would then follow from downward closure of exclusion that δ_1 must be excluded as well, leaving us with no reason to conclude P either. Given downward closure, we would

[12]Perry (1987, p. 223; see also 1989, p. 933).
[13]Dancy (2004, pp. 41–42).
[14]Schroeder (2005, pp. 10–11; see also 2011a).
[15]Horty (2007b, pp. 14–18).

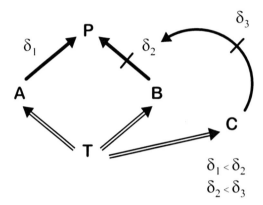

$$\delta_1 < \delta_2$$
$$\delta_2 < \delta_3$$

Figure 5.7: Downward closure of exclusion

thus have, in this situation, no reason to conclude $\neg P$ and no reason to conclude P either. Setting aside our formal account, and just considering the example from an intuitive perspective, let us now ask: is this the correct outcome?

The matter is complicated, because, under certain concrete interpretations of the abstract theory, it seems that this outcome might indeed be correct. Consider, for example, an epistemic interpretation involving three mathematicians of varying degrees of reliability: the second is more reliable than the first, and the third is more reliable than the second. Suppose A is an announcement by the first mathematician that he has proved P (previously an open problem), so that δ_1 represents the fact that this announcement favors the conclusion that P holds; suppose B is an announcement by the second mathematician that she has proved $\neg P$, so that δ_2 represents the fact that this announcement favors concluding $\neg P$; finally, suppose C is a statement by the third mathematician that the second mathematician is so unreliable and error-prone that her proofs cannot be trusted, so that δ_3 represents the fact that this statement favors the conclusion that δ_2 is to be excluded. The priority ordering among defaults corresponds to the reliability of the three mathematicians, so that δ_2 is stronger than δ_1 and δ_3 is stronger than δ_2.

Under this interpretation, the outcome suggested by downward closure is plausible, at least. As before, δ_3 provides us with a reason for excluding δ_2—the second mathematician is too unreliable to be trusted; her announcement cannot count as a reason to conclude $\neg P$. But it is part of our hard information that the first mathematician is less reliable than the second. If she cannot be trusted, and the first mathematician is even less reliable, than surely he cannot be trusted either. Just as downward closure would have it, then, it seems to follow from the exclusion of the stronger δ_2

that the weaker δ_1 must be excluded as well—the first mathematician's announcement likewise cannot count as a reason to conclude P. We are thus led very naturally, under this interpretation, to the outcome supported by downward closure: no reason for $\neg P$, and no reason for P either.

But there are other interpretations of the same abstract theory under which the downward closure outcome is less attractive. Consider a normative interpretation in which a soldier, Corporal O'Reilly, is subject to the commands of three officers. We now take A as a command by the Captain that O'Reilly is to perform some action, where P stands for the proposition that O'Reilly performs that action, so that δ_1 represents the fact that the Captain's command favors P; we take B as a command by the Major that O'Reilly is not to perform that action, so that δ_2 represents the fact that the Major's command favors $\neg P$; and we take C as a command by the Colonel that O'Reilly is to disregard the Major's command—perhaps the Colonel knows that the Major is drunk—so that δ_3 represents the fact that the Colonel's command favors the exclusion of δ_2. The priority ordering among defaults now corresponds to the rank, and so the authority, of the various officers, with the Major outranking the Captain and the Colonel outranking the Major.

Under this interpretation, it seems clear that the downward closure outcome is incorrect. Again, δ_3 provides a reason for excluding δ_2—the Colonel has ordered O'Reilly to disregard the Major's command; this command cannot, therefore, be taken as a reason for $\neg P$. But it is hard to see why δ_1 should be excluded, or why the Captain's command should be ignored. Imagine O'Reilly trying to explain to the Captain why he has ignored the Captain's command. O'Reilly might say: "The Colonel commanded me to ignore the Major." The Captain could reply: "But I am not the Major." O'Reilly might persist: "The Major outranks you. If I am not supposed to obey even a higher-ranking officer like the Major, why should I obey a lower-ranking officer like you?" But the Captain could again reply: "You were not commanded to ignore orders from the Major and also from all officers of lower rank. That would have been a different command from the one you were actually given, which was simply to ignore orders from the Major." At this point I think the Captain has won the dispute. Even though δ_2 should be excluded, and δ_2 has a higher priority than δ_1, that does not entail that δ_1 must be excluded as well—the Major's command favoring $\neg P$ should be disregarded, but not the Captain's command favoring P. The outcome supported by downward closure thus fails: there is no reason for $\neg P$, but there does seem to be reason for P.

Since there are interpretations of our abstract theory under which the downward closure outcome is incorrect, we must reject downward closure for exclusion at least as a general logical feature of exclusionary reasoning in prioritized default theories. And since, as we saw, the idea currently under consideration—that exclusion might be defined as a special case of priority adjustment—entails downward closure, we must reject that idea

as well. Fortunately, the account of exclusionary reasoning developed here
supports us in rejecting downward closure. The theory Δ_{23}, displayed in
Figure 5.7, for example, yields $\mathcal{S}_1 = \{\delta_1, \delta_3\}$ as its unique proper scenario,
supporting both P and $Out(d_2)$ as conclusions; accordingly, δ_2 is excluded
but δ_1 is not, even though δ_1 has a lower priority than δ_2.

But now the question arises: if downward closure is rejected as a logical feature of exclusionary reasoning, how do we account for examples,
such as our story about the mathematicians, in which downward closure
seems to be so natural? My feeling is that our intuition in these cases
is driven by information that is tacitly assumed as part of the example
but not explicitly represented, and that, once this information is explicitly
represented, the desired outcomes do then follow as a matter of logic. In
the case of the mathematicians, for example, where the priority ordering
represents reliability, the tacit information is that, whenever one mathematician's statements must be excluded due to unreliability, the statements
of any other mathematician who is even less reliable must be excluded as
well. This is simply a matter of the proper interaction between the twin
concepts of reliability and exclusion based on unreliability, which was appealed to in our informal argument justifying downward closure in the case
of the mathematicians, but which was not represented in our underlying
abstract theory.

Now suppose we did include this information about the interaction between reliability and exclusion based on unreliability explicitly in the underlying theory, by supplementing the set $\mathcal{W}$ of hard information from the
theory Δ_{23} with each instance of the general schema

$$(Out(d) \wedge d' \prec d) \supset Out(d'),$$

telling us that any default less reliable than an excluded default must likewise be excluded. As the reader can verify, the new theory would then
yield $\mathcal{S}_2 = \{\delta_3\}$ as its unique proper scenario, supporting only $Out(d_2)$ as
a conclusion. Both δ_2 and δ_1 would now be excluded, in the context of this
scenario, the first because we have $Out(d_2)$ as an explicit conclusion, and
the second because $Out(d_1)$ follows from this explicit conclusion together
with our new general schema as well as $d_1 \prec d_2$, both now contained in $\mathcal{W}$.

As this example shows, the information that leads to downward closure
in some particular case might lie among the hard facts of a default theory.
But it may just as easily be provided by the defaults. Consider again the
second interpretation of our abstract example. As the Captain noted in his
dialog with O'Reilly, the Colonel did not command O'Reilly to disregard
orders both from the Major and from any officer of lower rank—but he
easily could have. In that case, the force of the Colonel's command would
be represented, not by the inclusion of the simple default δ_3 in the set $\mathcal{D}$ of
defaults from Δ_{23}, but instead by the inclusion within $\mathcal{D}$ of each instance
of the more complex general default

$$C \;\rightarrow\; Out(d_2) \wedge (d' \prec d_2 \supset Out(d')).$$

If the theory Δ_{23} were modified in this way, it would again yield a unique proper scenario containing each instance of this new general default, supporting each instance of the schema $Out(d_2) \wedge (d' \prec d_2 \supset Out(d'))$ as a conclusion, and so a scenario in which downward closure holds and both δ_2 and δ_1 are excluded. In fact, orders of this form, with downward closure built in, can arise very naturally. Just imagine, for example, a scenario in which a high-ranking security official recruits O'Reilly as an agent to act for the official during a sensitive mission—Project Xerxes, say—and then constrains O'Reilly's behavior with the following command: "In all matters concerning Project Xerxes, you are to disregard any order issued by any officer below the rank of Lieutenant General."

In summary, then: downward closure of exclusion cannot be viewed as a logical feature of exclusionary default reasoning, since there are cases in which it fails; and so any view of exclusion that entails downward closure must be rejected. There are, however, many cases in which downward closure does seems to be natural. In these cases, the property can be seen as flowing from information contained in the underlying default theory, either in the hard information from the theory or among the defaults themselves.

5.3.2   Exclusion by weaker defaults

We now turn to a different issue concerning the relation between priorities and exclusion: is it possible that a stronger default might be excluded by a weaker default? This issue does not arise in the case of our previous abstract example, the theory Δ_{23} from Figure 5.7. Here, the excluding default δ_3 is stronger than the excluded default δ_2, a fact that is also reflected in our concrete interpretations of this example: the third mathematician, who excludes the second mathematician's announcement from consideration, is supposed to be a better mathematician than the second; the Colonel, who excludes the Major's announcement, outranks the Major. But what if it were otherwise? Could the first mathematician, who is even less reliable than the second, exclude the second mathematician's announcement; could the Captain, who is outranked by the Major, order O'Reilly to disregard the Major's command?

Of course, when it comes to ordinary defeat, it is part of our formal definition that a defeating default must be stronger than any default it defeats. But there is no such constraint built into our account of exclusion, and in fact, the account does allow defaults to be excluded by weaker defaults. Suppose that δ_1 is $A \to Out(d_2)$, and δ_2 is $B \to P$, and consider the theory $\Delta_{24} = \langle \mathcal{W}, \mathcal{D} \rangle$, depicted in Figure 5.8, in which $\mathcal{D}$ contains the defaults δ_1 and δ_2 and $\mathcal{W}$ contains the propositions A, B, and $d_1 \prec d_2$.[16] Then it is easy to verify that this theory yields $\mathcal{S}_1 = \{\delta_1\}$ as its unique

---

[16]This theory differes from the earlier Δ_{18} from Figure 5.3 only in containing priority information for the two defaults.

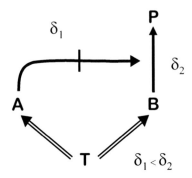

Figure 5.8: Exclusion by weaker defaults

proper scenario, supporting the proposition $Out(d_2)$, so that δ_2 is excluded by the weaker default δ_1.

Still, there is something odd about the possibility that a stronger default might be excluded by a weaker default; and at least one writer, Pollock, feels that it should be ruled out as a matter of logic, arguing that the idea "becomes incoherent when we take account of the fact that justification must always be relativized to a degree of justification," and basing his argument on the premise that "any adequate account of justification must have the consequence that if a belief is unjustified relative to a particular degree of justification, then it is unjustified relative to any higher degree of justification."[17]

It is easy enough to understand the source of Pollock's premise, and his argument. For Pollock, the degree of justification associated with a conclusion depends on the strength of the reasons, or defaults, appealed to in arriving at that conclusion; higher standards for justification require better reasons, or stronger defaults, so that conclusions supported only by weaker reasons, or defaults, must then be discounted.[18] Consider, for illustration, a theory containing only three defaults, δ_1, δ_2, and δ_3, where δ_1 is $\top \rightarrow A$, where δ_2 is $\top \rightarrow B$, and where δ_3 is $\top \rightarrow C$, and where the defaults are ordered so that $\delta_1 < \delta_2$ and $\delta_2 < \delta_3$. Suppose the agent begins with low standards for justification, so that all three defaults are accepted, supporting A, B, and C as conclusions. One can then imagine that, as the agent's standards for justification rise, the first default falls

---

[17]These remarks, as well as the argument described in the following two paragraphs, are found in Pollock (1995, pp. 103–104).

[18]See Pollock (1995, pp. 48, 101) for further discussion of his concept of degree of justification.

below threshold, so that only the second two can be accepted, supporting only B and C as conclusions; and that, as the agent's standards rise still further, the second default now falls below threshold as well, so that only the conclusion C is supported. This is Pollock's picture, and it is a natural one: higher standards for justification result in fewer conclusions—the set of supported conclusions decreases monotonically as the standards for justification increase.

Now, still supposing that stronger defaults can be excluded by weaker defaults, let us consider how Pollock's picture of changing standards for justification might work in the case of the theory Δ_{24} from Figure 5.8, where δ_1 is $A \rightarrow Out(d_2)$ and δ_2 is $B \rightarrow P$, with A and B among the hard information and with δ_1 weaker than δ_2. Suppose, once more, that the reasoner begins with low standards for justification, so that both δ_1 and δ_2 lie above threshold. The reasoner should thus accept δ_1, supporting the conclusion $Out(d_2)$; as a result, δ_2 is excluded and therefore not available to support P, its own conclusion. But again, imagine that the reasoner's standards for justification rise to the extent that δ_1, but not δ_2, now falls below threshold. In that case, since δ_1 falls below threshold, there is no longer any reason for the conclusion that δ_2 should be excluded, so that this default is now available to support P. Our example therefore provides a case in which raising the standards for justification actually leads to the acceptance of a conclusion—the proposition P—that was not accepted before, when the standards were lower. Pollock labels this outcome as "perverse," blames it on the possibility that a stronger default might be excluded by one that is weaker, and so concludes that this possibility cannot be allowed.

I am not so sure. Pollock's argument against exclusion by weaker defaults is based on two assumptions. The first—which we can describe as the *threshold view* of justification—is that a standard for justification corresponds to some particular threshold, that maintaining such a standard requires ignoring all defaults below that threshold, and that raising the standard is simply raising the threshold. The second—which we can describe as the *monotonicity* requirement—is that, on pain of perversion, as Pollock says, the set of supported conclusions must decrease monotonically as the standard of justification increases. As it turns out, both of these assumptions can be questioned. To begin with, even setting aside the possibility of exclusion by weaker defaults, the threshold view of justification already fails to imply satisfaction of the monotonicity requirement: there are situations without any exclusion at all, but in which raising the threshold below which defaults are to be ignored actually leads to the acceptance of new conclusions, and so to a violation of monotonicity.[19] More impor-

---

[19]One example is the theory Δ_{45}, to be discussed in detail in Section 8.2 and depicted in Figure 8.3. This theory contains three defaults δ_1, δ_2, and δ_3, ordered so that $\delta_1 < \delta_2$ and $\delta_2 < \delta_3$. As the reader can verify, the theory yields $\mathcal{S}_1 = \{\delta_1, \delta_3\}$ as its unique proper scenario, supporting the proposition O. However, if it were somehow decided that the

tant, though, it is not clear that the threshold view itself provides the only account, or the best account, of what it might mean to raise the standard for justification.

To see this, we turn to the legal domain, where practitioners are trained to work with various conventionally recognized standards for justification, or evidence. The weakest standard, typically appealed to in routine civil and administrative matters, requires nothing more than a *preponderance* of evidence, a demonstration only that some proposition in question is more likely than not. An intermediate standard, employed in important civil cases, requires *clear and convincing* evidence, a demonstration that the proposition is overwhelmingly likely, though some doubt is allowed. The highest standard, employed in criminal cases and familiar to all viewers of television courtroom drama, requires evidence *beyond any reasonable doubt*; this standard falls short of Cartesian certainty, but is still very strong.

Against the background of these various standards for justification, or evidence, let us return to our example, Δ_{24} from Figure 5.8, now fitted with a legal interpretation—as a case, say, in which the testimony of a reasonably credible defendant might be undermined by that of a much less credible witness, such as a jailhouse snitch. Suppose, more exactly, that δ_2 is interpreted with B as an assertion by the credible defendant in favor of the proposition P, and that δ_1 is interpreted with A as an assertion by the less credible jailhouse snitch in favor of the proposition that the defendant cannot be believed, so that δ_2 should be removed from consideration.

I think it would be plausible to conclude, in this case, that a preponderance of evidence favors the proposition P. After all, the jailhouse snitch is not very credible, and so we can assume that the statement supported by the snitch, that the defendant's testimony should be excluded, itself fails the preponderance of evidence test; since the defendant herself is credible, we can also plausibly assume that the statement she supports, the proposition P, is more likely than not, and so satisfies preponderance. On the threshold view, of course, the standard for justification, or evidence, at work in this situation would then have to be represented by a placement of the threshold somewhere between the defaults δ_1 and δ_2, so that the jailhouse snitch's δ_1 falls below threshold, and is to be ignored, while the credible defendant's δ_2 lies above threshold, and is to be taken seriously.

Suppose, now, that we move up the scale of standards for justification, past clear and convincing evidence, all the way to evidence beyond a reasonable doubt. Even if P passes the preponderance of evidence test, I think it is not inconceivable that this proposition might, all the same, fail to satisfy the much higher standard of having been established beyond a reasonable doubt—and, furthermore, that it might fail to satisfy this standard precisely because the statement by the snitch can be taken to cast

---

threshold representing the appropriate standard for justification should be raised to the extent that the weakest default, δ_1, is taken out of consideration, the theory would then yield $\mathcal{S}_2 = \{\delta_2\}$ as its proper scenario, supporting the new conclusion $\neg O$.

at least some doubt, and some reasonable doubt, on the defendant's testimony. But it is hard to see how this new assessment could be arrived at if we accept the threshold view of what it means to raise standards for justification. Notice that the source of doubt, in this case, is supposed to be the statement by the jailhouse snitch, whose force is carried by the default δ_1. This default, however, had previously been placed below threshold, and ignored, even when the standard for justification was lower. How, then, on the threshold view, can we now give any weight to this default, or the statement it represents, once the threshold has been raised to reflect our higher standard?

I do not intend, here, to address the interesting question of how varying standards for justification can actually be represented in the current framework; but my feeling is that, in contrast to the threshold view, there are situations in which raising the standard for justification might involve paying more, rather than less, attention to certain propositions supported only by weak reasons—to the proposition that the defendant is not to be trusted, for example, which is supported only by evidence from the jailhouse snitch. In any case, since Pollock's argument against exclusion by weaker defaults relies on the threshold view of justification as well as the monotonicity constraint, both of which I have now rejected, I can safely reject his argument as well, and allow exclusion by weaker defaults as a logical possibility at least.

But if exclusion by weaker defaults is not to be ruled out as a matter of logic, how can we account for the fact that this possibility frequently seems to be so unnatural? My suggestion is that, in many situations, we tend to treat defaults as if they were *protected* from exclusion, with the strength of the protection at least as great as that assigned to the protected default itself. There are different ways of implementing this general idea, with different advantages and disadvantages, and I will sketch only one here. Let us say that an *ordinary* default δ of the form $X \to Y$ is *explicitly self-protected* in a theory whenever that theory contains a *protection* default δ' of the form $X \to \neg Out(d)$, so that what δ tells us is that X favors Y and what δ' tells us is that X also favors not excluding δ; we can assume that the protection default δ' occupies a position in the priority ordering identical to that of the ordinary default δ that it protects. The suggestion, then, would be that, even when defaults are not explicitly self-protected, we often tend to treat them as implicitly self-protected, with the necessary protection defaults, spoken *sotto voce*, defeating attempts at exclusion of the original by weaker defaults.

This suggestion can be illustrated by providing our familiar example, Δ_{24} from Figure 5.8, now with a military interpretation. Let B be a command by the Major that O'Reilly should perform some action, represented by P, and let A be a command by the Captain that the Major's command is to be disregarded; the defaults δ_2 and δ_1 thus represent the facts that the Major's command favors performing the action and that the Captain's command favors disregarding the Major's command, with greater weight given to the Major's command. This theory, as we have seen, yields $\mathcal{S}_1 = \{\delta_1\}$ as its unique proper scenario, supporting the odd conclusion $Out(d_2)$, that the Major's command is to be disregarded, so that O'Reilly has no reason at all to perform the action. But suppose the default representing the Major's command is interpreted as implicitly self-protected, and that what is implicit is now rendered explicit—that is, suppose we introduce δ_3 as the protection default $B \rightarrow \neg Out(d_2)$, representing the Major's implicit view that her command is not to be ignored. To be precise: we are now dealing with the new theory $\Delta_{25} = \langle \mathcal{W}, \mathcal{D} \rangle$, where $\mathcal{D}$ contains δ_1, δ_2, and δ_3, with δ_1 and δ_2 as the previous $A \rightarrow Out(d_2)$ and $B \rightarrow P$ and with δ_3 as before, and where $\mathcal{W}$ contains the statements A, B, and $d_1 \prec d_2$ as before, but now $d_1 \prec d_3$ as well. This new theory yields $\mathcal{S}_2 = \{\delta_2, \delta_3\}$ as its unique proper scenario, supporting the conclusions P and $\neg Out(d_2)$. The default δ_1, supporting the conclusion that δ_2 is to be taken out of consideration, is now defeated by the stronger default δ_3, supporting the conclusion that it is not.

Two observations are now in order. First of all—just in case it seems that self-protection is an ad hoc idea, formulated only to avoid exclusion by weaker defaults—it is worth noting that protection from exclusion can come from various sources, with different effects depending on the source, and that self-protection is merely a special case. For example, the Brigadier General might say, "Don't disregard the Major's commands," thus protecting those commands from exclusion even by certain officers outranking the Major, such as the Colonel, though not from exclusion by officers outranking the Brigadier General, such as the Lieutenant General.[20] The Brigadier General can thus protect the Major's orders from exclusion by any other officer lying beneath the Brigadier General in the hierarchy of command; that is, the Brigadier General can protect the Major's commands with the authority available to a Brigadier General. And of course, in just the same way, the Major is able to protect the commands of still other officers, such as the Captain, with the authority available to a Major. So it is only natural to assume that the Major can likewise protect her own commands from exclusion, again with the authority available to a Major. Indeed, this assumption is so natural—and it is so reasonable to suppose that the Major would want all of her commands to be protected in this way, as

---

[20]Note that, in protecting the Major's commands from exclusion by the Colonel, the Brigadier General is not necessarily protecting them from defeat. Suppose the Major commands O'Reilly to perform some action, the Colonel commands O'Reilly not to perform that action, and the Brigadier General says "Don't disregard the Major's command." In this situation, the proper response is for O'Reilly to receive the Major's command, note that it is defeated by the Colonel's stronger, conflicting command, and so to refrain from the action. It is, of course, possible for the Brigadier General to oblige O'Reilly to perform the action, either by excluding the Colonel's command from consideration, in which case the Major's command would have its desired effect, or simply by directly commanding O'Reilly to perform the action, and so defeating the Colonel's weaker, conflicting command.

would anyone else issuing commands—that it is easy to see how the idea of self-protection from exclusion could become implicit in the notion of a command itself, perhaps in the notion of an assertion as well, and in defaults more generally.

As a second observation: We have now considered both exclusion by a stronger default, which is unproblematic, and also exclusion by a weaker default, which is a logical possibility, at least, but fails when defaults are self-protected. But what about exclusion by a default that is either identical or else incomparable in priority? Here, as it turns out, the notion of self-protection can again be appealed to, with useful results. To illustrate, let us consider an abstract theory like the previous Δ_{25} but with all information about priority removed—that is, the theory $\Delta_{26} = \langle \mathcal{W}, \mathcal{D} \rangle$, where $\mathcal{D}$ contains δ_1, δ_2, and δ_3, with δ_1 as $A \to Out(d_2)$, with δ_2 as $B \to P$, and with δ_3 as $B \to \neg Out(d_2)$, and where $\mathcal{W}$ now contains only A and B. The theory can be provided with a concrete interpretation if we imagine that Jack and Jo are equally (or incomparably) reliable sources of information, and take A as an assertion by Jo and B as an assertion by Jack. The default δ_2 can thus be taken to represent the fact that Jack's assertion favors the conclusion P, while δ_1 represents the fact that Jo's assertion favors the conclusion that Jack's assertion is to be excluded as a reason for P, and δ_3 represents Jack's contrary view that his assertion is to be taken seriously. The defaults are unordered with respect to priority, since neither Jack nor Jo is a more reliable source of information.

In this case, then, there is a definite issue on which Jack and Jo disagree—the issue of whether or not Jack's assertion is to be excluded. Since neither Jack nor Jo is more reliable, neither of the two defaults involved will defeat the other. We therefore have a simple conflict, as in the Nixon Diamond, and would naturally expect distinct proper scenarios. It is easy to verify that our account tracks this intuition: the formal theory yields both $\mathcal{S}_1 = \{\delta_1\}$ and $\mathcal{S}_2 = \{\delta_2, \delta_3\}$ as proper scenarios, the first supporting the single conclusion $Out(d_2)$, and the second supporting the pair of conclusions P and $\neg Out(d_2)$. According to the first of these scenarios, the reasoning agent accepts Jo's assertion as a conclusive reason that Jack's assertion is to be excluded. According to the second, the agent instead accepts Jack's assertion as a conclusive reason for P, and also for the implicit conclusion that his own assertion is not to be excluded from consideration as a reason.

5.3.3 Excluders, intensifiers, and attenuators

We saw earlier, in Chapter 2, how the notion of a reason could be defined against the background of a scenario based on an underlying default theory, and how certain technical ideas from default logic could then be used to reconstruct some of our more ordinary concepts concerning reasons and their interactions. These various definitions were developed in terms of the fixed priority default theories before us at the time, but can easily be adapted to the more sophisticated default theories developed in this chapter. To be precise, and also as a reminder: suppose that S is a scenario based on a variable priority exclusionary default theory $\Delta = \langle W, D \rangle$. Then, against the background of this theory and in the context of the scenario S, we can say that X is a *reason* for Y just in case there is some default δ of the form $X \to Y$ from D that is triggered in the context of that scenario, in which case we also say that δ provides X as a reason for Y; we can say that X is *conflicted* as a reason for Y if the default that provides X as a reason for Y is itself conflicted; that X is *defeated* as a reason for Y if the default that provides X as a reason for Y is defeated; and that X is a *good reason* for Y if the default that provides X as a reason for Y is binding.

We can now draw on technical ideas from the new default logics developed in the present chapter to explicate some additional concepts from our more ordinary talk of reasons. The most central of these is the concept of exclusion, or undercutting. Again working against the background of a variable priority exclusionary default theory $\Delta = \langle W, D \rangle$, and in the context of a scenario S based on this theory, the concept can be explicated as follows: where δ is a default of the form $X \to Y$ from the underlying set of defaults, we can say that X is *excluded*, or *undercut*, as a reason for Y just in case $W \cup \textit{Conclusion}(S) \vdash \textit{Out}(d)$—just in case, that is, it follows from the scenario in question together with the hard information from the background theory that the default δ should be taken out of consideration. As noted before, since this definition involves entailment based on information from both the background set W together with the scenario S, the responsibility for the conclusion that δ is to be taken out of consideration, so that X is excluded as a reason for Y, may well be distributed among a variety of sources. Nevertheless, often, and perhaps in the typical case, the scenario S will contain a particular default δ' of the form $Z \to \textit{Out}(d)$, so that the responsibility for exclusion is localized, and we can then say that the proposition Z itself *excludes*, or *undercuts*, X as a reason for Y.

This typical case can be illustrated by $\Delta_{20} = \langle W, D \rangle$, our initial drug example from Figure 5.5, where D contains δ_1, δ_2, and δ_3, with δ_1 as $L \to R$, with δ_2 as $S \to \neg R$, and with δ_3 as $D_1 \to \textit{Out}(d_1)$, and where W contains L and D_1—again, L, R, and D_1 are the propositions that the object looks red, that the object is red, and that I have taken Drug 1, which makes everything look red. As we have seen, this theory yields the unique proper scenario $S_2 = \{\delta_3\}$, supporting $\textit{Out}(d_1)$. In the context of this scenario, then, D_1 excludes L as a reason for R—the fact that I have taken Drug 1 excludes looking red as a reason for concluding that the object is red.

At this point, we can at last return to the example Dancy uses to introduce his distinction between reasons and enablers—between, that is, propositions providing positive support for actions or conclusions, and external considerations that enable these positive reasons to do their job.

The example, discussed earlier in Section 2.2.2 but repeated here for convenience, is this:

1. I promised to do it.
2. My promise was not given under duress.
3. I am able to do it.
4. There is no greater reason not to do it.
5. So I ought to do it.

As we saw earlier, Dancy's purpose in this example is to argue that only the first of these considerations, that I promised to do it, counts as a reason for the conclusion that I ought to do it. The other three considerations, he claims, are simply three different kinds of enablers, playing three different roles in allowing the reason to support its conclusion—though, earlier, we were able to discuss only one of these.

We are now in possession of the technical and conceptual resources to consider the entire example, and to show that the current analysis of the example coincides with Dancy's. Imagine, then, that I have promised to perform some action—perhaps, like Jack, I have promised to meet Jo for lunch. Let P be the proposition that I made this promise and M the proposition that I actually meet Jo; as possible confounding circumstances, let D be the proposition that the promise was made under duress and N the proposition that a drowning child needs to be rescued; let R be the proposition that I rescue the child. Suppose that δ_1 is the default $P \to M$, that δ_2 is $D \to Out(d_1)$, and that δ_3 is $N \to R$—so that δ_1 tells us that having promised to meet Jo favors doing so, δ_2 that having promised under duress favors removing δ_1 from consideration, and δ_3 that encountering a drowning child favors rescuing the child. A situation along the lines of Dancy's example could then be encoded as the theory $\Delta_{27} = \langle \mathcal{W}, \mathcal{D} \rangle$, where $\mathcal{D}$ contains each of δ_1, δ_2, and δ_3, and where $\mathcal{W}$ contains only P, $\neg(M \wedge R)$, and $d_1 \prec d_3$—I have promised to meet Jo, I cannot both do so and rescue the child, and rescuing the child, if need be, is more important than keeping my promise.

This theory now has $\mathcal{S}_1 = \{\delta_1\}$ as its unique proper scenario, supporting the conclusion M—or, in accord with our deontic logic, $\bigcirc(M)$, that I ought to meet Jo. Furthermore, the proposition identified by our analysis as the reason for this conclusion, provided by the default δ_1, is simply P, that I promised to perform the action—just as Dancy suggests. The other premises from the displayed argument are not classified as reasons at all, but, again following Dancy, simply as considerations that function in different ways to show how the reason already provided is able to support its conclusion.

It is easy to see, for example, that if the drowning child had needed to be rescued—if, that is, the set $\mathcal{W}$ of background information had contained N as an additional fact—then my promise would have been defeated as a reason for meeting Jo; there would then have been a greater reason not to perform that action, since we know that I cannot both meet Jo and rescue the child, and the priority ordering stipulates that rescuing the child is more important than keeping my promise to Jo. The purpose of the fourth premise, then, is simply to note that no such thing occurs: the reason set out in the first premise is not defeated. Likewise, if my promise had been given under duress—that is, if W had contained the proposition D as well— my promise, as we can now see, would then have been excluded as a reason for meeting Jo. The purpose of the second premise, again, is to register the fact that this does not occur either: the reason set out in the first premise is not excluded from consideration. Finally, as we saw earlier, in Section 3.2, the deontic logics formulated here respect the principle that ought implies can. If I were not able to perform the promised action, then my promise to do so—while still, on the present analysis, counting as a reason to perform the action—would not support the corresponding ought.[21] The purpose of the third premise, then, is simply to note that the promised action lies within my abilities, so that the promise itself, since it is neither defeated nor excluded as a reason, supports the conclusion that the action is one I ought to perform.

In addition to separating the idea of a reason from that of an enabler, Dancy isolates a number of other concepts to help us understand reasons and their interactions, notably the dual concepts of intensifiers and atten- uators. Beginning with the former, Dancy introduces the idea with the following example:

1. She is in trouble and needs help.
2. I am the only person around.
3. So I ought to help her.[22]

Now ask yourself, what is the function of the second consideration in this chain of argument? It is certainly not, as Dancy notes, a reason for the conclusion: the mere fact that I am the only person around would be no reason at all to help her if she were not in trouble. It is instead, he argues, a consideration that intensifies the strength of the first consideration, the fact that she is in trouble, as a reason for the conclusion that I ought to help her.

As it turns out, this concept of an intensifier can likewise be modeled, or approximated, within the current framework. Consider again a variable priority exclusionary default theory $\Delta = \langle W, \mathcal{D} \rangle$, where $\mathcal{D}$ contains a de- fault δ of the form $X \rightarrow Y$, along with a scenario S based on this theory. In such a context, the proposition Z can be defined as an *intensifier* of X as

---

[21] Here there is a minor point of disagreement with Dancy. On my analysis, the promise counts as a reason whether or not I am able to fulfill it, and lack of ability serves only to break the connection between this reason and the corresponding ought, while for Dancy (2004, p. 40), lack of ability would prevent the promise from being classified as a reason at all.

[22] Dancy (2004, p. 43); once again, I modify the example so that the displayed argu- ment terminates with an ought, rather than an action.

a reason for Y just in case S contains a default of the form $Z \to d' \prec d$ for some other default δ' from $\mathcal{D}$—just in case, that is, the scenario contains a default that provides Z as a reason for increasing the priority assigned to δ, and thus the weight given to X as a reason for Y, relative to some other default.

This rather complicated definition can be illustrated by encoding a situation just slightly more elaborate than Dancy's. Suppose that she is in trouble, which is a reason to help her, but that I have just been served a nice cup of coffee, giving me a reason to remain here and enjoy my coffee, which I cannot do if I go to help her; and suppose that, sadly, my morality is deficient enough that these two reasons are either balanced or incomparable for me, but not quite so deficient that I fail to give the first greater weight once I realize that I am the only person around to help. To represent the situation, let T, H, C, E and O be the respective propositions that she is in trouble, that I help her, that I have been served my coffee, that I remain here to enjoy my coffee, and that I am the only person around to help; let δ_1 be the default $T \to H$, let δ_2 be $C \to E$, and let δ_3 be $O \to d_2 \prec d_1$—so that the trouble favors helping, being served the coffee favors enjoying the coffee, and being the only one around to help favors placing more weight on the first default than the second. The situation can then be encoded as $\Delta_{28} = \langle W, \mathcal{D} \rangle$, where $\mathcal{D}$ contains δ_1, δ_2, and δ_3, and where W contains T, C, O, $\neg(H \wedge E)$—she is in trouble, I have been served the coffee, I am the only one around to help, but I cannot both help and enjoy my coffee.

It is easy to see that this theory yields $S_1 = \{\delta_1, \delta_3\}$ as its unique proper scenario, supporting the conclusions that I ought to give more weight to the first default, and help her with her trouble—that is, appealing once again to our deontic logics, the conclusions $\bigcirc(d_2 \prec d_1)$ and $\bigcirc(H)$. Furthermore, we can see that the proposition O is now classified as an intensifier of T as a reason for H—the fact that I am the only one around strengthens the fact that she is in trouble as a reason for helping her—since, in accord with our definition, the scenario contains the default δ_3, which provides O as a reason for increasing the priority of δ_1 relative to δ_2, and so for giving more weight to T as reason for H than to C as a reason for E.

Two points are worth noting. First of all, it is a consequence of our definition that an intensifier must make a reason stronger than some other reason—it cannot simply make a reason stronger *per se*. In our example, my being the only person around can strengthen the fact that she is in trouble as a reason to help her only because there is another reason, the coffee, that is then weaker by comparison. This first observation is itself dictated by our framework assumption that reasons are to be related to one another only through an ordinal ranking, rather than an assignment to each of some cardinal weight, so that strengthening one reason relative to another is the only form of strengthening there is.

Second, Dancy introduces the concept of an intensifier as part of his general project of distinguishing reasons from other considerations, such as enablers, that play a role in our reasoning but are not themselves reasons, and so suggests that intensifiers are not reasons either—he writes, in the case of our example, that my being the only person around is not still another reason to help her. Here, I agree with what I think is the spirit of Dancy's view, but not the letter. Intensifiers, on the current analysis, are indeed reasons, but not reasons for ordinary sorts of actions or conclusions. They are reasons, instead, for adjusting the priorities among other reasons. The fact that I am the only person around is not, then, just as Dancy says, a further reason to help her, but it is a reason: it is a reason for assigning a higher priority to the fact that she is in trouble as a reason for helping her.

An attenuator, for Dancy, is the opposite of an intensifier, a further consideration that weakens the force, or priority, of a reason; he illustrates the idea by imagining a situation in which she is again in trouble, but this time she got into the trouble through trying to spite someone else— where this second consideration might reasonably be thought to weaken, or attenuate, the fact that she is in trouble as a reason for helping her. Again, this concept can be introduced into the current framework in a parallel way: working against the background of a scenario S based on a default theory $\Delta = \langle \mathcal{W}, \mathcal{D} \rangle$, where $\mathcal{D}$ contains a default δ of the form $X \rightarrow Y$, we can define Z as an *attenuator* of X as a reason for Y just in case S contains a default of the form $Z \rightarrow d \prec d'$ for some other default δ' from $\mathcal{D}$.

Examples similar to those for intensifiers can be devised to illustrate the workings of attenuators, and similar remarks made, all of which I will spare the reader. But one cautionary reminder is necessary. Having introduced the notion of an attenuator as a consideration that weakens a reason, Dancy goes on, as we saw earlier, in Section 5.3.1, to define the further concept of a "disabler" for a reason—his analogue to our excluders, or undercutters— as a consideration that attenuates the strength of that reason entirely. He thus follows the strategy of treating exclusion, or undercutting, as a limiting case of attenuation; but this strategy leads to difficulties, as we also saw, and it is not the one adopted here.

Chapter 6

Particularism

I now want to apply the account of reasons developed in this book, and especially in the previous chapter, to an argument recently advanced by Dancy in support of particularism in moral theory. We begin with some general definitions.

It is often thought that our ability to settle on appropriate actions, or at least to justify these actions as appropriate, involves, at some level, an appeal to general principles. Let us refer to any view along these lines as a form of *generalism*. Certainly the view presented here qualifies, since it is based, ultimately, on a system of principles intended to capture defeasible, or default, generalizations.

Standing in contrast to generalism is the position known as *particularism*, which tends to downplay the importance of general principles, and to emphasize instead a kind of receptivity to the features of particular situations. It is useful, however, to distinguish different versions of this particularist perspective. We can imagine, first, a *moderate* particularism, which holds only that a significant part of our practical evaluation is not grounded in an appeal to general principles.

Moderate particularism is an irenic doctrine, which is compatible with generalism. The two ideas can be combined in a view according to which our everyday evaluative reasoning is typically based on principles, but which also admits the possibility of situations in which the accepted stock of principles yields incorrect results, and must then be emended by a process of reasoning that does not itself involve appeal to further principles. This is, I believe, a sensible view, and one that suggests a promising research agenda centered around questions concerning the update and maintenance of complex systems of principles. Many of these questions would have analogs in legal theory, and in the study of normative systems more generally.

In addition to moderate particularism, however, there is also a more radical position that might be called *extreme* particularism. While the moderate view allows for an appeal to principles in the course of our everyday practical evaluation, insisting only that there may be special circumstances in which a straightforward application of these rules yields incorrect results, extreme particularism holds that principles have no role to play in practical evaluation at all.

Since it denies the legitimacy of any appeal to principles whatsoever, extreme particularism is flatly inconsistent with generalism. Nevertheless, it is exactly this radical position that has been advanced by Dancy, who argues that extreme particularism follows from a broader *holism* about reasons—the idea that the force of reasons is variable, so that what counts as a reason for an action or conclusion in one setting need not support the same action or conclusion in another.[1]

6.1   Dancy's argument

In Dancy's view, holism is a general phenomenon that applies to both practical and epistemic reasons. Both, as he writes, are capable of shifting polarity: a consideration that functions as a reason for some action or conclusion in one context need not serve as a reason for the same action or conclusion in another, and indeed, might even be a reason against it. Dancy presents a variety of cases intended to establish this possibility, in both the practical and theoretical domains. Since these examples follow a common pattern, we consider only two representatives.

Beginning with the practical domain, imagine that I have borrowed a book from you. In most situations, the fact that I have borrowed a book from you would give me a reason to return it to you. But suppose I discover that the book I borrowed is one you had previously stolen from the library. In that context, according to Dancy, the fact that I borrowed the book from you no longer functions as a reason to return it to you, and indeed, I may no longer have any reason to return it to you at all.[2] In order to illustrate the same phenomenon in the epistemic domain, Dancy turns to a standard example along the lines of those considered in the previous chapter. In most situations, the fact that an object looks red functions as a reason for concluding that it is red. But suppose that I have now taken yet another drug—call this one Drug 3—which makes red things look blue and blue things look red. In this new context, according to Dancy, the fact that an object looks red no longer functions as a reason for thinking that it is red; it is, instead, a reason for thinking that the object is blue, and therefore not red.[3]

---

[1]The argument is set out with minor variations in a number of publications beginning with Dancy's (1983), but I focus here on the versions found in his (1993), (2000), (2001), and particularly the canonical (2004). Similar arguments have been advanced by others; an especially clear version is presented by Margaret Little (2000).

[2]This example can be found in Dancy (1993, p. 60); it is followed by a number of similar examples.

[3]Dancy (2004, p. 74); the example is discussed also in (2000, p. 132) and in Section 3 of his (2001).

Let us grant, for the moment, that examples like these are sufficient to establish a general holism of reasons. How is this holistic view supposed to lead to extreme particularism, a thoroughgoing rejection of any role for general principles in practical evaluation? To answer this question, we must consider the nature of the generalizations involved in these principles, and it is useful to focus on a concrete example. Consider, then, the principle that lying is wrong. What could this mean?

We might understand this principle, first of all, as a universally quanti-fied material conditional according to which any action that involves lying must be wrong, regardless of the circumstances. Although some writers have endorsed a view along these lines, very few people today would find such an unyielding conception to be tenable. It is, of course, possible to weaken the proposal by viewing the simple principle that lying is wrong as a sort of abbreviation for a much more complicated rule, still a material conditional, but one laden with exception clauses covering all the various circumstances in which it may be acceptable to lie: saving a life, avoiding a pointless insult, and so on. The problem with this suggestion is that no satisfactory rule of this form has ever been displayed, and it is legitimate to doubt our ability even to formulate such fully-qualified rules with any degree of confidence, let alone learn these rules or reason with them.

Alternatively, we might take the principle that lying is wrong to ex-press the idea, not that all acts that involve lying are wrong, or even all acts that involve lying and also satisfy some extensive list of qualifications, but simply that lying is always a feature that counts against an action, a "wrong-making" feature. On this view, the fact that an action involves lying would always count as some reason for taking it to be wrong, even though that action might be judged as the right thing to do overall, when various other reasons are taken into account. The function of principles, then, would be to articulate general reasons for or against actions or conclu-sions, which may not be decisive, but which would at least play an invariant role in our deliberation, always favoring one particular side or the other. This is the view suggested by some of Ross's remarks about prima facie duties, and it is, in addition, the view of principles that is endorsed by Dancy as the most attractive option available:

> Moral principles, however we conceive of them, seem to be all
> in the business of specifying features as *general* reasons. The
> principle that it is wrong to lie, for instance, presumably claims
> that mendacity is always a wrong-making feature wherever it
> occurs (that is, it always makes the same negative contribution,
> though it often does not succeed in making the action wrong
> overall).[4]

But now, suppose reason holism is correct, so that, for any consideration favoring an outcome in some situation, there is another situation in which

---

[4]Dancy (2004, p. 76).

that same consideration fails to favor that same outcome. In that case, there would be no general reasons at all, no considerations that play an invariant role in our deliberation, carrying the same force regardless of context. If the function of principles is to identify general reasons like this, then, there would simply be nothing for them to identify; any principle telling us that a reason plays some uniform role in our deliberation would have to be incorrect, since there would always be some context in which that reason plays a different role. This is Dancy's conclusion—that, as he says, "a principle-based approach to ethics is inconsistent with the holism of reasons."[5]

6.2   Evaluating the argument

This argument of Dancy's has been studied in some detail, and I cannot attempt here to review the resulting literature.[6] My intention is simply to analyze the argument from the perspective of the current theory of reasons.

Let us start with the epistemic example that Dancy offers to support reason holism. Take L, R, B and D_3 as the respective propositions that the object looks red, that it is red, that it is blue, and that I have taken Drug 3; and suppose that the default δ_1 is $L \to R$ and that δ_2 is $L \wedge D_3 \to B$, so that δ_1 tells us me that looking red favors the conclusion that the object is red, while δ_2 tells me that looking red once I have taken Drug 3 favors the conclusion that the object is blue. We consider two different formalizations of this example, beginning with $\Delta_{29} = \langle \mathcal{W}, \mathcal{D} \rangle$, depicted in Figure 6.1, where $\mathcal{D}$ contains δ_1 and δ_2 and where $\mathcal{W}$ contains L, D_3, $d_1 \prec d_2$, and $\neg(R \wedge B)$.[7] According to this theory, then: the object looks red but I have taken Drug 3; the default δ_1, that what looks red is red, is outweighed by the default δ_2, that what looks red once I have taken Drug 3 is blue; and the object cannot be both red and blue. It is easy to see that this theory yields $\mathcal{S}_1 = \{\delta_2\}$ as its unique proper scenario, supporting the conclusion B and, because of logical closure, $\neg R$ as well, that the object is blue and not red.

---

[5]Dancy (2004, p. 77). A couple of paragraphs later, Dancy admits that there may actually be a few factors whose role in normative evaluation is not sensitive to context, such as "causing of gratuitous pain on unwilling victims," for example, but he tends to downplay the theoretical significance of isolated exceptions like these, and I agree; a robust generalism would require a wide range of normative principles, not just an occasional principle here and there.

[6]A classic collection of papers has been assembled by Brad Hooker and Little (2000); a more recent and very useful overview of the issues is provided by Pekka Väyrynen (2011).

[7]The inference graph displayed in Figure 6.1 may seem to suggest that the truth of $L \wedge D_3$ is somehow independent of the separate truths of L and D_3, but this suggestion is an artifact of our very restricted graphical notation. Boolean relations like these among propositions can be encoded in structures only slightly more complex, known as *and/or graphs*; a description can be found in any standard introduction to artificial intelligence, such as the classic text of Nils Nilsson (1980).

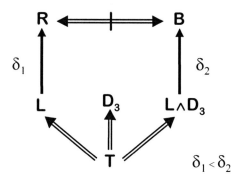

Figure 6.1: Drug 3, first interpretation

Dancy's argument depends, however, not so much on the conclusions supported by particular situations, but instead, on the propositions that are or are not to be classified as reasons in those situations. This is an issue that can usefully be explored from the standpoint of our theory of reasons as the premises of triggered defaults; and when we do explore the issue from this standpoint, we find that—with the situation represented as before—the proposition that the object looks red is indeed classified as a reason for the conclusion that the object is red. Why? Because a default is triggered in the context of a scenario just in case its premise is entailed in that context and it is not excluded from consideration. The premise of the default δ_1 already belongs to the hard information from the background theory, and so is entailed in the context of any scenario based on this theory, and nothing excludes this default. The default is therefore triggered, and so provides its premise, the proposition L, that the object looks red, as a reason for its conclusion, the proposition R, that the object is red. But if L is classified as a reason for the conclusion R, why do we not simply accept this conclusion? Well, because L is defeated, of course, by the stronger reason $L \wedge D_3$, that the object looks red once I have taken Drug 3, which supports the conflicting conclusion B, that the object is blue.

Our initial representation of this situation, then, illustrates the possibility of an alternative interpretation of one of the key examples that Dancy relies on to establish reason holism. On Dancy's view, the situation in which the object looks red but I have taken the drug provides a context in which, although looking red normally functions as a reason for the conclusion that an object is red, it now loses its status as a reason entirely; what is a reason in the normal run of cases is not a reason in this case, and so we are driven to reason holism. On our initial representation, by contrast,

looking red is still classified as a reason for the conclusion that the object
is red, but simply as a defeated reason.

I mention this possibility here only to show that there are different
ways of interpreting those situations in which some familiar consideration
appears not to play its usual role as a forceful or persuasive reason. In
each case, we must ask: does the consideration fail to function as a reason
at all, or does it indeed function as a reason, but simply as one that is
defeated? The answer often requires a delicate judgment, and at times
different interpretations of the same situation are possible—this is a point
we will return to when we consider Dancy's practical example.

In the particular case at hand, as it happens, the idea that looking red
still functions as a reason, but simply a defeated reason, is one that Dancy
entertains but immediately rejects:

> It is not as if it is some reason for me to believe that there is
> something red before me, though that reason is overwhelmed
> by contrary reasons. It is no longer *any reason at all* to believe
> that there is something red before me; indeed it is a reason for
> believing the opposite.[8]

And, in this particular case, I would have to agree. Once I have taken
the drug, it does not seem as if looking red still provides some reason for
concluding that the object is red, which is then defeated by a stronger
reason to the contrary; in this case, it just does seem that the status of
looking red as a reason is itself undermined.

What is crucial to see, however, is that this interpretation of the situation, Dancy's preferred interpretation, can likewise be accommodated
within the framework set out here, by appeal to our treatment of exclusionary default reasoning. Let δ_3 be the new default $D_3 \rightarrow Out(d_1)$, and
consider the exclusionary default theory $\Delta_{30} = \langle W, D \rangle$, depicted in Figure 6.2, just like the previous Δ_{29} except that, in addition, D now contains
the default δ_3. This new interpretation of Dancy's example, then, includes
all the information from our previous representation together with the additional information that having taken Drug 3 favors excluding the previous
δ_1 from consideration. And it can now be verified that this new theory
yields $S_2 = \{\delta_2, \delta_3\}$ as its unique proper scenario, supporting the conclusions B and $\neg R$ as before, as well as the new conclusion $Out(d_1)$—that the
object is blue rather than red, and also that δ_1 is to be excluded.

Given this new representation of the situation, the default δ_1, which
had previously provided L, looking red, as a reason for R, being red, is
no longer triggered. Why not? Because a default can triggered only if
its premise is entailed and, in addition, it is not excluded; and while the
premise of δ_1 is indeed entailed within the context of the scenario S_2, this
scenario tells us also that δ_1 itself is excluded. A reason, once again, is

---

[8]Dancy (2004, p. 74).

the premise of a triggered default; and since looking red is no longer the premise of a triggered default, it now loses its status as a reason for the conclusion that the object is red. What is a reason in the usual range of cases is, therefore, not just a defeated reason, but no longer any reason at all, exactly as Dancy claims.

With this observation in place, we can turn to an evaluation of Dancy's argument. The argument hinges on the idea that extreme particularism, the rejection of general principles, follows from reason holism. The framework developed here, however, supports reason holism, allowing for the possibility that a consideration that counts as a reason in one situation might not be classified as a reason in another. Yet this framework is itself based on a system of principles—default rules, which can be thought of as instances of defeasible generalizations. Indeed, what is and what is not a reason in any particular situation is determined by these defaults and their interactions. The framework thus provides a counter-instance to the idea that reason holism entails extreme particularism, or that holism is inconsistent with any form of generalism. Reason holism is consistent with the form of generalism set out here, at least, and so Dancy's argument is, strictly speaking, invalid.[9]

Clearly, there is a disagreement. How should it be diagnosed? Why is it that Dancy considers holism to be inconsistent with any appeal to general principles, while in the framework developed here, it seems that the two ideas, holism and generalism, can be accommodated together?

The disagreement has its roots, I believe, in our different views concerning the meaning of general principles—it is a semantic disagreement. We both acknowledge that, by and large, the principles guiding practical reasoning cannot usefully be taken to express universally generalized material conditionals: the practical principle that lying is wrong cannot mean that every action that involves lying is wrong. Instead, as we have seen, what Dancy suggests as the most attractive generalist option is that these principles should be taken to identify considerations that play an invariant role as reasons. The principle that lying is wrong should thus be taken to mean that lying always provides some reason for evaluating an action less favorably, even in those cases in which our overall evaluation is favorable. And presumably, the epistemic principle according to which things that

---

[9]The argument I have set out here is aimed at showing that reason holism is consistent with generalism because facts about which propositions count as reasons and when—as well as facts about defeat, exclusion, intensification, and attenuation—can themselves be explained through general principles. Another argument that attempts to establish the same conclusion in the same way, and an argument that was very influential in the development of my own, is set out by Schroeder, particularly in his (2009) and (2011a). There is, however, this difference: while the principles I appeal to are logical, or semantic, and concern reasons themselves, the principles that Schroeder appeals to are pragmatic and concern our way of speaking about reasons. These two modes of explanation are complimentary, not conflicting, and it would be an interesting project to figure out which of the holistic phenomena involving reasons are best explained in which way.

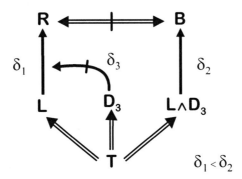

Figure 6.2: Drug 3, second interpretation

look red tend to be red should likewise be taken to mean that looking red always provides some reason for concluding that an object is red, even in those cases in which our overall conclusion is that the object is not red.

Now, given this understanding of general principles, it follows at once—it is *obvious*—that reason holism must lead to their rejection: if what counts as a reason in one situation need not count as a reason in another, then, of course, any principle that identifies some consideration as playing an invariant role as a reason has to be mistaken. If what it means to say that lying is wrong is that lying always favors a negative evaluation of an action, and there are certain situations in which it does not, then the practical principle itself is faulty, and cannot properly guide our actions; if what it means to say that looking red indicates being red is that looking red always provides some reason for concluding that an object is red, and there are certain situations in which it does not, then again, the epistemic principle is faulty.

I agree, then, that reason holism must entail the rejection of general principles, given Dancy's understanding of these principles. In developing a framework within which holism is consistent with general principles, therefore, I rely on a different understanding of these principles, not as identifying invariant reasons, but instead, as identifying the defaults that underlie our reasoning. On this view, the general principle that lying is wrong should be taken to mean simply that there is a default according to which actions that involve lying are wrong—or that, to a first approximation, once we learn that an action involves lying, we ought to judge that it is wrong, unless certain complicating factors interfere. And the principle that looking red indicates being red should likewise be taken to mean that this relation holds by default—that, once we notice that an object looks red, we ought to conclude that it is red, again in the absence of other complicating factors.

This explication of general principles as statements identifying defaults involves an explicit appeal to ceteris paribus restrictions; the principles tell us what to conclude only in the absence of complicating factors. Ceteris paribus statements like these are sometimes criticized as vacuous.[10] It is also argued that these statements, which specify the appropriate conclusions in the absence of complicating factors, tell us nothing about what to conclude in the more usual case in which complicating factors are present.

Both of these criticisms have, I believe, some merit when lodged against many appeals to ceteris paribus generalizations, since these appeals, often, do not move past the level of a first approximation. The criticisms have no merit in the present case, however. Here, our first approximation to the meaning of a general principle is nothing but a high level summary of the workings of this principle in the underlying default theory, which specifies in detail, not only what the complicating factors might be—when a default is conflicted, defeated, excluded—but also how the various issues introduced by these complicating factors are to be resolved, and the appropriate set of conclusions to be arrived at in each case. What the present account has to contribute, then, is a concrete theory of default reasoning to sustain the explication of general principles as defaults, a theory that is precise, supported by our intuitions, and consistent with reason holism.[11]

6.3   Discussion

Having explored Dancy's central argument for extreme particularism, I now want to consider three related issues. Two of these bear on Dancy's argument itself: first, the sense in which a reason supporting some con-

---

[10]The joke is that an explication of this kind reduces the apparently substantive claim "Lying is wrong" to the less substantive claim "Lying is wrong except when it isn't."

[11]In fact, the use of defaults and defeasibility in analyzing normative principles is so natural that the idea is often appealed to informally in the ethical literature, and especially in the literature on moral particularism. Dancy himself mentions default reasons as early as (1993) and discusses them at length in his (2004); together, Mark Lance and Little have written an important series of papers on the topics of defeasibility and particularism, beginning with (2004) and including (2007) and (2008); and the relations of defaults, and defeasibility, to particularism are explored by other writers as well, notably including Sean McKeever and Michael Ridge (2006), as well as Väyrynen (2004). None of this work, however, attempts to provide any concrete account of the structure of default reasoning, or alludes to the extensive literature on nonmonotonic logics; I hope, therefore, that the theory I have set out here will help to bridge this gap. One writer from the ethical tradition who does try to develop a logic of defeasible moral principles is Richard Holton (2002), who independently reconstructs ideas like those found in some of the early nonmonotonic logics. I have no objections to the philosophical aspects of Holton's work; he develops an account very much in line with that presented here, and does so first. Unfortunately, like so many of the early nonmonotonic logics, the logic that Holton uses to frame his account itself runs into problems; I hope to discuss some of these problems in future work.

clusion can properly be said, not simply to lose its force, but actually to shift polarity so that it supports a conflicting conclusion; second, the range of interpretations allowed by certain informal examples. The third is an argument for moderate particularism.

6.3.1   Pragmatic considerations

We have seen how the present account allows us to understand the idea that L, the proposition that the object looks red, which normally counts as a reason for R, the conclusion that the object is red, fails to count as a reason for this conclusion in the situation in which I have taken Drug 3. But in fact, Dancy claims more than this. What he claims is not only that L fails to count as a reason for R, but that it is actually, in this situation, a reason for B, the conclusion that the object is blue, and so not red. This further claim is not yet supported by the present framework. Can it be? Should it be? I believe that it should be, and it can be, but that it requires a different sort of explanation—roughly, pragmatic rather than semantic.

To see why it sometimes seems natural to think of the fact that an object looks red as a reason for the conclusion that it is blue, consider a slight variation on Dancy's example. Suppose you and I both know that I have taken the drug, which makes red things look blue and blue things look red—that is, we both know D_3—but that my eyes are closed, so that I cannot see the object before me. Now imagine that I open my eyes, see that the object looks red, and so announce, since I know I have taken the drug, that it must be blue. And suppose you ask me *why* I concluded that the object is blue. It would then be very natural for me to respond, "Because I realized that it looks red," apparently citing the fact that the object looks red as a reason for concluding that it is blue; and the ease of my response in this situation certainly suggests that there is a sense in which looking red can, in some cases, be taken as a reason for not being red.

What the current account tells us, by contrast, is that my real reason for concluding that the object is blue is, not just that it looks red, but that it looks red and I have taken the drug—not just L, but $L \wedge D_3$. Returning to the theory Δ_{30} from Figure 6.2, we can see that it is this conjunction that forms the antecedent of the triggered default δ_2, which supports the conclusion B, that the object is blue. In the present situation, however, I would argue that there is a pragmatic principle at work that allows me to cite this conjunctive reason by mentioning only a salient part, the simple statement L. Different propositions can be salient at different times and in different ways. In this case, what makes L salient is simply that it provides *new* information. The statement D_3 was already part of our background knowledge. Although I actually mean to cite the proposition $L \wedge D_3$ as my reason for concluding that the object is blue, then, a principle of conversational economy allows me to do so simply by mentioning the new information that, taken together with our shared background information, entails this proposition.

This pragmatic analysis can be supported by considering another variant of the situation. Suppose, this time, that my eyes are open and I can see that the object looks red, but I am not yet aware that I have taken Drug 3—perhaps it was administered to me secretly. Since the object looks red, my initial judgment would be that it is red. But imagine that I am now told about the drug and its effects, and so revise my judgment to conclude that the object is blue. In this case, if I were again asked why I changed my mind, it would no longer be appropriate to cite the fact that the object looks red. After all, I knew that it looked red before, when I judged it to be red. Instead, I would now be more likely to say, "Because I learned that I took the drug."

This response conforms to the pattern of the previous variant, and so suggests a common pragmatic principle at work. In both cases, my final state of information can be thought of as a set containing both L and D_3, which entails $L \wedge D_3$, the actual reason for my conclusion that the object is blue. In the first case, I arrive at this final state of information by adding L to a set of background information that at first contains only D_3; in the second, I arrive at this final state by adding D_3 to a set that at first contains only L. In both cases, then, I am able to cite the conjunction $L \wedge D_3$ itself as a reason for my conclusion that the object is blue in exactly the same way, by mentioning only the new information that, taken together with our shared background knowledge, entails this proposition—L in the first case, and D_3 in the second.

Neither of these cases conforms exactly to Dancy's example, of course. Yet I feel that a very similar explanation would apply there: we are able to refer to the proposition $L \wedge D_3$ by citing only its most salient part—where D_3 is now the most salient part of this proposition, not because it presents new information, but because the information it presents is more striking, or abnormal.

6.3.2 Borrowing a book

We now turn to the practical example offered by Dancy to illustrate reason holism, which has not yet been considered in any detail: I borrow a book from you, but then learn that this book is one you have previously stolen from the library. According to Dancy, this situation is one in which my borrowing the book from you, which generally functions as a reason for returning it to you, no longer counts as such a reason. What is generally a reason is not a reason in this particular situation, and so again we have holism.

In his discussion of this example, just as in his discussion of the epistemic example, Dancy explicitly considers and rejects the possibility that the consideration, having borrowed a book, is still functioning as a reason, but simply as a defeated reason:

> It isn't that I have *some* reason to return it to you and more reason to put it back in the library. I have no reason at all to return it to you.[12]

But here, in contrast to the epistemic case, I do not think the matter is so straightforward; I cannot agree that Dancy's reading of the situation provides the unique interpretation, or perhaps even the most natural. I myself would be inclined toward a very different interpretation. In the situation as described, I would tend to feel that my having borrowed the book from you gives me a personal obligation to return it to you, and that it is simply not my business to supervise your relations with the library: that is someone else's job.

I do not mean for this autobiographical detail—how I personally would view the matter—to carry any particular importance beyond suggesting a different and, I hope, coherent interpretation of the situation Dancy describes. This situation is especially interesting, in fact, precisely because it does serve so naturally to illustrate what I consider to be a pervasive phenomenon: situations described at this level of generality often allow for a number of different, equally coherent interpretations. In order to establish this point, I will now simply describe—first informally and then formally— five different interpretations of the situation Dancy sets out, arranged in a sort of spectrum depending on the relative strength assigned to my reasons for returning the book to you compared to my reasons for returning it to the library.

First, there is my own personal interpretation: borrowing the book from you gives me a reason to return it to you, but your having stolen the book from the library gives me no particular reason to do anything at all (though it might well count as a reason supporting certain actions by the library police), so that what I ought to do is return the book to you. Second, I can imagine someone who agrees that my borrowing the book gives me a reason for returning it to you, but who also feels that your having stolen the book gives me some reason for returning it to the library, though the reason for returning it to you is stronger, so that, on balance, what I ought to do is return the book to you. Third, I can imagine someone who feels that my borrowing the book gives me a reason for returning it to you, that your having stolen the book also gives me a reason for returning it to the library, and that these two reasons are, in fact, incomparable in priority, so that I am now faced with a dilemma, incomparable reasons supporting conflicting actions; I would then have to resolve the matter in whatever way I resolve dilemmas, perhaps by flipping a coin or seeking further advice. Fourth, I can imagine someone who feels that my borrowing

---

[12]Dancy (1993, p. 60).

the book gives me a reason for returning it to you, that your having stolen the book gives me a reason for returning it to the library, but in this case, that the reason for returning it to the library is stronger, so that what I ought to do is return the book to the library. And, fifth, we have Dancy's own preferred interpretation: your having stolen the book both gives me a reason for returning the book to the library and excludes any reason I might otherwise have had for returning it to you, so that what I ought to do is return it to the library and, in addition, there is no longer any reason at all for returning it to you.

In order to present these various interpretations formally, let us take B, S, Y, and L as the respective propositions that I borrowed the book from you, that you stole it from the library, that I return the book to you, and that I return it to the library; and we will assume the proposition $\neg(Y \wedge L)$ as a fact—I cannot return the book both to you and to the library. Let us also take the default δ_1 as $B \rightarrow Y$, the default δ_2 as $S \rightarrow L$, and the default δ_3 as $S \rightarrow Out(d_1)$, indicating respectively that borrowing the book from you favors returning it to you, that your having stolen it from the library favors returning it to the library, and that your having stolen it from the library also favors excluding δ_1 from consideration.

The first of our interpretations, my personal favorite, can then be captured through the theory $\Delta_{31} = \langle W, D \rangle$, where D contains only δ_1 and where W contains B, S and $\neg(Y \wedge L)$. The unique proper scenario based on this theory is $S_1 = \{\delta_1\}$. Here, the default δ_1 provides B, borrowing the book from you, as a reason for Y, returning it to you, which is what I ought to do; since there are no further defaults, there are no further reasons.

The second of our interpretations can be captured through the theory $\Delta_{32} = \langle W, D \rangle$, where D now contains both δ_1 and δ_2, and where W contains B, S, $\neg(Y \wedge L)$, and $d_2 \prec d_1$. The unique proper scenario based on this theory is again $S_1 = \{\delta_1\}$. In this case, however, the triggered default δ_2 now provides S, your having stolen the book, as a reason for L, returning it to the library; but this new default is defeated by the stronger δ_1, which again provides B as a reason for Y, so that Y is what I ought to do.

The third of our interpretations can be captured through the theory $\Delta_{33} = \langle W, D \rangle$, with D as before, and where W contains B, S, and $\neg(Y \wedge L)$, but no priority ordering on the defaults. This theory yields two proper scenarios, both $S_1 = \{\delta_1\}$ and $S_2 = \{\delta_2\}$. Here, both δ_1 and δ_2 are triggered in both scenarios, providing B as a reason for Y and S as a reason for L. Since there is no priority information, neither default is defeated and so there is a conflict; the two scenarios represent different ways of resolving the conflict.

The fourth of our interpretations can be captured through the theory $\Delta_{34} = \langle W, D \rangle$, depicted in Figure 6.3, with D as before, but where W contains B, S, $\neg(Y \wedge L)$, and now $d_1 \prec d_2$. This theory yields $S_2 = \{\delta_2\}$ as its unique proper scenario. Again, both δ_1 and δ_2 are triggered, providing B as a reason for Y and S as a reason for L. However, since δ_2 is now

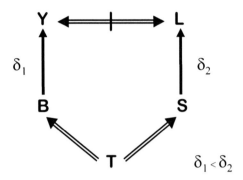

Figure 6.3: The borrowed book, fourth interpretation

assigned a higher priority than δ_1, the reason B for Y is defeated by the reason S for L, so that L is what I ought to do.

And finally, the fifth of our interpretations, Dancy's preferred reading, can be captured through the theory $\Delta_{35} = \langle \mathcal{W}, \mathcal{D} \rangle$, depicted in Figure 6.4, where $\mathcal{D}$ contains δ_1, δ_2, and now δ_3 as well, and with $\mathcal{W}$ as before. This theory yields $\mathcal{S}_3 = \{\delta_2, \delta_3\}$ as its unique proper scenario. The triggered defaults δ_2 and δ_3 assign to S a dual role, so that it functions as a reason both for L and also for $Out(d_1)$, excluding δ_1 from consideration, and this is exactly what I ought to do: return the book to the library, and ignore any favoring relation between B and Y. The default δ_1 is no longer triggered, since it is excluded, and so, just as Dancy suggests, no longer provides B as any sort of reason, even a defeated reason, for Y.

My purpose in presenting these five formalizations in detail is not just to bore the reader, though that may have been a side effect, but to show that each of our interpretations can, in fact, be represented and distinguished from the others within the framework developed here. The formal analysis of reasons facilitated by this framework thus carries benefits analogous to the benefits of formal work in other areas. By providing a precise representation of reasons and their interactions, it allows us to tease apart different interpretations of particular situations that might otherwise escape notice, to suggest new possibilities, and, where disagreement about interpretation occurs, to localize the source of that disagreement.

6.3.3   Moderate particularism

Let us return, finally, to moderate particularism, the idea that some significant part of our moral evaluation is not grounded in an appeal to general

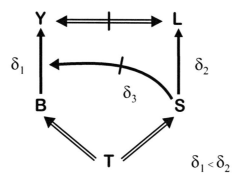

Figure 6.4: The borrowed book, fifth interpretation

principles. Once we reject Dancy's argument from reason holism to extreme particularism, why should we accept any form of particularism at all—why not suppose that our ethical reasoning is entirely based on general principles?

In fact, there is a simple argument in favor of moderate particularism. It frequently happens that the application of a finite set of principles in some particular situation yields what appears to be the wrong result, from an intuitive standpoint, and we therefore feel that these principles must themselves be revised. The phenomenon is widespread, but it is especially noticeable in three kinds of cases: first, when our principles yield conflicting oughts, yet we come to believe that the conflict can be resolved, so that the principles must be revised to reflect our resolution; second, when, even without a conflict, we come to believe that some ought generated by our principles is mistaken, so that the principles must be revised to avoid generating the offensive ought; and third, when our principles fail to yield any result at all, yet we come to believe that there is an important moral dimension to the situation, so that the principles must be revised, this time, in order to generate the desired ought.

But in cases like this—when our principles appear to yield the wrong result, and so require revision—how can we tell that the original result was wrong? It cannot be through an application of our principles, since it is these principles that led to the result we now disagree with. And what guides us as we revise our principles? Some writers have suggested that, in both recognition and revision, we appeal to a more fundamental set of principles, somehow lying in the background. Although this suggestion may be useful in many cases, as when we rely on moral principles to correct errors in a legal system, for example, there is a limit to its applicability.

As long as we admit that any finite, usable set of principles can lead to errors in moral evaluation, the appeal to still further principles for the diagnosis and repair of these errors must eventually result in either regress or circularity—which can only be avoided, therefore, if we allow for some non-principled mode of evaluation as well.

This argument depends, of course, on the assumption just stated—that, for any set of moral principles that is both finite and usable, there will be situations in which these principles yield results that seem, from an intuitive standpoint, to be mistaken. Why should we believe this? Let us define terms. By a finite set of principles, I mean a set containing only a finite number of principles, each of which is itself finite. I am less sure of what I mean, exactly, by calling a principle usable, but it is something like this: a principle that can be applied in a relatively straightforward manner. The principle must therefore involve only predicates that are uncontentious and, even if not purely descriptive, require, at least, no extensive theoretical investigation for the determination of applicability. The usability constraint thus rules out principles like "You ought to do what is right," since what is right is a contentious matter, as well as principles like "You ought to do what maximizes utility," since determining what maximizes utility can be both contentious and theoretically complex.

Given this understanding of the relevant terms, I can now offer two reasons for thinking that any finite set of usable moral principles must, at times, yield incorrect results. Neither reason is conclusive, but I think they are persuasive. The first is simply that, as far as I know, no finite and exception-free set of usable moral rules, in any reasonably rich domain, has ever been constructed.[13] The second is that, even setting aside morality, there are a variety of other normative systems in which the development of a set of authoritative rules follows exactly the course I have suggested, with procedures in place through which the results issued by these rules in particular situations are evaluated and the rules themselves then modified. Many of these normative systems are peripheral to society at large, such as the body of regulations governing the sport of American football, for example, which are reviewed each year by the National Football League Competition Committee, or the bylaws of the Takoma Park Food Coop, which can be modified by the Coop Board. Some, however, play a more central role, such as the United States Constitution, which can be amended by Congress and the state legislators, or the common law itself, which is based on a system of conventions through which the rules formulated by courts in previous cases can then be broadened, distinguished, overturned, or confirmed by later courts as they confront new situations.[14]

---

[13] If such a set of rules could be displayed, I would immediately abandon my position, of course.

[14] In related work, I have adapted the ideas set out in this book to provide an account of reasoning by precedent in common law, with case rules represented through defaults, with the reasons guiding the decisions in previous cases identified with the premises of

Of course, the standards by which rules are evaluated in these different domains—football, a food cooperative, the Constitution, common law—can vary wildly, ranging from concerns with a balance between entertainment and player safety, to concrete concerns about the creation of a harmonious society in the small, or in the large, to abstract concerns about justice or equity. What these different domains all have in common, though, is that, in each case, the standards by which the rules governing that domain are evaluated and revised generally lie outside the body of rules itself, in some broader conception of excellence appropriate to the domain, which is not necessarily well-articulated in advance and may, for all we know, not be fully-articulable. My suggestion is simply that moral principles, or at least the principles of common sense morality, may be like that as well, with some form of reasoning that is not manifestly based on principles playing an important role in their maintenance.

The general idea that a set of moral principles might need to be refined as it is applied in practice is not unfamiliar, of course; but I do feel that advocates of this idea tend to underplay the extent to which the process of refining such a set of principles requires a form of reasoning that is not itself guided by principles. This is not a position that I can defend with any care here, but I will mention two examples.

R. M. Hare, in his early work, presents a detailed picture according to which we are supposed to be guided in much of our action, moral and otherwise, by a progressively refined set of principles; he illustrates this process of refinement by noting the way in which the naive principle "Never say what is false" might be qualified to allow for some of the familiar exceptions, or the way in which the simple principle "Signal before you stop or turn the car" might be refined to yield the more subtle "Signal before you stop or turn the car, except in an emergency."[15] Hare is concerned to emphasize the cognitive, or rational, nature of this process of refinement, and writes that:

> decisions of this kind are decisions, and not, as Aristotle seems sometimes to think, exercises of a peculiar kind of perception. We *perceive*, indeed, a difference in the class of case; but we *decide* whether this difference justifies us treating it as exceptional.[16]

But here it seems fair to ask, since this decision concerns our own principles—which, we can assume, do not initially classify the case at hand as exceptional, or recommend any exceptional treatment—how, exactly, we are to recognize this case as special, and what guides us as we decide both

---

those case rules, and with precedential constraint then determined by those reasons; see Horty (2011).

[15]See especially Sections 3.6 through 4.3 of Hare (1952); the topic is also discussed throughout Chapter 3 of Hare (1963).

[16]Hare (1952, p. 54).

whether it warrants an exception and how any such exception should be
formulated. If these decisions are to be made entirely through the application of further, possibly more fundamental principles, we are again faced
either with regress or circularity—Hare himself admits, immediately following the passage just cited, that the process of modifying our principles
is "never completed." Otherwise, it is hard to avoid the conclusion that,
at some point, at least some of the decisions involved in the maintenance
and refinement of our principles will call for reasoning that is not based on
principles.

A related, but more contemporary, example is found in the work of
Henry Richardson, who is also concerned with the application of general
moral principles in particular situations.[17] Richardson argues—for broadly
Aristotelian reasons, drawing on the variability of the situations in which
we might find ourselves—that it is impossible to qualify general moral
principles so carefully that they will not clash under some circumstances
or other, leading to moral conflicts. How, then, are these conflicts to be
handled, once they arise? A common idea is that the conflicting principles
can be balanced, or weighed, against one another by some faculty of intuition, judgment, or perception. But Richardson objects to this idea on the
grounds that it is not rationally defensible. Instead, he suggests that conflicts are to be resolved by specifying, or further specifying, the principles
involved, to incorporate exceptions or further exceptions.

The central example that Richardson relies on to motivate his approach
is one in which a lawyer is required by a principle of professional conduct
to protect her client's interests by any legal means necessary, but also
required by a principle of morality not to knowingly distort the character
of a witness—and he imagines a situation in which the most effective means
available to the lawyer for protecting her client's interests would, in fact,
involve distorting the character of a witness.[18] In this case, Richardson
claims that the matter can be resolved by further qualifying the principle
of professional conduct so that it requires the lawyer, not simply to protect
her client's interests by any legal means, but to protect her client's interests
by any means that are both legal and ethical, where we can suppose that
knowingly distorting the character of a witness is not ethical.

Since Richardson, in contrast to Hare, considers only those situations in
which our principles actually conflict, he is able to avoid the question of how
we can recognize that these principles require revision; we can safely assume
that an explicit conflict among principles can be detected without appeal
either to further principles or to any special faculty of insight. But it is hard
to see how he can avoid the further question of how one particular revision
in our principles, rather than another, can be justified. In the case of
Richardson's central example, for instance, why should we not suppose that
it is the second, rather than the first, of the two conflicting principles that

---

[17]The arguments I summarize here are from Richardson (1990).

[18]Richardson's more complex example is simplified for present purposes.

requires qualification—leading, perhaps, to the more specific principle that the lawyer is required not to knowingly distort the character of a witness unless doing so would provide the most effective means for protecting her client's interests? With this modification, just as before, the formal conflict would be avoided. So what is the justification for favoring one modification over the other?

Richardson recognizes this problem, of course, and devotes a good deal of thought to the matter of defining rational constraints on the specification of moral principles. He settles, ultimately, on a "coherence standard," according to which, as he writes: "a specification is rationally defensible ... so long as it enhances the mutual support among the set of norms found acceptable on reflection."[19] I have no complaints about this proposal. And certainly I agree that it is the first, rather than the second of Richardson's two principles that should be modified, and modified in the way he suggests.

But remember, my purpose here is not to select the proper specification of our principles, or even to identify the standard through which a revision of our principles is to be evaluated, but only to make room for a moderate particularism by arguing that, whatever standard is at work, the application of this standard will involve some form of reasoning that is itself not entirely guided by principles. The appeal to coherence does not tell against this purpose. As a standard of evaluation, coherence has many virtues, but theoretical transparency is not among them: I do not know of any successful, generally applicable characterization of the conditions under which one set of principles can be classified as more coherent than another. It may well be correct, then, to define a rationally defensible specification of a set of principles as one that is found to be acceptable on reflection, but doing so does not, I believe, take us very far beyond the Aristotelian idea that the correct specification is the one that would be perceived to be right by the practically wise person.

---

[19]Richardson (1990, pp. 300, 301).

Part IV

Some complications

Chapter 7

Skepticism and floating conclusions

In the first part of this book, we set out a simple prioritized default logic and presented a theory of reasons constructed on the basis of this logic. In the second part, we saw how this default logic could serve as a foundation for two different deontic logics; and in the third, how this logic could be elaborated to allow both for reasoning about priorities and for exclusionary reasoning, and also how these elaborations could then be incorporated into our theory of reasons.

In this fourth part of the book, we now return to the simple prioritized default logic set out in the first part and consider two issues that were discussed there but left unsettled: first, the problem of characterizing skeptical reasoning in the face of multiple extensions, and second, the problem of accounting for the impact on our reasoning of the priority ordering among defaults. I focus here on these two particular issues, not because they are the only issues remaining in the development of default logic, and not, unfortunately, in order to resolve them—indeed, both problems remain open—but because I believe they hold special philosophical interest.

We begin, in this chapter, with the problem presented for the standard characterization of skeptical reasoning by the phenomenon of floating conclusions.

7.1   Floating conclusions

One of the most striking ways in which default logics can differ from classical logic, and even from standard philosophical logics, is in allowing for multiple extensions, rather than a single conclusion set. The canonical example, once again, is the Nixon Diamond—the theory $\Delta_3 = \langle \mathcal{W}, \mathcal{D}, < \rangle$, depicted in Figure 1.3, where $\mathcal{W} = \{Q, R\}$, where $\mathcal{D} = \{\delta_1, \delta_2\}$ with δ_1 and δ_2 as the defaults $Q \rightarrow P$ and $R \rightarrow \neg P$, and where the priority ordering $<$ is empty. As a reminder: Q, R, and P are the propositions that Nixon is a Quaker, a Republican, and a pacifist. In the case of this theory, as we have seen, there are two proper scenarios, $\mathcal{S}_1 = \{\delta_1\}$ and $\mathcal{S}_2 = \{\delta_2\}$. These two proper scenarios generate the two extensions $\mathcal{E}_1 = Th(\{Q, R, P\})$ and $\mathcal{E}_2 = Th(\{Q, R, \neg P\})$, one containing P, the proposition that Nixon is a pacifist, and the other containing $\neg P$, the proposition that he is not.

In our earlier discussion, from Section 1.3.1, we isolated three broad options for reasoning with default theories like this, which allow for multiple extensions. According to the first, described there as the "choice" option, the reasoner is to be thought of simply as selecting one or another of the theory's several extensions as its conclusion set—and so, in this case, either the extension $\mathcal{E}_1$, containing the proposition that Nixon is a pacifist, or the extension $\mathcal{E}_2$, containing the proposition that he is not. According to the second, described as the "credulous" option, the reasoner is to be thought of as giving some weight, either epistemic or deontic, to each proposition contained in any extension of the underlying theory—and so, in this case, both to the proposition that Nixon is a pacifist and to the proposition that he is not. According to the third, the standard version of the "skeptical" option, the reasoner is to be thought of as accepting a proposition just in case that proposition is contained in each extension of the underlying default theory—and so, in this case, rejecting both the conclusion that Nixon is a pacifist and the conclusion that Nixon is not a pacifist, since neither of these propositions is contained in both extensions.

This third option, the "proposition intersection" version of skepticism, is surely the most popular approach for reasoning with multiple extensions. My goal in this chapter, however, is to show that the intuitions underlying the general skeptical approach fragment in the presence of floating conclusions—which can be defined, very briefly, as propositions that are contained in each of a theory's various extensions, but which are supported by different, and conflicting, justifications in these different extensions. For ease of exposition, I will concentrate throughout the chapter on very simple default theories, representable as simple inference graphs, in which the justifications of propositions can then be represented as paths through these graphs. I begin, therefore, with a general discussion of justification in default logic, and with a rationale for treating paths through graphs, in certain cases, as justifications. Any reader who is willing to take this rationale on faith is invited to skim quickly through these preliminary matters, simply to fix vocabulary, and then jump at once to the substantive discussion that begins in Section 7.1.2.

7.1.1   Arguments and paths

In my initial treatment of default logic, from Chapter 1, I introduced a direct, unmediated relation between a proper scenario based on a default theory and the extension generated by that scenario. More exactly, where S is a proper scenario based on the theory $\Delta = \langle \mathcal{W}, \mathcal{D}, < \rangle$, we characterized the extension generated by this scenario, in Definition 8 from Section 1.2.2, simply as

$$\mathcal{E} = Th(\mathcal{W} \cup Conclusion(S)),$$

the set of propositions formed by combining the hard information from $\mathcal{W}$ with the conclusions of the default rules from S, and then closing the result under logical consequence.

But it is also possible, rather than moving at once from proper scenarios to the extensions they generate, to pause at an intermediate stage in which the propositions belonging to extensions are associated with the justifications that support them. What are these justifications? It is natural to take them as *defeasible arguments*, where a defeasible argument constructed from a scenario S is like a proof in ordinary logic, except that it allows for appeal, not just to the usual rules of logic, but also to the special default rules belonging to S.

Let us be precise. Ordinary propositional logic is often formulated as an axiomatic system containing a number of axioms, but with modus ponens as its sole rule of inference. Against the background of this formulation, a proof, originating from a set $\mathcal{W}$ of assumptions, is then defined as a sequence $X_1, X_2, \ldots, X_n$ of propositions such that each member X_i of the sequence satisfies one of the following conditions: (1) X_i is one of the axioms of propositional logic; (2) X_i belongs to the set $\mathcal{W}$ of assumptions; or (3) X_i follows from previous members of the sequence by modus ponens, the unique rule of inference.[1] Working with this same formulation of propositional logic, then, a defeasible argument from $\mathcal{W}$ can be characterized simply by relaxing the standard definition of a proof so that it allows later members of the sequence to follow from previous members, not just by modus ponens, but by appropriate default rules as well.

Definition 19 (Defeasible arguments) Where S is a set of default rules and $\mathcal{W}$ is a set of propositions, a defeasible argument, originating from $\mathcal{W}$ and constructed from S, is a sequence of propositions $X_1, X_2, \ldots, X_n$ such that each member X_i of the sequence satisfies one of the following conditions: (1) X_i is an axiom of propositional logic; (2) X_i belongs to $\mathcal{W}$; (3) X_i follows from previous members of the sequence by modus ponens; or (4) there is some default δ from S such that $Conclusion(\delta)$ is X_i and $Premise(\delta)$ is a previous member of the sequence.

This concept of a defeasible argument can be illustrated by returning to the Nixon Diamond, with $\mathcal{W} = \{Q, R\}$ as its hard information, and considering the scenario $S_1 = \{\delta_1\}$ based on this theory, where δ_1 is the default $Q \rightarrow P$. According to our definition, the simple two-member sequence Q, P is a defeasible argument, originating from $\mathcal{W}$ and constructed

---

[1] This definition of a proof occurs in nearly every introduction to modern logic, but a canonical formulation can be found in Chapter 2 of the classic text by Alonzo Church (1956).

from S_1, since Q belongs to W and P follows from Q by the default rule δ_1, which is contained in S_1.

Earlier, toward the beginning of Chapter 1, we defined the *Conclusion* function so that it picks out the conclusion of a default rule, given that default rule as an argument, or the set of conclusions belonging to a set of default rules, given that set as argument. We can now overload this notation so that *Conclusion* also picks out the final proposition in an argument as its conclusion, and likewise the set of conclusions of a set of arguments. More exactly, where α is an argument of the form $X_1, X_2, \ldots, X_n$, then *Conclusion*(α) is X_n, and where Φ is some set of arguments, then *Conclusion*(Φ) is the set of conclusions of the arguments belonging to Φ.

Having defined the notion of a defeasible argument, originating from a set of propositions W and constructed from a scenario S, let us take *Argument*$_W(S)$ as the entire set of such arguments—the entire collection of arguments from W based on S. We can then define an *argument extension* of a default theory as a set of arguments originating from the hard information in that theory and constructed from one of its proper scenarios.

Definition 20 (Argument extensions) Let $\Delta = \langle W, D, < \rangle$ be a fixed priority default theory. Then Φ is an argument extension of Δ just in case, for some proper scenario S based on this theory,

$$\Phi = Argument_W(S).$$

These new extensions are described as "argument" extensions in order to distinguish them from the ordinary extensions introduced earlier—which will now be referred to as "proposition" extensions when there is any possibility of confusion. But of course, the two concepts are related, and related in the natural way: the set of conclusions of any argument extension of a default theory is a proposition extension of that theory. This observation can be put formally by noting that, where $\Delta = \langle W, D, < \rangle$ is a default theory and S is a proper scenario based on that theory, then

$$Conclusion(Argument_W(S)) = Th(W \cup Conclusion(S));$$

here, the inclusion from left to right is obvious, while the more difficult inclusion, from right to left, is established as Theorem 2 in Appendix A.1.[2]

The goal, thus far, has been to introduce a new notion of an argument extension in which supported propositions are explicitly associated with the justifications that support them. This has now been accomplished, and in some generality. The generality is desirable, of course, but it can also make it difficult to visualize or reason about the resulting structures, which

---

[2] Note that the verification of this right to left inclusion requires our more general definition of proper scenarios, itself to be supplied in Definition 27 from Appendix A.1; the inclusion fails to hold if we rely only on the preliminary definition presented earlier, in Definition 7 from Section 1.2.2.

are both large and, in some sense, full of unnecessary information (each argument extension will contain every proof of every classical tautology, for example). For the sake of simplicity, then—and even though the issues surrounding floating conclusions could, in fact, be introduced in terms of the general argument extensions already before us—I will concentrate here on a class of elementary default theories, representable by simple inference graphs, in which all the important arguments are linear, and can therefore be represented as paths through these inference graphs.

To be precise, let us define a *chain* as a sequence of positive strict or defeasible links, of the form $X \Rightarrow Y$ or $X \rightarrow Y$, subject to the constraint that the conclusion of each link in the chain matches the premise of its successor; thus, for example, the sequence $X \rightarrow Y$, $Y \Rightarrow Z$, $Z \rightarrow \neg W$ is a chain, which we can write with the matched propositions merged as $X \rightarrow Y \Rightarrow Z \rightarrow \neg W$, while the sequence $X \rightarrow Y$, $Z \rightarrow \neg W$ is not a chain. An *argument path*, then, is simply a chain beginning with the special proposition $\top$. Such a path can represent an argument, of a very restricted form, with the final displayed proposition on the path as its conclusion. As an abstract example, the argument path $\top \Rightarrow X \rightarrow Y \Rightarrow \neg Z$ represents an argument of the form "X is true, which defeasibly implies Y, which strictly implies $\neg Z$," supporting the conclusion $\neg Z$. As a less abstract example, the path $\top \Rightarrow Q \rightarrow P$ can be taken as the argument that Nixon is a Quaker and so a pacifist, while the path $\top \Rightarrow R \rightarrow \neg P$ can be taken as the argument that Nixon is a Republican and so not a pacifist.

Since argument paths—like default rules, and like full-fledged defeasible arguments—also have conclusions, we can overload the *Conclusion* function still further so that, if α is an argument path, then $Conclusion(\alpha)$ is the conclusion of that path, and if Φ is a set of argument paths, then $Conclusion(\Phi)$ is the set of their conclusions.

Where $\mathcal{S}$ is a scenario based on the default theory $\Delta = \langle \mathcal{W}, \mathcal{D}, < \rangle$, let us say that an argument path α is *constructed from* $\mathcal{S}$ just in case: (1) for every defeasible link $X \rightarrow Y$ from the path α, there is a default δ of the form $X \rightarrow Y$ belonging to $\mathcal{S}$, and (2) for every strict link $X \Rightarrow Y$ from α, it follows from the hard information $\mathcal{W}$ belonging to the underlying default theory that X implies Y—or more formally, that $\mathcal{W} \vdash X \supset Y$. If we suppose that $\mathcal{S}$ is, not just any scenario, but a proper scenario based on the underlying theory Δ, we can then define a *path extension* of this theory as a set Φ of argument paths constructed from $\mathcal{S}$ subject to the further conditions that: (3) for each default δ belonging to $\mathcal{S}$, there is some argument path in Φ with δ as its terminal link, so that the conclusion of that path is the conclusion of δ, and (4) for each proposition X belonging to the set $\mathcal{W}$ of hard information from the underlying theory, there is likewise some argument path in Φ with X as its conclusion.

It can be verified—and I will spare the reader—that for default theories of the elementary sort considered in this chapter, the conclusion set supported by any path extension constructed from a proper scenario will have, as its logical closure, the ordinary proposition extension generated by that scenario.

These various concepts can be illustrated through the Nixon Diamond, again—the theory $\Delta_3 = \langle \mathcal{W}, \mathcal{D}, < \rangle$, depicted in Figure 1.3, where $\mathcal{W} = \{Q, R\}$, where $\mathcal{D} = \{\delta_1, \delta_2\}$ with δ_1 and δ_2 as the defaults $Q \rightarrow P$ and $R \rightarrow \neg P$, and where $<$ is empty. Here, as we know, there are two proper scenarios, $\mathcal{S}_1 = \{\delta_1\}$ and $\mathcal{S}_2 = \{\delta_2\}$, from which we can now construct the respective path extensions

$$\Phi_1 = \{ \top \Rightarrow Q, \ \top \Rightarrow R, \ \top \Rightarrow Q \rightarrow P \},$$
$$\Phi_2 = \{ \top \Rightarrow Q, \ \top \Rightarrow R, \ \top \Rightarrow R \rightarrow \neg P \},$$

one containing the argument path that moves up the left side of the diamond, the other containing the argument path that moves up the right side. The reader is invited to note that each of these two extensions contains only paths that are constructed from the corresponding proper scenarios, in the sense given by the previous conditions (1) and (2), and also that each is indeed a path extension in the sense of (3) and (4), containing individual paths supporting the conclusions of each default from the corresponding proper scenario, as well as each proposition from the underlying set of facts. These two path extensions support the conclusion sets $\mathcal{E}_1 = \{Q, R, P\}$ and $\mathcal{E}_2 = \{Q, R, \neg P\}$, respectively, which then have as their respective logical closures the familiar proposition extensions for the underlying default theory.

Once again, not every default theory can be analyzed in this way, through path extensions; some are too complex for the relevant defeasible arguments to be representable by linear paths alone. But as long as we are willing to confine our attention to sufficiently elementary theories, as we do in this chapter, path extensions provide a convenient intermediary between ordinary proposition extensions, which contain supported propositions but not their justifications, and full argument extensions, which do contain justifications but at the cost of considerable complexity. Path extensions are simple, often finite, and can be constructed to contain justifications for the propositions that concern us and little more.

7.1.2   Two versions of skepticism

Having considered how justifications can be worked into default logic, and associated with the propositions belonging to extensions or their surrogates, let us now return to the idea, generally described as "skeptical," that the way to arrive at a unique conclusion set in the face of multiple extensions is by, somehow, intersecting the information contained in these various extensions. Previously, when we were working directly with proposition extensions—that is, with sets of propositions alone as extensions—there was really only one way of implementing this idea: by intersecting the various extensions themselves, to arrive at the set of propositions contained in each. Suppose, however, that we now work with path extensions—that is, with sets of argument paths as extensions—so that each proposition supported by an extension is associated with an argument path that provides its justification. And suppose, in particular, that our goal is to get from a multitude of such path extensions to a single set of propositions, taken to represent the core conclusions of a reasoning agent, and from which a full belief set can then be derived by ordinary logic. In that case, there are two distinct options for implementing the general policy of constructing a unique set of core conclusions by intersecting the information contained in the different path extensions.

We might decide, first of all, that the reasoning agent should endorse an argument path just in case it is contained in each path extension associated with an underlying default theory, and then endorse a conclusion just in case that conclusion is supported by an endorsed argument path. More exactly, if we suppose that the underlying theory is Δ, then this first, or *argument intersection*, option leads to the suggestion that the appropriate core conclusion set should be defined as

$$Conclusion(\bigcap\{\Phi : \Phi \text{ is a path extension of } \Delta\}),$$

where, of course, $\bigcap$ is the function that maps a set of sets into the intersection of its members. Or second, we might decide that the agent should endorse a conclusion just in case that conclusion is itself supported by each of the original path extensions. This *conclusion intersection* option leads to the suggestion that the appropriate core conclusion set should instead be defined as

$$\bigcap\{Conclusion(\Phi) : \Phi \text{ is a path extension of } \Delta\},$$

where the order of the conclusion function *Conclusion* and the intersection function $\bigcap$ is reversed. According to the argument intersection option, then, the agent first intersects the various path extensions to get the set of argument paths common to each, and then projects this set of common arguments onto the set of conclusions they support; according to the conclusion intersection option, the agent first projects each of the various path extensions onto the set of conclusions supported by the argument paths in that extension, and then intersects the resulting conclusion sets.

These two options for implementing the skeptical policy—argument intersection, conclusion intersection—often come to the same thing, as they do with the standard Nixon Diamond, whose path extensions were displayed previously. Here, as the reader can verify, both options lead to $\mathcal{E} = \{Q, R\}$ as the appropriate core conclusion set. But there are other situations in which the two options yield different results. A well-known example, due to Matthew Ginsberg, is the theory $\Delta_{36} = \langle \mathcal{W}, \mathcal{D}, < \rangle$, depicted in Figure 7.1, where $\mathcal{W} = \{Q, R, D \supset E, H \supset E, \neg(D \wedge H)\}$, where $\mathcal{D} = \{\delta_1, \delta_2\}$ with δ_1 as $Q \rightarrow D$ and δ_2 as $R \rightarrow H$, and where $<$ is empty.

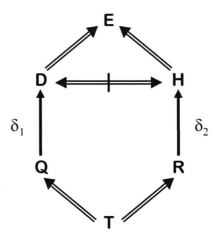

Figure 7.1: Is Nixon politically extreme?

Ginsberg's example is a variant of the Nixon Diamond, with Q and R as the familiar propositions that Nixon is a Quaker and a Republican, and with D, H, and E as the new propositions that Nixon is, respectively, a dove, a hawk, and politically extreme (regarding the appropriate use of military force). What the theory tells us, then, is that Nixon is both a Quaker and a Republican, that there is good reason to suppose that Nixon is a dove if he is a Quaker, a hawk if he is a Republican, that he cannot be both a dove and a hawk, but that he is politically extreme if he is either a dove or a hawk.

It is easy to see that this theory allows two proper scenarios, $\mathcal{S}_1 = \{\delta_1\}$ and $\mathcal{S}_2 = \{\delta_2\}$, leading to the two path extensions

$$
\begin{aligned}
\Phi_1 \;=\; \{\; & \top \Rightarrow Q,\ \top \Rightarrow R, \\
& \top \Rightarrow D \supset E,\ \top \Rightarrow H \supset E, \\
& \top \Rightarrow \neg(D \wedge H), \\
& \top \Rightarrow Q \rightarrow D, \\
& \top \Rightarrow Q \rightarrow D \Rightarrow \neg H, \\
& \top \Rightarrow Q \rightarrow D \Rightarrow E \;\},
\end{aligned}
$$

$$
\begin{aligned}
\Phi_2 \;=\; \{\; & \top \Rightarrow Q,\ \top \Rightarrow R, \\
& \top \Rightarrow D \supset E,\ \top \Rightarrow H \supset E, \\
& \top \Rightarrow \neg(D \wedge H), \\
& \top \Rightarrow R \rightarrow H, \\
& \top \Rightarrow R \rightarrow H \Rightarrow \neg D, \\
& \top \Rightarrow R \rightarrow H \Rightarrow E \;\}.
\end{aligned}
$$

The first five paths in each of these extensions are nothing but trivial arguments justifying the five propositions that already belong to the underlying
set of hard information, and hold little interest. In each case, though, the
next three paths do represent interesting arguments constructible from the
two proper scenarios. These arguments support, in the case of Φ_1, the conclusions that Nixon is a dove, and so not a hawk, but politically extreme,
and in the case of Φ_2, the conclusions that Nixon is a hawk, and so not a
dove, but still politically extreme.

Since no paths except those representing the trivial arguments are contained in both Φ_1 and Φ_2, the argument intersection option for implementing the general skeptical policy leads to

$$\Phi_3 \;=\; \{\; \top \Rightarrow Q, \;\; \top \Rightarrow R,$$
$$\top \Rightarrow D \supset E, \;\; \top \Rightarrow H \supset E,$$
$$\top \Rightarrow \neg(D \wedge H) \;\}$$

as the intersection of these extensions, and so to $\mathcal{E}_3 = \mathcal{W}$, the set of conclusions of the paths belonging to this intersection, as the appropriate core
conclusion set, containing nothing beyond our initial information. According to the conclusion intersection option, by contrast, we begin by projecting the two extensions Φ_1 and Φ_2 to their individual conclusion sets,
$\mathcal{E}_1 = \mathcal{W} \cup \{D, \neg H, E\}$ and $\mathcal{E}_2 = \mathcal{W} \cup \{H, \neg D, E\}$, and then intersecting
these conclusion sets to reach $\mathcal{E}_4 = \mathcal{W} \cup \{E\}$ as the appropriate core conclusions set, now containing, not just the initial information from $\mathcal{W}$, but
the further conclusion E, that Nixon is politically extreme.

Why is the proposition E in $\mathcal{E}_4$ but not in $\mathcal{E}_3$? Because, although
this proposition is supported in each of the original path extensions, Φ_1
and Φ_2, it is supported by different argument paths in each—by the path
$\top \Rightarrow Q \rightarrow D \Rightarrow E$ in Φ_1, by the path $\top \Rightarrow R \rightarrow H \Rightarrow E$ in Φ_2—neither of
which, therefore, is contained in the intersection of the two path extensions.
Propositions like this, which are supported in each path extension of an
underlying default theory, but only by different arguments, are known as
floating conclusions. The phrase, coined by David Makinson and Karl
Schlechta, nicely captures the picture of these conclusions as floating above
the different, and conflicting, arguments that might be taken to support
them.[3]

The phenomenon of floating conclusions was first investigated in the
context of path-based reasoning in inference graphs, particularly in connection with the theory developed by Richmond Thomason, David Touretzky,
and myself.[4] In contrast to the accounts considered in this book, which
allow for multiple extensions, from which a skeptical result is then supposed to be defined through some form of intersection, that theory defined
a single path extension directly. This single path extension was thought of

---

[3]See Makinson and Schlechta (1991).
[4]See Horty, Thomason, and Touretzky (1990) for the canonical formulation.

as containing the skeptically acceptable argument paths based on a given inference graph; the skeptical conclusions based on that inference graph were then identified with the statements supported by those skeptically acceptable argument paths.

Ginsberg's political extremist example was meant to show, by means of the following argument, that no "directly skeptical" approach of this sort, relying only on a single path extension, could correctly represent skeptical reasoning. First, a single path extension could not consistently contain both the argument paths $\top \Rightarrow Q \to D \Rightarrow E$ and $\top \Rightarrow R \to H \Rightarrow E$, since path extensions are naturally thought of as closed under subpaths, and the two propositions D and H, that Nixon is a dove and a hawk, are inconsistent. Second, a single path extension could not contain either of these argument paths without the other, since the decision to favor either the path through D or the path through H would be arbitrary. And third, if a single path extension failed to contain either of these two argument paths, it would likewise fail to support the conclusion E, which Ginsberg considers to be an intuitive consequence of the initial information from the default theory: "given that both hawks and doves are politically [extreme], Nixon certainly should be as well."[5]

Both Makinson and Schlechta, as well as Lynn Stein and Pollock, have likewise considered floating conclusions in the context of defeasible inference graphs. Makinson and Schlechta share Ginsberg's view that the appropriate conclusions to derive from a graphical default theory are those supported by each of its path extensions:

> It is an oversimplification to take a proposition A as acceptable ... iff it is supported by some path α in the intersection of all extensions. Instead, A must be taken as acceptable iff it is in the intersection of all *outputs* of extensions, where the output of an extension is the set of all propositions supported by some path within it.[6]

From this they argue, not only that the particular theory developed by Thomason, Touretzky, and myself is incorrect, but more generally, that any theory attempting to define the skeptically acceptable conclusions by reference to a single set of acceptable arguments will be mistaken. Stein reaches a similar judgment, for similar reasons:

> The difficulty lies in the fact that some conclusions may be true in every credulous extension, but supported by different paths in each. Any path-based theory must either accept one of these paths—and be unsound, since such a path is not in

---

[5] See Ginsberg (1993, p. 221); the example was first published in this textbook, but it had been part of the oral tradition for many years.

[6] Makinson and Schlechta (1991, pp. 201–204).

every extension—or reject all such paths—and with them the ideally skeptical conclusion, and be incomplete.[7]

And, as it turns out, Pollock explicitly tailored his most important and influential system of defeasible reasoning so that it guarantees the acceptability of floating conclusions.[8]

What lies behind these various criticisms and constructions is the assumption, widely held in the nonmonotonic reasoning community, that the second, rather than the first, of our two skeptical options is correct—conclusion intersection, rather than argument intersection—so that floating conclusions should be accepted, and a system that fails to classify them among the consequences of a default theory is therefore in error. My goal in this chapter is to cast doubt on that assumption.

7.2 The problem with floating conclusions

7.2.1 An example

Why not accept floating conclusions? Their precarious status can be illustrated through any number of examples, but we might as well choose a dramatic one.[9]

Suppose, then, that my parents have a net worth of one million dollars, but that they have divided their assets in order to avoid an inheritance tax, so that each parent currently possesses half a million dollars apiece. And suppose that, because of their simultaneous exposure to a fatal disease, it is now settled that both of my parents will shortly pass away. This is a fact: medical science is certain.

Imagine also, however, that there is some expensive item—a yacht, say—whose purchase I believe would help to soften the blow of my impending loss. Although the yacht I want is currently available, the price is low enough that it is sure to be sold by the end of the month. I can now reserve the yacht for myself by putting down a large deposit, with the balance due within half a year. But there is no way I can afford to pay off the balance unless I happen to inherit at least half a million dollars from my parents within that period; and if I fail to pay the balance on time, I will lose my large deposit. Setting aside any doubts concerning the real depth of my grief, let us suppose that my utilities determine the following conditional preferences: if I believe I will inherit half a million dollars from

---

[7]Stein (1992, p. 204).

[8]The system is that of Pollock (1995). Although it is easy to see that this system does, in fact, allow for floating conclusions, it was not clear to me that supporting floating conclusions was one of Pollock's explicit goals until I read his (2007, pp. 12–14), where he discusses the ways in which he had to modify the original idea underlying this system in order to guarantee their acceptability.

[9]This example was developed in conjunction with Tamara Horowitz.

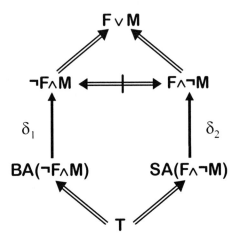

Figure 7.2: Should I buy the yacht?

my parents within six weeks, it is very much in my benefit to place a deposit on the yacht; if I do not believe this, it is very much in my benefit not to place the deposit.

Now suppose I have a brother and a sister, both of whom are extraordinarily reliable as sources of information. Neither has ever been known to be mistaken, to deceive, or even to misspeak—although of course, like nearly any source of information, they must be regarded as defeasible. My brother and sister have both talked with our parents about their estate plans, and feel that they understand the situation. I have written to each of them describing my delicate predicament regarding the yacht, and receive letters back. My brother writes: "Father is going to leave his money to me, but Mother will leave her money to you." My sister writes: "Mother is going to leave her money to me, but Father will leave his money to you." No further information is now available: the wills are sealed, my brother and sister are trekking together through the Andes, and our parents, unfortunately, have each slipped into a coma.

Based on my current information, what should I conclude? Should I form the belief that I will inherit half a million dollars—and therefore place a large deposit on the yacht—or not?

Suppose that: F is the proposition that I will inherit half a million dollars from my father, M is the proposition that I will inherit half a million dollars from my mother, $BA(\neg F \wedge M)$ is the proposition that my brother asserts that I will inherit my mother's money but not my father's, and $SA(F \wedge \neg M)$ is the proposition that my sister asserts that I will inherit my father's money but not my mother's. The situation can then be represented through the default theory $\Delta_{37} = \langle \mathcal{W}, \mathcal{D}, < \rangle$, where $\mathcal{W} = \{BA(\neg F \wedge M),$ $SA(F \wedge \neg M)\}$, where $\mathcal{D} = \{\delta_1, \delta_2\}$ with δ_1 as $BA(\neg F \wedge M) \rightarrow \neg F \wedge M$ and δ_2 as $SA(F \wedge \neg M) \rightarrow F \wedge \neg M$, and where $<$ is empty. The hard information from $\mathcal{W}$, then, records the facts of my brother's and sister's assertions, while δ_1 and δ_2 can be seen as instances of general defaults according to which any assertion by my brother or sister provides good reason for concluding that the content of that assertion is true. This theory is depicted in Figure 7.2, where the other strict links simply reflect various logical implications and inconsistencies. Notice that, although the contents of my brother's and sister's assertions—the propositions $\neg F \wedge M$ and $F \wedge \neg M$—are jointly inconsistent, the truth of either entails the disjunctive claim $F \vee M$, which is, of course, all I really care about. As long as I can conclude that I will inherit half a million dollars from either my father or my mother, I should go ahead and place a deposit on the yacht.

This theory again allows two proper scenarios, $\mathcal{S}_1 = \{\delta_1\}$ and $\mathcal{S}_2 = \{\delta_2\}$, leading to the two path extensions

$$
\begin{aligned}
\Phi_1 \;=\; \{\; &\top \Rightarrow BA(\neg F \wedge M), \\
&\top \Rightarrow SA(F \wedge \neg M), \\
&\top \Rightarrow BA(\neg F \wedge M) \rightarrow \neg F \wedge M, \\
&\top \Rightarrow BA(\neg F \wedge M) \rightarrow \neg F \wedge M \Rightarrow \neg(F \wedge \neg M), \\
&\top \Rightarrow BA(\neg F \wedge M) \rightarrow \neg F \wedge M \Rightarrow F \vee M \;\},
\end{aligned}
$$

$$
\begin{aligned}
\Phi_2 \;=\; \{\; &\top \Rightarrow BA(\neg F \wedge M), \\
&\top \Rightarrow SA(F \wedge \neg M), \\
&\top \Rightarrow SA(F \wedge \neg M) \rightarrow F \wedge \neg M, \\
&\top \Rightarrow SA(F \wedge \neg M) \rightarrow F \wedge \neg M \Rightarrow \neg(\neg F \wedge M), \\
&\top \Rightarrow SA(F \wedge \neg M) \rightarrow F \wedge \neg M \Rightarrow F \vee M \;\}.
\end{aligned}
$$

Just as in Ginsberg's political extremist example, the argument intersection option for implementing the skeptical reasoning policy would lead to

$$
\Phi_3 \;=\; \{\; \top \Rightarrow BA(\neg F \wedge M), \\
\top \Rightarrow SA(F \wedge \neg M) \;\}
$$

as the intersection of these two path extensions, Φ_1 and Φ_2, and then to $\mathcal{E}_3 = \mathcal{W}$ as the core conclusion set supported by this intersection, thus telling me nothing beyond the original information that my brother and sister asserted what they did. And again, the conclusion intersection option would begin by projecting Φ_1 and Φ_2 to their individual conclusion sets

$$
\begin{aligned}
\mathcal{E}_1 \;&=\; \mathcal{W} \cup \{\neg F \wedge M, \neg(F \wedge \neg M), F \vee M\}, \\
\mathcal{E}_2 \;&=\; \mathcal{W} \cup \{F \wedge \neg M, \neg(\neg F \wedge M), F \vee M\},
\end{aligned}
$$

and then continue by intersecting these sets to reach $\mathcal{E}_4 = \mathcal{W} \cup \{F \vee M\}$ as the appropriate result. Since each of the initial path extensions contains some argument supporting the proposition $F \vee M$, this second option would thus tell me—as a floating conclusion—that I will inherit half a million dollars from either my father or my mother.

In this situation, then, there is a vivid practical difference between the two skeptical options. If I were to reason according to the first, I would not be justified in concluding that I am about to inherit half a million dollars, and so it would be foolish for me to place a deposit on the yacht. If I were to reason according to the second, I would be justified in drawing this conclusion, and so it would be foolish for me not to place a deposit.

Which option is correct? I have not done a formal survey, but most of the people to whom I have presented this example are suspicious of the floating conclusion, and so favor the argument intersection option. Most do not feel that the initial information from the default theory would provide sufficient justification for me to conclude, as the basis for an important decision, that I will inherit half a million dollars. Certainly, this is my own opinion—I believe the example shows, contrary to the widely held assumption, that it is at least coherent for a skeptical reasoner to withhold judgment from floating conclusions. Although both my brother and sister are reliable, and each supports the conclusion that I will inherit half a million dollars, the support provided by each of these reliable sources is undermined by that provided by the other; there is no argument for the conclusion that does not involve appeal to some proposition that is opposed with no less strength than it is supported. Since either my brother or sister must be wrong, it is possible to imagine that they might both be wrong, and wrong in this way: perhaps my father will leave his money to my brother and my mother will leave her money to my sister, so that I will inherit nothing.

In case this example does not yet seem sufficient as an objection to floating conclusions, it might help to consider the information it presents in stages. So suppose I had written, at first, only to my brother, and received his response—that my father had named him as sole beneficiary, but that my mother would leave her money to me. That is, suppose my starting point is the information depicted in the left-hand side of Figure 7.2. In this new situation, should I conclude that I will inherit half a million dollars, and therefore place a deposit on the yacht?

Some might say no—that even in this simplified situation I should not make such an important decision on the basis of my brother's word alone. But this objection misses the point. Most of what we know, we know through sources of information that are, in fact, defeasible. By hypothesis, we can suppose that my brother is arbitrarily reliable, as reliable as any defeasible source of information could possibly be—as reliable as perception, for instance, or the bank officer's word that the money has actually been deposited in my account. If we were to reject information like this, it is hard to see how we could get by in the world at all. When a source of defeasible information that is, by hypothesis, arbitrarily reliable tells me that I will inherit half a million dollars, and there is no conflicting evidence in sight, it is reasonable for me to accept this statement, and to act on it. Note that both of the two skeptical options yield this outcome in our simplified situation, since the initial information, represented by the left-hand side of Figure 7.2, generates only a single path extension, in which the conclusion that I will inherit half a million dollars is supported by a single argument.

Now suppose that, at this point, I hear from my equally reliable sister with her conflicting information—that she is my mother's beneficiary, but that my father will leave his money to me. As a result, I am again in the situation depicted in the full Figure 7.2, with two path extensions, and in which the statement that I will inherit half a million dollars is supported only as a floating conclusion. Ask yourself: should my confidence in the statement that I will inherit half a million dollars be weaker in this new situation, now that I have heard from my sister as well as my brother? If it seems that my confidence can legitimately be diminished—that this new information casts any additional doubt on the outcome—then it follows that floating conclusions are somewhat less secure than conclusions that are uniformly supported by a common argument. And that is all we need. The point is not that floating conclusions might be wrong; any conclusion drawn through defeasible reasoning might be wrong. The point is that a statement supported only as a floating conclusion is less secure than the same statement when it is uniformly supported by a common argument. As long as there is this difference in principle, it is coherent to imagine a skeptical reasoner whose standards are calibrated so as to accept propositions that receive uniform support, but to reject propositions that are supported only by different, and conflicting, arguments in different extensions.

7.2.2 Objections to the example

I have heard two objections worth noting to the yacht example as an argument for rejecting the conclusion intersection option—the standard option, that is, of defining the skeptical outcome of a theory by intersecting only the conclusion sets supported by that theory's various path extensions.

The first objection focuses on the underlying methodology of logical formalization. Even though what my brother literally said is, "Father is going to leave his money to me, but Mother will leave her money to you," one might argue that the actual content of his statement is better conveyed through the two separate sentences "Father is going to leave his money to me" and "Mother will leave her money to you." In that case, rather than treating the content of my brother's assertion as the single, conjunctive proposition $\neg F \wedge M$, it would be more natural to treat it as two separate propositions, $\neg F$ and M; and the content of my sister's assertion could likewise be taken as the separate propositions F and $\neg M$.

Since the conclusion intersection option, which ignores justifications, yields the same results as ordinary default logic, from which justifications are absent, the easiest way to understand the effects of this proposed reformulation is to consider it from the standpoint of default logic. The situation could then be represented through the new default theory $\Delta_{38} = \langle \mathcal{W}, \mathcal{D}, < \rangle$, in which $\mathcal{W}$ contains the four propositions $BA(\neg F)$, $BA(M)$, $SA(F)$, and $SA(\neg M)$, describing what now appear to be the four independent assertions made by my brother and sister, in which $\mathcal{D}$ contains the defaults δ_1, δ_2, δ_3, and δ_4, with δ_1 as $BA(\neg F) \to \neg F$, with δ_2 as $BA(M) \to M$, with δ_3 as $SA(F) \to F$, and with δ_4 as $SA(\neg M) \to \neg M$, and in which $<$ is empty. There would then be four proper scenarios based on this new theory—$\mathcal{S}_1 = \{\delta_1, \delta_2\}$, $\mathcal{S}_2 = \{\delta_1, \delta_4\}$, $\mathcal{S}_3 = \{\delta_2, \delta_3\}$, and $\mathcal{S}_4 = \{\delta_3, \delta_4\}$—leading to four proposition extensions:

$$
\begin{aligned}
\mathcal{E}_1 &= Th(\mathcal{W} \cup \{\neg F, M\}), \\
\mathcal{E}_2 &= Th(\mathcal{W} \cup \{\neg F, \neg M\}), \\
\mathcal{E}_3 &= Th(\mathcal{W} \cup \{F, M\}), \\
\mathcal{E}_4 &= Th(\mathcal{W} \cup \{F, \neg M\}).
\end{aligned}
$$

Since not all of these extensions contain the statement $F \vee M$, their intersection no longer leads, in this case, to the problematic conclusion that I will inherit half a million dollars.

The idea behind this objection is that the problems presented by floating conclusions might be avoided if we were to adopt a different strategy for formalizing the statements taken as inputs by the logical system, which would involve, among other things, articulating conjunctive inputs into their conjuncts. This idea is interesting, has some collateral benefits, and bears affinities to proposals that have been suggested in other contexts.[10] Nevertheless, in the present setting, the strategy of factoring conjunctive statements into their conjuncts in order to avoid undesirable

---

[10] Imagine, for example, that my brother asserts a statement of the form $P \wedge Q$, where it turns out that P is a logical contradiction—perhaps a false mathematical statement—but Q expresses a perfectly sensible proposition that just happens to be conjoined with P for reasons of conversational economy. And suppose this situation were represented in the most natural way, through the default theory $\Delta_{39} = \langle \mathcal{W}, \mathcal{D}, < \rangle$, where $\mathcal{W}$ contains $BA(P \wedge Q)$, where $\mathcal{D}$ contains δ_1, with δ_1 as $BA(P \wedge Q) \to P \wedge Q$, and where $<$ is empty. In that case, the theory would have as its extension only $\mathcal{E}_1 = Th(\mathcal{W})$, allowing us to conclude neither P nor Q, since the default δ_1 would be conflicted in every scenario. But if the situation were represented instead through the articulated theory $\Delta_{40} = \langle \mathcal{W}, \mathcal{D}, < \rangle$ in which $\mathcal{W}$ contains $BA(P)$ and $BA(Q)$, and in which $\mathcal{D}$ contains δ_2 and δ_3, with δ_2 as $BA(P) \to P$ and δ_3 as $BA(Q) \to Q$, the resulting extension would then be $\mathcal{E}_2 = Th(\mathcal{W} \cup \{Q\})$—allowing us the benefit of concluding Q, at least, in spite of its incidental affiliation with P in my brother's statement. This idea of articulating premises into simpler components, in order to draw the maximum amount of information out of a set of input statements without actually reaching contradictory conclusions, has also been studied in the context of relevance logic; a proposal along these lines was originally formulated by Belnap (1979) and then refined by Alan Anderson, Belnap, and Michael Dunn (1992, Section 82.4).

floating conclusions suggests a procedure that might be described as "wishful formalization"—carefully tailoring the inputs to a logical system so that the system then yields the desired outputs. Ideally, a logic should take as its inputs formulas conforming as closely as possible to the natural language premises provided by a situation, and then the logic itself should tell us what conclusions follow from those premises. Any time we are forced to adopt a less straightforward representation of the input premises in order to avoid inappropriate conclusions—replacing conjunctions with their conjuncts, for example—we are backing away from that ideal. By tailoring the inputs in order to assure certain outputs, we are doing some work for the logic that, in the ideal case, the logic should be doing for us.

The second objection to the yacht example as an argument against floating conclusions concerns the method for evaluating supported statements. Part of what makes this example convincing as a reason for rejecting the floating conclusion that I will inherit half a million dollars is the fact that it is developed within the context of an important practical decision, where an error carries significant consequences: I will lose my large deposit. But what if the consequences were less significant? Suppose the deposit were trivial: one dollar, say. In that case, many people would then argue that the support provided for the proposition that I will inherit half a million dollars—even as a floating conclusion—would be sufficient, when balanced against the possibility for gain, to justify the risk of losing my small deposit. The general idea behind this objection is that the proper notion of consequence in defeasible reasoning is sensitive to the risk of being wrong. The evaluation of a logic for defeasible reasoning cannot—so the argument goes—be made outside of some particular decision-theoretic setting, with particular costs assigned to errors; and there are certain settings in which the cost of error may be small enough that we might well want to act even on the basis of propositions supported only as floating conclusions.

This is an intriguing objection. I will point out only that, if accepted, it suggests a major revision in our attitude toward nonmonotonic logics. Traditionally, a logic—unlike a system for probabilistic or evidential reasoning—is thought to classify statements into only two categories: those that follow from some set of premises, and those that do not. The force of this objection is that nonmonotonic logics should be viewed, instead, as placing statements into several categories, depending on the degree to which they are supported by a set of premises, with floating conclusions then classified, not necessarily as unsupported, but perhaps only as less firmly supported than statements that are justified by the same argument in every extension.

7.3   Discussion

7.3.1   Other examples

Once the structure of the yacht example is understood, it is easy to construct other examples along similar lines: just imagine a situation in which two sources of information support a common conclusion, but also undermine each other, and therefore undermine the support that each provides for the common conclusion.

Suppose you are a military commander pursuing an enemy that currently holds a strong defensive position. It is suicide to attack while the enemy occupies this position in force, but you have orders to press ahead as quickly as possible, and so you send out your reliable scouts. After a few days, one scout reports back that there can now be only a skeleton force remaining in the defensive position; he has seen the main enemy column retreating through the mountains, although he also noticed that they sent out a diversionary group to make it appear as if they were retreating along the river. The other scout agrees that only a skeleton force remains in the defensive position; she has seen the main enemy column retreating along the river, although she notes that they also sent out a diversionary group to make it appear is if they were retreating through the mountains. Based on this information, should you assume at least that the main enemy force has retreated from the defensive position—a floating conclusion that is supported by both scouts—and therefore commit your troops to an attack? Not necessarily. Although they support a common conclusion, each scout undermines the support provided by the other. Perhaps the enemy sent out two diversionary groups, one through the mountains and one along the river, and managed to fool both your scouts into believing that a retreat was in progress. Perhaps the main force still occupies the strong defensive position, awaiting your attack.

Or suppose you attend a macroeconomics conference during a period of economic health, with low inflation and strong growth, and find that the community of macroeconomic forecasters is now split right down the middle. One group, working with an economic model that has been reliable in the past, predicts that the current strong growth rate will lead to higher inflation, triggering an economic downturn. By modifying a few assumptions in the same model, the other group arrives at a prediction according to which the current low inflation rate will actually continue to decline, leading to a dangerous period of deflation and triggering an economic downturn. Both groups predict an economic downturn, but for different and conflicting reasons—higher inflation versus deflation—and so the prediction is supported only as a floating conclusion. Based on this information, should you accept the prediction, adjusting your investment portfolio accordingly? Not necessarily. Perhaps the extreme predictions are best seen as undermining each other and the truth lies somewhere in between: the inflationary and deflationary forces will cancel each other out, the inflation rate will remain pretty much as it is, and the period of economic health will continue.

There is no need to labor the point by fabricating further examples in which floating conclusions are suspect. But what about the similar cases, exemplifying the same pattern, that have been advanced as supporting floating conclusions, such as Ginsberg's political extremist example, depicted in Figure 7.1?

I have always been surprised that this example has seemed so persuasive to so many people. The example relies on our understanding that individuals adopt a wide spectrum of attitudes regarding the appropriate use of military force, but that Quakers and Republicans tend to be doves and hawks, respectively—where doves and hawks take the extreme positions that the use of military force is never appropriate, or that it is very often appropriate. Of course, Nixon's own position on the matter is well known. But if I were told of some other individual that she is both a Quaker and a Republican, I would not be sure what to conclude. It is possible that this individual would adopt an extreme position, as either a dove or a hawk. But it seems equally reasonable to imagine that such an individual, rather than being pulled to one extreme or the other, would combine elements of both views into a more balanced, measured position falling toward the center of the political spectrum—perhaps believing that the use of military force is sometimes appropriate, but only as a response to serious provocation. Given this real possibility, it may be sensible to take a skeptical attitude, not only toward the questions of whether this individual would be a dove or a hawk, but also toward the question whether she would adopt a politically extreme position at all.

Another example appears in Reiter's original paper on default logic, where he suggests defaults representing the facts that people tend to live in the same cities as their spouses, but also in the cities in which they work, and then asks us to consider the case of Mary, whose spouse lives in Toronto but who works in Vancouver.[11] Coded into default logic, this information leads to a theory with two extensions, in one of which Mary lives in Toronto and in one of which she lives in Vancouver. Reiter seems to favor the credulous policy of embracing a particular one of these extensions, either concluding that Mary lives in Toronto or concluding that Mary lives in Vancouver. But then, in a footnote, he also mentions what amounts to the skeptical possibility of forming the belief only that Mary lives in either Toronto or Vancouver—where this proposition is supported, of course, as a floating conclusion.

Given the information from this example, I would, in fact, be likely to conclude that Mary lives either in Toronto or Vancouver. But I am not sure this conclusion should follow as a matter of logic, even default

---

[11]See Reiter (1980, pp. 86–87).

logic, from the information provided thus far. In this case, the conclusion seems to rely on a good deal of additional knowledge about the particular domain involved, including the vast distance between Toronto and Vancouver, which effectively rules out any sort of intermediate solution to Mary's two-body problem.

By contrast, consider the happier situation of Carol, who works in College Park, Maryland, but whose spouse works in Alexandria, Virginia; and assume the same two defaults—that people tend to live in the same cities as their spouses, but also tend to live in the cities in which they work. Represented in default logic, this information would again lead to a theory with multiple extensions, in each of which, however, Carol would live either in College Park or in Alexandria. Nevertheless, I would be reluctant to accept the floating conclusion that Carol lives either in College Park or in Alexandria. Just thinking about the situation, I would consider it equally likely that Carol and her spouse live together in Washington, DC, within easy commuting distance of both their jobs.

Having now considered a number of cases in which, I believe, floating conclusions fail, I want to mention one example in which our intuitions lie on the other side—the evidence is not unambiguous. The example, due to Henry Prakken, concerns Brigt Rykkje, the Dutch speed skater, who was born in Holland but has a Norwegian name.[12] As a rule, people born in Holland tend to be Dutch citizens, while people with Norwegian names tend to be Norwegian citizens. Suppose that no one is a citizen of both Holland and Norway, but that both the Dutch and the Norwegians uniformly like ice skating. The question is: setting aside what we know about Brigt Rykkje as an individual—that he is a speed skater—can we conclude from the information provided that he likes ice skating?

Let us take BH as the proposition that Rykkje was born in Holland, NN as the proposition that he has a Norwegian name, D as the proposition that he is Dutch, N as the proposition that he is Norwegian, and S as the proposition that he likes ice skating. The situation can be represented, then, through the theory $\Delta_{41} = \langle \mathcal{W}, \mathcal{D}, < \rangle$, depicted in Figure 7.3, where $\mathcal{W} = \{BH, NN, D \supset S, N \supset S, \neg(D \wedge N)\}$, where $\mathcal{D} = \{\delta_1, \delta_2\}$ with δ_1 as $BH \to D$ and δ_2 as $NN \to N$, and where $<$ is empty. Here, the hard information from $\mathcal{W}$ tells us about Rykkje's birth and name, about the fondness of the Dutch and Norwegians for ice skating, and about the impossibility of joint citizenship between Holland and Norway. The default δ_1 tells us that having been born in Holland favors the conclusion that Rykkje is Dutch, while the default δ_2 tells us that having a Norwegian name favors the conclusion that he is Norwegian.

It is evident that this theory shares the structure of our two central examples, Ginsberg's political extremist example and my own yacht example, and leads to a similar formal result. There are two proper scenarios,

---

[12]See Prakken (2002).

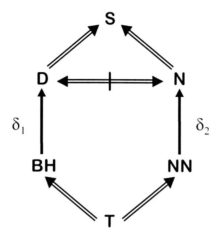

Figure 7.3: Does Brigt Rykkje like ice skating?

$S_1 = \{\delta_1\}$ and $S_2 = \{\delta_2\}$, from which conflicting path extensions can be constructed: one will contain the argument paths $\top \Rightarrow BH \to D \Rightarrow S$ and $\top \Rightarrow BH \to D \Rightarrow \neg N$, while the other contains $\top \Rightarrow NN \to N \Rightarrow S$ and $\top \Rightarrow NN \to N \Rightarrow \neg D$. Each path extension, then, will contain some path with S as its conclusion, but no path supporting this conclusion will be contained in all extensions. The conclusion—that Brigt Rykkje likes ice skating—is therefore supported only as a floating conclusion.

What is different about this case, however, is that the floating conclusion is much more plausible; it seems to many people—and I am among them—that even a skeptical reasoner should accept this conclusion that Brigt Rykkje likes ice skating, in the situation as Prakken describes it. How, then, can we account for the difference between this case and our previous yacht example, for instance, where most people feel that the floating conclusion should be rejected? I am not sure what to say, though the space of alternatives seems clear enough. We might suppose, first, that the floating conclusions either are, or are not, uniformly acceptable in both situations, and then appeal to pragmatic phenomena of some sort to explain why it appears in the yacht case that these conclusions are unacceptable, or why it appears in the ice skating case that they are. Second, we might suppose that, although floating conclusions are in general acceptable, there are structural features present in situations such as the yacht example, but not yet captured in our formal representations of these examples, that block these conclusions. Or third, we might suppose that, although floating conclusions are not in general acceptable, there are structural features present in situations such as the ice skating example, but again, not yet in our formal representations, that allow these conclusions to go through. As it happens, Prakken leans toward the second of these explanations, while I lean toward the third, though neither of us has been able to offer any conclusive explanation of what these structural features might be, or of why they are present in some situations and not others.

7.3.2   Skepticism

Supposing I am right that floating conclusions are problematic, it is worth asking: why was it so widely thought, at least until recently, that floating conclusions must be accepted by a skeptical reasoner, so that a system that fails to generate these conclusions is therefore incorrect? It is hard to be sure, since this point of view was generally taken as an assumption, rather than argued for, but we can speculate.

Imagine an agent who believes that either the proposition X or the proposition Y holds, that X implies Z, and that Y also implies Z. Classical logic then allows the agent to draw Z as a conclusion; this is a valid principle of inference, sometimes known as the principle of constructive dilemma. The inference to a floating conclusion is in some ways similar. Suppose a default theory has two extensions, $\mathcal{E}_1$ and $\mathcal{E}_2$, that the extension $\mathcal{E}_1$ contains the proposition Z, and that the extension $\mathcal{E}_2$ also contains the proposition Z. The standard view is that a skeptical reasoner should then draw Z as a conclusion, even if it is supported only as a floating conclusion, and not by any common argument in the two extensions.

Notice the difference between these two cases, though. In the first case, the classical reasoning agent believes both that X and Y individually imply Z, and also that either X or Y holds. In the second case, we might as well suppose that the skeptical reasoner knows that Z belongs to both the extensions $\mathcal{E}_1$ and $\mathcal{E}_2$, so that both $\mathcal{E}_1$ and $\mathcal{E}_2$ individually imply Z. The reasoner is therefore justified in drawing Z as a conclusion by something like the principle of constructive dilemma—as long as it is reasonable to suppose, in addition, that either $\mathcal{E}_1$ or $\mathcal{E}_2$ is correct. This is the crucial assumption, which underlies the standard view of skeptical reasoning and the acceptance of floating conclusions. But is this assumption required? Is it necessary for a skeptical reasoner to assume, when a theory leads to multiple extensions, that one of those extensions must be correct?

Earlier, we described the choice option for handling multiple extensions as the strategy followed by a reasoning agent that simply selects one or another of these extensions, and then endorses the conclusions contained in that extension. The assumption that one of the theory's extensions must be correct is therefore equivalent to the assumption that some reasoning agent following the choice option must be right. But why should a reasoner following a skeptical strategy assume that some reasoner or another following an entirely different reasoning strategy must be correct? Of course, there may be situations in which it is appropriate for a skeptical reasoner to adopt this standard view—that some reasoner following the choice option must be right, but that it is simply unclear which one. That might be the extent of the skepticism involved. But there also seem to be situations in which a deeper form of skepticism is appropriate—where each of a theory's multiple extensions is undermined by another to such an extent that it seems like a real possibility that every reasoner following the choice option could be wrong. The yacht, scout, and economist examples illustrate situations that seem to call for this deeper form of skepticism.

As a policy for reasoning with conflicting defaults, the notion of skepticism was originally introduced into the field of nonmonotonic logic to characterize the particular system developed by Thomason, Touretzky, and myself—which did not, in fact, involve the assumption that one of a theory's multiple extensions must be correct, and did not support floating conclusions. By now, however, the term is used almost uniformly to describe approaches that do rely on this assumption, so that the "skeptical conclusions" of a theory are generally identified as the propositions supported by each of its multiple extensions, including the floating conclusions. There is nothing wrong with this usage of the term, as a technical description of the propositions supported by each extension, except that it might tend to cut off avenues for research, suggesting that we now know exactly how to characterize the skeptical conclusions of a theory. On the contrary, if we think of skepticism as the general policy of withholding judgment in the face of conflicting defaults, rather than arbitrarily favoring one default or another, there is a complex space of reasoning policies—including the two skeptical options described in this chapter, the separate theory of Thomason, Touretzky, and myself, as well as many others—that could all legitimately be described as skeptical.[13]

---

[13]There is, furthermore, an evident analogy between the problem presented by floating conclusions and the "doctrinal paradox" first identified in the field of legal theory by Lewis Kornhauser and Lawrence Sager (1986) and since studied by a number of philosophers, logicians, and political theorists (sometimes as the "discursive dilemma," or as the "paradox of judgment aggregation"); more exactly, the argument intersection option described in this chapter, which rejects floating conclusions, corresponds to what is sometimes called the "premise-based" reasoning procedure in the literature on the doctrinal paradox, while the conclusion intersection option, which accepts floating conclusions, corresponds to what is called the "conclusion-based" procedure in that literature.

Chapter 8

Problems with priorities

A central feature of the theories studied in this book is that the defaults involved are ordered by a priority relation; no such ordering was present in Reiter's original default logic. Earlier, in Chapter 1, I attempted to account for the impact of this priority ordering among defaults by introducing a notion of defeat, according to which a default is defeated in the context of a scenario whenever there is a stronger default triggered in that scenario that supports a conflicting conclusion. I noted at the time, however, that, although this definition led to correct results in a wide variety of examples, including all of those considered thus far, it failed in more complex cases, and so could be regarded only as preliminary.

The present chapter addresses some of these more complex cases by exploring two further accounts of default reasoning with fixed priorities. The first fits within the general framework developed in this book, simply refining the concept of defeat presented earlier. The second, presented here both for contrast and because it is, in some ways, the industry standard, shifts to an entirely different, more procedural framework, in which priorities among defaults are accommodated by controlling the order in which these defaults are applied. I argue that the account developed here, based on defeat, compares favorably to the more familiar, procedural account. But this account is not without problems of its own—once again, I do not know of any account that is entirely satisfactory—and I close the chapter by discussing some of the issues it raises.

8.1 Refining the concept of defeat

Let us begin by reviewing our preliminary idea that a default is defeated in a scenario if that scenario triggers a stronger default supporting a conflicting conclusion. More exactly, given a scenario S based on an underlying theory $\Delta = \langle W, D, < \rangle$, this idea was introduced, in Definition 4 from Section 1.2.1, through the specification of a set $Defeated_{W,D,<}(S)$, containing the defaults defeated in the context of S, according to which a default δ belongs

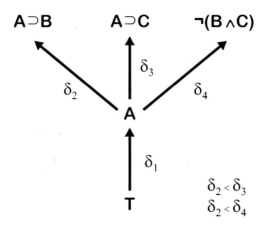

Figure 8.1: Difficulties with defeat

to $Defeated_{\mathcal{W},\mathcal{D},<}(\mathcal{S})$ just in case there is another default δ' belonging to the set $Triggered_{\mathcal{W},\mathcal{D}}(\mathcal{S})$ of triggered defaults and satisfying the additional conditions that (1) $\delta < \delta'$ and (2) $\mathcal{W} \cup \{Conclusion(\delta')\} \vdash \neg\, Conclusion(\delta)$, so that δ' is stronger than δ and supports a conflicting conclusion.

The canonical example of defeat was provided by the Tweety Triangle—the theory $\Delta_1 = \langle \mathcal{W}, \mathcal{D}, < \rangle$, depicted in Figure 1.1, where $\mathcal{W} = \{P, P \supset B\}$, where $\mathcal{D} = \{\delta_1, \delta_2\}$ with δ_1 and δ_2 as the defaults $B \to F$ and $P \to \neg F$, and where $\delta_1 < \delta_2$. Consider the scenario $\mathcal{S}_1 = \emptyset$ based on this theory. Then, as we recall, the default δ_1 is defeated in the context of this scenario, since the default δ_2 belongs to $Triggered_{\mathcal{W},\mathcal{D}}(\mathcal{S}_1)$ and we have both $\delta_1 < \delta_2$ and $\mathcal{W} \cup \{Conclusion(\delta_2)\} \vdash \neg\, Conclusion(\delta_1)$.

In fact, this preliminary treatment of defeat is nothing but a straightforward adaptation of the notion of preemption developed for the very restricted language of inheritance hierarchies; but unfortunately, it is too simple to work in the present, more general setting of full default logic, and for two reasons. First, it seems possible for a default to be defeated, not just by a single stronger default, but by a set of stronger defaults—a *defeating set*—each of which may be individually consistent with the original default, but which are inconsistent with this default when taken together. And second, in determining whether one default, or set of defaults, conflicts with another in the context of a scenario, it seems that we can legitimately appeal, not only to hard information from the underlying default theory, but also to certain facts supported by the scenario to which the agent is already committed.

Both these difficulties can be illustrated by an abstract example in which the default δ_1 is $\top \to A$, in which δ_2 is $A \to (A \supset B)$, in which δ_3 is

$A \to (A \supset C)$, and in which δ_4 is $A \to \neg(B \wedge C)$. Consider the theory $\Delta_{42} = \langle \mathcal{W}, \mathcal{D}, < \rangle$, depicted in Figure 8.1, with $\mathcal{W}$ empty, with $\mathcal{D} = \{\delta_1, \delta_2, \delta_3, \delta_4\}$, and with $\delta_2 < \delta_3$ and $\delta_2 < \delta_4$; and suppose that the agent's current scenario, based on this theory, is $\mathcal{S}_1 = \{\delta_1\}$. Here, it seems reasonable to say that the single default δ_2 is defeated by the set $\mathcal{D}' = \{\delta_3, \delta_4\}$ in the context of the scenario $\mathcal{S}_1$. Why? Because both defaults belonging to $\mathcal{D}'$ are triggered in the context of this scenario, both of these defaults have a higher priority than δ_2, and the conclusions of these defaults, when taken together with the conclusion of the default from $\mathcal{S}_1$, to which the agent is already committed, conflict with the conclusion of δ_2.

Generalizing from this abstract example, it may now appear that we reach a satisfactory analysis of defeat by stipulating that the default δ is defeated in the context of a scenario $\mathcal{S}$ just in case there is a set $\mathcal{D}'$ of defaults triggered in the context of $\mathcal{S}$, satisfying the conditions that the defaults from $\mathcal{D}'$ are uniformly stronger than δ, and also that the conclusions of these defaults, taken together with the conclusions of the defaults from $\mathcal{S}$, conflict with the conclusion of δ. In order to represent the idea that one set of defaults has a higher priority than another, we lift the familiar priority relation from individual defaults to sets of defaults, so that $\mathcal{D} < \mathcal{D}'$ means that $\delta < \delta'$ for each δ in $\mathcal{D}$ and each δ' in $\mathcal{D}'$; and for convenience, we abbreviate $\{\delta\} < \mathcal{D}'$ as $\delta < \mathcal{D}'$. Our new proposal can then be captured, more formally, as the stipulation that δ is defeated in the context of $\mathcal{S}$ just in case there is a defeating set $\mathcal{D}' \subseteq \mathit{Triggered}_{\mathcal{W}, \mathcal{D}}(\mathcal{S})$ such that (1) $\delta < \mathcal{D}'$ and (2) $\mathcal{W} \cup \mathit{Conclusion}(\mathcal{S} \cup \mathcal{D}') \vdash \neg \mathit{Conclusion}(\delta)$.

Let us refer to this proposal as the *candidate definition*. In fact, this candidate definition is nearly correct, but requires further refinement in order to handle certain problems that arise when a potential defeating set is inconsistent with the agent's current scenario.

The problems can be illustrated by an example that extends the earlier Nixon Diamond with a weaker but irrelevant default. As before, let Q, R, and P represent the propositions that Nixon is a Quaker, a Republican, and a pacifist; let δ_1 be $Q \to P$ and δ_2 be $R \to \neg P$. But this time, let S represent some proposition that is entirely irrelevant to Nixon's pacifism, perhaps the proposition that Nixon enjoys the seashore; and let δ_3 be the default $\top \to S$, an instance for Nixon of the rule that people in general tend to enjoy the seashore. Suppose the reasoning agent is provided with the new theory $\Delta_{43} = \langle \mathcal{W}, \mathcal{D}, < \rangle$ as initial information, where $\mathcal{W} = \{Q, R\}$, where $\mathcal{D} = \{\delta_1, \delta_2, \delta_3\}$, and where the ordering tells us that the new default has a lower priority than the previous two: $\delta_3 < \delta_1$ and $\delta_3 < \delta_2$. And imagine that the agent has selected the default δ_1 over the conflicting default δ_2, so that its current scenario is $\mathcal{S}_1 = \{\delta_1\}$.

Now, once the conflict concerning Nixon's pacifism has been settled, can the agent then simply accept the additional default δ_3 and so conclude S, that Nixon likes the seashore? The intuitive answer is Yes. The new default provides a reason for this conclusion, and there is apparently nothing in the vicinity to oppose this reason. Unfortunately, the candidate definition tells us otherwise—that, in the agent's current scenario, the new default δ_3 is actually defeated. How can this be? Well, taking $\mathcal{D}' = \{\delta_2\}$ as a potential defeating set, it is clear to begin with that $\mathcal{D}' \subseteq \mathit{Triggered}_{\mathcal{W},\mathcal{D}}(\mathcal{S}_1)$. Furthermore, we have (1) $\delta_3 < \mathcal{D}'$, and since the set $\mathcal{W} \cup \mathit{Conclusion}(\mathcal{S}_1 \cup \mathcal{D}')$—that is, $\mathcal{W} \cup \{P, \neg P\}$—is inconsistent, entailing anything at all, we also have (2) $\mathcal{W} \cup \mathit{Conclusion}(\mathcal{S}_1 \cup \mathcal{D}') \vdash \neg \mathit{Conclusion}(\delta_3)$.

This example might seem to suggest that the candidate definition should be supplemented with a restriction according to which the defeating set $\mathcal{D}'$ should be consistent with the current scenario $\mathcal{S}$. Perhaps the original clause (2) should be replaced with a pair of clauses requiring both (2a) that $\mathcal{W} \cup \mathit{Conclusion}(\mathcal{S} \cup \mathcal{D}')$ is consistent, and (2b) that $\mathcal{W} \cup \mathit{Conclusion}(\mathcal{S} \cup \mathcal{D}') \vdash \neg \mathit{Conclusion}(\delta)$. However, this suggestion will not work either, as we can see by returning to the Tweety Triangle, the theory Δ_1 depicted in Figure 1.1. Suppose, in this example, that the reasoning agent has mistakenly come to accept δ_1—that is, the default $B \rightarrow F$, according to which Tweety flies because he is a bird—so that the agent's current scenario is $\mathcal{S}_1 = \{\delta_1\}$. From an intuitive standpoint, we would nevertheless like δ_1 to be defeated by δ_2—the stronger default $P \rightarrow \neg F$, according to which Tweety does not fly because he is a penguin. But this defeat relation would no longer hold, since the new clause (2a) requires that a default can be defeated only by another that is consistent with the agent's current scenario, and δ_2 is not consistent with $\mathcal{S}_1$.

What I would like to suggest, instead, is that the defeating set $\mathcal{D}'$ may be consistent, not necessarily with the agent's current scenario $\mathcal{S}$ as it stands, but only with another scenario that results when a certain subset $\mathcal{S}'$ is retracted from the agent's current scenario, so that the defeating set can then be consistently accommodated. For convenience, we let

$$\mathcal{S}^{\mathcal{D}'/\mathcal{S}'} = (\mathcal{S} - \mathcal{S}') \cup \mathcal{D}'$$

be the result of retracting the defaults belonging to $\mathcal{S}'$ from the scenario $\mathcal{S}$, and then supplementing what remains with the defaults from $\mathcal{D}'$—or more simply, as the notation indicates, replacing $\mathcal{S}'$ by $\mathcal{D}'$ in $\mathcal{S}$. The suggestion, then, is to require, not that the defeating set $\mathcal{D}'$ must be consistent with the scenario $\mathcal{S}$, but simply that there should be some appropriate set $\mathcal{S}'$ such that $\mathcal{S}^{\mathcal{D}'/\mathcal{S}'}$ is consistent. Returning to our variant of the Tweety Triangle, again taking $\mathcal{S}_1 = \{\delta_1\}$ as the agent's current scenario, if we now suppose that $\mathcal{D}' = \{\delta_2\}$ and $\mathcal{S}' = \{\delta_1\}$, then it turns out that $\mathcal{S}_1^{\mathcal{D}'/\mathcal{S}'} = \{\delta_2\}$ is consistent; and since this set entails $\neg \mathit{Conclusion}(\delta_1)$, the desired defeat relation is restored.

The key to this proposal is that, in order to accommodate a defeating set, we are free to retract certain defaults to which the agent is already committed. But are there any constraints on this process of accommodation; can we retract just anything at all from the agent's current scenario? No, there are limits. The definition to be presented here is based on the idea that the set $\mathcal{S}'$ of retracted defaults and the defeating set $\mathcal{D}'$ are subject to the constraint that $\mathcal{S}' < \mathcal{D}'$—the defaults belonging to $\mathcal{S}'$ must be uniformly weaker than those belonging to $\mathcal{D}'$. We can retract as many defaults from the agent's current scenario as necessary in order to accommodate a defeating set, as long as the defaults we retract are themselves lower in priority than those we are attempting to accommodate.

Definition 21 (Defeated defaults) Let $\Delta = \langle \mathcal{W}, \mathcal{D}, < \rangle$ be a fixed priority default theory, and $\mathcal{S}$ a scenario based on this theory. Then the defaults from $\mathcal{D}$ that are defeated in the context of the scenario $\mathcal{S}$ are those belonging to the set

$Defeated_{\mathcal{W},\mathcal{D},<}(\mathcal{S}) =$

$\quad \{\delta \in \mathcal{D} : \quad$ there is a set $\mathcal{D}' \subseteq Triggered_{\mathcal{W},\mathcal{D}}(\mathcal{S})$ such that
$\qquad\qquad (1)\ \delta < \mathcal{D}',$
$\qquad\qquad (2)$ there is a set $\mathcal{S}' \subseteq \mathcal{S}$ such that
$\qquad\qquad\qquad (a)\ S' < \mathcal{D}',$
$\qquad\qquad\qquad (b)\ \mathcal{W} \cup Conclusion(\mathcal{S}^{\,\mathcal{D}'/\mathcal{S}'})$ is consistent,
$\qquad\qquad\qquad (c)\ \mathcal{W} \cup Conclusion(\mathcal{S}^{\,\mathcal{D}'/\mathcal{S}'}) \vdash \neg\ Conclusion(\delta)\}.$

When a default δ is defeated in accord with this definition, with $\mathcal{D}'$ as its defeating set, we say that $\mathcal{S}'$ is an *accommodating set* for $\mathcal{D}'$, a set of defaults whose retraction from the current scenario $\mathcal{S}$ enables the defeating set to be accommodated.

Evidently, this definition of defeat allows an accommodating set to be larger than necessary, in the sense that it might contain defaults that do not actually need to be retracted from the current scenario in order to accommodate the defeating set. We can, however, define the stricter notion of a minimal accommodating set, as follows: where some default is defeated in the scenario $\mathcal{S}$, with $\mathcal{D}'$ as a defeating set, $\mathcal{S}^*$ is a *minimal accommodating set* for $\mathcal{D}'$ just in case $\mathcal{S}^*$ is an accommodating set for $\mathcal{D}'$ and, for any proper subset $\mathcal{S}'$ of $\mathcal{S}^*$, the set $\mathcal{W} \cup Conclusion(\mathcal{S}^{\,\mathcal{D}'/\mathcal{S}'})$ is inconsistent. A minimal accommodating set, then, is some minimal set of defaults that must be retracted from the current scenario in order to accommodate a defeating set. And it is easy to see, first of all, that the concept of defeat remains unchanged if we allow for the retraction only of minimal accommodating sets, and second, that any defeating set which is already consistent with the current scenario has the empty set as its unique minimal accommodating set; these two facts are established as Observations 1 and 2 in Appendix A.2.

The reader is invited to verify that our definition of a defeated default yields the correct defeat relations in the various examples considered here, as well as others of his or her own devising. Any definition this complicated, however, needs a justification apart from its application to particular examples, and I offer two.

We have, in the first place, a clear rationale for preferring conclusions based on $\mathcal{S}^{\,\mathcal{D}'/\mathcal{S}'}$—the new scenario, which results from the original by retracting the accommodating set and adding the defeating set—to conclusions based on $\mathcal{S}$, the agent's original scenario. For there is a precise sense in which the new scenario provides a stronger set of reasons than the original: setting aside those defaults shared by the two scenarios, it follows from our definition that each default belonging to the new but not to the original scenario will have a higher priority than any default belonging to the original scenario but not to the new one. This observation depends, of course, on our requirement that the defaults belonging to the defeating set must be uniformly stronger than those belonging to the accommodating set. Without this requirement, it would be hard to draw any meaningful strength comparisons between the new scenario and the original, and so hard to see why conclusions based on the new scenario should be preferred.

And second, since what is most distinctive about our definition of defeat is its appeal to an accommodating set, to be retracted from the agent's current scenario, it is worth focusing on the defaults belonging to this set; how can we justify retracting defaults to which the agent is already committed? As we have already seen, there is no need to justify the retraction of defaults belonging to arbitrary accommodating sets, possibly containing defaults that do not actually need to be retracted in order to accommodate some defeating set. It is enough to limit our attention to defaults from minimal accommodating sets, those whose retraction is necessary; and in this case, there is no real difficulty justifying the retraction of these defaults at all, since it turns out that any default belonging to such a set must itself be defeated; this fact is established as Observation 3 in Appendix A.2.

8.2 Controlling the order of application

Of course, the problem of reasoning with complex patterns of priority in default logic is not new. There has been previous work along several paths, but the most popular approaches rely on the general idea that priorities should function as control information to guide the application of defaults, so that those defaults with higher priority must be satisfied before those of lower priority can be considered; among the various theories based on this idea, which differ in detail, the most prominent is due to Gerhard Brewka.[1]

---

[1]See Brewka (1994a; 1994b). Other theories based on the same idea have been explored by Franz Baader and Bernhard Hollunder (1995) and by Wiktor Marek and Mirek Truszczyński (1993); and the approach has recently been developed in a more sophisticated form by Brewka together with Thomas Eiter (2000). An entirely different approach has been followed by Delgrande and Schaub (2000a; 2000b), who explore techniques for compiling priority information into ordinary default rules, revitalizing in a much more general and systematic way an idea that was first hinted at by Reiter and Giovanni Criscuolo (1981), and developed in a different direction by Etherington and Reiter (1983). Jussi Rintanen (1998) has explored the idea of ordering extensions on the basis of the defaults generating them, with higher priority defaults leading to better

The approach is adapted here to fit the pattern, followed in this book, of first defining a class of acceptable scenarios, and then defining extensions in terms of these acceptable scenarios.

The architecture of Brewka's approach is straightforward. The acceptable scenarios are viewed as being constructed in a series of stages, represented by a sequence of scenarios, with the defaults that are *active* at any given stage defined as those that are triggered, not conflicted, but also not yet accepted.

Definition 22 (Active defaults) Let $\Delta = \langle \mathcal{W}, \mathcal{D}, < \rangle$ be a fixed priority default theory, and $\mathcal{S}$ a scenario based on this theory. Then the defaults from $\mathcal{D}$ that are active in the context of the scenario $\mathcal{S}$ are those belonging to the set

$$Active_{\mathcal{W},\mathcal{D}}(\mathcal{S}) \;=\; \{\delta \in \mathcal{D} : \quad \delta \in Triggered_{\mathcal{W},\mathcal{D}}(\mathcal{S}),$$
$$\delta \notin Conflicted_{\mathcal{W},\mathcal{D}}(\mathcal{S}),$$
$$\delta \notin \mathcal{S}\}.$$

At any given stage, then, the active defaults are those among the defaults not yet accepted that provide reasons for their conclusions, since they are triggered, and whose conclusions are consistent with the information at hand, since they are not conflicted either. These defaults are therefore, in a sense, primed to be accepted.

Brewka's idea is simply to accept, at each stage, the most important of the defaults that are active at that stage. Where $\mathcal{S}$ is some scenario ordered by $<$, we can define $Maximal_<(\mathcal{S})$ as the subset of $\mathcal{S}$ containing only the highest ranking, or most important, defaults from this scenario, so that a default δ from $\mathcal{S}$ belongs to $Maximal_<(\mathcal{S})$ just in case there is no other default δ' from $\mathcal{S}$ with $\delta < \delta'$. Now let us begin with the special case of a theory in which the priority ordering on the entire set $\mathcal{D}$ of defaults is total—or linear, or connected. The ordering on each subset $\mathcal{S}$ of $\mathcal{D}$ will likewise be total, so that the set $Maximal_<(\mathcal{S})$ will contain a single member, a unique most important default, as long as $\mathcal{S}$ itself is nonempty. In this simple case, then, we can define the acceptable scenarios—which I refer to as *simple control scenarios*—by taking the union of a sequence of scenarios that begins with $\mathcal{S}_0$ as the empty scenario, and then, at each stage, constructs the next scenario $\mathcal{S}_{i+1}$ by supplementing the previous scenario $\mathcal{S}_i$ with the unique most important default that is still active in the previous scenario.

Definition 23 (Simple control scenarios) Let $\Delta = \langle \mathcal{W}, \mathcal{D}, < \rangle$ be a fixed priority default theory for which the priority ordering $<$ is total. Then

---

outcomes, and then defining the acceptable extensions as those that are maximal in the ordering. More recently, Jörg Hansen (2006; 2008) has developed a sophisticated new approach, drawing on Brewka's idea, but incorporating a number of fresh elements as well.

$\overline{S}$ is a simple control scenario based on this theory just in case $\overline{S} = \bigcup_{i \geq 0} S_i$, where

$$S_0 = \emptyset,$$

$$S_{i+1} = \begin{cases} S_i & \text{if } Active_{W,D}(S_i) = \emptyset \\ S_i \cup Maximal_<(Active_{W,D}(S_i)) & \text{otherwise.} \end{cases}$$

But what about the more general case, in which the priority ordering on defaults is partial but not necessarily total? Here, Brewka recommends the familiar strategy of reasoning about a partial ordering by reasoning about each total ordering with which it is consistent, or to which it can be extended. The acceptable scenarios based on an arbitrary prioritized default theory—which I refer to simply as *control scenarios*, without qualification—are therefore identified with the simple control scenarios based on all the various theories like the original theory, but in which the original partial ordering is extended to a total ordering.

Definition 24 (Control scenarios) Let $\Delta = \langle W, D, < \rangle$ be a fixed priority default theory. Then $\overline{S}$ is a control scenario based on Δ just in case there is some total ordering $<'$ extending $<$ such that $\overline{S}$ is a simple control scenario based on $\Delta' = \langle W, D, <' \rangle$.

And of course, once this new class of acceptable scenarios has been introduced, we can then define the new class of extensions generated by these scenarios—the *control extensions*—in the usual fashion, by combining conclusions of defaults from the acceptable scenarios with hard information from the original theory, and then closing under consequence.

Definition 25 (Control extensions) Let $\Delta = \langle W, D, < \rangle$ be a fixed priority default theory. Then $\mathcal{E}$ is a control extension of Δ just in case, for some control scenario $\overline{S}$ based on this theory,

$$\mathcal{E} = Th(W \cup Conclusion(\overline{S})).$$

Once again, the crucial difference between Brewka's approach and my own is that, on Brewka's approach, the impact of priorities among defaults is supposed to be accounted for without appeal to any explicit concept of defeat. Instead, the idea is that it is sufficient to control the order in which defaults are to be applied, or accepted. A conflict among a group of defaults is then supposed to be resolved in favor of the more important members of the group, since these defaults are accepted first. Once these defaults are placed in the agent's scenario, the less important defaults are then conflicted; they are therefore no longer active, and so cannot be accepted themselves.

This basic idea is clean and attractive, and leads to results that coincide with my own in many of the most central examples. Consider the Tweety

Triangle—the theory $\Delta_1 = \langle \mathcal{W}, \mathcal{D}, < \rangle$, where $\mathcal{W} = \{P, P \supset B\}$, where $\mathcal{D} = \{\delta_1, \delta_2\}$ with δ_1 and δ_2 as the defaults $B \to F$ and $P \to \neg F$, and where $\delta_1 < \delta_2$. Here, the defaults are totally ordered, so that the unique control scenario based on this theory coincides with its unique simple control scenario, which is all we need to calculate. The process begins with $\mathcal{S}_0 = \emptyset$, in the context of which both defaults are classified as active. Selecting the most important of these defaults leads to $\mathcal{S}_1 = \{\delta_2\}$, in which both defaults are now inactive, δ_1 because it is now conflicted and δ_2 because it has been accepted. The process thus levels out, resulting in $\overline{\mathcal{S}_1} = \{\delta_2\}$ as the unique simple control scenario, and so the unique control scenario, for this theory.

Or consider the Nixon Diamond—the theory $\Delta_3 = \langle \mathcal{W}, \mathcal{D}, < \rangle$, where $\mathcal{W} = \{Q, R\}$, where $\mathcal{D} = \{\delta_1, \delta_2\}$ with δ_1 and δ_2 as the defaults $Q \to P$ and $R \to \neg P$, and where $<$ is empty. This partial ordering on defaults is consistent with two total orderings, one in which $\delta_1 < \delta_2$ and one in which $\delta_2 < \delta_1$, and so we must calculate simple control scenarios for each of the two theories like the Nixon Diamond but in which the empty partial ordering from the original Nixon Diamond is extended, respectively, to each of these two total orderings. In the case of the first, with $\delta_1 < \delta_2$, we are then led to $\overline{\mathcal{S}_1} = \{\delta_2\}$ as a simple control scenario, and so as a control scenario, for the original Nixon Diamond. In the case of the second, with $\delta_2 < \delta_1$, we are likewise led to $\overline{\mathcal{S}_2} = \{\delta_1\}$ as a simple control scenario, and so a control scenario, for the Nixon Diamond.

In both of these examples, therefore, the control scenarios generated by Brewka's analysis coincide with our proper scenarios. There are other cases, however, in which these two approaches yield different results.

Consider, for example, the theory $\Delta_{44} = \langle \mathcal{W}, \mathcal{D}, < \rangle$, depicted in Figure 8.2, where $\mathcal{W}$ is empty, where $\mathcal{D} = \{\delta_1, \delta_2, \delta_3, \delta_4\}$ with δ_1 as the default $\top \to A$, with δ_2 as $\top \to B$, with δ_3 as $A \to C$, and with δ_4 as $B \to \neg C$, and where the priority ordering tells us only that $\delta_3 < \delta_4$. There are, of course, many total orderings extending the partial ordering on defaults from this theory, but one of these is the ordering according to which

$$\delta_2 < \delta_3 < \delta_4 < \delta_1.$$

One of the control scenarios for the original default theory, therefore, will be identified with the simple control scenario that results when the partial ordering from this theory is replaced with this particular total ordering, so let us calculate. The process begins with $\mathcal{S}_0 = \emptyset$, in the context of which both δ_1 and δ_2 are classified as active. Selecting the most important of these, according to this particular total ordering, leads to $\mathcal{S}_1 = \{\delta_1\}$, in which δ_2 and δ_3 are now active; the default δ_3 is now active, since it is triggered, and δ_1 is no longer active, since it has been accepted. Again, selecting the most important of the active defaults leads to $\mathcal{S}_2 = \{\delta_1, \delta_3\}$, in which only δ_2 is now active; the default δ_3 has been accepted. Finally, selecting the remaining active default leads to $\mathcal{S}_3 = \{\delta_1, \delta_2, \delta_3\}$, in which

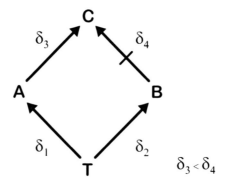

Figure 8.2: A control scenario anomaly

no further defaults are active; only δ_4 has not been accepted, and, although now triggered, it is conflicted.

Taking the union, we thus have $\overline{\mathcal{S}_1} = \{\delta_1, \delta_2, \delta_3\}$ as the simple control scenario for the default theory that results from Δ_{44} when the partial ordering from that theory is replaced with the total ordering displayed earlier, and so as one control scenario for the theory Δ_{44} itself. This recommendation fails to coincide with the approach adopted in this book, based on defeat, according to which Δ_{44} has the set $\mathcal{S} = \{\delta_1, \delta_2, \delta_4\}$ as its unique proper scenario. Moreover, I feel that the suggestion of the proper scenario $\mathcal{S} = \{\delta_1, \delta_2, \delta_4\}$ as an acceptable scenario for this theory is correct, while the suggestion of the control scenario $\overline{\mathcal{S}_1} = \{\delta_1, \delta_2, \delta_3\}$ as an acceptable scenario is anomalous. Both δ_1 and δ_2 are triggered, and nothing stands in the way of accepting both of these defaults; so they must be contained in any acceptable scenario, thus triggering the conflicting δ_3 and δ_4. The reasoning agent must therefore choose between these. But δ_4 is the stronger of the two, defeating δ_3, and should therefore be selected.

What this particular anomaly seems to challenge is the general strategy of reasoning about a theory whose defaults are only partially ordered by reasoning about the cluster of theories in which this partial order is extended to a total order. But, more interestingly, the order of application approach also differs from the account presented in this book in the case of certain theories in which the priority ordering on defaults is already total.

A representative example—which I refer to as the Order Puzzle, because of the interpretation I will attach to it—is the theory $\Delta_{45} = \langle \mathcal{W}, \mathcal{D}, < \rangle$, depicted in Figure 8.3, where $\mathcal{W} = \{W\}$, where $\mathcal{D} = \{\delta_1, \delta_2, \delta_3\}$ with δ_1 as $W \rightarrow H$, with δ_2 as $W \rightarrow \neg O$, and with δ_3 as $H \rightarrow O$, and where the priority ordering places $\delta_1 < \delta_2$ and $\delta_2 < \delta_3$. It is easy to see that the order of application approach leads to $\overline{\mathcal{S}_1} = \{\delta_1, \delta_2\}$ as the unique simple control scenario for this totally ordered theory, and so as the unique control scenario as well. The process of constructing this control scenario would begin with δ_1 and δ_2 as the only active defaults, from which δ_2 would be selected as most important, leaving δ_1 active, which would be selected next. At that point, there are no more active defaults; the default δ_3 , although now triggered, is conflicted by the prior selection of δ_2.

This particular example has a curious history. It had been part of the oral tradition in nonmonotonic reasoning for many years, was discussed in print by Prakken, and also by Brewka, who, as an order of application theorist, argued that the scenario $\overline{\mathcal{S}_1}$ is correct.[2] Later, Brewka and Thomas Eiter rejected $\overline{\mathcal{S}_1}$ in favor of the scenario $\mathcal{S}_2 = \{\delta_1, \delta_3\}$.[3] This is also, as it happens, the unique proper scenario recommended by the theory developed in this book; the control scenario $\overline{\mathcal{S}_1}$ is not proper, since δ_2 is defeated in the context of that scenario by δ_3.

The argument advanced by Brewka and Eiter against $\overline{\mathcal{S}_1}$ as an acceptable scenario runs, roughly, along the following lines: since the original theory assigns δ_3 a higher priority than δ_2, any approach that takes priority seriously must favor a scenario containing δ_3 to a scenario that is otherwise identical except that it contains δ_2 instead. Even if one accepts this argument, however, all it actually shows is that $\overline{\mathcal{S}_1}$ should not lie among the acceptable scenarios based on the original theory, not that $\mathcal{S}_2$ should, which leaves open a third possibility: perhaps the theory is incoherent, and has no acceptable scenarios at all. This possibility is embraced by James Delgrande and Torsten Schaub, who argue that the original theory is indeed meaningless, since the priority ranking of its defaults does not correspond to the order in which the propositions at work in this example would naturally be established.[4]

So what is the correct result in the case of the Order Puzzle? Is it $\overline{\mathcal{S}_1} = \{\delta_1, \delta_2\}$, as the order of application approach would suggest? Is it $\mathcal{S}_2 = \{\delta_1, \delta_3\}$, as suggested by Brewka and Eiter, and by the present approach? Or is it better to conclude with Delgrande and Schaub that the original theory is incoherent, and that it fails to allow an acceptable extension at all? The problems presented by the Order Puzzle are problems of coherence and interpretation. To establish that this theory is even coherent, we need to find a sensible interpretation, suggesting that the theory should actually allow some acceptable scenario; the interpretation will then support the present approach only if the acceptable scenario it suggests is our $\mathcal{S}_2$.

How could we construct such an interpretation? We cannot appeal to the idea that default priority tracks specificity, as Delgrande and Schaub note; on any view of specificity, the default δ_1 would provide more specific information than δ_3, yet in this case, δ_3 is assigned the higher priority. A reliability interpretation is possible, with each default indicating something

---

[2]See Prakken (1993) and Brewka (1994a).

[3]See Brewka and Eiter (2000), especially their Principle I.

[4]See Delgrande and Schaub (2000a), particularly Sections 3.1 and 4.2.

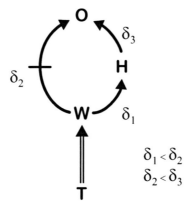

Figure 8.3: The Order Puzzle

like a high conditional probability that its conclusion is satisfied, given that its premise is satisfied, and with the priority ordering measuring relative strength of these conditional probabilities. But notice that the acceptable scenario naturally suggested by such an interpretation is actually $\overline{S}_1$, rather than S_2. For the default δ_2 then tells us that $\neg O$ follows with high probability, given that W holds. And the potential competing argument has no force, since δ_1 already supports H given W less strongly than δ_2 supports $\neg O$ given W. As a result, even if the conditional support provided by δ_3 for O given H is arbitrarily strong, it still follows that the conditional probability of O given W will be less than that of $\neg O$ given W.

Is there, then, an interpretation of the Order Puzzle that is intuitively coherent and also supports S_2 as the acceptable scenario? There is. Consider a command interpretation along the lines of those sketched earlier, in Sections 5.3.1 and 5.3.2, but slightly different: rather than taking a command as the premise of a default rule, so that it is the command that stands as a reason for some action, we now interpret default rules themselves as commands, which then specify that certain facts about the world are to function as reasons for action. More precisely, a default of the form $X \to Y$ will now be taken to represent a *conditional command*, or conditional imperative, enjoining some agent to guarantee the truth of Y in any situation in which X holds; the priorities among defaults will represent the levels of authority associated with these various commands. In the context of a scenario that supports the proposition X, we can then say that the conditional command $X \to Y$ is *obeyed* if that scenario supports the truth of Y as well, and *disobeyed* otherwise. And in selecting a scenario, the agent can now be viewed as choosing an appropriate set of commands to obey.

Once again, we suppose that the agent is the hapless Corporal O'Reilly, and that he is subject to the commands of three superior officers: a Captain, a Major, and a Colonel. The Captain, who does not like to be cold, issues a standing order that, during the winter, the heat should be turned on. The Major, who is concerned about energy conservation, issues an order that, during the winter, the window should not be opened. And the Colonel, who does not like to be too warm and does not care about energy conservation, issues an order that, whenever the heat is on, the window should be opened. If we now take W, H, and O as the propositions that it is winter, the heat is turned on, and the window is open, then the defaults δ_1, δ_2, and δ_3 can be taken to represent the respective commands issued by the Captain, the Major, and the Colonel. And since the Major outranks the Captain and the Colonel outranks the Major, we have the desired priority ordering: $\delta_1 < \delta_2$ and $\delta_2 < \delta_3$. Finally, suppose it is winter. The situation is then exactly as specified in the Order Puzzle.

Although there are many things wrong with this set of commands (the Colonel's order is especially odd), I hope we can agree that it is at least coherent, in the sense that O'Reilly might, in fact, be subject to a set of commands like these. A thinking soldier could perhaps grasp the intentions behind the various imperatives and arrive at a plan of action that would satisfy all three officers. But it is not O'Reilly's job to think, or to help the officers express their intentions more effectively by issuing more subtle or carefully qualified commands. O'Reilly's job is to obey his orders exactly as they have been issued. If he fails to obey an order issued by an officer without an excuse, he will be court-martialed. And, let us suppose, there is only one *excuse* for failing to obey such an order: that, under the circumstances, he is prevented from obeying the order issued by this officer by having chosen to obey another order or set of orders issued by officers of equal or higher rank. Again, some of us may feel that there must be more to the concept of an excuse than this, but I hope we can agree that the present notion is at least coherent, in the sense that this narrow concept of an excuse may actually be the one at work in some normative system.

Under the current interpretation, a scenario is supposed to represent an appropriate selection of commands to obey, where we can suppose, in this case, that a selection is appropriate if it does not involve disobeying any command without an excuse—so that, in particular, the agent can avoid court-martial. Given the set of commands that O'Reilly has been issued in the Order Puzzle, can he, then, avoid court-martial? Yes, he can, by choosing the proper scenario $\mathcal{S}_2 = \{\delta_1, \delta_3\}$, obeying the orders issued by the Captain and the Colonel, thus guaranteeing H and O. In this scenario, O'Reilly fails to obey the Major's order, the default δ_2, but he has an excuse: he was prevented from doing so by obeying an order issued by the

Colonel, an officer of higher rank. What if O'Reilly were instead to select the control scenario $\overline{\mathcal{S}_1} = \{\delta_1, \delta_2\}$, guaranteeing H and $\neg O$? In that case, he would obey the Captain and the Major, but fail to obey the Colonel, and he would do so, furthermore, without an excuse: although O'Reilly is prevented from obeying the Colonel by complying with an order issued by the Major, that is no excuse, since the Colonel outranks the Major. What this interpretation offers, then, is a way of understanding why the proper scenario $\mathcal{S}_2$, but not the control scenario $\overline{\mathcal{S}_1}$, might be classified as acceptable, or appropriate: $\mathcal{S}_2$ allows O'Reilly to avoid court-martial, while $\overline{\mathcal{S}_1}$ does not.

Are there, however, any other options to consider, apart from the two scenarios $\overline{\mathcal{S}_1}$ and $\mathcal{S}_2$? Well, it may seem that O'Reilly could reason in the following way.[5] If he obeys the Captain's command δ_1 to turn the heater on, then he will find himself in a situation in which he has no choice but to disobey either the Colonel's command δ_3 to open the window, or else the Major's command δ_2 to keep the window closed. Both the Colonel and the Major outrank the Captain. Therefore, it is best to disobey the Captain's command in order to avoid being placed in a situation in which he is then forced to disobey one or the other of two higher ranking officers. But of course, if he does disobey the Captain's command δ_1, and the heater is left off, there can then be no possible justification for failing to obey the Major's command δ_2, to keep the window closed.

This line of reasoning suggests the scenario $\mathcal{S}_3 = \{\delta_2\}$. Is $\mathcal{S}_3$, then, an acceptable scenario? Not according to the approach taken in this book, since this scenario fails to contain the default δ_1, representing the Captain's command, which is triggered in the context but neither conflicted nor defeated; the scenario is, therefore, not proper. Nor is this scenario one that allows O'Reilly to avoid court-martial. O'Reilly has no excuse at all for failing to obey the Captain's command: the Captain has ordered him to turn on the heater, and he is not prevented from doing so by obeying the commands of any other officers at all, let alone officers of equal or higher rank.[6]

There is one further complication worth noting, both because it highlights the ability of the present system to capture an important ambiguity, and also because it may be—I am not certain—that this ambiguity plays some role in accounting for the attractions of the form of hypothetical reasoning just discussed. Suppose that what the Colonel actually says in issuing his command is: "If the heater is on, the window should be open." This statement could naturally be interpreted as a conditional command,

---

[5]This line of reasoning was suggested to me by Paul Pietroski.

[6]Of course, in an effort to justify his actions, O'Reilly might advance an argument along the lines set out above, explaining how obeying the Captain would inevitably have led to disobeying either the Major or the Colonel. The argument is interesting, and it would be interesting to try to develop a version of prioritized default logic that allowed this form of hypothetical reasoning.

along the lines of "If the heater is on, you have an order to open the window," formalized here through our δ_3, the default $H \rightarrow O$. But it is also possible to interpret the same statement, not as a conditional command, but as an unconditional, or categorical, command whose content happens to be a conditional, along the lines of "You have an order to open the window if the heater is on." On this latter interpretation, the Colonel's command could best be represented, not through δ_3, but through the new default $\top \rightarrow (H \supset O)$.

Now imagine that the Colonel's order is interpreted in this way, as a command of a conditional, rather than a conditional command. In that case, the situation would be represented, not through the original Order Puzzle, but through the new theory $\Delta_{46} = \langle \mathcal{W}, \mathcal{D}, < \rangle$, a slight variant, where again $\mathcal{W} = \{W\}$, where $\mathcal{D} = \{\delta_1, \delta_2, \delta_4\}$ with δ_1 and δ_2 as before and with δ_4 as the new default $\top \rightarrow (H \supset O)$, and where $\delta_1 < \delta_2$ and $\delta_2 < \delta_4$. The unique proper scenario associated with this new default theory would then be $\mathcal{S}_4 = \{\delta_2, \delta_4\}$, supporting the propositions $\neg O$ and $H \supset O$, and so $\neg H$ as well.

The two interpretations of the Colonel's command, then, lead to strikingly different results. If the Colonel is interpreted as issuing a conditional command, then, as we have seen, what O'Reilly ought to do is obey the Colonel and the Captain, turning the heater on and opening the window, while disobeying the Major's command to keep the window closed. If the Colonel is interpreted as commanding a conditional, then what O'Reilly ought to do is obey the Colonel and the Major, keeping the window closed but making sure the heater is off, while disobeying the Captain's command to turn the heater on. In both the scenario $\mathcal{S}_4$ associated with the latter interpretation and the scenario $\mathcal{S}_3$, suggested by the process of hypothetical reasoning, O'Reilly obeys the Major and does not necessarily obey the Captain; and it may be—though again, I am not sure—that $\mathcal{S}_3$ gains whatever plausibility it has simply by running together the two distinct ways of interpreting the Colonel's order, as a conditional command or a command of a conditional.

8.3   Discussion

Having studied a number of situations in which the current treatment of defeat seems to yield desirable results, or at least results for which straightforward justifications can be found, I now want to conclude by considering some situations that raise more difficult issues.

8.3.1   Inappropriate equilibria

The first can be illustrated with the theory $\Delta_{47} = \langle \mathcal{W}, \mathcal{D}, < \rangle$ where $\mathcal{W} = \{\neg(A \wedge B)\}$, where $\mathcal{D} = \{\delta_1, \delta_2, \delta_3\}$ with δ_1 as $\top \rightarrow A$, with δ_2 as $\top \rightarrow B$, and with δ_3 as $A \rightarrow \neg B$, and where $\delta_1 < \delta_2$ and $\delta_2 < \delta_3$. Again, this theory can usefully be interpreted as a set of commands issued to O'Reilly by the officers, where δ_1 represents the Captain's command to see to it that A, where δ_2 represents the Major's command to see to it that B, and where δ_3 represents the Colonel's command, conditional on the truth of A, to see to it that $\neg B$. Once more, the Colonel's command is peculiar, since the background information from W already tells us that A and B are incompatible, but there is nothing to prevent the Colonel from issuing a peculiar command.

This theory leads to two proper scenarios. The first is the entirely reasonable $\mathcal{S}_1 = \{\delta_2\}$, supporting B and so $\neg A$. On this scenario, O'Reilly obeys the Major's command δ_2; he disobeys the Captain's command δ_1, but has an excuse, since he is prevented from obeying the Captain by obeying the Major, who outranks the Captain. The Colonel's command δ_3 does not come into play, since it is conditional on the truth of A. There is also, however, the second proper scenario $\mathcal{S}_2 = \{\delta_1, \delta_3\}$, supporting A and $\neg B$. On this scenario, O'Reilly obeys the Captain's command δ_1 and the Colonel's command δ_3; he disobeys the Major's command δ_2, but has an excuse, since he is prevented from obeying the Major by instead obeying the Colonel, who outranks the Major.

Now, although this second scenario, $\mathcal{S}_2$, is indeed proper—and does allow O'Reilly to avoid court-martial—there is something anomalous about the scenario all the same. From an intuitive standpoint, it seems almost as if the defaults have been considered in the wrong order. The initial conflict, one wants to say, lies between the Captain's command δ_1 and the Major's command δ_2. This conflict should of course be resolved in favor of the Major, in which case the Colonel's command δ_3 is never even triggered, as in the scenario $\mathcal{S}_1$. In the case of $\mathcal{S}_2$, by contrast, it is as if O'Reilly has made the wrong initial decision, favoring the Captain over the Major, but is absolved from his error by the fact that this incorrect decision triggers the Colonel's command, which provides, in our technical sense, an excuse for his earlier decision to disobey the Major. Once he arrives at the scenario $\mathcal{S}_2$, then, O'Reilly has reached a sort of equilibrium state—the scenario is proper, there is no risk of court-martial—but it is not a state he would have arrived at if his reasoning had followed the correct path to begin with.

Let us turn to another example, illustrating the same point but more disturbing. Since the example is somewhat complicated, we rely on mnemonic abbreviations, focusing on a particular individual, Susan, and taking RC, RN, CC, CU, and VU as the respective propositions that Susan is a resident of Cuba, a resident of North America, a citizen of Cuba, a citizen of the United States, and a person with voting rights in the United States. We consider the default theory $\Delta_{48} = \langle W, \mathcal{D}, < \rangle$, depicted in Figure 8.4, where W contains the propositions RC, $RC \supset RN$, $\neg(CC \wedge CU)$, and $\neg(CC \wedge VU)$, where $\mathcal{D} = \{\delta_1, \delta_2, \delta_3\}$ with δ_1 as $RN \rightarrow CU$, with δ_2 as $RC \rightarrow CC$, and with δ_3 as $CU \rightarrow VU$, and where the defaults are ordered so that $\delta_1 < \delta_2$ and $\delta_2 < \delta_3$.

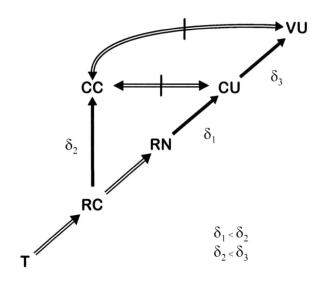

Figure 8.4: Can Susan vote in the United States?

The strict information from W tells us that Susan is a resident of Cuba, and contains instances for Susan of the general facts that residents of Cuba are residents of North America (since Cuba is part of North America), and that citizens of Cuba can neither be citizens of nor have voting rights in the United States. The set D contains instances for Susan of three general defaults. First, there is a weak default—with some statistical justification— according to which residents of North America tend to be citizens of the United States. Second, there is a stronger default according to which residents of Cuba tend to be citizens of Cuba. And third, there is a very strong default—stronger than any of the others, and violated only by a few select groups, such as convicted felons—according to which citizens of the United States tend to have voting rights in the United States.

Now, given this information, what are we to conclude about Susan? Well, on the present approach, the theory leads to two proper scenarios. The first is $S_1 = \{\delta_2\}$, supporting CC and so $\neg CU$ and $\neg VU$—Susan is a citizen of Cuba, rather than the United States, and so has no voting rights in the United States. Here, the default δ_1, supporting the proposition that Susan is a citizen of the United States, is defeated by the stronger default δ_2, and so the default δ_3, supporting Susan's claim to voting rights, is not even triggered. This is, I feel, a reasonable scenario, leading to an intuitively acceptable set of conclusions.

Again, however, there is also a second proper scenario, $S_2 = \{\delta_1, \delta_3\}$, supporting CU and VU, and so $\neg CC$—Susan is a citizen of the United States with voting rights, and so not a citizen of Cuba. Here, the default δ_2

is now defeated by the stronger default δ_3. This second scenario is much less reasonable than the first. And again, I would offer the same diagnosis: from an intuitive standpoint, it seems that the defaults are being considered in the wrong order. The initial conflict lies between the defaults δ_1, suggesting that Susan is a citizen of the United States, and δ_2, suggesting that she is a citizen of Cuba. This conflict should be resolved in favor of δ_2, the stronger of the two defaults, in which case δ_3 is not even triggered, as in the reasonable scenario $\mathcal{S}_1$. In the case of the less reasonable $\mathcal{S}_2$, it is as if we have made the wrong initial decision, favoring δ_1 over δ_2, but as a result, the very strong default δ_3 is now triggered, which then defeats δ_3 and provides a sort of justification for our initial mistake.

Our discussion in the previous section highlighted certain problems with the pure order of application approach, but what the two examples presented here suggest is the need for defining some appropriate order on defaults so that, by considering defaults in that order, we will avoid unintuitive scenarios, like the scenarios $\mathcal{S}_2$ in each of these theories. This is, as far as I know, an open problem in prioritized default reasoning, and the lack of a solution affects a number of the most promising approaches, as well as this one.[7]

8.3.2 Other orderings

The second difficulty I consider raises a different kind of issue, concerning our strength ordering on sets of defaults, according to which one set of defaults $\mathcal{D}'$ is stronger than another set $\mathcal{D}$ just in case $\mathcal{D} < \mathcal{D}'$—that is, just in case $\delta < \delta'$ for each δ in $\mathcal{D}$ and δ' in $\mathcal{D}'$.

A possible problem for this definition is posed by examples such as $\Delta_{49} = \langle \mathcal{W}, \mathcal{D}, < \rangle$, depicted in Figure 8.5, where $\mathcal{W}$ is empty, where $\mathcal{D} = \{\delta_1, \delta_2, \delta_3, \delta_4\}$ with δ_1 as $\top \to A$, with δ_2 as $\top \to \neg A$, with δ_3 as $\top \to A$, and with δ_4 as $\top \to \neg A$, and where the defaults are ordered so that $\delta_1 < \delta_2$ and $\delta_3 < \delta_4$. It is useful to think of this theory as representing a set of commands issued to the agent by officials belonging to two separate systems of authority—say, military and ecclesiastical. Let us imagine that δ_1 represents the Captain's command to see to it that A and δ_2 represents the Colonel's command to see to it that $\neg A$, while δ_3 likewise represents the Priest's command to see to it that A and δ_4 represents the Bishop's command to see to it that $\neg A$. The Colonel outranks the Captain and the Bishop outranks the Priest, but the military and ecclesiastical ranks are incomparable.

---

[7]The theory of Brewka and Eiter (2000), for example, supports both the correct scenario $\mathcal{S}_1$ and the incorrect $\mathcal{S}_2$ in both of our examples. In Horty, Thomason, and Touretzky (1990), a "degree" ordering is defined on the defaults present in the very simple language of defeasible inheritance networks, and the correct results are generated when defaults are considered in order of their degree; but this notion of degree has not been extended to richer languages.

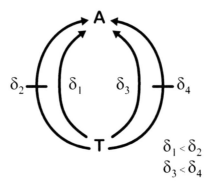

Figure 8.5: Unrelated hierarchies

On the present approach, this theory again supports two proper scenarios. The first is the reasonable $\mathcal{S}_1 = \{\delta_2, \delta_4\}$, in which the agent obeys the commands of the higher ranking officials from each of the two systems of authority, the Colonel and the Bishop. The second is $\mathcal{S}_2 = \{\delta_1, \delta_3\}$—not as evidently reasonable—in which the agent obeys the lower ranking officials, the Captain and the Priest.

It is worth pausing at this point to note why $\mathcal{S}_2$ should count as a proper scenario. Why is the default δ_1, for instance, not defeated in the context of $\mathcal{S}_2$ by the stronger δ_2, or at least by the defeating set $\mathcal{D}' = \{\delta_2, \delta_4\}$? The reason is that, as we recall from our earlier discussion, a defeating set $\mathcal{D}'$ must be consistent with the set that results when some accommodating set $\mathcal{S}'$ is removed from the current scenario—that is, $\mathcal{S}_2^{\mathcal{D}'/\mathcal{S}'}$ must be consistent—where we require in addition that $\mathcal{S}' < \mathcal{D}'$; the defeating set $\mathcal{D}'$ must be stronger than the accommodating set $\mathcal{S}'$. In this case, the only possible accommodating set $\mathcal{S}'$ is, in fact, $\mathcal{S}_2$ itself; and of course, $\mathcal{S}_2^{\mathcal{D}'/\mathcal{S}_2}$ is consistent. But it turns out that $\mathcal{D}'$ is not stronger than $\mathcal{S}_2$ according to our current strength ordering. We do not have $\mathcal{S}_2 < \mathcal{D}'$, since it is not the case that every default from $\mathcal{D}'$ is stronger than every default from $\mathcal{S}_2$; the Colonel's command δ_2 is not stronger than the Priest's command δ_3, and the Bishop's command δ_4 is not stronger than the Captain's command δ_1.

There are two possible reactions to $\mathcal{S}_2$ as a proper scenario. It is, first of all, conceivable to imagine that, although this scenario is apparently less reasonable than $\mathcal{S}_1$, the difficulties are only apparent, and the scenario should indeed be accepted as a legitimate outcome of the theory. Consider, for example, our earlier idea that an agent has an excuse for disobeying an officer if that agent is forced to do so by obeying other officers of equal or higher rank. This idea works well in the military setting, where the system of ranks forms a total order, but how could it be generalized to apply more broadly? One natural proposal is that an agent should then have an excuse for disobeying an official if that agent is forced to do so by obeying other officials whose ranks are at least not lower. And in this sense, the agent who adopts the scenario $\mathcal{S}_2$ is, in fact, able to provide excuses for the neglected commands. The agent is prevented from obeying the Bishop's command δ_4 by instead obeying the command δ_1 issued by the Captain, whose rank is not lower than that of the Bishop; and the agent is prevented from obeying the Colonel's command δ_2 by obeying the command δ_3 issued by the Priest, whose rank is not lower than that of the Colonel.

This line of reasoning supports the current account of defeat exactly as it stands, since this account does generate $\mathcal{S}_2$ as a proper scenario, along with $\mathcal{S}_1$. Another reaction, of course, is to reject $\mathcal{S}_2$ as a legitimate outcome. One can imagine the Colonel saying, when δ_3 is offered as an excuse for disobeying δ_2, something along the lines of: "Don't bring up that odd command issued by your Priest—even your Bishop thinks he's wrong."[8] And surely, from an external perspective, it is hard not to share the intuition that $\mathcal{S}_1$ is, in some sense, a better scenario than $\mathcal{S}_2$.

What this second reaction suggests is that the current strength ordering on sets of defaults must be modified. Our current definition of strength through the $<$ ordering on sets—according to which one set of defaults is stronger than a second only if every member of the first is stronger than every member of the second—is extremely severe. The question is not whether it can be weakened, but which of the various weakenings result in an acceptable overall theory.

This is, of course, a question that can be answered only after detailed experimentation. But just to hint at the direction such a weakening might take, I display one option with some prima facie plausibility. Suppose we define a new strength ordering $\ll$ on sets of defaults so that $\mathcal{D} \ll \mathcal{D}'$ just in case: (1) for all δ from $\mathcal{D}$ there is a δ' from $\mathcal{D}'$ such that $\delta < \delta'$; and (2) for all δ' in $\mathcal{D}'$ there is a δ in $\mathcal{D}$ such that $\delta < \delta'$; and (3) there is no δ from $\mathcal{D}$ and δ' from $\mathcal{D}'$ such that $\delta' < \delta$. Then, returning to the scenarios generated by our example, we can see that $\mathcal{S}_2 \ll \mathcal{S}_1$, as desired; the set of orders issued by the Colonel and the Bishop is preferred to that issued by the Priest and the Captain. And as the reader can verify, with the new $\ll$ relation substituted for the previous $<$ in our definition of defeat, the example would now support only $\mathcal{S}_1$, no longer $\mathcal{S}_2$, as a proper scenario.

8.3.3   Reinstatement

The final difficulty I consider concerns the vexed topic of reinstatement. We saw earlier that, when a first default is excluded by a second, then a third default that itself excludes the second typically allows the first to reemerge from exclusion to support its original conclusion—this was the point of our discussion of Drug 2 from Section 5.2.2. But what about the case in which

---

[8]A response suggested by Hansen.

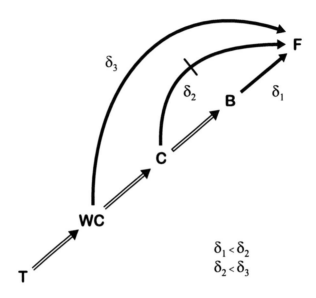

Figure 8.6: Does Bob fly because he is a bird?

a default is, not excluded, but defeated in the more ordinary sense? Does a third default that defeats a second default that defeats a first then reinstate the first default, allowing it to support its conclusion? Interestingly, the answer to this question differs depending on which treatment of defeat is adopted—the preliminary Definition 4 from Chapter 1, or the more refined Definition 21 from the current chapter.

We begin with an example. Let B, F, C, and WC be the propositions that Bob is a bird, that he flies, that he is a chicken, and that he is a wild chicken, respectively. And consider the theory $\Delta_{50} = \langle \mathcal{W}, \mathcal{D}, < \rangle$, depicted in Figure 8.6, where $\mathcal{W} = \{WC, WC \supset C, C \supset B\}$, where $\mathcal{D} = \{\delta_1, \delta_2, \delta_3\}$ with δ_1 as $B \to F$, with δ_2 as $C \to \neg F$, and with δ_3 as $WC \to F$, and where the priority ordering places $\delta_1 < \delta_2$ and $\delta_2 < \delta_3$. The story that goes along with this theory is mostly familiar—as a rule, birds tend to fly and chickens tend not to—but there is one fresh twist: we have discovered a new kind of chicken, known as a wild chicken, that is able to fly, and we are told that Bob is a wild chicken.[9]

Now, if we analyze this example, first, on the basis of our preliminary treatment of defeat—again, Definition 4 from Chapter 1—we then see that the theory leads to $\mathcal{S}_1 = \{\delta_3\}$ as its unique proper scenario, supporting F. This scenario thus supports the conclusion that Bob flies, and the reason for this conclusion is that he is a wild chicken. Notice that this theory does not contain the default δ_1, which supports exactly the same con-

---

[9]Wild chickens were first introduced into the literature on nonmonotonic reasoning by Touretzky, Thomason, and Horty (1991).

clusion. According to our preliminary treatment, this default is defeated by δ_2, a stronger triggered default supporting an inconsistent proposition. Although δ_3 defeats δ_2, this does not lead to the reinstatement of δ_1. According to our preliminary treatment, Bob flies because he is a wild chicken, but not because he is a bird.

According to our more refined treatment of defeat—Definition 21 from the current chapter—it turns out, instead, that the same theory leads to $S_2 = \{\delta_1, \delta_3\}$ as its unique proper scenario, where both defaults support F. Here, the default δ_3 again defeats δ_2, but as the reader can verify, the default δ_1 is no longer classified as defeated: although δ_2 is stronger than δ_1, it cannot be consistently accommodated in S_2 unless δ_3 is removed, but our definition does not allow δ_3 to be removed to accommodate δ_2, since δ_3 is stronger than δ_2. In defeating δ_2, the default δ_3 thus reinstates δ_1, allowing this default to support its conclusion as well. According to our refined treatment, then, Bob flies because he is a wild chicken, but also because he is a bird.

In this case, of course, the difference between our two treatments of defeat, preliminary and refined, may not seem to be terribly significant. After all, although the two approaches lead to different proper scenarios, the two scenarios do not differ in the conclusions they support, but only in the propositions they classify as reasons for those conclusions. If the choice between accepting or rejecting reinstatement had no effects beyond this, it could well be argued that the choice did not really matter at all— or, it could be argued that the choice did matter, since reasons as well as conclusions are important. But, as it turns out, this is an argument we need not engage in, since there are other cases in which whether or not we accept or reject reinstatement affects the set of supported conclusions, not just the reasons for those conclusions.

This possibility can be illustrated with a story. Imagine that, in virtue of stock options accrued over the years, most Microsoft employees are by now millionaires; imagine it is at least a weak default that Microsoft employees are millionaires.[10] Suppose also, as a slightly stronger default, that most new Microsoft employees, many of them just out of college, have not yet accumulated so much as half a million dollars. Finally, imagine that Beth is a new Microsoft employee, but suppose there is reason to believe, as a very strong default—perhaps someone has actually seen a recent list of assets—that Beth does happen to have half a million dollars. And let us supplement this defeasible information by explicitly noting the strict truths that any new Microsoft employee is necessarily a Microsoft employee, and that anyone with a million dollars also has half a million dollars.

Suppose we take *NME* and *ME* as the propositions that Beth is a new Microsoft employee and a Microsoft employee, and we take *1M* and $^1/_2M$ as the propositions that Beth has a million dollars, and that she

---

[10]This default was suggested by Allan Sloan (1997).

has half a million dollars. The story can be represented, then, through the default theory $\Delta_{51} = \langle \mathcal{W}, \mathcal{D}, < \rangle$, depicted in Figure 8.7, where $\mathcal{W} = \{NME, NME \supset ME, 1M \supset {}^1\!/_2M\}$, where $\mathcal{D} = \{\delta_1, \delta_2, \delta_3\}$ with δ_1 as $ME \to 1M$, with δ_2 as $NME \to \neg \, {}^1\!/_2M$, and with δ_3 as $\top \to {}^1\!/_2M$, and where $\delta_1 < \delta_2$ and $\delta_2 < \delta_3$. Here, once again, our preliminary treatment of defeat, which blocks reinstatement, leads to $\mathcal{S}_1 = \{\delta_3\}$ as a unique proper scenario; the default δ_1 is defeated by δ_2, and so excluded from the proper scenario, even though δ_2 is itself defeated by δ_3. On this preliminary treatment, then, only the conclusion ${}^1\!/_2M$ is supported. And just as before, our refined treatment of defeat, which allows reinstatement, leads instead to $\mathcal{S}_2 = \{\delta_1, \delta_3\}$; as the reader can verify, the default δ_3 now defeats δ_2 in such a way that it prevents δ_2 from defeating δ_1. Thus, on the refined treatment, the conclusions $1M$ and ${}^1\!/_2M$ are both supported.

The Microsoft example, therefore, provides an illustration of a case in which reinstatement matters. Our preliminary and refined treatments of defeat actually support different conclusions, not just different reasons for the same conclusion: the refined treatment supports the conclusion that Beth has a million dollars, not just the half a million dollars allowed her by the preliminary treatment. Moreover, it is clear that the stronger conclusion supported by the refined treatment is wrong. Our only reason for believing that Beth has a million dollars is that she is a Microsoft employee, but this reason seems to be legitimately defeated by the fact that Beth is a new Microsoft employee, a special kind of Microsoft employee that is unlikely to have even half a million dollars. As it happens, we do have an independent reason for believing that Beth has half a million dollars, but this gives us no reason at all to conclude that Beth has a million dollars. The additional half million dollars supported by the refined treatment is due to reinstatement alone.

This discussion appears to leave us in an awkward position. On one hand, our preliminary treatment of defeat really was preliminary, and the refined analysis was put forth as an improvement. On the other hand, the refined analysis allows for reinstatement, which leads us, as it now seems, to incorrect conclusions in cases such as the Microsoft example. How do we escape this impasse?

In previous work, I relied on situations such as the Microsoft example to argue against reinstatement.[11] I now believe, however, that the prob-

---

[11]The issue has a complicated history in the literature on inheritance reasoning. The original skeptical theory of inheritance developed by Horty, Thomason, and Touretzky (1990) allowed for reinstatement. Because of concerns with this pattern of reasoning—some of which can be found in Touretzky, Thomason, and Horty (1991)—I developed an alternative skeptical theory of inheritance that blocks reinstatement in Horty (1994b); the topic is discussed at length, but without using the terminology of "reinstatement," in Section 4.3 of that paper. Arguments based on the Microsoft example and similar situations were first presented in Horty (2001b), and directed against systems for defeasible reasoning developed in the style of Dung (1995), which rely on reinstatement as a defining idea.

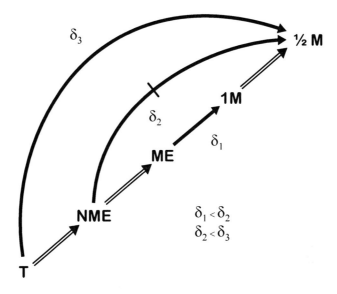

Figure 8.7: Is Beth a millionaire?

lem lies, not with reinstatement itself, but with our formalization of these situations—and that, once they are represented properly, reinstatement can be seen as innocuous. How, then, should our representation of the Microsoft example be changed? Well, recall our earlier discussion, from Section 6.2, of Drug 3, which makes red things look blue and blue things look red. There we decided that, while looking red generally functions as a reason for concluding that some object is red, looking red once Drug 3 has been taken is a stronger reason to the contrary, and so defeats mere looking red as a reason; but we also decided—following Dancy—that, once Drug 3 has been taken, looking red no longer functions as a reason at all for concluding that the object is red. In our technical language, having taken Drug 3 both helps to defeat and also excludes, or undercuts, looking red as a reason for concluding that the object is red; the fact that the agent has taken Drug 3 is both a defeater and an excluder.

My proposal is that a similar sort of thing is going on in the Microsoft example. Being a new Microsoft employee, as we have seen, defeats being a Microsoft employee as a reason for concluding that Beth has one million dollars, but what I would like to suggest is that being a new Microsoft employee should be taken to exclude this reason as well. Once we learn that Beth is a new Microsoft employee, and so unlikely to have even half a million dollars, it is hard to see how the mere fact that she is a Microsoft employee could function as an independent reason for concluding that she has a million dollars. If this analysis is correct, then the excluding default must be made explicit in our representation of the situation. More exactly, we must move from the previous Δ_{51} to the new $\Delta_{52} = \langle \mathcal{W}, \mathcal{D}, < \rangle$, where $\mathcal{W}$ is as before, where $\mathcal{D} = \{\delta_1, \delta_2, \delta_3, \delta_4\}$ with δ_1, δ_2, and δ_3 as before and with δ_4 as the new exclusionary default $NME \rightarrow Out(d_1)$, and where the priority ordering is as before except that, now, we have $\delta_1 < \delta_4$ as well. As the reader can verify, our refined analysis of defeat would then lead to $\mathcal{S}_3 = \{\delta_3, \delta_4\}$ as a unique proper scenario, supporting $^1\!/_2 M$ and $Out(d_1)$—that Beth has half a million dollars and that δ_1 is removed from consideration. We avoid the unfortunate conclusion that Beth has a million dollars, then, not by blocking reinstatement in general, but by excluding the particular default that leads to that conclusion.

Is this proposal ad hoc, constructed only to avoid odd results in the Microsoft example and related cases? I do not think so. As we have seen, a similar idea was already advanced by Dancy, on the basis of independent intuitions. And the general idea that certain defeaters—particularly those whose priority is derived from specificity—exclude as well as defeat finds further support from cases in which specificity seems to support exclusion even without ordinary defeat.

Imagine, for example, that a naturalist studying the distribution of birds among a remote chain of islands has identified two new kinds of finches.[12] There is, first of all, the species of Ruffed Finches, whose nests are largely though not entirely confined to Green Island; and second, there is a particular subspecies of the Ruffed Finches, known as the Least Ruffed Finches, whose nests are distributed almost evenly between Green Island and Sand Island, with only a few strays found elsewhere. Now consider a particular individual, Frank, who happens to be a Least Ruffed Finch. What should the naturalist conclude, by default, about the location of Frank's nest? Take R, L, G, and S as the respective propositions that Frank is a Ruffed Finch, that he is a Least Ruffed Finch, that his nest is on Green Island, and that his nest is on Sand Island; and take δ_1 as the default $R \rightarrow G$ and δ_2 as the default $L \rightarrow G \vee S$, instances of the generalizations that Ruffed Finches live on Green Island while Least Ruffed Finches are distributed between Green and Sand Islands. Our story could, perhaps, be represented through the theory $\Delta_{53} = \langle \mathcal{W}, \mathcal{D}, < \rangle$ where $\mathcal{W} = \{L, L \supset R\}$, where $\mathcal{D} = \{\delta_1, \delta_2\}$, and where $\delta_1 < \delta_2$. This theory tells us that Frank is a Least Ruffed Finch and so a Ruffed Finch; and it contains the two defaults, with the second, based on more specific information, preferred to the first. It is easy to see that this theory has $\mathcal{S}_1 = \{\delta_1, \delta_2\}$ as its unique proper scenario, supporting both G and $G \vee S$.

But that does not seem right. It is Ruffed Finches in general that tend to live on Green Island; the Least Ruffed Finches are a particular subspecies of Ruffed Finches whose population tends to be distributed over Green and Sand Islands—so the fact that he lives on one of these islands is all we want to conclude about Frank. Of course, if the conclusions of our

---

[12]This example arose in discussion with Bijan Parsia and Michael Morreau.

two defaults were inconsistent, the second, as the higher priority default, would defeat the first; but their conclusions are not inconsistent. I believe, therefore, that the most natural way of avoiding the inappropriately strong conclusion that Frank lives on Green Island is by supposing that the fact that he is a Least Ruffed Finch excludes the fact that he is a Ruffed Finch as a reason for this conclusion. More exactly, I believe that the information from our story should be represented as $\Delta_{54} = \langle \mathcal{W}, \mathcal{D}, < \rangle$, where $\mathcal{W}$ is as before, and where $\mathcal{D} = \{\delta_1, \delta_2, \delta_3\}$ with δ_1 and δ_2 as before and with δ_3 as $L \rightarrow Out(d_1)$. This new theory leads to $\mathcal{S}_2 = \{\delta_2, \delta_3\}$ as its unique proper scenario, supporting the conclusions $G \vee S$ and $Out(d_1)$—that Frank lives on either Green or Sand Island, and that δ_1 is removed from consideration, so that the fact that Frank is a Ruffed Finch no longer functions as a reason at all for the stronger conclusion that he lives on Green Island.

This general proposal—that specificity defeaters exclude as well as defeat—would, however, have wide-ranging effects in our representation of any number of central examples, going all the way back to the Tweety Triangle—again, the initial theory $\Delta_1 = \langle \mathcal{W}, \mathcal{D}, < \rangle$, depicted in Figure 1.1, where $\mathcal{W} = \{P, P \supset B\}$, where $\mathcal{D} = \{\delta_1, \delta_2\}$ with δ_1 and δ_2 as the defaults $B \rightarrow F$ and $P \rightarrow \neg F$, and where $\delta_1 < \delta_2$. In that case, it would then be natural to suppose that being a penguin not only defeats but also excludes being a bird as a reason for flying—so that the situation would have to be represented through the new theory $\Delta_{55} = \langle \mathcal{W}, \mathcal{D}, < \rangle$, with $\mathcal{W}$ and $<$ as in the initial representation, but where $\mathcal{D} = \{\delta_1, \delta_2, \delta_3\}$, with δ_1 and δ_2 as before but with δ_3 as the new default $P \rightarrow Out(d_1)$. This theory, of course, yields $\mathcal{S}_1 = \{\delta_2, \delta_3\}$ as its unique proper scenario, supporting the conclusions $\neg F$ and $Out(d_1)$, and so telling us, not only that Tweety does not fly, but that there is no reason at all for thinking he does.

Part V

Appendices

Appendix A

Notes on the default logics

This appendix has three parts. The first part provides a correct definition of the proper scenarios for fixed priority default theories; the second formulates and verifies some observations concerning the notion of defeat; the third maps out some relations between the fixed priority default theories formulated here and Reiter's original approach.

A.1 Proper scenarios

We noted earlier that the preliminary idea of identifying the proper scenarios with the stable scenarios, codified in Definition 7 from Section 1.2.2, fails to yield correct results for certain aberrant default theories containing self-triggering defaults, or chains of defaults. To illustrate, let δ_1 be the default $A \to A$, and consider the theory $\Delta_{56} = \langle W, D, < \rangle$ in which W is empty, $D = \{\delta_1\}$, and $<$ is empty. Here, the set $S_1 = \{\delta_1\}$ is a stable scenario based on this theory, since the single default δ_1 is triggered in the context of this scenario, but neither conflicted nor defeated. But should S_1 be classified as a proper scenario? No, as we can see by considering $\mathcal{E}_1 = Th(\{A\})$, the belief set generated by this scenario. This set contains the proposition A, of course, but we would not want the agent to accept this proposition, since it is not, in an intuitive sense, grounded in the agent's initial information.

As this example shows, a stable scenario can contain too much information, but perhaps there is a simple solution to the problem. Even though, in the example, S_1 is a stable scenario, it is not a *minimal* stable scenario. The only minimal stable scenario based on the underlying default theory is $S_2 = \emptyset$, generating the belief set $\mathcal{E}_2 = Th(\emptyset)$, which does seem to be appropriate. Is it possible, then, to identify the proper scenarios with the minimal stable scenarios?

No again. Let δ_1 be the default $A \to A$, let δ_2 be $\top \to \neg A$, and consider the theory $\Delta_{57} = \langle W, D, < \rangle$ in which $W = \emptyset$, $D = \{\delta_1, \delta_2\}$, and $<$ is empty. Here, $S_1 = \{\delta_1\}$ is again a stable scenario, containing exactly the defaults that are binding in this scenario; the default δ_2 is not binding, since it is conflicted. In this case, however, the scenario $\mathcal{S}_2 = \emptyset$ is not stable, since the default δ_2 is binding in the context of that scenario, but not included. It follows that $\mathcal{S}_1$ is not only a stable scenario, but a minimal stable scenario. But again, we would not want to classify $\mathcal{S}_1$ as proper; the only proper scenario, in this case, is $\mathcal{S}_3 = \{\delta_2\}$, which generates the belief set $\mathcal{E}_3 = Th(\{\neg A\})$.

Rather than attempting to define the proper scenarios in terms of the notion of stability, then, we will adapt a quasi-inductive construction of the kind employed by Reiter. We begin by introducing the notion of an approximating sequence.

Definition 26 (Approximating sequences) Let $\Delta = \langle \mathcal{W}, \mathcal{D}, < \rangle$ be a fixed priority default theory and $\mathcal{S}$ a scenario based on this theory. Then $\mathcal{S}_0, \mathcal{S}_1, \mathcal{S}_2, \ldots$ is an approximating sequence that is based on the theory Δ and constrained by the scenario $\mathcal{S}$ just in case

$$
\begin{aligned}
\mathcal{S}_0 &= \emptyset, \\
\mathcal{S}_{i+1} &= \{\delta : \quad \delta \in \mathit{Triggered}_{\mathcal{W},\mathcal{D}}(\mathcal{S}_i), \\
&\qquad\quad \delta \notin \mathit{Conflicted}_{\mathcal{W},\mathcal{D}}(\mathcal{S}), \\
&\qquad\quad \delta \notin \mathit{Defeated}_{\mathcal{W},\mathcal{D},<}(\mathcal{S})\}.
\end{aligned}
$$

An approximating sequence is supposed to provide an abstract representation of the reasoning process carried out by an ideal agent in arriving at some scenario, a set of acceptable defaults. The sequence depends on two parameters: a base default theory representing the agent's initial information, and a constraining scenario against which the agent checks defaults for conflict or defeat. The agent begins its reasoning process, at the initial stage $\mathcal{S}_0$, without having accepted any defaults; and then, at each successive stage $\mathcal{S}_{i+1}$, it supplements its current stock of defaults with those that have been triggered at the previous stage $\mathcal{S}_i$, as long as they are neither conflicted nor defeated in the constraining set $\mathcal{S}$. It is easy to see that the scenarios belonging to an approximating sequence are nested, each a subset of the next, so that the sequence really can be thought of as providing better and better approximations of some end result. The *limit* of an approximating sequence—defined as $\bigcup_{i \geq 0} \mathcal{S}_i$—represents this end result, the scenario that the agent will arrive at after carrying out the reasoning process indefinitely.

We are particularly interested in the special case of an approximating sequence that is *constrained by its own limit*—a sequence, that is, representing a reasoning process in which defaults are evaluated for conflict or defeat with respect to the scenario that the agent will eventually arrive at after carrying out that very process. A proper scenario can be defined as the limit of an approximating sequence of this kind.

Definition 27 (Proper scenarios) Let $\Delta = \langle \mathcal{W}, \mathcal{D}, < \rangle$ be a fixed priority default theory and $\mathcal{S}$ a scenario based on this theory, and let $\mathcal{S}_0, \mathcal{S}_1, \mathcal{S}_2, \ldots$

be an approximating sequence that is based on Δ and constrained by $\mathcal{S}$. Then $\mathcal{S}$ is a proper scenario based on Δ just in case $\mathcal{S} = \bigcup_{i \geq 0} \mathcal{S}_i$.

It is easy to see that, as desired, this definition yields $\mathcal{S}_2 = \emptyset$ and $\mathcal{S}_3 = \{\delta_2\}$ as the unique proper scenarios based on the theories Δ_{56} and Δ_{57}, respectively; combined with our earlier characterization of extensions in terms of proper scenarios, found in Definition 8 from Section 1.2.2, this new treatment of proper scenarios thus yields $\mathcal{E}_2 = Th(\emptyset)$ and $\mathcal{E}_3 = Th(\{\neg A\})$ as the unique extensions for these two theories.

As we have seen, there are stable scenarios, and even minimal stable scenarios, that are not proper. But it is easy to verify that each proper scenario is stable.

Theorem 1 Let $\Delta = \langle \mathcal{W}, \mathcal{D}, < \rangle$ be a fixed priority default theory and $\mathcal{S}$ a proper scenario based on this theory. Then $\mathcal{S}$ is also a stable scenario based on the theory Δ.

Proof Assuming that $\mathcal{S}$ is a proper scenario, so that $\mathcal{S}$ is the limit of an approximating sequence based on Δ and constrained by $\mathcal{S}$, we need to show that $\mathcal{S} = Binding_{\mathcal{W},\mathcal{D},<}(\mathcal{S})$.

So suppose, first, that $\delta \in \mathcal{S}$. Then there is some $\mathcal{S}_{i+1}$ from the approximating sequence for $\mathcal{S}$ such that $\delta \in \mathcal{S}_{i+1}$. From the definition of an approximating sequence, we know, therefore, that $\delta \in Triggered_{\mathcal{W},\mathcal{D}}(\mathcal{S}_i)$, that $\delta \notin Conflicted_{\mathcal{W},\mathcal{D}}(\mathcal{S})$, and that $\delta \notin Defeated_{\mathcal{W},\mathcal{D},<}(\mathcal{S})$. Because the triggering function is monotonic in its argument, it follows that $\delta \in Triggered_{\mathcal{W},\mathcal{D}}(\mathcal{S})$ as well, since $\mathcal{S}_i \subseteq \mathcal{S}$. Hence the conditions are satisfied to have $\delta \in Binding_{\mathcal{W},\mathcal{D},<}(\mathcal{S})$.

Next, suppose $\delta \in Binding_{\mathcal{W},\mathcal{D},<}(\mathcal{S})$, so that the definition of a binding default tells us that $\delta \in Triggered_{\mathcal{W},\mathcal{D}}(\mathcal{S})$, that $\delta \notin Conflicted_{\mathcal{W},\mathcal{D}}(\mathcal{S})$, and that $\delta \notin Defeated_{\mathcal{W},\mathcal{D},<}(\mathcal{S})$. Because $\delta \in Triggered_{\mathcal{W},\mathcal{D}}(\mathcal{S})$, we have $\mathcal{W} \cup Conclusion(\mathcal{S}) \vdash Premise(\delta)$, from which it follows by compactness, along with the fact that the members of the approximating sequence are nested, that $\mathcal{W} \cup Conclusion(\mathcal{S}_i) \vdash Premise(\delta)$ for some $\mathcal{S}_i$ from the sequence. Therefore, $\delta \in Triggered_{\mathcal{W},\mathcal{D}}(\mathcal{S}_i)$. The conditions are thus satisfied to have $\delta \in \mathcal{S}_{i+1}$, and so $\delta \in \mathcal{S}$. ∎

What the concept of a proper scenario adds to that of a stable scenario, from an intuitive standpoint, is simply the requirement that the set of defaults accepted by an agent must be properly grounded in the hard information from the underlying default theory: a default can belong to a proper scenario only if it belongs to some scenario from the approximating sequence, and it can belong to such a scenario only if it is triggered in the empty scenario, or in some other scenario that occurs earlier in the sequence.

Membership in an approximating sequence guarantees groundedness by ensuring that the conclusion of a default rule cannot be appealed to until its premise is actually established—by, in effect, treating a default as a rule of inference. One way of arriving at a firm understanding of this concept of groundedness, therefore, is by relying on our earlier Definition 19 from Section 7.1.1, which introduced the notion of a defeasible argument constructed from a scenario $\mathcal{S}$—or more simply, an $\mathcal{S}$-*argument*—as a sequence like an ordinary proof, but in which the standard proof rules are supplemented with the defaults from $\mathcal{S}$ as additional rules of inference. In that earlier discussion, we likewise took $Argument_{\mathcal{W}}(\mathcal{S})$ as the entire set of $\mathcal{S}$-arguments based on the initial information in $\mathcal{W}$, and so $Conclusion(Argument_{\mathcal{W}}(\mathcal{S}))$ as the set of conclusions of these arguments—the set of propositions, that is, that can be established through $\mathcal{S}$-arguments from the information in $\mathcal{W}$.

Using these ideas, we can now explicate the concept of groundedness by stipulating that a scenario $\mathcal{S}$ is grounded in an underlying default theory $\Delta = \langle \mathcal{W}, \mathcal{D}, < \rangle$ just in case the belief set generated by $\mathcal{S}$ contains only propositions that can be established through $\mathcal{S}$-arguments from the hard information $\mathcal{W}$ contained in this theory.

Definition 28 (Grounded scenarios) Let $\Delta = \langle \mathcal{W}, \mathcal{D}, < \rangle$ be a fixed priority default theory and $\mathcal{S}$ a scenario based on this theory. Then $\mathcal{S}$ is *grounded* in the theory Δ just in case

$$Th(\mathcal{W} \cup Conclusion(\mathcal{S})) \subseteq Conclusion(Argument_{\mathcal{W}}(\mathcal{S})).$$

The concept can be illustrated by returning to the earlier $\Delta_{56} = \langle \mathcal{W}, \mathcal{D}, < \rangle$, in which $\mathcal{W}$ is empty, in which $\mathcal{D} = \{\delta_1\}$ where δ_1 is $A \to A$, and in which $<$ is empty. We noted earlier that the stable scenario $\mathcal{S}_1 = \{\delta_1\}$ is not, in an intuitive sense, grounded in the agent's initial information; and this intuition can now be confirmed by appeal to our formal definition, since $Th(\mathcal{W} \cup Conclusion(\mathcal{S}_1)) = Th(\{A\})$ while $Conclusion(Argument_{\mathcal{W}}(\mathcal{S}_1)) = Th(\emptyset)$.

The stable scenarios, then, need not be grounded, but it can now be verified that the proper scenarios are grounded.

Theorem 2 Let $\Delta = \langle \mathcal{W}, \mathcal{D}, < \rangle$ be a fixed priority default theory and $\mathcal{S}$ a proper scenario based on this theory. Then $\mathcal{S}$ is also grounded in the theory Δ.

Proof Assuming that $\mathcal{S}$ is a proper scenario, so that $\mathcal{S}$ is the limit of an approximating sequence based on Δ and constrained by $\mathcal{S}$, we need to show that $Th(\mathcal{W} \cup Conclusion(\mathcal{S})) \subseteq Conclusion(Argument_{\mathcal{W}}(\mathcal{S}))$.

We show by induction that, for each i,

$$Th(\mathcal{W} \cup Conclusion(\mathcal{S}_i)) \subseteq Conclusion(Argument_{\mathcal{W}}(\mathcal{S})),$$

from which it follows that by compactness, along with the fact that the members of the approximating sequence are nested, that

$$Th(\mathcal{W} \cup Conclusion(\mathcal{S})) \subseteq Conclusion(Argument_{\mathcal{W}}(\mathcal{S})).$$

The base of the induction is obvious, since $\mathcal{S}_0 = \emptyset$. So suppose for hypothesis that $Th(\mathcal{W} \cup Conclusion(\mathcal{S}_i)) \subseteq Conclusion(Argument_{\mathcal{W}}(\mathcal{S}))$, and consider some proposition $X \in Th(\mathcal{W} \cup Conclusion(\mathcal{S}_{i+1}))$.

From this it follows that there must be an ordinary proof of X from $\mathcal{W} \cup Conclusion(\mathcal{S}_{i+1})$—that is, a sequence of propositions $X_1, X_2, \ldots, X_n$ such that X_n is X and, for $j \leq n$, each X_j either satisfies one of the conditions (1), (2), or (3) from Definition 19, or else the following new condition: (∗) X_j belongs to $Conclusion(\mathcal{S}_{i+1})$. In order to show that $X \in Conclusion(Argument_{\mathcal{W}}(\mathcal{S}))$, we show how this ordinary proof can be transformed into an $\mathcal{S}$-argument of X from $\mathcal{W}$. Since the conditions (1), (2), and (3) are already $\mathcal{S}$-argument conditions, we consider only the case in which X_j is justified by the new condition (∗).

In that case, we know there is some $\delta \in \mathcal{S}_{i+1}$ with X_j as $Conclusion(\delta)$, from which it follows that that $\delta \in Triggered_{\mathcal{W},\mathcal{D}}(\mathcal{S}_i)$ by the definition of the approximating sequence, and by the definition of triggering, that $\mathcal{W} \cup Conclusion(\mathcal{S}_i) \vdash Premise(\delta)$, or put another way, that $Premise(\delta) \in Th(\mathcal{W} \cup Conclusion(\mathcal{S}_i))$. We can conclude from the inductive hypothesis that $Premise(\delta) \in Conclusion(Argument_{\mathcal{W}}(\mathcal{S}))$, so that there is an $\mathcal{S}$-argument $Y_1, Y_2, \ldots, Y_m$ of $Premise(\delta)$ from $\mathcal{W}$. This new argument can then be inserted directly ahead of X_j in the original sequence, and X_j can now be justified by appeal to condition (4) from Definition 19.

Since each appeal to the new condition (∗) can be eliminated in this way in favor of an appeal to condition (4), our original proof of X from $\mathcal{W} \cup Conclusion(\mathcal{S}_{i+1})$ can be transformed into an $\mathcal{S}$-argument of X from $\mathcal{W}$. We therefore have $X \in Conclusion(Argument_{\mathcal{W}}(\mathcal{S}))$ and the induction is complete. ∎

Together with the preceding theorem, this result tells us that the proper scenarios are both stable and grounded. And indeed, the other direction can be established as well, leading to an alternative characterization of the proper scenarios based on a default theory as those that are stable and grounded in that theory.

Theorem 3 Let $\Delta = \langle \mathcal{W}, \mathcal{D}, < \rangle$ be a fixed priority default theory. Then $\mathcal{S}$ is a proper scenario based on the theory Δ just in case $\mathcal{S}$ is both stable and also grounded in this theory.

Proof It follows from Theorems 1 and 2 that $\mathcal{S}$ is stable and grounded if it is proper; we need only establish the other direction. Assume, then, that the scenario $\mathcal{S}$ is both stable and grounded—that $\mathcal{S} = Binding_{\mathcal{W},\mathcal{D},<}(\mathcal{S})$ and $Th(\mathcal{W} \cup Conclusion(\mathcal{S})) \subseteq Conclusion(Argument_{\mathcal{W}}(\mathcal{S}))$—and suppose $\mathcal{S}_0, \mathcal{S}_1, \mathcal{S}_2, \ldots$ is an approximating sequence constrained by $\mathcal{S}$. In order to show that $\mathcal{S}$ is proper, we verify that $\mathcal{S} = \bigcup_{i \geq 0} \mathcal{S}_i$.

For inclusion from right to left, we show by induction that $\mathcal{S}_i \subseteq \mathcal{S}$ for each i, from which it follows that $\bigcup_{i \geq 0} \mathcal{S}_i \subseteq \mathcal{S}$. The base case is obvious, since $\mathcal{S}_0 = \emptyset$. So suppose as inductive hypothesis that $\mathcal{S}_i \subseteq \mathcal{S}$, and consider some default $\delta \in \mathcal{S}_{i+1}$. From our definition of the approximating sequence, we know that $\delta \in Triggered_{\mathcal{W},\mathcal{D}}(\mathcal{S}_i)$, so that $\delta \in Triggered_{\mathcal{W},\mathcal{D}}(\mathcal{S})$ by inductive hypothesis together with the monotonicity of triggering. From the definition of the sequence, again, we also have $\delta \notin Conflicted_{\mathcal{W},\mathcal{D}}(\mathcal{S})$ and $\delta \notin Defeated_{\mathcal{W},\mathcal{D},<}(\mathcal{S})$, so that, all together, we now have $\delta \in Binding_{\mathcal{W},\mathcal{D},<}(\mathcal{S})$. Given our initial assumption that $\mathcal{S} = Binding_{\mathcal{W},\mathcal{D},<}(\mathcal{S})$, we can conclude from this that $\delta \in \mathcal{S}$, and the induction is complete.

For left to right inclusion, suppose $\delta \in \mathcal{S}$. Since $\mathcal{S} = Binding_{\mathcal{W},\mathcal{D},<}(\mathcal{S})$, we know that $\delta \in Triggered_{\mathcal{W},\mathcal{D}}(\mathcal{S})$, that $\delta \notin Conflicted_{\mathcal{W},\mathcal{D}}(\mathcal{S})$, and that $\delta \notin Defeated_{\mathcal{W},\mathcal{D},<}(\mathcal{S})$. Given our definition of the approximating sequence, then, we need only show that there is some i such that $\delta \in Triggered_{\mathcal{W},\mathcal{D}}(\mathcal{S}_i)$ in order to establish that $\delta \in \mathcal{S}_{i+1}$—from which it will then follow that $\delta \in \bigcup_{i \geq 0} \mathcal{S}_i$.

Since $\delta \in Triggered_{\mathcal{W},\mathcal{D}}(\mathcal{S})$, we have $\mathcal{W} \cup Conclusion(\mathcal{S}) \vdash Premise(\delta)$, or put another way, $Premise(\delta) \in Th(\mathcal{W} \cup Conclusion(\mathcal{S}))$. Given our assumption that $Th(\mathcal{W} \cup Conclusion(\mathcal{S})) \subseteq Conclusion(Argument_{\mathcal{W}}(\mathcal{S}))$, we therefore have $Premise(\delta) \in Conclusion(Argument_{\mathcal{W}}(\mathcal{S}))$. But we can now show that $(*)$ for any proposition X, if $X \in Conclusion(Argument_{\mathcal{W}}(\mathcal{S}))$, there is some i such that $X \in Th(\mathcal{W} \cup Conclusion(\mathcal{S}_i))$. Since we have $Premise(\delta) \in Conclusion(Argument_{\mathcal{W}}(\mathcal{S}))$, this allows us to conclude that there is some i such that $Premise(\delta) \in Th(\mathcal{W} \cup Conclusion(\mathcal{S}_i))$, or put another way, that $\mathcal{W} \cup Conclusion(\mathcal{S}_i) \vdash Premise(\delta)$. From this, we get the desired result that there is some i such that $Premise(\delta) \in Triggered_{\mathcal{W},\mathcal{D}}(\mathcal{S}_i)$, completing the proof.

Our verification of $(*)$ proceeds by induction on length of $\mathcal{S}$-arguments. We show that for any $\mathcal{S}$-argument establishing that some proposition belongs to $Conclusion(Argument_{\mathcal{W}}(\mathcal{S}))$, there is some i such that the very same proof sequence is an ordinary proof establishing that the same proposition belongs to $Th(\mathcal{W} \cup Conclusion(\mathcal{S}_i))$. In the base case, where the $\mathcal{S}$-proof is of length 1, the result is obvious, since the single proposition belonging to the proof must be either an axiom or a member of $\mathcal{W}$. So suppose as inductive hypothesis that, for each $\mathcal{S}$-proof of length less than or equal to j establishing that some proposition belongs to $Conclusion(Argument_{\mathcal{W}}(\mathcal{S}))$, there is some i such that the same sequence counts as an ordinary proof establishing that the same proposition belongs to $Th(\mathcal{W} \cup Conclusion(\mathcal{S}_i))$.

Now consider some $\mathcal{S}$-argument $X_1, \ldots, X_j, X_{j+1}$ which establishes that X_{j+1} belongs to $Conclusion(Argument_{\mathcal{W}}(\mathcal{S}))$, with length $j+1$. By hypothesis, there is some i such that the sequence $X_1, \ldots, X_j$ is an ordinary proof establishing that X_j belongs to $Th(\mathcal{W} \cup Conclusion(\mathcal{S}_i))$. If the proposition X_{j+1} is justified by condition (1), (2), or (3) of Definition 19, then of course $X_1, \ldots, X_j, X_{j+1}$ is likewise an ordinary proof showing that X_{j+1} belongs to $Th(\mathcal{W} \cup Conclusion(\mathcal{S}_i))$. So suppose X_{j+1} is justified by condition (4)—that is, that there is some δ from $\mathcal{S}$ such that $Conclusion(\delta)$ is X_{j+1} and $Premise(\delta)$ is a previous member of the sequence. Again, the inductive hypothesis allows us to conclude that $Premise(\delta)$ belongs to $Th(\mathcal{W} \cup Conclusion(\mathcal{S}_i))$, so that $\delta \in Triggered_{\mathcal{W},\mathcal{D}}(\mathcal{S}_i)$. Since $\delta \notin Conflicted_{\mathcal{W},\mathcal{D}}(\mathcal{S})$ and $\delta \notin Defeated_{\mathcal{W},\mathcal{D},<}(\mathcal{S})$, the definition of the sequence tells us that $\delta \in \mathcal{S}_{i+1}$, so that $X_{j+1} \in Conclusion(\mathcal{S}_{i+1})$. This allows us to conclude that $X_1, \ldots, X_j, X_{j+1}$ is an ordinary proof showing that X_{j+1} belongs to $Th(\mathcal{W} \cup Conclusion(\mathcal{S}_{i+1}))$, and so the induction is complete. ∎

A.2 Some observations on defeat

This section formulates and verifies three observations concerning the more refined notion of defeat from Section 8.1, bearing particularly on the ideas introduced there of defeating sets, accommodating sets, and minimal accommodating sets.

Observation 1 Let $\Delta = \langle \mathcal{W}, \mathcal{D}, < \rangle$ be a fixed priority default theory, $\mathcal{S}$ a scenario based on this theory, and suppose δ is defeated in $\mathcal{S}$, with $\mathcal{D}'$ as a defeating set and $\mathcal{S}'$ as an accommodating set for $\mathcal{D}'$. Then there is some $\mathcal{S}^* \subseteq \mathcal{S}'$ such that δ is likewise defeated in $\mathcal{S}$ with $\mathcal{D}'$ as a defeating set and $\mathcal{S}^*$ as a minimal accommodating set for $\mathcal{D}'$.

Proof Using standard techniques, define $\mathcal{S}''$ as a maximal subset of $\mathcal{S}'$ such that $Conclusion(\mathcal{S}'')$ is consistent with $\mathcal{W} \cup Conclusion((\mathcal{S} - \mathcal{S}') \cup \mathcal{D}')$. Then set $\mathcal{S}^* = \mathcal{S}' - \mathcal{S}''$. ∎

Observation 2 Let $\Delta = \langle \mathcal{W}, \mathcal{D}, < \rangle$ be a fixed priority default theory, $\mathcal{S}$ a scenario based on this theory, and suppose δ is defeated in $\mathcal{S}$, with $\mathcal{D}'$ as a defeating set. Then $\mathcal{S}^* = \emptyset$ is a minimal accommodating set for $\mathcal{D}'$ just in case $\mathcal{W} \cup Conclusion(\mathcal{S} \cup \mathcal{D}')$ is consistent.

Proof First, suppose $\mathcal{S}^* = \emptyset$, where $\mathcal{S}^*$ is a minimal accommodating set for $\mathcal{D}'$. Then since $\mathcal{S}^*$ is an accommodating set for $\mathcal{D}'$, it follows that $\mathcal{W} \cup Conclusion((\mathcal{S} - \mathcal{S}^*) \cup \mathcal{D}')$ is consistent. So $\mathcal{W} \cup Conclusion(\mathcal{S} \cup \mathcal{D}')$ is consistent, since $\mathcal{S}^* = \emptyset$. Next, suppose $\mathcal{W} \cup Conclusion(\mathcal{S} \cup \mathcal{D}')$ is consistent. Then $\mathcal{S}^* = \emptyset$ is an accommodating set for $\mathcal{D}'$, and so a minimal accommodating set, since it has no proper subsets. ∎

Observation 3 Where $\mathcal{S}$ is a scenario based on the fixed priority default theory $\Delta = \langle \mathcal{W}, \mathcal{D}, < \rangle$, suppose δ is defeated in $\mathcal{S}$, with $\mathcal{D}'$ as a defeating set and $\mathcal{S}^*$ as a minimal accommodating set for $\mathcal{D}'$. Then each default belonging to $\mathcal{S}^*$ is likewise defeated in $\mathcal{S}$, with $\mathcal{D}'$ as a defeating set and $\mathcal{S}^*$ as a minimal accommodating set for $\mathcal{D}'$.

Proof If $\mathcal{S}^*$ is empty, the result is trivial, so suppose otherwise, and pick some δ^* belonging to $\mathcal{S}^*$. We show that δ^* is likewise defeated as follows. Since $\mathcal{S}^*$ is an accommodating set for $\mathcal{D}'$, we know that (2a)

$\mathcal{S}^* < \mathcal{D}'$ by hypothesis, so that (1) $\delta^* < \mathcal{D}'$, since δ^* belongs to $\mathcal{S}^*$. We know that (2b) $\mathcal{W} \cup Conclusion((\mathcal{S} - \mathcal{S}^*) \cup \mathcal{D}')$ is consistent, also by hypothesis. And since $\mathcal{S}^*$ is a minimal accommodating set for $\mathcal{D}'$, we know that $\mathcal{W} \cup Conclusion((\mathcal{S} - (\mathcal{S}^* - \{\delta^*\})) \cup \mathcal{D}')$—that is, $\mathcal{W} \cup Conclusion((\mathcal{S} - \mathcal{S}^*) \cup \mathcal{D}' \cup \{\delta^*\})$—is inconsistent, from which it follows that (2c) $\mathcal{W} \cup Conclusion((\mathcal{S} - \mathcal{S}^*) \cup \mathcal{D}') \vdash \neg\, Conclusion(\delta^*)$. ∎

A.3   Normal default theories

The defaults in Reiter's original theory are rules of the form $(X : Z / Y)$, with the rough interpretation: if X belongs to the agent's stock of beliefs, and Z is consistent with these beliefs, then the agent should believe Y as well. A *normal default* is a default rule in which the second and third of these elements match—that is, a rule of the form $(X : Y / Y)$, which we can write as $X \to Y$, thus identifying Reiter's normal defaults with the default rules presented here. A *normal default theory*, in Reiter's sense, can be defined as a pair consisting of a set $\mathcal{W}$ of ordinary propositions together with a set $\mathcal{D}$ of normal defaults, but without any priority ordering on the defaults.

Definition 29 (Normal default theories) A normal default theory Δ is a structure of the form $\langle \mathcal{W}, \mathcal{D} \rangle$, in which $\mathcal{W}$ is a set of ordinary propositions and $\mathcal{D}$ is a set of default rules.

Using the notation of the current paper, the extensions defined by Reiter for these normal default theories—which I will refer to here as *Reiter extensions*—can be characterized as follows.

Definition 30 (Reiter extensions) Let $\Delta = \langle \mathcal{W}, \mathcal{D} \rangle$ be a normal default theory. Then $\mathcal{E}$ is a *Reiter extension* of the theory Δ just in case $\mathcal{E} = \bigcup_{i \geq 0} \mathcal{E}_i$, where the sequence $\mathcal{E}_0, \mathcal{E}_1, \mathcal{E}_2, \ldots$ is defined by taking

$$
\begin{aligned}
\mathcal{E}_0 &= \mathcal{W}, \\
\mathcal{E}_{i+1} &= Th(\mathcal{E}_i) \ \cup \ Conclusion(\{\delta \in \mathcal{D} :\ \mathcal{E}_i \vdash Premise(\delta), \\
&\qquad\qquad\qquad\qquad\qquad\quad \mathcal{E} \nvdash \neg\, Conclusion(\delta)\}).
\end{aligned}
$$

Let us say that the normal default theory $\langle \mathcal{W}, \mathcal{D} \rangle$ *corresponds* to any fixed priority default theory of the form $\langle \mathcal{W}, \mathcal{D}, < \rangle$, sharing the same set $\mathcal{W}$ of ordinary propositions and the same set $\mathcal{D}$ of defaults. The normal default theory corresponding to a fixed priority default theory is arrived at, then, simply by removing all priority information from the fixed priority theory. What is the relation between the extensions of a fixed priority default theory, as defined here, and the Reiter extensions of its corresponding normal default theory?

The first thing to note is that the current account is a conservative generalization of Reiter's account, in the sense that the extensions of a fixed priority default theory without any real ordering information coincide with those of the corresponding normal default theory.

Theorem 4 Let $\Delta = \langle \mathcal{W}, \mathcal{D}, < \rangle$ be a fixed priority default theory in which the ordering $<$ is empty. Then $\mathcal{E}$ is an extension of the theory Δ just in case $\mathcal{E}$ is a Reiter extension of $\langle \mathcal{W}, \mathcal{D} \rangle$, the corresponding normal default theory.

    Proof (sketch) Left to right. Suppose $\mathcal{E}$ is an extension of $\langle \mathcal{W}, \mathcal{D}, < \rangle$. Then $\mathcal{E} = Th(\mathcal{W} \cup Conclusion(\mathcal{S}))$, where $\mathcal{S}$ is a proper scenario based on $\langle \mathcal{W}, \mathcal{D}, < \rangle$—that is, $\mathcal{S} = \bigcup_{i \geq 0} \mathcal{S}_i$, where $\mathcal{S}_0, \mathcal{S}_1, \mathcal{S}_2, \ldots$ is an approximating sequence constrained by $\mathcal{S}$. Define the sequence $\mathcal{E}_0, \mathcal{E}_1, \mathcal{E}_2, \ldots$ by putting

$$
\begin{aligned}
\mathcal{E}_0 &= \mathcal{W}, \\
\mathcal{E}_{i+1} &= Th(\mathcal{E}_i) \cup Conclusion(\mathcal{S}_{i+1}),
\end{aligned}
$$

and let $\mathcal{E}' = \bigcup_{i \geq 0} \mathcal{E}_i$. It is easy to see that $\mathcal{E}' = \mathcal{E}$. Hence, it is necessary only to show that $\mathcal{E}'$ is a Reiter extension, by verifying that the $\mathcal{E}_i$ sequence meets the conditions of Definition 30.

    We begin by noting that (∗) $Th(\mathcal{E}_i) = Th(\mathcal{W} \cup Conclusion(\mathcal{S}_i))$ for each i, and also that (∗∗) $Th(\mathcal{E}) = Th(\mathcal{W} \cup Conclusion(\mathcal{S}))$. The first of these results can be established by induction. The base case, with $i = 0$, is evident from the definition of the $\mathcal{E}_i$ sequence. As inductive hypothesis, suppose that $Th(\mathcal{E}_i) = Th(\mathcal{W} \cup Conclusion(\mathcal{S}_i))$ for some i. The inductive step can then be established through the chain of reasoning

$$
\begin{aligned}
Th(\mathcal{E}_{i+1}) &= Th(Th(\mathcal{E}_i) \cup Conclusion(\mathcal{S}_{i+1})) \\
&= Th(Th(\mathcal{W} \cup Conclusion(\mathcal{S}_i)) \cup Conclusion(\mathcal{S}_{i+1})) \\
&= Th(Th(\mathcal{W}) \cup Conclusion(\mathcal{S}_{i+1})) \\
&= Th(\mathcal{W} \cup Conclusion(\mathcal{S}_{i+1})),
\end{aligned}
$$

in which the first equation follows from the definition of the $\mathcal{E}_i$ sequence, the second from the inductive hypothesis, the third from the fact that $\mathcal{S}_i \subseteq \mathcal{S}_{i+1}$, and the fourth from general properties of the Th operator.

    The second result can be established by reasoning as follows:

$$
\begin{aligned}
Th(\mathcal{E}) &= Th(\textstyle\bigcup_{i \geq 0} \mathcal{E}_i) \\
&= \textstyle\bigcup_{i \geq 0}(Th(\mathcal{E}_i)) \\
&= \textstyle\bigcup_{i \geq 0}(Th(\mathcal{W} \cup Conclusion(\mathcal{S}_i))) \\
&= Th(\mathcal{W} \cup Conclusion(\textstyle\bigcup_{i \geq 0} \mathcal{S}_i)) \\
&= Th(\mathcal{W} \cup Conclusion(\mathcal{S})),
\end{aligned}
$$

where the first equation holds because $\mathcal{E} = \bigcup_{i \geq 0} \mathcal{E}_i$, the second by compactness and because the $\mathcal{E}_i$ sequence is nested, the third due to the previous (∗), the fourth by compactness and because the $\mathcal{S}_i$ sequence is nested, and the fifth because $\mathcal{S} = \bigcup_{i \geq 0} \mathcal{S}_i$.

In order to verify that the $\mathcal{E}_i$ sequence meets the conditions of Definition 30, it is enough to verify the equation

$$\mathcal{S}_{i+1} \;=\; \{\delta \in \mathcal{D} : \;\; \mathcal{E}_i \vdash Premise(\delta),$$
$$\mathcal{E} \not\vdash \neg\, Conclusion(\delta)\}.$$

Since the $<$ ordering is empty, no default can be defeated in any scenario. Hence, by the definition of the $\mathcal{S}_i$ sequence, $\delta \in \mathcal{S}_{i+1}$ just in case $\delta \in Triggered_{\mathcal{W},\mathcal{D}}(\mathcal{S}_i)$ and $\delta \notin Conflicted_{\mathcal{W},\mathcal{D}}(\mathcal{S})$. By definition, $\delta \in Triggered_{\mathcal{W},\mathcal{D}}(\mathcal{S}_i)$ just in case $\mathcal{W} \cup Conclusion(\mathcal{S}_i) \vdash Premise(\delta)$, which is equivalent by $(*)$ to the condition that $\mathcal{E}_i \vdash Premise(\delta)$. And $\delta \notin Conflicted_{\mathcal{W},\mathcal{D}}(\mathcal{S})$ just in case $\mathcal{W} \cup Conclusion(\mathcal{S}) \not\vdash \neg\, Conclusion(\delta)$, which is equivalent by $(**)$ to the condition that $\mathcal{E} \not\vdash \neg\, Conclusion(\delta)$. The equation is therefore established.

Right to left (sketch). Suppose $\mathcal{E}$ is a Reiter extension of $\langle \mathcal{W}, \mathcal{D} \rangle$. Then $\mathcal{E} = \bigcup_{i \geq 0} \mathcal{E}_i$, with the sequence $\mathcal{E}_0, \mathcal{E}_1, \mathcal{E}_2, \ldots$ specified as in Definition 30. Define the sequence $\mathcal{S}_0, \mathcal{S}_1, \mathcal{S}_2, \ldots$ by putting

$$\mathcal{S}_0 \;=\; \emptyset,$$
$$\mathcal{S}_{i+1} \;=\; \{\delta \in \mathcal{D} : \;\; \mathcal{E}_i \vdash Premise(\delta),$$
$$\mathcal{E} \not\vdash \neg\, Conclusion(\delta)\};$$

let $\mathcal{S} = \bigcup_{i \geq 0} \mathcal{S}_i$, and let $\mathcal{E}' = Th(\mathcal{W} \cup Conclusion(\mathcal{S}))$. The result can then be verified by showing that $\mathcal{E}' = \mathcal{E}$, and that the $\mathcal{S}_i$ sequence is an approximating sequence constrained by the scenario $\mathcal{S}$. $\blacksquare$

But what about the more general case, when the ordering information from a fixed priority default theory is not empty? In fact, the definitions presented here do allow theories of this kind to have extensions without corresponding Reiter extensions, as we can see by considering $\Delta_{58} = \langle \mathcal{W}, \mathcal{D}, < \rangle$, defined as follows: $\mathcal{W}$ is empty; $\mathcal{D}$ contains an infinite number of defaults, where each default δ_i has the form $\top \rightarrow A$ when i is an odd integer and the form $\top \rightarrow \neg A$ when i is an even integer; and the defaults are ordered so that $\delta_i < \delta_j$ whenever $i < j$. The normal default theory $\langle \mathcal{W}, \mathcal{D} \rangle$ corresponding to this fixed priority theory allows just two Reiter extensions: $\mathcal{E}_1 = Th(\{A\})$ and $\mathcal{E}_2 = Th(\{\neg A\})$. But there are three proper scenarios based on the fixed priority theory itself: both the scenarios $\mathcal{S}_1 = \{\delta_i : i \text{ is odd}\}$ and $\mathcal{S}_2 = \{\delta_i : i \text{ is even}\}$, which generate the extensions $\mathcal{E}_1$ and $\mathcal{E}_2$ above, but also the scenario $\mathcal{S}_3 = \emptyset$, generating the extension $\mathcal{E}_3 = Th(\emptyset)$, which is not a Reiter extension of the corresponding normal theory.

Still, even though it does not hold in general that the extensions of fixed priority default theories form a subset of the Reiter extensions of the corresponding normal default theories, this relation can be established for certain well-behaved fixed priority default theories, and particularly, for those that contain only a finite set of defaults. The verification of this result relies on three initial observations, which have some interest on their own. The first, which holds of fixed priority default theories in general, not just finite theories, is that, whenever a default is defeated in the context of a stable scenario, the defeating set for that default must be consistent with the scenario. The second is that, in the special case of finite theories, any set that defeats a default in the context of a stable scenario must already be contained within that scenario. And the third, also restricted to finite theories, is that any default that is defeated in the context of a stable scenario must be conflicted in that context as well.

Observation 4 Let $\Delta = \langle \mathcal{W}, \mathcal{D}, < \rangle$ be a fixed priority default theory, and suppose $\mathcal{S}$ is a stable scenario based on this theory. Then if some default δ is defeated in $\mathcal{S}$, with $\mathcal{D}'$ as a defeating set, it follows that $Conclusion(\mathcal{S} \cup \mathcal{D}')$ is consistent.

Proof Assume that the default δ is defeated in the scenario $\mathcal{S}$ with $\mathcal{D}'$ as a defeating set and $\mathcal{S}'$ as an accommodating set for $\mathcal{D}'$. By Observation 1, it follows that there is some $\mathcal{S}^* \subseteq \mathcal{S}'$—so that $\mathcal{S}^* \subseteq \mathcal{S}$, of course—such that δ is likewise defeated with $\mathcal{D}'$ as a defeating set and $\mathcal{S}^*$ as a minimal accommodating set for $\mathcal{D}'$. Now suppose $Conclusion(\mathcal{S} \cup \mathcal{D}')$ is not consistent. By Observation 2, it follows that $\mathcal{S}^*$ is nonempty, and by Observation 3, that each default belonging to $\mathcal{S}^*$ is itself defeated in $\mathcal{S}$. But this is impossible, since $\mathcal{S}^* \subseteq \mathcal{S}$, and, because $\mathcal{S} = Binding_{\mathcal{W}, \mathcal{D}, <}(\mathcal{S})$, no default belonging to $\mathcal{S}$ can be defeated. ∎

Observation 5 Let $\Delta = \langle \mathcal{W}, \mathcal{D}, < \rangle$ be a fixed priority default theory in which the set $\mathcal{D}$ of defaults is finite, and suppose $\mathcal{S}$ is a stable scenario based on this theory. Then if some default δ is defeated in $\mathcal{S}$, with $\mathcal{D}'$ as a defeating set, it follows that $\mathcal{D}' \subseteq \mathcal{S}$.

Proof Since $\mathcal{D}$ is finite, we can define the degree of a default δ— written, $degree(\delta)$—as follows: if there is no δ' such that $\delta < \delta'$, then $degree(\delta) = 0$, and otherwise,

$$degree(\delta) = 1 + maximum(\{degree(\delta') : \delta < \delta'\}).$$

The result can then be established by induction on the degree of the defeated default. The base case, with $degree(\delta) = 0$, is trivial, since defaults can be defeated only by other defaults having higher priority. But if $degree(\delta) = 0$, then δ has a maximal priority, and so can never be defeated.

As inductive hypothesis, suppose we know that, for any default whose degree is less than n, whenever that default is defeated in some scenario $\mathcal{S}$, any defeating set for the default must be a subset of that scenario. And where δ is a particular default with $degree(\delta) = n$, suppose that δ is defeated in the scenario $\mathcal{S}$ with defeating set $\mathcal{D}'$.

From the definition of defeat, and from Observation 4, which tells us that $Conclusion(\mathcal{S} \cup \mathcal{D}')$ is itself consistent, so that the accommodating set can be empty, we know that $\mathcal{D}'$ is a subset of $Triggered_{\mathcal{W},\mathcal{D}}(\mathcal{S})$, and also that (1) $\delta < \mathcal{D}'$, that (2b) $\mathcal{W} \cup Conclusion(\mathcal{S} \cup \mathcal{D}')$ is consistent, and that (2c) $\mathcal{W} \cup Conclusion(\mathcal{S} \cup \mathcal{D}') \vdash \neg\ Conclusion(\delta)$. In order to show that $\mathcal{D}'$ is a subset of $\mathcal{S}$, pick some default δ' from $\mathcal{D}'$. We know that $\mathcal{D}'$ is triggered in the scenario $\mathcal{S}$, and also, from (2b), that it is not conflicted. Because $\mathcal{S} = Binding_{\mathcal{W},\mathcal{D},<}(\mathcal{S})$, therefore, δ' must belong to $\mathcal{S}$ unless it is defeated.

Assume, then, that δ' is defeated in $\mathcal{S}$, with $\mathcal{D}''$ as a defeating set. Then from the definition of defeat and Observation 4, again, we know that $\mathcal{D}''$ is also a subset of $Triggered_{\mathcal{W},\mathcal{D}}(\mathcal{S})$, and as before, that (1') $\delta' < \mathcal{D}''$, that (2b') $\mathcal{W} \cup Conclusion(\mathcal{S} \cup \mathcal{D}'')$ is consistent, and that (2c') $\mathcal{W} \cup Conclusion(\mathcal{S} \cup \mathcal{D}'') \vdash \neg\ Conclusion(\delta')$. From the fact that $degree(\delta) = n$, as well as (1) above, we know that $degree(\delta') < n$. Our inductive hypothesis therefore tells us that $\mathcal{D}'' \subseteq \mathcal{S}$, which together with (2c') allows us to conclude that $\mathcal{W} \cup Conclusion(\mathcal{S}) \vdash \neg\ Conclusion(\delta')$. Since δ' belongs to $\mathcal{D}'$, however, this contradicts the previous (2b), and so the assumption that δ' is defeated fails.

Therefore δ' belongs to $\mathcal{S}$, and the proof is complete. ∎

Observation 6 Let $\langle \mathcal{W}, \mathcal{D}, < \rangle$ be a fixed priority default theory in which the set $\mathcal{D}$ of defaults is finite, and suppose $\mathcal{S}$ is a stable scenario based on this theory. Then any default that is defeated in $\mathcal{S}$ must also be conflicted in $\mathcal{S}$.

Proof Suppose δ is defeated in $\mathcal{S}$, with $\mathcal{D}'$ as a defeating set. Then by the definition of defeat we have, among other things, $\mathcal{W} \cup Conclusion(\mathcal{S} \cup \mathcal{D}') \vdash \neg\ Conclusion(\delta)$. Observation 5 tells us that $\mathcal{D}' \subseteq \mathcal{S}$. Therefore $\mathcal{W} \cup Conclusion(\mathcal{S}) \vdash \neg\ Conclusion(\delta)$ as well, so that δ is conflicted in $\mathcal{S}$. ∎

With these observations in place, we can now establish that, at least in the case of fixed priority default theories containing only a finite number of defaults, each extension must also be a Reiter extension of the corresponding normal default theory.

Theorem 5 Let $\Delta = \langle \mathcal{W}, \mathcal{D}, < \rangle$ be a fixed priority default theory in which the set $\mathcal{D}$ of defaults is finite. Then if $\mathcal{E}$ is an extension of $\langle \mathcal{W}, \mathcal{D}, < \rangle$, it follows that $\mathcal{E}$ is also a Reiter extension of $\langle \mathcal{W}, \mathcal{D} \rangle$, the corresponding normal default theory.

Proof The proof follows the pattern of the first half of the proof of the earlier Theorem 4. We begin, as before, by noting that $\mathcal{E} = Th(\mathcal{W} \cup Conclusion(\mathcal{S}))$ where $\mathcal{S}$ is a proper scenario—that is, $\mathcal{S} = \bigcup_{i \geq 0} \mathcal{S}_i$, where $\mathcal{S}_0, \mathcal{S}_1, \mathcal{S}_2, \ldots$ is an approximating sequence constrained by $\mathcal{S}$. As before, we define the sequence $\mathcal{E}_0, \mathcal{E}_1, \mathcal{E}_2, \ldots$ by putting

$$\begin{aligned} \mathcal{E}_0 &= \mathcal{W}, \\ \mathcal{E}_{i+1} &= Th(\mathcal{E}_i) \cup Conclusion(\mathcal{S}_{i+1}). \end{aligned}$$

Setting $\mathcal{E}' = \bigcup_{i \geq 0} \mathcal{E}_i$, it is again easy to see that $\mathcal{E}' = \mathcal{E}$. Hence, it remains only to show that $\mathcal{E}'$ is a Reiter extension, by verifying that the $\mathcal{E}_i$ sequence meets the conditions of Definition 30, which we can accomplish, as before, by showing that

$$\mathcal{S}_{i+1} = \{ \delta \in \mathcal{D} : \quad \mathcal{E}_i \vdash Premise(\delta), \\ \mathcal{E} \nvdash \neg Conclusion(\delta) \}.$$

From the definition of the $\mathcal{S}_i$ sequence, we have $\delta \in \mathcal{S}_{i+1}$ just in case $\delta \in Triggered_{\mathcal{W},\mathcal{D}}(\mathcal{S}_i)$. and $\delta \notin Conflicted_{\mathcal{W},\mathcal{D}}(\mathcal{S})$, and $\delta \notin Defeated_{\mathcal{W},\mathcal{D},<}(\mathcal{S})$. It is again possible to establish the earlier $(*)$ and $(**)$ from the proof of Theorem 4, and then to use these preliminary facts to verify that $\delta \in Triggered_{\mathcal{W},\mathcal{D}}(\mathcal{S}_i)$ just in case $\mathcal{E}_i \vdash Premise(\delta)$, and $\delta \notin Conflicted_{\mathcal{W},\mathcal{D}}(\mathcal{S})$ just in case $\mathcal{E} \nvdash \neg Conclusion(\delta)$. The right hand side of the equation therefore contains those defaults that are triggered in $\mathcal{S}_i$ and not conflicted in $\mathcal{S}$, exactly as before.

In this new case, however, since the priority ordering $<$ is not empty, it is now possible for a default to be defeated in $\mathcal{S}$, and as we have seen, the membership conditions for $\mathcal{S}_{i+1}$ specify that $\delta \notin Defeated_{\mathcal{W},\mathcal{D},<}(\mathcal{S})$. Since defaults that are defeated in $\mathcal{S}$ cannot belong to the left hand side of the equation, we must be able to show that they cannot belong to the right hand side either. Fortunately, Observation 6 allows us to conclude that any default that is defeated in $\mathcal{S}$ is also conflicted—that $Defeated_{\mathcal{W},\mathcal{D},<}(\mathcal{S}) \subseteq Conflicted_{\mathcal{W},\mathcal{D}}(\mathcal{S})$. By ruling out conflicted defaults, the right hand side therefore rules out defeated defaults as well, and the result is established. ∎

Appendix B

Notes on the deontic logics

The purpose of this appendix is to establish two results mentioned in Chapter 3 of the text. The first is that the logic presented there as the conflict account is a conservative generalization of that defined by van Fraassen; the second is that both the conflict and disjunctive accounts can be seen to agree with standard deontic logic, and therefore with each other, when applied to a consistent set of background reasons, or oughts.

B.1   A comparison with van Fraassen's logic

In van Fraassen's account, simple ought statements of the form $\bigcirc(Y)$ are derived from an underlying set $\mathcal{I}$ of imperatives, each of the form $!(Y)$.[1] For convenience, we extend our *Conclusion* notation so that, if i is the imperative $!(Y)$, then *Conclusion*(i) is the proposition Y, and if $\mathcal{I}$ is a set of imperatives, then *Conclusion*$(\mathcal{I})$ is $\{\, Conclusion(i) : i \in \mathcal{I} \,\}$.

The account relies on a notion of *score*. Where v is an ordinary model of the underlying propositional language—that is, a simple valuation mapping proposition letters into truth values—the score of the valuation v, relative to a set $\mathcal{I}$ of imperatives, is defined as the particular subset of imperatives from $\mathcal{I}$ that are satisfied by v. Formally, where $\models$ represents the ordinary satisfaction relation between models and propositions, so that $v \models Y$ tells

---

[1]The account is first sketched in Section 7 of van Fraassen (1973). That paper also contains an account of conditional oughts, which I criticize in Horty (1994a); the treatment of conditional oughts from Section 3.1 of the text is supposed to improve on van Fraassen's account, but a treatment that is entirely correct would require a resolution of the problems with priorities described here in Chapter 8. Lou Goble (2009) makes the point that the systems I have defined in Chapter 3 of this book are not deontic logics in the usual sense, since they do not tell us how to derive ought statements from other, possibly conflicting ought statements, but only how to generate ought statements from an underlying set of reasons, codified in a default theory; he then goes on to remedy the situation by proposing a logic for reasoning sensibly with conflicting ought statements themselves. Goble's observation would apply equally to van Fraassen's logic, which likewise does not provide a calculus for deriving some ought statements from others, but only for deriving oughts from imperatives.

us that Y is satisfied by the model v, the score of a model v relative to a set $\mathcal{I}$ of imperatives can then be defined as

$$score_{\mathcal{I}}(v) = \{i \in \mathcal{I} : v \models Conclusion(i)\}.$$

Against this background, we take $|Y|$ as the ordinary model class of Y, the set of models in which Y holds, and where $\mathcal{F}$ is a set of propositions, we take $|\mathcal{F}|$ as the intersection of the model classes of the propositions in this set: formally, $|Y| = \{v : v \models Y\}$ and $|\mathcal{F}| = \bigcap\{|Y| : Y \in \mathcal{F}\}$. Van Fraassen's account of deontic consequence is then defined as follows.

Definition 31 (Simple oughts: van Fraassen's account) Let $\mathcal{I}$ be a set of imperatives. Then the simple ought statement $\bigcirc(Y)$ follows from $\mathcal{I}$ according to van Fraassen's account—written, $\mathcal{I} \mathrel{\vdash}_F \bigcirc(Y)$—just in case there is a model $v_1 \in |Y|$ for which there is no model $v_2 \in |\neg Y|$ such that $score_{\mathcal{I}}(v_1) \subseteq score_{\mathcal{I}}(v_2)$.

The idea is that Y ought to be the case, given some background set of imperatives, just in case the truth of Y is a necessary condition for achieving a maximal score based on those imperatives.

Our goal, now, is to show that van Fraassen's framework can be interpreted within the framework of default logics in such a way that his account of simple oughts can be seen as a special case of the conflict account presented here. The key to the interpretation is that simple imperatives are represented as simple defaults, those with trivial premises: if i is an imperative of the form $!(Y)$, then the default δ_i representing i will have the form $\top \rightarrow Y$. Formally, then, where $\mathcal{I}$ is a set of imperatives, we define the fixed priority default theory *generated* by $\mathcal{I}$ as the theory $\Delta = \langle \mathcal{W}, \mathcal{D}, < \rangle$ in which $\mathcal{W}$ and $<$ are both empty, and in which $\mathcal{D} = \{\delta_i : i \in \mathcal{I}\}$ is the set of defaults representing the imperatives from $\mathcal{I}$. We can describe a default theory of this form—with no hard information, no priorities, and in which all defaults have the proposition $\top$ as premise—as an *imperative default theory*.

These imperative default theories have a number of simplifying properties. First, because all defaults have the trivial proposition as premise, they are all triggered in the context of any scenario whatsoever; and second, because the priority ordering is empty, no default can be defeated. Taken together with our earlier treatment of the binding defaults and stable scenarios—Definitions 5 and 6 from Sections 1.2.1 and 1.2.2 —these properties now allow us to characterize the stable scenarios based on an imperative default theory $\Delta = \langle \mathcal{W}, \mathcal{D}, < \rangle$ very simply as those satisfying the condition

$$\mathcal{S} = \{\delta \in \mathcal{D} : \delta \notin Conflicted_{\mathcal{W},\mathcal{D}}(\mathcal{S})\}.$$

Furthermore, since the set $\mathcal{W}$ of hard information from an imperative default theory is empty, our earlier account of conflicted defaults—Definition 3 from Section 1.2.1—can be modified so that this simple characterization of stable scenarios for imperative theories can be replaced with an even simpler characterization, according to which the stable scenarios are those satisfying the condition

$$(*) \quad S = \{\delta \in \mathcal{D} : \mathit{Conclusion}(\mathcal{S}) \not\vdash \neg \, \mathit{Conclusion}(\delta)\}.$$

Finally, and again because the premises of all defaults are trivial, the kind of anomaly addressed in Appendix A.1 cannot arise, and the proper scenarios based on imperative default theories can be identified with their stable scenarios.

These observations support yet another characterization of the proper scenarios for imperative theories as maximal sets of defaults whose conclusions are consistent.

Observation 7 Let $\Delta = \langle \mathcal{W}, \mathcal{D}, < \rangle$ be an imperative default theory. Then $\mathcal{S}$ is a proper scenario based on this theory just in case $\mathcal{S}$ is a maximal set of defaults from $\mathcal{D}$ such that $\mathit{Conclusion}(\mathcal{S})$ is consistent.

    Proof   Supposing, first, that $\mathcal{S}$ is a proper scenario based on this theory, so that it satisfies $(*)$, we show that $\mathcal{S}$ is a maximal set of defaults from $\mathcal{D}$ such that $\mathit{Conclusion}(\mathcal{S})$ is consistent. It is easy to see that $\mathit{Conclusion}(\mathcal{S})$ must be consistent because, if not, then $\mathit{Conclusion}(\mathcal{S}) \vdash \neg\, \mathit{Conclusion}(\delta)$ for each $\delta \in \mathcal{D}$, from which it follows by $(*)$ that $\mathcal{S} = \emptyset$; but the set of conclusions of the empty set of defaults is consistent. So suppose $\mathcal{S}$ is not maximal: there is some δ from $\mathcal{D}$ such that $\delta \notin \mathcal{S}$ but $\mathit{Conclusion}(\mathcal{S} \cup \{\delta\})$ is consistent. Since $\mathit{Conclusion}(\mathcal{S} \cup \{\delta\})$ is consistent, it follows that $\mathit{Conclusion}(\mathcal{S}) \not\vdash \neg\, \mathit{Conclusion}(\delta)$, from which we can conclude by $(*)$ that, in fact, $\delta \in \mathcal{S}$.

    Next, supposing that $\mathcal{S}$ is a maximal set of defaults from $\mathcal{D}$ such that $\mathit{Conclusion}(\mathcal{S})$ is consistent, we show that $\mathcal{S}$ satisfies $(*)$ and so is proper. Moving from left to right, if we assume $\delta \in \mathcal{S}$, then it follows that $\mathit{Conclusion}(\mathcal{S}) \not\vdash \neg\, \mathit{Conclusion}(\delta)$, since $\mathit{Conclusion}(\mathcal{S})$ is consistent. And from right to left, if we assume that $\mathit{Conclusion}(\mathcal{S}) \not\vdash \neg\, \mathit{Conclusion}(\delta)$ for some δ from $\mathcal{D}$, then we must have $\delta \in \mathcal{S}$ since $\mathcal{S}$ is maximal. ∎

Because the hard information $\mathcal{W}$ from an imperative default theory $\Delta = \langle \mathcal{W}, \mathcal{D}, < \rangle$ must be empty, it is easy to see that an ought statement $\bigcirc(Y)$ follows from such a theory according to the conflict account— written, $\Delta \mathrel{|\!\sim}_C \bigcirc(Y)$—just in case Y itself is entailed by the conclusions of the defaults belonging to some proper scenario.

Observation 8 Let $\Delta = \langle \mathcal{W}, \mathcal{D}, < \rangle$ be an imperative default theory. Then $\Delta \mathrel{|\!\sim}_C \bigcirc(Y)$ just in case $\mathit{Conclusion}(\mathcal{S}) \vdash Y$ for some proper scenario $\mathcal{S}$ based on this theory.

    Proof   Our general characterization of the conflict account, Definition 9 from Section 3.1.1, stipulates that $\Delta \mathrel{|\!\sim}_C \bigcirc(Y)$ just in case $Y \in \mathcal{E}$ for some extension $\mathcal{E}$ of Δ—just in case, that is, $Y \in Th(\mathcal{W} \cup Conclusion(\mathcal{S}))$ for some proper scenario $\mathcal{S}$ based on this theory, or $\mathcal{W} \cup Conclusion(\mathcal{S}) \vdash Y$. But since the set $\mathcal{W}$ is empty in the case of an imperative default theory, we have $\Delta \mathrel{\vdash_C} \bigcirc(Y)$ just in case $Conclusion(\mathcal{S}) \vdash Y$. ∎

The interpretation of van Fraassen's account within the current framework, which establishes that van Fraassen's account is a special case of the conflict account presented here, or that the conflict account is a generalization, can then be stated as follows.

Theorem 6 Let $\mathcal{I}$ be a set of imperatives and $\Delta = \langle \mathcal{W}, \mathcal{D}, < \rangle$ the default theory generated by $\mathcal{I}$. Then $\mathcal{I} \mathrel{\vdash_F} \bigcirc(Y)$ just in case $\Delta \mathrel{\vdash_C} \bigcirc(Y)$.

Proof   Suppose, first, that $\mathcal{I} \mathrel{\vdash_F} \bigcirc(Y)$. Then there is a model $v_1 \in |Y|$ for which there is no model $v_2 \in |\neg Y|$ such that $score_{\mathcal{I}}(v_1) \subseteq score_{\mathcal{I}}(v_2)$. Taking $Theory(v)$ as the set of formulas true in the model v—that is, $Theory(v) = \{A : v \models A\}$—we let

$$\mathcal{F} = Theory(v_1) \cap Conclusion(\mathcal{I}).$$

Clearly, $\mathcal{F}$ is consistent and a subset of $Conclusion(\mathcal{I})$; and it is clear also that $score_{\mathcal{I}}(v) = score_{\mathcal{I}}(v')$ for any two models $v, v' \in |\mathcal{F}|$. To see that $\mathcal{F} \vdash Y$, suppose otherwise: then there exists a model $v_2 \in |\mathcal{F}| \cap |\neg Y|$; but in that case we have $score_{\mathcal{I}}(v_2) = score_{\mathcal{I}}(v_1)$, contrary to the definition of $\mathrel{\vdash_F}$. The set $\mathcal{F}$ is therefore a consistent subset of $Conclusion(\mathcal{I})$ such that $\mathcal{F} \vdash Y$.

Now consider the scenario $\mathcal{S} = \{\top \to X : X \in \mathcal{F}\}$ formed from the propositions belonging to $\mathcal{F}$. Since $\mathcal{F}$ is a consistent subset of $Conclusion(\mathcal{I})$, and since Δ is the default theory generated by $\mathcal{I}$, it follows that $\mathcal{S}$ is a subset of the set $\mathcal{D}$ of defaults from this theory such that $Conclusion(\mathcal{S})$ is consistent. Standard techniques allow $\mathcal{S}$ to be extended to a maximal set $\mathcal{S}'$ from $\mathcal{D}$ such that $Conclusion(\mathcal{S}')$ is consistent, from which we can conclude by Observation 7 that $\mathcal{S}'$ is a proper scenario based on Δ. Further, it is immediate from our definition of $\mathcal{S}$ that $\mathcal{F} \subseteq Conclusion(\mathcal{S})$, and since $\mathcal{S}'$ extends $\mathcal{S}$, we have $\mathcal{F} \subseteq Conclusion(\mathcal{S}')$ as well. Therefore, since $\mathcal{F} \vdash Y$, we know that $Conclusion(\mathcal{S}') \vdash Y$, and so it follows from Observation 8 that $\Delta \mathrel{\vdash_C} \bigcirc(Y)$.

Next, suppose that $\Delta \mathrel{\vdash_C} \bigcirc(Y)$, so that we have, by Observations 7 and 8, $Conclusion(\mathcal{S}) \vdash Y$ for some maximal subset $\mathcal{S}$ of $\mathcal{D}$ such that $Conclusion(\mathcal{S})$ is consistent—for some $\mathcal{S}$, that is, such that $Conclusion(\mathcal{S})$ is a maximal consistent subset of $Conclusion(\mathcal{D})$. Since Δ is the default theory generated by the set $\mathcal{I}$ of imperatives, it follows at once that $Conclusion(\mathcal{D}) = Conclusion(\mathcal{I})$, from which we can conclude that $Conclusion(\mathcal{S})$ is likewise a maximal consistent subset of $Conclusion(\mathcal{I})$. Since $Conclusion(\mathcal{S})$ is consistent, and since $Conclusion(\mathcal{S}) \vdash Y$, we have some model $v_1 \in |Conclusion(\mathcal{S})| \subseteq |Y|$; and then since $Conclusion(\mathcal{S})$ is maximal, it follows that there can be no $v_2 \in |\neg Y|$ such that $score_{\mathcal{I}}(v_1) \subseteq score_{\mathcal{I}}(v_2)$. So $\mathcal{I} \not\vdash_F \bigcirc (Y)$. ∎

B.2   A comparison with standard deontic logic

Unlike van Fraassen's account, standard deontic logic is a species of modal logic, developed using the usual possible worlds techniques; accessible treatments can be found in most texts on modal logic.

Very briefly, standard deontic logic is the modal logic based on *standard deontic models*—structures of the form $\mathcal{M} = \langle W, f, v \rangle$, with W a set of possible worlds, v a modal valuation mapping sentence letters into sets of worlds at which they are thought of as true, and f a function mapping each world α into a set of worlds $f(\alpha)$, subject only to the constraint that this set of worlds should be nonempty: $f(\alpha) \neq \emptyset$. Where α is an individual world, $f(\alpha)$ can be thought of as the set of worlds that are ideal from the standpoint of α, those in which all the oughts in force at α are satisfied.

Following the usual pattern in modal logics, formulas are assigned truth values relative to a pair consisting of a model $\mathcal{M}$ and a world α from that model. For a sentence letter p, we have the evaluation rule

$$\mathcal{M}, \alpha \models p \text{ just in case } \alpha \in v(p),$$

telling us simply that p is true at the world α if α is among the worlds assigned by v to p. The rules for the truth functional connectives mirror those of ordinary logic:

$$\mathcal{M}, \alpha \models X \wedge Y \text{ just in case } \mathcal{M}, \alpha \models X \text{ and } \mathcal{M}, \alpha \models Y,$$
$$\mathcal{M}, \alpha \models \neg X \text{ just in case it is not the case that } \mathcal{M}, \alpha \models X.$$

And the rule for the deontic operator $\bigcirc$ follows the standard recipe:

$$\mathcal{M}, \alpha \models \bigcirc(Y) \text{ just in case } \mathcal{M}, \beta \models Y \text{ for each } \beta \in f(\alpha).$$

The idea is that $\bigcirc(Y)$ holds at a world α in the model $\mathcal{M}$ just in case Y holds in all the worlds that are ideal from the standpoint of α.

As usual, we will say that $\mathcal{M} \models X$ just in case X holds at each world in $\mathcal{M}$—just in case, that is, $\mathcal{M}, \alpha \models X$ for each world α from the model. Where Γ is a set of formulas, we will say that $\mathcal{M} \models \Gamma$ whenever $\mathcal{M} \models X$ for each formula X from Γ. And we will say that the set of formulas Γ semantically entails the formula X according to standard deontic logic— written $\Gamma \Vdash_{SDL} X$—just in case $\mathcal{M} \models \Gamma$ implies $\mathcal{M} \models X$ for each standard deontic model $\mathcal{M}$.

In order to establish the appropriate connection between standard deontic logic and the theories presented here, based on default logic, we impose two restrictions on the formalisms. First, from the side of default logic, we consider only imperative default theories as defined in the previous section—those theories of the form $\langle \mathcal{W}, \mathcal{D}, < \rangle$ in which both $\mathcal{W}$ and

$<$ are empty, and in which each default from $\mathcal{D}$ has the form $\top \rightarrow Y$. Second, from the side of standard deontic logic, since this system allows nested deontic operators, while the theories presented in this book do not, we explicitly restrict ourselves only to the nonnested fragment of standard deontic logic.

Given these restrictions, we now describe the way in which both the conflict and disjunctive accounts defined in this book coincide with standard deontic logic when applied to a consistent imperative default theory $\Delta = \langle \mathcal{W}, \mathcal{D}, < \rangle$—where such a theory is defined as *consistent* whenever the set $Conclusion(\mathcal{D})$ is itself consistent. As a preliminary observation, we note that, when the theory Δ is consistent in this sense, the set $Conclusion(\mathcal{D})$ will be its own unique maximal consistent subset. We are thus led, in this case, to the following characterization of the conflict and disjunctive consequence relations—represented, once again, as $\vdash_C$ and $\vdash_D$—which shows that these relations coincide when applied to consistent theories.

Observation 9 Let $\Delta = \langle \mathcal{W}, \mathcal{D}, < \rangle$ be a consistent imperative default theory. Then we have both $\Delta \vdash_C \bigcirc(Y)$ and $\Delta \vdash_D \bigcirc(Y)$ just in case $Conclusion(\mathcal{D}) \vdash Y$.

Since $Conclusion(\mathcal{D})$ is maximal, the verification of this fact for the conflict account follows immediately from the previous Observations 7 and 8, and the verification for the disjunctive account is similar.

Because the conflict and disjunctive accounts coincide in the special case in which the underlying theory $\Delta = \langle \mathcal{W}, \mathcal{D}, < \rangle$ is consistent, we can, in this case, take $\Delta \vdash \bigcirc(Y)$ to mean that $\bigcirc(Y)$ follows from the theory Δ according to either the conflict or the disjunctive account, indiscriminately. Where $\mathcal{D}$ is the set of defaults from such a theory, we can define the set $\mathcal{D}^* = \{\bigcirc(Y) : \top \rightarrow Y \in \mathcal{D}\}$, so that $\mathcal{D}^*$ represents, in a sense, the interpretation of $\mathcal{D}$ in standard deontic logic. Our primary result, establishing the agreement in case of consistency between the theories set out here and standard deontic logic, can therefore be stated as follows.

Theorem 7 Let $\Delta = \langle \mathcal{W}, \mathcal{D}, < \rangle$ be a consistent imperative default theory, and let $\mathcal{D}^* = \{\bigcirc(Y) : \top \rightarrow Y \in \mathcal{D}\}$. Then $\Delta \vdash \bigcirc(Y)$ just in case $\mathcal{D}^* \Vdash \bigcirc(Y)$.

Proof We begin by supposing that $\mathcal{D}^* \Vdash \bigcirc(Y)$—that is, that $\mathcal{M} \models \mathcal{D}^*$ implies $\mathcal{M} \models \bigcirc(Y)$ for each standard deontic model $\mathcal{M}$.

In order to show that $\Delta \vdash \bigcirc(Y)$, we begin by constructing a particular standard deontic model $\mathcal{M}_{\mathcal{D}} = \langle W, f, v \rangle$, whose components are defined as follows. (1) W contains the set of models, ordinary valuations, for the underlying propositional language. Note that this stipulation is potentially confusing, since the same objects—α, β, γ, and so on—now play two roles: they are both models or valuations for the underlying propositional language and also possible worlds in a particular model for the deontic language. (2) f is the constant function mapping each possible world α into the set $|\,Conclusion(\mathcal{D})|$. What this means is that f associates each world, each ordinary valuation, with the set of ordinary valuations that satisfy the conclusions of all the defaults from $\mathcal{D}$. (3) v is the modal valuation defined by taking $v(p) = \{\alpha : \alpha \models p\}$. What this means is that v maps each sentence letter p into the set of possible worlds that, considered now as ordinary propositional models, assign the value of truth to p.

At this point, we need to establish two preliminary facts.

First, to show that $\mathcal{M}_{\mathcal{D}}$ is, in fact, a standard deontic model, we need to guarantee that $f(\alpha) \neq \emptyset$, but this is trivial: $f(\alpha) = |\,Conclusion(\mathcal{D})|$ is simply the set of ordinary propositional models satisfying the set of sentences $Conclusion(\mathcal{D})$, but by hypothesis, $Conclusion(\mathcal{D})$ is a consistent set, and so we know that it must have at least one model.

Second, we need to show that, for each ordinary propositional formula Y, we have

$$(**)\qquad \mathcal{M}_{\mathcal{D}}, \beta \models Y \text{ just in case } \beta \models Y,$$

telling us that Y is satisfied by the world β in the model $\mathcal{M}_{\mathcal{D}}$ just in case β, now considered as an ordinary propositional valuation, assigns the value truth to Y—or, put another way, that $\mathcal{M}_{\mathcal{D}}, \beta \models Y$ just in case $\beta \in |Y|$, where again, $|Y| = \{\beta \models Y\}$ is the set of ordinary propositional valuations satisfying Y. This fact can be established by induction on the complexity of the formula Y. The base case is guaranteed by the definition of v in (3) above; the inductive step is straightforward.

We can now proceed with our main argument. Since $\mathcal{D}^* \Vdash \bigcirc(Y)$, and since $\mathcal{M}_{\mathcal{D}}$ is a standard deontic model, we know that $\mathcal{M}_{\mathcal{D}} \models \bigcirc(Y)$ whenever $\mathcal{M}_{\mathcal{D}} \models \mathcal{D}^*$. It is easy to verify that $\mathcal{M}_{\mathcal{D}} \models \mathcal{D}^*$, and so we can conclude that $\mathcal{M}_{\mathcal{D}} \models \bigcirc(Y)$. According to the deontic evaluation rule, however, we have $\mathcal{M}_{\mathcal{D}} \models \bigcirc(Y)$ only if $\mathcal{M}, \beta \models Y$ for each $\beta \in f(\alpha)$. From $(**)$ above, we can now conclude that $f(\alpha) \subseteq |Y|$: each model belonging to $f(\alpha)$—that is, each model satisfying $Conclusion(\mathcal{D})$—is also a model of Y. From this, it follows by the completeness theorem for ordinary propositional logic that $Conclusion(\mathcal{D}) \vdash Y$, from which we can conclude that $\Delta \mathrel{|\!\sim} \bigcirc(Y)$ by Observation 9.

The argument in the other direction is easier. If we suppose that $\Delta \mathrel{|\!\sim} \bigcirc(Y)$, we know by Observation 9 that $Conclusion(\mathcal{D}) \vdash Y$, so that $\{X_1, \ldots X_n\} \vdash Y$ for some finite subset $\{X_1, \ldots X_n\}$ of $Conclusion(\mathcal{D})$ by compactness. From this it follows that $\vdash (X_1 \wedge \ldots \wedge X_n) \supset Y$, by the deduction theorem for propositional logic. Since standard deontic logic is a normal modal logic, we therefore have $\Vdash (\bigcirc(X_1) \wedge \ldots \wedge \bigcirc(X_n)) \supset \bigcirc(Y)$, from which we can conclude that $\mathcal{D}^* \Vdash \bigcirc(Y)$, since $\bigcirc(X_1), \ldots, \bigcirc(X_n) \in \mathcal{D}^*$.

∎

Bibliography

Anderson, Alan, Belnap, Nuel, and Dunn, J. Michael (1992). *Entailment: The Logic of Relevance and Necessity, Volume 2*. Princeton University Press.

Antonelli, G. Aldo (1999). A directly cautious theory of defeasible consequence for default logic via the notion of a general extension. *Artificial Intelligence*, 109:71–109.

Apt, Krzysztof, Blair, Howard, and Walker, Adrian (1988). Towards a theory of declarative knowledge. In Minker, Jack, editor, *Foundations of Deductive Databases and Logic Programming*, pages 89–148. Morgan Kaufmann Publishers Inc.

Baader, Franz and Hollunder, Bernhard (1995). Priorities on defaults with prerequisites, and their applications in treating specificity in terminological default logic. *Journal of Automated Reasoning*, 15:41–68.

Baier, Kurt (1958). *The Moral Point of View: A Rational Basis of Ethics*. Cornell University Press.

Belnap, Nuel (1979). Rescher's hypothetical reasoning: an amendment. In Sosa, Ernest, editor, *The Philosophy of Nicholas Rescher: Discussion and Replies*, pages 19–28. D. Reidel Publishing Company.

Belnap, Nuel, Perloff, Michael, and Xu, Ming (2001). *Facing the Future: Agents and Choices in Our Indeterministic World*. Oxford University Press.

Brachman, Ronald and Levesque, Hector, editors (1985). *Readings in Knowledge Representation*. Morgan Kaufmann Publishers.

Bradley, F. H. (1927). *Ethical Studies (Second Edition)*. Oxford University Press.

Brewka, Gerhard (1994a). Adding priorities and specificity to default logic. In *Proceedings of the European Workshop on Logics in Artificial Intelligence (JELIA-94)*, Springer Verlag Lecture Notes in Artificial Intelligence, pages 247–260. Springer Verlag.

Brewka, Gerhard (1994b). Reasoning about priorities in default logic. In *Proceedings of the Twelveth National Conference on Artificial Intelligence (AAAI-94)*, pages 940–945. AAAI/MIT Press.

Brewka, Gerhard (1996). Well-founded semantics for extended logic programs with dynamic preferences. *Journal of Artificial Intelligence Research*, 4:19–36.

Brewka, Gerhard and Eiter, Thomas (2000). Prioritizing default logic. In Hölldobler, St., editor, *Intellectics and Computational Logic: Papers in Honor of Wolfgang Bibel*. Kluwer Academic Publishers.

Brink, David (1994). Moral conflict and its structure. *The Philosophical Review*, 103:215–247.

Broome, John (1999). Normative requirements. *Ratio*, 12:398–419.

Broome, John (2004). Reasons. In Wallace, R. Jay, Smith, Michael, Scheffler, Samuel, and Pettit, Philip, editors, *Reason and Value: Essays on the Moral Philosophy of Joseph Raz*, pages 28–55. Oxford University Press.

Chellas, Brian (1974). Conditional obligation. In Stenlund, Søren, editor, *Logical Theory and Semantic Analysis*, pages 23–33. D. Reidel Publishing Company.

Chisholm, Roderick (1964). The ethics of requirement. *American Philosophical Quarterly*, 1:147–153.

Chisholm, Roderick (1966). *Theory of Knowledge*. Prentice Hall.

Chisholm, Roderick (1974). Practical reason and the logic of requirement. In Körner, Stephan, editor, *Practical Reason*, pages 2–13. Blackwell Publishing Company. Reprinted in Raz (1978).

Church, Alonzo (1956). *Introduction to Mathematical Logic, Volume I*. Princeton University Press.

Conee, Earl (1982). Against moral dilemmas. *Philosophical Review*, 91:87–97.

Dancy, Jonathan (1983). Ethical particularism and morally relevant properties. *Mind*, 92:530–547.

Dancy, Jonathan (1991). An ethic of prima facie duties. In Singer, Peter, editor, *A Companion to Ethics*. Basic Blackwell Publishers.

Dancy, Jonathan (1993). *Moral Reasons*. Basil Blackwell Publisher.

Dancy, Jonathan (2000). The particularist's progress. In Hooker, Brad and Little, Margaret, editors, *Moral Particularism*, pages 130–156. Oxford University Press.

Dancy, Jonathan (2001). Moral particularism. In Zalta, Edward, editor, *The Stanford Encyclopedia of Philosophy (Summer 2001 Edition)*. Stanford University. Available at http://plato.stanford.edu/archives/sum2001/entries/moral-particularism/.

Dancy, Jonathan (2004). *Ethics Without Principles*. Oxford University Press.

Davidson, Donald (1970). How is weakness of the will possible? In Feinberg, Joel, editor, *Moral Concepts*. Oxford University Press.

Delgrande, James and Schaub, Torsten (2000a). Expressing preferences in default logic. *Artificial Intelligence*, 123:41–87.

Delgrande, James and Schaub, Torsten (2000b). The role of default logic in knowledge representation. In Minker, Jack, editor, *Logic Based Artificial Intelligence*, pages 107–126. Kluwer academic Publishers.

Delgrande, James and Schaub, Torsten (2004). Reasoning with sets of defaults in default logic. *Computational Intelligence*, 20:56–88.

Delgrande, James, Schaub, Torsten, and Jackson, W. Ken (1994). Alternative approaches to default logic. *Artificial Intelligence*, 70:167–237.

Donagan, Alan (1984). Consistency in rationalist moral systems. *The Journal of Philosophy*, 81:291–309.

Donagan, Alan (1993). Moral dilemmas, genuine and spurious: a comparative anatomy. *Ethics*, 104:7–21.

Dung, Phan Minh (1995). On the acceptability of arguments and its fundamental role in nonmonotonic reasoning, logic programming, and n-person games. *Artificial Intelligence*, 77:321–357.

Edmundson, William (1993). Rethinking exclusionary reasons: a second edition of Joseph Raz's 'Practical Reason and Norms'. *Law and Philosophy*, 12:329–343.

Etherington, David and Reiter, Raymond (1983). On inheritance hierarchies with exceptions. In *Proceedings of the Third National Conference on Artificial Intelligence (AAAI-83)*, pages 104–108.

Fahlman, Scott (1979). *NETL: A System for Representing and Using Real-world Knowledge*. The MIT Press.

Føllesdal, Dagfinn and Hilpinen, Risto (1971). Deontic logic: an introduction. In Hilpinen, Risto, editor, *Deontic Logic: Introductory and Systematic Readings*, pages 1–35. D. Reidel Publishing Company.

Foot, Philippa (1983). Moral realism and moral dilemmas. *Journal of Philosophy*, 80:379–398. Reprinted in Gowans (1987b), pages 250–270; pagination refers to this version.

Franklin, Benjamin (1772). Letter to Joseph Priestly. Reprinted in Frank Mott and Chester Jorgenson, editors, *Benjamin Franklin: Representative Selections*, pages 348–349, American Book Company, 1936; pagination refers to this version.

Gans, Chaim (1986). Mandatory rules and exclusionary reasons. *Philosophia*, 615:373–394.

Ginsberg, Matthew (1993). *Essentials of Artificial Intelligence*. Morgan Kaufmann Publishers.

Goble, Lou (2009). Normative conflicts and the logic of 'ought'. *Noûs*, 43:450–489.

Gordon, Thomas (1993). *The Pleadings Game: An Artificial-Intelligence Model of Procedural Justice*. PhD thesis, Technische Hochschule Darmstadt.

Gowans, Christopher (1987a). Introduction: the debate on moral dilemmas. In Gowans, Christopher, editor, *Moral Dilemmas*, pages 3–33. Oxford University Press.

Gowans, Christopher, editor (1987b). *Moral Dilemmas*. Oxford University Press.

Hansen, Jörg (2006). Deontic logic for prioritized imperatives. *Artificial Intelligence and Law*, 14:1–34.

Hansen, Jörg (2008). Prioritized conditional imperatives: problems and a new proposal. *Autonomous Agents and Multi-agent Systems*, pages 11–35.

Hansson, Bengt (1971). An analysis of some deontic logics. In Hilpinen, Risto, editor, *Deontic Logic: Introductory and Systematic Readings*, pages 121–147. D. Reidel Publishing Company.

Hansson, Sven Ove (2001). *The Structure of Values and Norms*. Cambridge University Press.

Hare, R. M. (1952). *The Language of Morals*. Oxford University Press.

Hare, R. M. (1963). *Freedom and Reason*. Oxford University Press.

Harman, Gilbert (1975). Reasons. *Critica*, 7:3–18. Reprinted in Raz (1978); pagination refers to this version.

Harman, Gilbert (1978). *The Nature of Morality: An Introduction to Ethics*. Oxford University Press.

Hart, H. L. A. (1948). The ascription of responsibility and rights. *Proceedings of the Aristotelian Society*, pages 171–194.

Hohfeld, Wesley (1919). *Fundamental Legal Conceptions as Applied in Judicial Reasoning*. Yale University Press.

Holton, Richard (2002). Principles and particularisms. In *Proceedings of the Aristotelian Society, Supplementary Volume 76*, pages 191–210. Harrison and Sons.

Hooker, Brad and Little, Margaret, editors (2000). *Moral Particularism*. Oxford University Press.

Horty, John (1994a). Moral dilemmas and nonmonotonic logic. *Journal of Philosophical Logic*, 23:35–65. A preliminary version appears in *Proceedings of the First International Workshop on Deontic Logic in Computer Science*, J.-J. Ch. Meyer and R.M. Wieringa (eds.), Free University of Amsterdam, 1991, pp. 212–231.

Horty, John (1994b). Some direct theories of nonmonotonic inheritance. In Gabbay, D., Hogger, C., and Robinson, J., editors, *Handbook of Logic in Artificial Intelligence and Logic Programming, Volume 3: Nonmonotonic Reasoning and Uncertain Reasoning*, pages 111–187. Oxford University Press.

Horty, John (2001a). *Agency and Deontic Logic*. Oxford University Press.

Horty, John (2001b). Argument construction and reinstatement in logics for defeasible reasoning. *Artificial Intelligence and Law*, 9:1–28.

Horty, John (2001c). Nonmonotonic logic. In Goble, Lou, editor, *The Blackwell Guide to Philosophical Logic*, pages 336–361. Basil Blackwell Publisher.

Horty, John (2002). Skepticism and floating conclusions. *Artificial Intelligence*, 135:55–72.

Horty, John (2003). Reasoning with moral conflicts. *Nous*, 37:557–605.

Horty, John (2007a). Defaults with priorities. *Journal of Philosophical Logic*, 36:367–413.

Horty, John (2007b). Reasons as defaults. *Philosopher's Imprint*, 7(3).

Horty, John (2011). Rules and reasons in the theory of precedent. *Legal Theory*, 17:1–33.

Horty, John and Belnap, Nuel (1995). The deliberative stit: a study of action, omission, ability, and obligation. *Journal of Philosophical Logic*, 24:583–644.

Horty, John, Thomason, Richmond, and Touretzky, David (1990). A skeptical theory of inheritance in nonmonotonic semantic networks. *Artificial Intelligence*, 42:311–348. A preliminary version appears in *Proceedings of the Sixth National Conference on Artificial Intelligence*, Morgan Kaufmann Publishers, 1987, pp. 358–363.

Jackson, Frank (1985). On the semantics and logic of obligation. *Mind*, 94:177–195.

Johnson, Steven (2008). *The Invention of Air*. Riverhead Books.

Kagan, Shelly (1988). The additive fallacy. *Ethics*, 99:5–31.

Konolige, Kurt and Myers, Karen (1989). Representing defaults with epistemic concepts. *Computational Intelligence*, 5:32–44.

Kornhauser, Lewis and Sager, Lawrence (1986). Unpacking the court. *Yale Law Journal*, 96:82–117.

Lance, Mark and Little, Margaret (2004). Defeasibility and the normative grasp of context. *Erkenntnis*, 61:435–455.

Lance, Mark and Little, Margaret (2007). Where the laws are. In Shafer-Landau, Russ, editor, *Oxford Studies in Metaethics*, volume 2, pages 149–171. Oxford University Press.

Lance, Mark and Little, Margaret (2008). From particularism to defeasibility in ethics. In Potrc, Matjaa, Strahovnik, Vojko, and Lance, Mark, editors, *Challenging Moral Particularism*. Routledge Publishers.

Lewis, David (1973). *Counterfactuals*. Oxford University Press.

Lewis, David (1974). Semantic analyses for dyadic deontic logic. In Stenlund, Søren, editor, *Logical Theory and Semantic Analysis*, pages 1–14. D. Reidel Publishing Company.

Little, Margaret (2000). Moral generalities revisited. In Hooker, Brad and Little, Margaret, editors, *Moral Particularism*. Oxford University Press.

Loui, Ronald (1995). Hart's critics on defeasible concepts and ascriptivism. In *Proceedings of the Fifth International Conference on Artificial Intelligence and Law (ICAIL-95)*, pages 21–30. The ACM Press.

Makinson, David (1994). General patterns in nonmonotonic reasoning. In Gabbay, D., C.Hogger, and Robinson, J., editors, *Handbook of Logic in Artificial*

Intelligence and Logic Programming, Volume 3: Nonmonotonic Reasoning and Uncertain Reasoning, pages 35–110. Oxford University Press.

Makinson, David (2005). *Bridges from Classical to Nonmonotonic Logic.* Texts in Computing, Volume 5. King's College Publications.

Makinson, David and Schlechta, Karl (1991). Floating conclusions and zombie paths: two deep difficulties in the "directly skeptical" approach to defeasible inheritance nets. *Artificial Intelligence*, 48:199–209.

Mandelbaum, Maurice (1955). *The Phenomenology of Moral Experience.* The Free Press.

Marcus, Ruth Barcan (1980). Moral dilemmas and consistency. *Journal of Philosophy*, 77:121–136. Reprinted in Gowans (1987b), pages 188–204; pagination refers to this version.

Marek, Wiktor and Truszczyński, Mirek (1993). *Nonmonotonic Logic: Context-dependent Reasoning.* Springer Verlag.

McCarthy, John (1959). Programs with common sense. In Blake, D. V. and Uttley, A. M., editors, *Proceedings of the Symposium on Mechanization of Thought Processes*, pages 77–84. H. M. Stationary Office. Expanded version reprinted in Brachman and Levesque (1985).

McCarthy, John (1977). Epistemological problems in artificial intelligence. In *Proceedings of the Fifth International Joint Conference on Artificial Intelligence (IJCAI-77)*, pages 1038–1044. Morgan Kaufmann Publishers. Reprinted in Brachman and Levesque (1985).

McCarthy, John (1980). Circumscription—a form of non-monotonic reasoning. *Artificial Intelligence*, 13:27–39.

McCarthy, John (1986). Applications of circumscription to formalizing common-sense knowledge. *Artificial Intelligence*, 28:89–116.

McCarthy, John and Hayes, Patrick (1969). Some philosophical problems from the standpoint of artificial intelligence. In Meltzer, B. and Michie, D., editors, *Machine Intelligence, volume 4*. Edinburgh Press.

McDermott, Drew (1982). Non-monotonic logic II. *Journal of the Association for Computing Machinery*, 29:33–57.

McDermott, Drew and Doyle, Jon (1980). Non-monotonic logic I. *Artificial Intelligence*, 13:41–72.

McKeever, Sean and Ridge, Michael (2006). *Principled Ethics: Generalism as a Regulative Ideal.* Oxford University Press.

Moore, Michael (1989). Authority, law, and Razian reasons. *Southern California Law Review*, 62:827–896.

Nagel, Thomas (1970). *The Possibility of Altruism.* Princeton University Press.

Nilsson, Nils (1980). *Principles of Artificial Intelligence.* Morgan Kaufmann Publishers.

Nute, Donald (1988). Defeasible reasoning and decision support systems. *Decision Support Systems*, 4:97–110.

Nute, Donald (1994). Defeasible logic. In Gabbay, D., Hogger, C., and Robinson, J., editors, *Handbook of Logic in Artificial Intelligence and Logic Programming, Volume 3: Nonmonotonic Reasoning and Uncertain Reasoning*, pages 355–395. Oxford University Press.

Parfit, Derek (2011). *On What Matters*. Oxford University Press.

Perry, Stephen (1987). Judicial obligation, precedent, and the common law. *Oxford Journal of Legal Studies*, 7:215–257.

Perry, Stephen (1989). Second-order reasons, uncertainty, and legal theory. *Southern California Law Review*, 62:913–994.

Pietroski, Paul (1993). Prima facie obligations, ceteris paribus laws in moral theory. *Ethics*, 103:489–515.

Pollock, John (1970). The structure of epistemic justification. In *Studies in the Theory of Knowledge*, American Philosophical Quarterly Monograph Series, number 4, pages 62–78. Basil Blackwell Publisher, Inc.

Pollock, John (1974). *Knowledge and Justification*. Princeton University Press.

Pollock, John (1987). Defeasible reasoning. *Cognitive Science*, 11:481–518.

Pollock, John (1995). *Cognitive Carpentry: A Blueprint for How to Build a Person*. The MIT Press.

Pollock, John (2007). Defeasible reasoning. Unpublished manuscript.

Pollock, John and Cruz, Joseph (1999). *Contemporary Theories of Knowledge*. Rowman and Littlefield Publishers, Inc.

Prakken, Henry (1993). An argumentation framework in default logic. *Annals of Mathematics and Artificial Intelligence*, 9:91–132.

Prakken, Henry (2002). Intuitions and the modelling of defeasible reasoning: some case studies. In Benferhat, Salem and Giunchiglia, Enrico, editors, *Proceedings of the Ninth International Workshop on Nonmonotonic Reasoning*.

Prakken, Henry (2005). A study of accrual of arguments, with applications to evidential reasoning. In *Proceedings of the Tenth International Conference on Artificial Intelligence and Law (ICAIL-05)*, pages 85–94. The ACM Press.

Prakken, Henry and Sartor, Giovanni (1995). On the relation between legal language and legal argument: assumptions, applicability, and dynamic priorities. In *Proceedings of the Fifth International Conference on Artificial Intelligence and Law (ICAIL-95)*. The ACM Press.

Prakken, Henry and Sartor, Giovanni (1996). A dialectical model of assessing conflicting arguments in legal reasoning. *Artificial Intelligence and Law*, 4:331–368.

Prakken, Henry and Vreeswijk, Gerard (2002). Logical systems for defeasible argumentation. In Gabbay, Dov and Guethner, F., editors, *Handbook of Philosophical Logic (Second Edition)*, pages 219–318. Kluwer Academic Publishers.

Raz, Joseph (1975). *Practical Reasoning and Norms*. Hutchinson and Company. Second edition with new Postscript printed in 1990 by Princeton University Press, and reprinted by Oxford University Press in 2002; pagination refers to the Oxford edition.

Raz, Joseph, editor (1978). *Practical Reasoning*. Oxford University Press.

Raz, Joseph (1989). Facing up: a reply. *Southern California Law Review*, 62:1153–1235.

Raz, Joseph (2000). The truth in particularism. In Hooker, Brad and Little, Margaret, editors, *Moral Particularism*, pages 48–78. Oxford University Press.

Reiter, Raymond (1980). A logic for default reasoning. *Artificial Intelligence*, 13:81–132.

Reiter, Raymond and Criscuolo, Giovanni (1981). On interacting defaults. In *Proceedings of the Seventh International Joint Conference on Artificial Intelligence (IJCAI-81)*, pages 270–276.

Richardson, Henry (1990). Specifying norms as a way to resolve concrete ethical problems. *Philosophy and Public Affairs*, 19:279–310.

Rintanen, Jussi (1998). Lexicographic priorities in default logic. *Artificial Intelligence*, 106:221–265.

Ross, W. D. (1930). *The Right and the Good*. Oxford University Press.

Sartre, Jean-Paul (1946). *L'Existentialisme est un Humanisme*. Nagel. Translated as "Existentialism is a Humanism" in W. Kaufmann, editor, *Existentialism from Dostoevsky to Sartre*. Meridian Press, 1975.

Scanlon, T. M. (1998). *What We Owe to Each Other*. Harvard University Press.

Schroeder, Mark (2005). Instrumental mythology. *Journal of Ethics and Social Philosophy*, Symposium I.

Schroeder, Mark (2007). *Slaves of the Passions*. Oxford University Press.

Schroeder, Mark (2009). A matter of principle. *Nous*, 43:568–580.

Schroeder, Mark (2011a). Holism, weight, and undercutting. *Nous*, 45:328–344.

Schroeder, Mark (2011b). *Ought*, agents, and actions. *Philosophical Review*, 120:1–41.

Searle, John (1980). Prima-facie obligations. In van Straaten, Zak, editor, *Philosophical Subjects: Essays Presented to P. F. Strawson*, pages 238–259. Oxford University Press.

Skourpski, John (1997). Reasons and reason. In Cullity, Garret and Gaut, Berys, editors, *Ethics and Practical Reason*, pages 345–368. Oxford University Press.

Sloan, Allan (1997). Millionaires next door—that is, if your neighbors work for Microsoft. *Newsweek (December 8)*.

Slote, Michael (1985). Utilitarianism, moral dilemmas, and moral cost. *American Philosophical Quarterly*, 22:161–168.

Stein, Lynn (1992). Resolving ambiguity in nonmonotonic inheritance hierarchies. *Artificial Intelligence*, 55:259–310.

Thomason, Richmond (1991). Logicism, AI, and common sense: John McCarthy's program in philosophical perspective. In Lifschitz, Vladimir, editor, *Artificial Intelligence and Mathematical Theory of Computation*, pages 449–466. Academic Press.

Thomason, Richmond (1992). NETL and subsequent path-based inheritance theories. *Computers and Mathematics with Applications*, 23:179–204.

Thomason, Richmond (2009). Logic and artificial intelligence. In Zalta, Edward, editor, *The Stanford Encyclopedia of Philosophy (Spring 2009 Edition)*. Stanford University. Available at http://plato.stanford.edu/archives/spr2009/entries/logic-ai/.

Thomson, Judith Jarvis (1990). *The Realm of Rights*. Harvard University Press.

Touretzky, David (1984). Implicit ordering of defaults in inheritance systems. In *Proceedings of the Fourth National Conference on Artificial Intelligence (AAAI-84)*, pages 322–325. Morgan Kaufmann.

Touretzky, David (1986). *The Mathematics of Inheritance Systems*. Morgan Kaufmann.

Touretzky, David, Horty, John, and Thomason, Richmond (1987). A clash of intuitions: the current state of nonmonotonic multiple inheritance systems. In *Proceedings of the Tenth International Joint Conference on Artificial Intelligence (IJCAI-87)*, pages 476–482. Morgan Kaufmann.

Touretzky, David, Thomason, Richmond, and Horty, John (1991). A skeptic's menagerie: conflictors, preemptors, reinstaters, and zombies in nonmonotonic inheritance. In *Proceedings of the Twelfth International Joint Conference on Artificial Intelligence (IJCAI-91)*, pages 478–483. Morgan Kaufmann Publishers.

van Fraassen, Bas (1972). The logic of conditional obligation. *The Journal of Philosophical Logic*, 72:417–438.

van Fraassen, Bas (1973). Values and the heart's command. *The Journal of Philosophy*, 70:5–19.

Väyrynen, Pekka (2004). Particularism and default reasons. *Ethical Theory and Moral Practice*, 7:53–79.

Väyrynen, Pekka (2011). Moral particularism. In Miller, Christian B., editor, *Continuum Companion to Ethics*. Continuum Books.

Wedgwood, Ralph (2006). The meaning of 'ought'. In Shafer-Landau, Russ, editor, *Oxford Studies in Metaethics*, volume 1, pages 127–160. Oxford University Press.

Williams, Bernard (1965). Ethical consistency. *Proceedings of the Aristotelian Society*, 39 (supplemental):103–124. A revised version appears in *Problems of the Self: Philosophical Papers 1956–1972*, Cambridge University Press, 1973, pages 166–186.

Index

Copy Kathy Dee, Bleakely's Report?
55 mph — Signage stuff, in
argument

CPSIA information can be obtained at www.ICGtesting.com
Printed in the USA
BVOW01s1320060514

352673BV00001B/1/P